Counterinsurgency

Counterinsurgency has staked its claim in the new century as the new American way of war. Yet, the wars in Afghanistan and Iraq have revived a historical debate about the costs – monetary, political, and moral – of operations designed to eliminate insurgents and build nations. Today's counterinsurgency proponents point to "small wars" past to support their view that the enemy is "biddable" if the correct tactical formulae are applied. Douglas Porch's sweeping history of counterinsurgency campaigns carried out by the three "providential nations" of France, Britain, and the United States, ranging from nineteenth-century colonial conquests to General Petraeus' "surge" in Iraq, challenges the contemporary mythologizing of counterinsurgency as a humane way of war. The reality, he reveals, is that "hearts and minds" has never been a recipe for lasting stability and that past counterinsurgency campaigns have succeeded not through state-building but by shattering and dividing societies while unsettling civil-military relations.

Douglas Porch is Distinguished Professor of National Security Affairs at the Naval Postgraduate School, Monterey, California. A specialist in military history, he advises on security issues all over the world. His most recent book, *The Path to Victory: The Mediterranean Theater in World War II*, received the Award for Excellence in US Army Historical Writing from the Army Historical Foundation.

Counterinsurgency

Exposing the Myths of the New Way of War

Douglas Porch

CAMBRIDGE
UNIVERSITY PRESS

CAMBRIDGE
UNIVERSITY PRESS

University Printing House, Cambridge CB2 8BS, United Kingdom

Cambridge University Press is part of the University of Cambridge.

It furthers the University s mission by disseminating knowledge in the pursuit of education, learning and research at the highest international levels of excellence.

www.cambridge.org
Information on this title: www.cambridge.org/9781107699847

First published 2013
3rd printing 2014

Printed in the United States of America by Sheridan Books Inc.

A catalogue record for this publication is available from the British Library

Library of Congress Cataloguing in Publication data
Porch, Douglas.
Counterinsurgency: exposing the myths of the new way of war / Douglas Porch.
  p.   cm.
Includes bibliographical references.
ISBN 978-1-107-69984-7
1. Counterinsurgency – Case studies.   2. Small wars – Case studies.
3. Counterinsurgency – History.   I. Title.
U240.P66   2013
355.02′18–dc23

2012038690

ISBN 978-1-107-02738-1 Hardback
ISBN 978-1-107-69984-7 Paperback

CONTENTS

ILLUSTRATIONS

MAPS

PREFACE AND ACKNOWLEDGMENTS

This book was conceived in the classrooms of the Naval Postgraduate School where I teach company and field grade US and international officers. Some of them have returned from Iraq and Afghanistan in recent years not only unsettled by their experiences in those countries, but also persuaded that the hearts and minds counterinsurgency doctrines they were dispatched to apply from 2007 were idealistic, when not naïve, impracticable, unworkable, and perhaps institutionally fraudulent. In short, they had been sent on a murderous errand equipped with a counterfeit doctrine that became the rage in 2007 following the publication of *FM 3–24: Counterinsurgency* as prologue to the surge commanded by General David Petraeus in Iraq. This was surely the case of US Air Force Major John Loftis, a former Peace Corps volunteer, sterling student, and a gentle, smiling man who fell victim to green-on-blue violence in Afghanistan in February 2012.

In 2010, Professor Jan Hoffenaar, President of the Netherlands Commission of Military History, invited me to address their 35th Congress at Amsterdam on the theme of counterinsurgency. My argument continues to be that what has long been called small war in its various reiterations as imperial policing or COIN (counterinsurgency operations) does not constitute a specialized category of warfare. Rather, it consists of the application of petty war tactics that its advocates since the 1840s have puffed as infallible prescriptions for effortless conquest, nation-building, and national grandeur. Small wars enthusiasts basically reject the Clausewitzian character of war in favor of a Jominian tactical and operational approach, in large part to evade democratic civilian control. Claims in doctrine for success in small wars, at least at a reasonable strategic, financial, and moral cost, have relied on mythologized versions of the past too often supported by shoddy research and flawed, selective analysis of cases. History cooked as COIN folklore can lead to people getting killed because it fails to convey that each insurgency is a contingent event in which doctrine, operations, and tactics must support a viable policy and strategy, not the other way around.

Although this message contradicted the official COIN optimism generated by neo-conservative "end of history" hubris combined with the triumphalism of the "surge" celebrated in Thomas Ricks' 2009 Pulitzer Prize hagiography of Petraeus,[1] the Amsterdam talk was far better received than I anticipated. My colleague Thomas Young was kind enough to publish my article which laid out these themes in more detail in *Small Wars and Insurgencies*.[2] Donald Abenheim encouraged me to expand my arguments into a short book, which Michael Watson at Cambridge University Press was persuaded to contract based on a brief prospectus. My plan was to chronicle with concision the parallel small wars experiences of the three providential democratic nations – Britain, France, and the United States – to illustrate against the assertions of Niall Ferguson and others that non-Western societies were seldom receptive to Western values and mores, especially when they were proselytized at the end of a bayonet. The result was that counterinsurgency methods supposedly calculated to win the hearts and minds of foreign folk invariably relied on coercion rather than persuasion. My motivation in the present work remains to create a historical record so that, in fifteen or twenty-five years' time, revisionists in the style of the "better war" school of the Vietnam conflict, tempted to conjure up a stab-in-the-back explanation for failure in Iraq and Afghanistan, will at least have to contend with a formulated, relatively comprehensive counter-argument, rather than wait for damage to reach disturbing proportions, failure to become evident, and critics to assemble to begin the laborious, painful, humiliating, and divisive process of disengagement. Those who advocate future imperial adventures in the manner of the George W. Bush wars of the last decade should have to face the fact that they seldom achieve their goals at an acceptable price. Finally, this cautionary volume might help to avert much misery, and save lives and resources in future.

This book would not have seen the light of day without the assistance of many people. Donald Abenheim has been a source both of inspiration and ideas, and kept me focused on the task. Another of my colleagues, Carolyn Halladay, generously helped to tighten the arguments and organization of the earliest version of the manuscript. John Lynn made many helpful comments on the proposal, as did David French who read the manuscript, suggested other sources, and allowed me to consult the proofs of his *The British Way in Counter-insurgency, 1945–1967*. William Fuller graciously allowed me access to the manuscript chapter on the Troubles in his forthcoming book on terrorism. Harold Trinkunas and Thomas Bruneau helped to shape the chapter on Latin America, Philip Williams that on the surge, and John Bew and Huw Bennett kindly saved me from errors of fact and interpretation in the case of Northern Ireland. Obviously, the opinions and interpretations remain my own and do not reflect those of the Department of the Navy or the Department of Defense. Throughout, Gian Gentile has been a kindred spirit, a voice simultaneously of reason and passion, and a model of professional integrity. I am also grateful to Michael Watson, Chloe Howell, and the editorial staff at Cambridge University Press who have been professional and supportive. Finally, it remains for me to thank my wife, Françoise, as ever for her love and support.

Douglas Porch
Monterey, California

1 A "HAPPY COMBINATION OF CLEMENCY WITH FIRMNESS": THE SMALL WARS PROLOGUE

Western powers have been engaged in counterinsurgency operations at least since the *Reconquista* of the Iberian Peninsula. The requirement to occupy the Western Hemisphere from 1492 – and later the Indian subcontinent, East Asia, and Africa – involved Western powers in armed conflict with local populations, much of it irregular warfare. Contemporary US COIN doctrine in its twenty-first-century form is an outgrowth of the belief, common in nineteenth-century France and Britain, that military action provided the mechanism for the dissemination of modern, Western values and attitudes as a foundation for indigenous governance and social, political, and economic transformation of pivotal regions.

The nineteenth century witnessed the establishment of small wars as a discrete category of warfare in France and Britain, one that required a special doctrine, an uncommon type of officer with a mindset and outlook distinct from those who prepared for and fought continental conflicts. Not only must colonial warriors prove to be excellent tacticians, but also they must prepare to engage non-Western populations on a political and cultural level. Because irregular or "small wars" were associated with imperial expansion, colonial soldiers had also to assemble a cast of influential supporters among journalists, geographic societies, army and navy leagues, and politicians to sell what was in effect a political project. The bid for the recognition of small wars as a separate category of service came about for several reasons, the increasing professionalization and industrialization of continental warfare most prominent among them.[1] Intensifying democratization of the political systems in these countries in an era of mass politics before 1914 also stimulated advocates of strategic superiority via small wars to fashion their own professional and doctrinal universe. In both Britain and France, demands for increased civilian control of the military that grew with the approach of the Great War joined with concerns about the barbarity of small war tactics and operations and questions about the risks and utility of imperial expansion. Especially from the turn of the twentieth century, sharpened tensions in the international system in the final phases of imperial expansion, caused in part by heated competition for diminishing swaths of unclaimed terrain, intensified diplomatic resistance to and journalistic scrutiny of small wars. Increasingly, stealth encroachments and territorial *faits accomplis* – standards in the small war repertoire – threatened to unsettle the international order. Their inherent brutality became a public relations liability for Western imperial powers that nonetheless were functioning democracies.

In this environment, small wars proponents had to rebrand rough methods of conquest and exploitative governance as an extension of "soft power" that benefited the governed (and flattered the West's sense of cultural hubris). Indigenous resistors to these civilizing ministrations were delegitimized as thugs, bandits, criminal tribes, bitter-enders, or fanatics. In this way, COIN promises to operationalize humanitarianism. Indeed, *FM 3–24: Counterinsurgency* of 2006 replicates the righteousness of nineteenth- century imperialists when it brands the enemies of coalition occupations of Iraq and Afghanistan as "elusive, unethical and indiscriminate foes" organized in an insurgency "characterized by violence, immorality, distrust and deceit."[2] This may indeed provide an accurate description of enemies of coalition occupations. On the other hand, populations of those countries who not for the first time have endured invasions and occupations by outsiders who employ indiscriminate violence, justified by trumped up security threats, and followed by occupations based on governance pacts with opportunists or sectarian and political rivals may perhaps be forgiven for failing to draw the stark moral distinctions that appear so obvious to the authors of *FM 3–24*.

Meanwhile, back at the staff colleges, continental warfare increasingly focused on the management and maneuver of technologically complex armies of millions to fight cataclysmic battles that decided the fate of nations. In this context, small warriors regressed in the eyes of their conventional colleagues into semi-warriors, quasi-professionals who misrepresented their skirmishes followed by forays into municipal governance as a skill comparable to big war management. Some conventional soldiers began to develop a distaste for those who went native in the worst sense, by adopting savage, degrading, primitive styles of warfare. Nowhere was this aversion more pronounced than in the United States, where at the US Military Academy at West Point, and in the wake of the Mexican (1846–1848) and Civil Wars (1861–1865), a category of military man who desired to reorganize the American army along European lines decried the total war savagery inflicted by "citizen soldiers" upon Native Americans as incompatible with American values.[3]

Hoche, Suchet, and Bugeaud: the French antecedents of counterinsurgency

Popular insurrection against authority and occupation is an age-old phenomenon. As American strategist and historian Edward Luttwak has noted, Romans, Ottomans, Russians, and World War II Germans controlled vast empires without resorting to a specialized category of soldier possessed of asymmetrical savvy. Counter terror, rather than counterinsurgency, was their preferred deterrent – "A massacre once in a while remained an effective warning for decades," concludes Luttwak.[4] The idea of counterinsurgency is linked to democracy, and the notion that a government's legitimacy is anchored in the consent of the governed. Therefore, when the French Revolution's evangelization of modern, democratic ideas through the empowerment of a centralized state and later empire in turn provoked popular resistance in some quarters, the occasional massacre no longer seemed compatible with democratic humanism. Therefore, a package of tactics that allied force with persuasion and clemency had to be devised. The Battle of Algiers, Mai Lai, Abu Ghraib, Haditha, or killing rampages by a soldier in Afghanistan's Panjwayi district,[5] could henceforth be explained as anomalies inflicted by stressed-out conscripts, by conventional soldiers untutored in the hearts and minds fundamentals of war among the people, or a regrettable collateral byproduct of necessary night raids or drone attacks rather than as patterns of racialized violence endemic to small wars. This was an evolutionary process in part because counter terror remained an effective tactic against groups whose culture, customs, religion, or previous encounters with occupation made them resistant to Westernized concepts of modernization. In Africa and parts of the Americas, the notion persisted into the twentieth century that lands had first to be emptied of their indigenous inhabitants to be made productive. But the increasing ambivalence of Western populations to the moral hazards and expense of empire required the codification of prescriptions that made conquest appear efficient, humane, and altruistic, as well as an act of economic and political self-interest for the ruling nations.

That the French were modern counterinsurgency pioneers whose practitioners continued to refine and guide the evolution of techniques and doctrine is well established in the community of counterinsurgency scholars. This is hardly surprising as French soldiers were the first to confront and work out techniques to master contemporary rebellions against their authority, both in France and in the Iberian birthplace of guerrilla warfare. British Major General Sir Charles Callwell is generally credited with first delineating in 1896 the prescriptions that established small wars as a distinct category of warfare with a glorious lineage and a professional codex equal to that of conventional war as celebrated in the proliferating general staff and war academies of the era. Callwell defined small wars at its most basic as "operations of regular armies against irregular, or comparatively speaking irregular forces."

> *Whenever a regular army finds itself engaged upon hostilities against irregular forces, or forces which in their armament, their organization, and their discipline are palpably inferior to it, the conditions of the campaign become distinct from the conditions of modern regular warfare.*[6]

Guerrilla warfare was of course a translation of small war, a much older tactic by which relatively diminutive groups of fighters utilized surprise as a force multiplier to carry out ambushes, sabotage, and raids to harass and forage on the margins of large clashes of armies.

Callwell credited Lazare Hoche with laying down tactical principles later followed by successors during his 1794 campaign against royalists in western France in rebellion against the French Revolution. Callwell's acknowledgment of the French provenance of counterinsurgency is shared by John Arquilla, a special operations specialist at the Naval Postgraduate School, who believes that the three central counterinsurgency concepts – information operations, the role of swarm tactics in battle, and the need to understand how networks fight – can be discovered in the histories of the campaigns of Louis-Gabriel Suchet in Spain from 1808–1812, those of Thomas-Robert Bugeaud in Algeria in the 1840s, and Joseph Gallieni in Tonkin in the 1890s.[7]

As a founder of the small wars school, Callwell was eager to detect an ancestry, identify techniques that distinguished small from big war, and create a compendium of best practices as befitted a professional military institution. Callwell designated General Lazare Hoche, "whose conduct of the campaign against the *Chouans* and insurgents from La Vendée will ever remain a model of operations of this kind," as, if not the Messiah of counterinsurgency, at least its John the Baptist who pioneered the light touch technique in small wars. Hoche, Callwell asserted, "achieved success as much by his happy combination of clemency with firmness, as by his masterly dispositions in the theater of war . . . It was a case of civil war, and the brilliant French soldier-administrator substituted this system for the devastation which had been tried by his predecessors."[8] In truth, Hoche's record belies this fiction of the light touch. Indeed, Hoche's clemency succeeded precisely *because of*, not in contrast to, the "devastation . . . tried by his predecessors."

A corporal in the Gardes Françaises when the Revolution erupted in 1789, Hoche was catapulted in four short years to the rank of major general in the Army of the Rhine by demonstrating his skills and courage in set-piece battles against Coalition forces on France's northern and eastern frontiers. With this experience, in August 1794 he headed west as commander-in-chief of the armies of Brittany where he was to marshal his big war skills to tame a two-year-old royalist insurrection that the scorched-earth tactics of his predecessors had diminished but not completely extinguished. A change of approach was in order, and was made possible largely because the previous counter-terror campaign had reduced the popular revolt to a handful of holdouts. Hoche divided the theater into sections, each with its network of posts linked by mobile patrols, informed by an active intelligence service. The fittest soldiers were organized into fast-moving mobile columns that hunted down and surprised hardcore bands of insurgents. Adolphe Thiers, a self-styled military expert and convinced Orleanist with shallow sympathies for ostensibly pro-Bourbon revolts, praised Hoche's use of "entrenched camps" from which he progressively enveloped

> *the whole country . . . so as to leave no free space by which an enemy who was at all numerous could pass. These posts were*

*directed to occupy every hamlet and village and disarm them.
To accomplish this they were to seize the cattle which usually
grazed together and the corn stowed away in the barns; they
were also to secure the principal inhabitants; they were not to
restore the cattle and corn, nor to release the persons taken as
hostages, till the peasants should have voluntarily delivered
up their arms.[9]*

Depriving peasants of their food and livelihoods while seizing hostages
would seem to situate Hoche (and Thiers) more in the "firmness" than
the "clemency" school of counterinsurgency that would have been
familiar to any Roman governor or Persian satrap. But his "population-
centric" tactics proved temporarily effective because of the nature of the
insurgency, because of lucky timing, and because of the context in which
they were applied.

More importantly, Hoche's measures were linked to a political
strategy. The wave of peasant insurrection that surged through western
France in the spring of 1793 had been triggered by the Convention's
February 24 conscription decree, made necessary because the supply of
patriotic volunteers who initially flocked to defend the Revolution was
no longer sufficient to fill the ranks of French armies expanded to cope
with the European coalition that that very revolution had called into
being. French historian of the counter-revolution Jacques Godechot
argues that the pro-Bourbon Breton Association, which had been organized by the local nobility and stockpiling muskets and gunpowder and
organizing counter-revolutionary committees in the smaller towns since
1791, transformed these anti-conscription protests into a pro-royalist
and pro-clerical insurrection. Together with peasants, the leaders of
these groupings, eventually called the *Chouans*,[10] were able to mobilize
those – and there were many – harmed by the changes brought by the
Revolution which had confiscated Church lands, abolished the hated salt
tax, which put both tax collectors and smugglers out of work, forced
many nobles to emigrate leaving their households, estate workers,
agents, managers, and solicitors without employment, and issued a
worthless paper currency that had sent prices through the roof, which
accentuated the hard times caused by poor harvests. One republican
official categorized the *Chouans* as an "army composed of refractory
priests, ex-salt-tax-collectors, bankrupts, excise men, solicitors' clerks,
valets of *émigrés*, monks and nuns, marquises, countesses and former

nobles."[11] With British encouragement, these losers of the French Revolution organized into military formations that soon numbered around 40,000 men, whom they christened the Catholic and Royal Army.

The rebels met early success in what was deemed the War of the Vendée, capturing some of the smaller towns and routing a diminutive republican force sent to defeat them. However, in late May 1793, just as the Republic appeared to have captured the initiative in the west and was poised to crush the rebellion, the Committee of Public Safety under Maximilian Robespierre in Paris was distracted by similar "federalist" rebellions from Bordeaux to Normandy, as well as in Toulouse, Marseilles, and Lyons, sparked by the arrest of the Girondin leaders in the Paris Convention. The six weeks required to quell the federalists handed the *Chouans* a new lease on life. But poor organization and discipline, a lack of weapons, London's inability to sustain support for the rebels (largely because the latter failed to capture the port cities of Nantes or Grandville), and the absence of an offensive strategy opened the *Chouans* to a counterstroke. Three Republican armies composed largely of fanaticized Parisian and German volunteers spearheaded an offensive of such savagery that one French historian has labeled it a genocide.[12] The remnants of the Catholic and Royal Army were cornered and slaughtered at Savenay by Jean-Baptiste Kléber on December 23, 1793, after which he relapsed into conventional soldiering until he was assassinated in Cairo in 1800.

Repressions continued into 1794 as military commissions crisscrossed the region executing, often wholesale and in gruesome fashion, those suspected of aiding the rebellion, while "infernal columns" of soldiers laid waste to the countryside. *Chouan* leaders retaliated with attacks on those who had purchased confiscated Church and émigré noble properties, republican mayors, and priests who swore allegiance to the Republic. They also launched a profitable sideline in kidnapping and ransoming pro-Republican citizens. But such harassment constituted a feeble response to the Republican occupation.

Hoche's (comparatively) more conciliatory strategy flowed from the toppling of Robespierre on 9 Thermidor, Year II (July 27, 1794), which effectively terminated the Revolution's most radical phase, broke the stranglehold of the radical Parisian *sans culottes* on France's political dynamic, and introduced a series of more moderate governments that sought to assuage public opinion rather than enflame it. In December, the

Committee of Public Safety in Paris offered amnesty to all rebels who surrendered their muskets. Negotiations led to a ceasefire in January 1795, followed by local peace treaties; insurgents were indemnified for lost or damaged property and allowed to retain their weapons. Conscription, the original spark of discontent, was modified so that young men served in territorial militias rather than in Republican armies eligible for foreign deployment. The worthless paper currency issued by the Vendéen rebels was redeemed in Republican *assignats*, and the principal *Chouan* leaders received incentives of up to £200,000 to lay down their arms.

These peace treaties nearly came unstuck in the summer of 1795, when Hoche blocked British attempts to land émigré royalists on the coast of Brittany to link up with the vestiges of the Vendée revolt. Following another flare-up of *Chouannerie* in 1799, royalists abandoned popular insurrection in favor of plots to assassinate Napoleon.[13] Generous concessions and indemnities, the substitution of local militia service for national conscription, and Napoleon's 1801 *Concordat* with the Church took the wind out of the insurgents' sails. Afterward, eager to avoid another insurgency as he dealt with a multi-front European conflict, Napoleon exempted the Vendée completely from the empire's tax and conscription policies.[14]

So what are the relevant historical insights from Hoche's putative success? First, Hoche had no particular counterinsurgency experience when he arrived to clean up a rebellion already much diminished in the winter of 1793–1794 by brutal military means. He simply employed "petty war" tactics that any regular soldier of the period would have recognized and practiced. Second, the groundwork for war termination was laid by the scorched-earth campaign of Kléber and others, which smashed and demoralized the insurgent base. Third, the insurgents were severed from outside support because they failed to capture a port town through which London might have funneled arms and cash. Finally, while Callwell, like Thiers, emphasized the effectiveness of Hoche's counterinsurgent tactics, they neglect to mention that political concessions and a downward shift in the overall violence of the Revolution ended a conflict that, in effect, the insurgency won. The Convention, and subsequently Napoleon, had plenty of conscripts. So what was the point of forcing a French uniform on refractory Vendéen and Breton peasants who would quickly desert in any case? Paris simply did not want a Bourbon Restoration. The vast majority of the Vendée rebels cared little about who ruled in Paris. They simply did not want to be soldiers. Amnesty combined with indemnities, bribes, property restitution, the restoration of Church–State relations, and a softening, and subsequently suspension, of conscription appeased the rebels and split them from die-hard royalists and common criminals – mainly *ci-devant* nobles, former salt smugglers, and domestic servants put out of work by the Revolution and now severed from royalist and English backing.

So the Hoche story has far less relevance for the doctrine of counterinsurgency than Callwell or his followers in more recent times would like, particularly in their attempt to establish COIN's legitimacy by tracing its lineage to Revolutionary France. Still, counterinsurgency aficionados, convinced that tactics, not strategy, hold the key to success in conflict, continue to ransack history to unearth primordial versions of key COIN concepts with which to decorate their doctrine's pedigree. One such tactical archeologist of COIN's past, John Arquilla, credits General Louis-Gabriel Suchet with formulating a successful information operations (IO) campaign to win over the populations of French-occupied Aragon and Catalonia in the Peninsular War (1808–1814). Arquilla makes two assertions in his effort to historicize IO. First, if the occupier is on message, the locals will buy into it, even if the occupation is inimical to their values and interests. And second, Suchet successfully suppressed the anti-French insurgency. Arquilla is wrong on both counts.

According to Arquilla, between 1808 and 1813 Suchet seduced the Aragonese and Catalans with a program that included the devolution of authority, infrastructure improvements, and the Napoleonic promise of modernization, administrative efficiency, and social progress.[15] The idea that good governance and material improvements in the standards of living win the hearts and minds of the target population is central to "information" or "psychological operations."[16] Arquilla is correct to point out that Aragon did in fact briefly enjoy a reputation as the most pacified province in Spain in the early months of the French invasion. But this had nothing to do with the fact that occupied Spaniards bought into French IO, or that Suchet's counterinsurgency tactics were effective. Suchet's achievement was temporary, contingent, and a success only when contrasted with the ultimately catastrophic outcome of Napoleon's Spanish project. Other than in Aragon and the sliver of bordering Catalonia over which Suchet had charge, the French totally lost the psychological warfare narrative in Spain. Napoleon's deposition and imprisonment of the Bourbon Ferdinand VII – whom he replaced with his brother Joseph Bonaparte in 1808 – established a government regarded as illegitimate not only in Spain but in Europe and Latin America as well. Napoleon's requirement that the Spaniards pay the costs of occupation translated into higher taxes and requisitions of Church lands. French liberation included a package of modern Revolutionary secularism that outraged conservative Spaniards already aghast that Napoleon had imprisoned two popes and annexed the Papal States to the Roman Republic. The fact that Napoleon was unable to vanquish Britain, combined with the presence of a significant and grow-ing British Army on the Iberian Peninsula, kept hope of re-liberation alive.

How, allegedly, did Suchet manipulate IO to surmount these circumstances in Aragon? While a crust of Liberal opinion in Madrid anticipated the French ignition of a modernizing project, in Aragon and especially Catalonia, the Napoleonic invasion briefly revived medieval autonomist aspirations – at least until it became apparent that Napoleon planned to incorporate Catalonia, part of Aragon and Navarre into the French state (Catalonia became a French department in 1812). The fall of Zaragoza in February 1809, after a successful resistance the previous summer, followed by defeat of the main Spanish armies in the first half of 1809 stunned the population, removed immediate hope of liberation, and quieted the province. Suchet initially kept the Spanish administra-tion in place because technically they still answered to the King of Spain, Joseph, not to the French. Meanwhile, nobles, the Church, and the administration in Aragon, concluding that France had won the war, collaborated with Suchet, not because French propaganda convinced them that they had been "liberated" by the occupiers, but to keep order and preserve their property and jobs.

It took two years for resistance to mobilize in Aragon and to acquire the arms and tactical skills necessary to battle the French. Wellington's force remained small and active on the relatively distant Spanish–Portuguese frontier – that is, the other side of the country. Thus, Suchet could concentrate his entire 20,000-man corps on collecting resources and putting down opposition brutally, though not indiscrim-inately. In short, if Aragon and Catalonia initially remained quiet, it was despite "information operations," not because of them.

Then things began to unravel. In February 1810 Napoleon decreed the Second Military Government. Henceforth, French commanders and the Spanish administration under them answered not to the Spanish king but to the War Ministry in Paris. Taxes and requisitions increased to pay for Napoleon's wars. This combined with entirely justified fears that Napoleon planned to incorporate Spain's northern provinces into France made the *Afrancesados* (Francophiles) very unpopular in Spain. Wellington began to supply insurgent forces, which he saw as vital adjuncts to his Anglo-Portuguese-Spanish conventional units as intelligence gatherers and threats to French communications and supplies. This strategy was particularly successful in Galicia from 1809, where Ney's 10,000 troops were unable either to guard against an amphibious assault or to control the interior of the province against combinations of insurgents and regular Spanish forces. The situation was also boiling in neighboring Navarre, where an insurgency had erupted instantaneously in the wake of Napoleonic suspension of Navarre's historic *fueros* – local rights and privileges.

From the outset of the French occupation, thousands of Aragonese and Catalonians – mainly the gentry and yeomanry – had flocked to the mountainous neighboring province to join Navarrese guerrilla bands fighting roughly 2,500 French troops.[17] Indeed, already in May 1810, Suchet complained that his force laying siege to Lerida in Western Catalonia was harassed by these guerrillas, whose numbers continued to swell in the wake of what historians describe as Suchet's "harsh" and "crushing tax obligations" in Aragon.[18] By the autumn of 1811, many of the exiles returned from Navarre to Aragon and Catalonia as battle-hardened *partidas* who, increasingly armed by the British, were able to operate in larger bands and who knew the terrain far better than did the French. Far from being able, as Arquilla asserts, to "go about unarmed amid the people," guerrillas under Espoz y Mina inflicted on average twenty-six casualties a day on Suchet's forces – who, in fact, could venture out only in large groups. Episodic "search and destroy" sweeps in 1812 had only limited impact, in part because the French increasingly had to shift forces south to deal with Anglo-Spanish forces under Wellington, who seized Madrid in August. By 1813, with many French soldiers recalled from Iberia following the Russian debacle, Suchet's soldiers controlled only a dozen strong points and Zaragoza. The *Afrancesado* administration outside these enclaves had collapsed; French troops went unpaid and starving.

The historian of Suchet's Aragon occupation, Don Alexander, concludes that the myth of Suchet's "deceptive and fleeting" success in

Aragon was initiated by Napoleon's praise for his methods (reinforced by Suchet's own memoirs), the relative quiet of Aragon in 1809–1811 as compared to full-blown insurgencies in Galicia and Navarre, and the difficulties for the British of supplying an insurgency on the Mediterranean coast, especially after Suchet seized Tarragona, fifty miles southwest of Barcelona, in June 1811. The record demonstrates that Suchet was not a particularly adept guerrilla fighter, while his occupation policies engendered at best a wary neutrality from the summer of 1809 to the autumn of 1811 – after which the IO and the military advantage tilted toward the *partidas*.[19] In short, unlike Hoche in the Vendée, Suchet's counterinsurgency tactics were applied in a legitimacy vacuum. In fact, French information operations that hyped a secular, centralizing monarchy, the annexation of some border provinces to France, and a French alliance as the focus of Spanish foreign policy managed to unify against France a fissiparous country in support of a reactionary Bourbon monarchy and the Church.

Nor was the Iberian Peninsula an exception – revolts occurred as well in the Tyrolean Alps, southern Italy, and the Illyrian Provinces as the legitimacy of Napoleon's modernizing project was rejected because it increased the tax burden, jettisoned customary legal practices, broke down traditional social relationships and land tenure arrangements, challenged belief systems, and opened confiscatory opportunities for corrupt, profit-seeking speculators and entrepreneurs, and rapacious French soldiers.[20]

"Navigating the Lake of Geneva": the yawning counterinsurgency/conventional warfare chasm

The Napoleonic campaigns irretrievably transformed continental warfare as well as military thought, to say nothing of military professionalism generally. The size of armies, lethality of combat, complexity of maneuver and the logistical and resource requirements had expanded exponentially between the military practices of 1789 and those of Europe by 1815. Small wars offered a subtext to the Napoleonic era, but they were eclipsed by the quest for the "decisive battle" on the model of Austerlitz in 1805 that determined the fate of empires. While conventional war entered an era of perpetual transformation and spiraling complexity – to the point that "the future of war" became a question of national survival in continental staff colleges – the basic contours of the Vendée rebellion would remain as familiar to Callwell in 1896 as they are to the current era's "global jihadis." Perceptive Western European soldiers detected this bifurcation of big and small wars, to the point that by the dawn of the nineteenth century, it was said that, "an English general, who returns from India, is like an Admiral who has been navigating the Lake of Geneva."[21]

The judgment was premature in the case of Sir Arthur Wellesley, a "sepoy general" whose India experience from 1797 to 1805 did not disqualify him for European command – though even the general himself understood that his colonial service, where a mix of locally recruited units run by the East India Company fortified by British regiments gradually extended British control over local rulers, might register as inferior. Indeed, while Wellesley doubted that "military services in India would be considered in the scale in which are considered similar services in other parts of the world," he allowed that he had learned "as much of military matters" in India as he had "done ever since." He also acknowledged that his imperial service had "opened opportunities for distinction, and then opened the road to fame,"[22] without which he might not have been selected for European command. Likewise, the notion that small wars constituted a professional specialization would have struck French soldiers, who rotated from set-piece battles and sieges to counterinsurgency operations without having to consult a therapist, as ludicrous.

The fact that small wars remained a core tactical manifestation of war beyond Europe's shores, even in epic historical movements like the wars of South American independence (1808–1825), could be safely ignored by those who believed that European conflict under Napoleon had acquired a scale and conventionality that allowed Clausewitz to elucidate war's strategic syntax; and Jomini, its operational and tactical grammar. However, the separation between continental and colonial warfare was not immediately obvious; at the beginning of the nineteenth century, the technological differential between European and non-European forces was not as disproportionate as they were to become by century's end once the Industrial Revolution had unfolded its full implications on the face of armies and battle. As the nineteenth century progressed, European and even American soldiers would be forced to acquire significant technical and managerial skills to mobilize, coordinate, combine, maneuver, and motivate mass armies of (hopefully) patriotic conscripts prepared to die for the Fatherland. And while an enduring image of imperial warfare is that of British soldiers blasting spear-wielding natives with Maxim guns, small wars became ever smaller and more tactically rudimentary in comparison with their continental counterpart as the century progressed.

But at the dawn of the nineteenth century, the differences between European and non-European fighters, technology, and organization were not so readily apparent. While Callwell in particular would contrast the savagery of the Oriental fighter with the disciplined European as one of the demarcations of conventional and small war, the truth was that European soldiers of the Napoleonic period and beyond were hardly studies in nobility of character – *au contraire*! Wellington noted that the ranks of "the scum of the earth (enlisted) as common soldiers" totally liquefied "when plunder or wine is within their reach." But then, the Iron Duke opined that most simple soldiers merely followed the example of their officers, who were in the forefront of the looting. "The discipline of the regiments is relaxed," Wellington recounted with typical understatement, especially when the capture of a town initiated an orgy of "enormous, incredible, indescribable barbarity" that could last for days.[23]

In contrast, with the exception of China, soldiering in many non-European lands was frequently viewed as an honorable, sometimes even a religious, calling. The founders of the American Republic in the eighteenth century considered the "citizen-soldier" fighting for patriotic ideals far superior to the European mercenary so typical of the armies of the old regime. Furthermore, European soldiers campaigning in India, China, even Africa, encountered relatively sophisticated indigenous armies equipped with technology that largely matched their own, with a discipline underpinned by clan, family, and sectarian loyalties. Marathan and Sikh forces in India were conventionally organized, well supplied with muskets and artillery, and instructed by European soldiers of fortune – the forerunner of private security companies – in modern tactics. Wellington for one believed that Waterloo paled in comparison to Assaye, his 1803 defeat of the Marathans, which was "the bloodiest for the numbers that I ever saw" as well as "the best thing" he ever accomplished in the way of fighting.[24] Technology developed for European battlefields was often ill-adapted to colonial conditions, so that artillery or even Gatling or Maxim guns seldom supplied the critical edge abroad. For instance, sepoy mutineers in 1857 did not fail for lack of firepower, even artillery, but because of poor leadership, the absence of viable political objectives, and a coherent strategy to achieve them. In

Algeria, Abd-e-Kader organized a large army that was defeated in pitched battle on the Sikkak River in 1836 and again at Isly in 1844. South of the Sahara, the Tokolor Empire, which stretched from Senegal to Timbuktu by the 1860s, tapped the gold mines of West Africa to purchase European weapons via Sierra Leone to arm its 20,000 *sofas* (warriors). So, without obvious technological or tactical advantages, the best European commanders sought an "operational edge" through feats of organization, logistics, matching indigenous mobility with the creation of light, mobile formations, and the establishment of intelligence collection agencies run by men who acquired cultural and linguistic tools to operate in theater, rather than modern firepower. Callwell's contribution to the formation of a "small wars" school of warfare in which European soldiers might lack a technological, logistical, or even disciplinary edge over their indigenous opponents, was to create a coda of tactical and operational methods that worked best against "savages." "From the days of Clive down to the present time, victory has been achieved by vigor and dash rather than by force of numbers," declared Callwell in 1896.[25]

The problem for the indigenous resistance was that even relatively advanced societies, like those found in China or India, lacked the administrative capacity or professionalized officer corps to take full advantage of new military technology. The clan, family, and sectarian bonds that united them, could also provide flashpoints of internal friction and division. After one or two defeats, indigenous commanders, assuming they survived, quickly learned not to confront Europeans on their own terms. Rather, the better tactic for the defender was to refuse battle, draw the lumbering European army deep into one's territory, and force them to cut their way out. In such circumstances, the dilemma for the European commander became to craft an invasion force to avoid being overwhelmed, but small enough to escape starvation. Oversized expeditions organized on conventional European lines with thousands of horses, pack animals, and porters forfeited mobility, frittered away soldiers as guards for supply convoys that offered tempting targets for the enemy, and thus seldom enjoyed success against an elusive foe. The British learned this hard lesson in Afghanistan in 1842; the Russians, in the Caucasus in the 1840s; and the French, in North Africa in the 1830s and 1840s. Imperial expeditions were more often "campaigns against nature," in the words of Callwell,[26] where disease and geography proved more formidable opponents than the weapons of the indigenous resistance. Battles were seldom decided on the basis of superior firepower alone, and in fact cumbersome heavy weapons like artillery became a liability in remote and tumultuous terrain, while European-style volley firing was too often ineffective against an irregular foe. In these circumstances, mobility and surprise usually brought greater dividends than did throwing a weight of lead in linear tactics.

L'armée en France est un sujet qui fâche[27]

If Hoche and Suchet merit footnotes in the history of French counter-insurgency, Thomas-Robert Bugeaud, who pioneered tactical practices in 1840s North Africa that subsequent generations of French colonial soldiers acknowledged had institutionalized their standard small wars repertoire, commands an opening chapter.[28] Born in 1784, the son of minor gentry from the Perigord in southwestern France, Bugeaud's family was made destitute when the French Revolution branded them aristocrats. A rustic childhood and perfunctory education left him un-credentialed for a direct commission, so in 1804 he enlisted as a private in the elite Imperial Grenadiers, where his energy singled him out for fast-track promotion.

He saw action at Austerlitz in 1805, participated in the 1806 invasion of Prussia, and was commissioned as a second lieutenant in December after being wounded in Poland fighting the Russians. For the remainder of the Napoleonic Wars, he distinguished himself in Spain as a guerrilla fighter, rising to regimental command by 1813, at the age of twenty-nine. The Bourbons retired him for rallying to Napoleon during the Emperor's brief return from Elba in 1815, so the Restoration (1814–1830) found him back on the farm experimenting with carrots and sugar beets, in the process cultivating a reputation as an agronomist of regional repute. Bugeaud was a self-made aristocrat, a son of the soil who embodied the paramount virtues of the French peasantry – independence, tenacity, craftiness, Voltairian skepticism, pragmatism, and a complete absence of sentimentality.

Like a number of Napoleonic veterans, Bugeaud leveraged the *trois glorieuses* of July 1830 – the three-day revolution that sent the French Bourbons packing and issued in the July Monarchy – to reactivate his commission with promotion to brigadier, while simultaneously representing his native Perigord in the Chamber of Deputies. In both venues he earned a reputation as a caustic critic who expressed his contempt for "intellectuals" and Republicans in a "corporal's language." Nor was

Bugeaud a man to be trifled with: In January 1834, he opened a vacancy in a neighboring constituency when, following a difference of opinion in a debate, he challenged a fellow representative to a duel – and killed the man. Three months later, in an incident memorialized in a Daumier lithograph, French soldiers murdered all the inhabitants of a house on la rue Transnonian in the process of quelling a minor Parisian disturbance. Although it was unclear whether the offending troops were under Bugeaud's direct command, for French Republicans, Bugeaud and Transnonian became henceforth indelibly linked. He reciprocated their contempt by suggesting in 1836 that they be deported to Algeria "to be killed. That would serve the country well." Such sentiments won him the nickname "the Achilles of the conservatives."[29] Bugeaud's clashes with the left heralded the growing divide between Republicans and a French army that in the 1790s and beyond they had embraced as the embodiment of the patriotic and equalitarian ideals of the French Revolution, a sentiment reinforced by the army's lukewarm defense of the Bourbon monarchy in 1830. However, Bugeaud's scorched-earth tactics in North Africa raised a growing protest in France. The return from Algeria of General Louis Eugène Cavaignac to crush the Revolution of 1848 in June of that year with singular severity demonstrated, not for the last time, the perils of colonial violence imported into the homeland by an expatriated military exempted from legal and political supervision. This is what the German-Jewish philosopher Hannah Arendt called "the boomerang effect of imperialism upon the homeland."[30]

Ironically, Bugeaud, whose name would become synonymous with Algeria and small war, was actually both a late convert to North African colonization and something of a conventional war snob. The agronomist opined that the climate and soil would never support productive European settlement, while soldiers like Bugeaud's later military critic General the Comte Pierre de Castellane, scorned the "manhunt" conducted on the Mediterranean's Left Bank as bearing "no resemblance" to warfare.[31] These opinions had been formed during a brief 1836 deployment to France's "North African Possession," during which he relieved the French garrison besieged at Tafna, then turned to smash the army of Algerian resistance leader Abd-el-Kader on the Sikkak River. Bugeaud's victory resulted in the 1837 Treaty of Tafna, in which Abd-el-Kader agreed to acknowledge the umbrella of French sovereignty along a section of the North African coast in return for Paris ceding effective control over most of it to him.

1 Marshal Thomas-Robert Bugeaud pioneered the idea that petty war should be elevated into a category of warfare distinct from continental warfare.

Following the 1839 collapse of the Treaty of Tafna, Bugeaud campaigned actively to be named Governor General for reasons not totally clear. Bugeaud the warrior-farmer was keen to open France's North African "frontier" to profitable European settlement. And indeed, the military colonization projects that proliferated during the Bugeaud decade of the 1840s may be seen as an attempt to reclaim France's imperial dynamism that had been squandered first by *ancien régime* and subsequently by Napoleonic overstretch. However, unlike North America, North Africa was not a "wilderness" to be emptied of its inhabitants, as the Muslims were too numerous and disease-resistant to kill or to confine to reservations. Furthermore, Bugeaud found most European settlers to be "amateurs" and "incompetents" who preferred city life to tilling an unyielding countryside.[32] Therefore, conquest seemed to offer no larger nation-building project as an outlet for national energies, and France's small war in North Africa became hardly more than military maneuvers in search of a strategic rationale. Small warriors became a self-serving, self-reverential collective devoid of national purpose – what Charles de Gaulle was later to term *l'armée pour l'armée.*

It was also true that, because the bulk of Bugeaud's Napoleonic War experience had been spent fighting Spanish *partidas*, he was less inclined to view what contemporaries, including Clausewitz, called *Kleinkrieg* or "petty war" as an inefficient, sub-professional fighting style encountered on the margins of conventional conflagrations.[33] For Bugeaud, who had mastered his profession on the field of battle fighting insurgents, not in the classroom, victory in war sprang from the individual qualities of instinct, resolve, and fervor, not through the applied science of maneuver and ever more doctrinized logistics.

It was just as well as, having learned his lesson on the Sikkak in 1836, Abd-el-Kader now shunned set-piece battles and harassed French forces with raids and ambushes that kept them off balance. Furthermore, the greatest generation of aging Napoleonic veterans, to which Bugeaud belonged, was being eclipsed by a new cohort of French soldier heroes. Newspapers recounted the martial exploits of young commanders like La Moricière, Changarnier, Cavaignac, and Bedeau, so that hostesses competed for their presence in chic capital *salons* when they returned on leave or to testify before the legislative Chamber. Nearing sixty, Bugeaud probably concluded that Algerian command offered him a last chance at battlefield fame.

It was also clear that France's governor general in Algeria – distinguished artilleryman and Napoleonic veteran Marshal Sylvain-Charles, Count Valée – was a completely clueless Arab-fighter. Valée scattered his troops in disease-ridden garrisons where they were sickened by putrid rations and harassed by Muslim raiders. Elephantine French columns lumbered across a blistered landscape in search of the decisive battle that the elusive Abd-el-Kader declined to award. Sick and wounded often chose suicide over abandonment to Muslim mercy. French military hospitals in Algeria were ill-disguised mortuaries. Bugeaud argued that Algeria resembled the Peninsular War minus Wellesley, and won Valée's job in December 1840 by promising to build a mobile force capable of taking the fight to the enemy – which is precisely what he did.

Bugeaud arrived in Algiers already learned in the techniques of small wars, fruit of his previous 1836 deployment there, his observation of the failures of his predecessors, and above all of familiarity gained in the Peninsular campaign fighting Spanish *partidas*. Bugeaud admonished his troops to "forget those orchestrated and dramatic battles that civilized peoples fight against one another, and realize that unconventional tactics are the soul of this war." His small wars success was based on the four principles of mobility, morale, leadership, and firepower. Fixed posts were replaced with scouting parties to locate resisting populations against which troops could be rapidly deployed. His mobile columns violated every principle of continental warfare but incorporated the basic attributes of small wars success – light on artillery and logistics, indifferent to European conventions like securing lines of communications as a precondition to an advance, they divided and converged in the face of a superior enemy on an objective identified by intelligence reports. Equipment was redesigned and much of the infantryman's load was shifted to mules to allow them to cover more territory with greater speed. With lighter, faster forces, Bugeaud penetrated hitherto inviolate tribal sanctuaries with an agility and speed that, he boasted, was "even more Arab than the Arabs." This kind of operational idea was destined to become the stock in trade of counterinsurgent soldiers in the years to come.

It would be easy to imagine that these lighter, faster, smaller French units "swarmed" Abd-el-Kader's forces so that in 1847, the celebrated Arab chief was forced to surrender to the French. And indeed, Bugeaud's mobile columns, which replicated Hoche's tactics in the Vendée and what Bugeaud had experienced in the Peninsula, usually worked in unison to converge on an objective from different directions. Unfortunately, even "swarming," another familiar tactical term in the present day COIN lexicon, failed to lock down Abd-el-Kader. Until May 1843, when, according to John Arquilla, Abd-el-Kader's *smala* ("*zmâla*" – encampment of the extended families of the chiefs) was detected and "swarmed" by French forces.[34] Abd-el-Kader was elsewhere with the bulk of his commanders and fighters when a reconnaissance party of Muslim tribesmen in French pay pinpointed the camp. The scouts alerted a group of French cavalry, who "swarmed" it. Of course, what they "swarmed" was a refugee camp composed principally of women, children, and their flocks – in short, non-combatants who had been driven from their homes by Bugeaud's relentless attacks on Muslim settlements. Swarming civilians – called the *razzia* or raid – became standard practice under Bugeaud and fundamental to the success of French conquest. Therefore, when contemporary COIN practitioners

2 *La Prise de la Smallah d'Abd-el-Kader:* The May 1843 "swarm" of Abd-el-Kader's refugee camp was celebrated in the Vernet painting as a decisive military victory in the manner of Austerlitz. In fact, counterinsurgencies prove to be long, destructive wars of attrition.

refer to their craft as "war among the people," they inherit a mode of operations that in effect targeted "the people" for assassination, rape, destitution, internment, and intimidation with the goal of depriving the resistors of their support base and indeed of any reason to go on living.

The deployment of indiscriminate violence against non-combatants went against the trends of continental warfare, which saw combat as an activity led and managed by professional soldiers to achieve the more or less limited political goals of sovereign nation-states. Clausewitz, whose *On War* appeared posthumously in 1832, saw insurgents as non-professional warriors whose methods were both ineffective and uncivilized. Small warriors in the years since, on the other hand, have dismissed Clausewitz as irrelevant precisely because their enemies were not sovereign entities but savages and infidels to whom the rules of civilized warfare did not apply. Clausewitz was declared obsolete on arrival in Africa, a mere theoretical gimmick of interstate war.[35] "In Europe, once [you are] master of two or three large cities, the entire country is yours," Marshal de Castellane wrote in defense of Bugeaud's *razzias.* "But in Africa, how do you act against a population whose only link with the land is the pegs of their tents? . . . The only way is to take the grain which feeds them, the flocks which clothe them. For this reason, we make war on silos, war on cattle, the *razzia*."[36]

German scholar Thomas Rid recounts how the French conquest of Algeria puzzled mid-century European strategists because it failed to fit the Napoleonic decisive battle paradigm, but instead seemed only to engender a string of inconclusive clashes fought in the middle of nowhere. The French had been drawn into a pre-modern system of warfare traditionally practiced among transhumant North African tribes, called the *ghaziya*, during which raiding parties lifted livestock and other goods, but generally left women and children unmolested.[37] The tactic was to surprise and frighten with noise, but to avoid if possible actually killing anyone so as not to initiate a blood feud that could persist for generations.

In the 1840s, Bugeaud tailored the tactic of the *ghaziya* but not its spirit into a population-centric strategy of attrition and economic warfare to break the back of the resistance. It offered a tactic that would reappear in countless counterinsurgency campaigns in the form of internment, resettlement, curfews, collective fines, house demolitions, food control, deportations, and so on. In the process, counterinsurgency became brutalized as French soldiers chopped down fruit trees, destroyed villages, raped women, and murdered children. A total war, which targeted the economic and psychological underpinnings of resistance and exceeded any definition of military necessity much less respected any recognized conventions of war, accelerated the trend by which warfare abroad increasingly departed from European norms and practices. Senior officers tolerated a different standard of behavior in some cases because they were unable to impose strict discipline on troops who acted, in the words of one observer of the French conquest of the Algerian oasis of Zaatcha in 1848, "like a pack of running dogs unleashed on their prey."[38]

Swarming indigenous villages and camps also offered collateral advantages to French colonial soldiers. First, the ability to live off the land lightened logistical demands, removed concerns about lines of communications, and made the mobile columns truly mobile. Second, captured grain, flocks, or women could be sold to support the costs of the expeditions in a colonial interpretation of the Napoleonic maxim of war that nourishes war. Making warfare pay became important within the civil-military relations of the era as the punitive expedition, just short of

18,000 soldiers launched in 1830 with the short-term goal of chastising the insolence of the Dey of Algiers, had ballooned by 1846 into an army of conquest and occupation, numbering almost 108,000 men – between a quarter and a third of French military strength in the day. Critics complained that while Bugeaud may have lightened his fighting columns, acting on the logic that it was impossible to carry out "half a conquest,"[39] he had surged his army into an occupation force too big to fail.

Third, the tactic of devastating the indigenous economy, which Bugeaud's lieutenant, the future Marshal of France, Jacques Leroy de Saint-Arnaud, called "ruining the countryside," terrorized tribes into submitting even before they were attacked – in fact, "ruin" became a favorite tactical expression among French soldiers in North Africa applied to anyone or anything thing that stood in their way.[40] Finally, the prospect of plunder attracted tribal allies and recruits to French-led indigenous regiments, like those who had actually located Abd-el-Kader's *smala*. Therefore, violence against non-combatants that deprived them of a livelihood was central to small wars amid imperial conquest, while colonial officers justified their methods as a prerequisite for the settlement, development, and hence the "civilizing" of Algeria.

Having concluded that the small war in Algeria was proving to be nasty, brutish, interminable, and incompatible with France's enlightened self-image, Parliament nevertheless found itself powerless to hold Bugeaud in check. He ignored direct orders: "I have received your note," Bugeaud replied to the War Minister, who instructed him to stay out of the Kabylia, a mountainous region of northeastern Algeria. "It is too late. My troops ... have already set out ... If we are successful, the government and France will have the honor ... In the opposite case, the entire responsibility will fall upon me. I claim it."[41] Thus, their principal mechanism of democratic civil-military control – budgetary constraints – was easily subverted by small warrior-heroes, a fact with profound implications for such wars in the future. The War Minister agreed in 1841 to limit conquests as a condition for parliamentary approval of the budget for Algeria. But the next year, certain military outposts required funding, and their number grew annually. In 1844, Parliament imposed geographic limits and only agreed to fund "defensive" posts. But this policy only forced the pace of Bugeaud's advances. He erected an elaborate public relations structure, another important feature of the civil-military relations in small wars that also impacted military professionalism, that enlisted a friendly press to praise his operations, discredit detractors, extol the benefits of French rule for the colonized, and pressure Parliament to recognize his *faits accomplis*.[42] In this way, parliamentary efforts to contain Bugeaud's expansion could be portrayed as anti-patriotic acts that placed the lives of French soldiers in jeopardy.

Thus, it was not as Arquilla claims the tactic of swarming that brought Abd-el-Kader to his knees, but the systemic devastation of the indigenous economy and disaggregation of Muslim society. That Arquilla interprets the loot of Abd-el-Kader's *smala* as the Austerlitz of Bugeaud's North Africa campaign is hardly surprising as that's how the French advertised the event at the time. Callwell, too, extolled the dispersing of Abd-el-Kader's *smala* as evidence that, if properly executed by small groups of intrepid horsemen, small wars could be both decisive and cheap, even though *la prise de la smala d'Abd-el-Kader* was in fact hardly a comma in a chapter of conquest and occupation that lasted from 1830 until 1962.[43] In this way, the litany of cruelty, pitiless violence, and human misery inflicted by Bugeaud on the Muslim population of North Africa could be depicted to the French public as both noble combat, a heroic *mano-a-mano* encounter with the enemy fighters, and decisive. The fact that the plunder was commanded by King Louis-Philippe's son, the Duc d'Aumale, also offered a propaganda coup, an information/ psychological operations deception to bolster an insecure Orleanist regime. Louis-Philippe commissioned the artist Horace Vernet to commemorate *La Prise de la smala d'Abd-el-Kader* in a painting of Napoleonic dimensions for an event in which nine French soldiers had perished. Although the 21-by-5 meter painting was fêted in the *salon* of 1845, as IO it failed to save the July Monarchy that in 1848 joined its Bourbon predecessor in exile.

But some French soldiers at least refused to celebrate Bugeaud's conquests as a glorious new chapter for French arms, among them Marshal de Castellane who told the French Chamber of Peers on July 4, 1845:

> *We have reduced the country by an arsenal of axes and phosphorus matches. The trees were cut down, the crops were burned, and soon the mastery was obtained of a population reduced to famine and despair ... Few soldiers perished by the hand of the enemy in this war – a sort of man hunt on a large scale, in which the Arabs, ignorant of European tactics, having no cannon-balls to exchange against ours, do not fight with equal arms.*[44]

Nor did *la prise de la smala d'Abd-el-Kader* terminate resistance in North Africa, which cost the French another four-and-a-half years of campaigning that included an invasion of Morocco, where Abd-el-Kader and, by French estimates, as many as 40,000 Algerian Muslims had sought refuge from French depredations.[45] *La prise de la smala* did nothing to dent Abd-el-Kader's support base in the Kabylia and Western Algeria, which continued to be swarmed employing tactics that today would qualify as serious war crimes and which caused an uproar even at the time. At one point, Britain facilitated lengthy diplomatic negotiations between Paris and the Sultan of Morocco to settle Algerian-Moroccan frontier disputes. Bugeaud's war of attrition finally induced Abd-el-Kader to surrender in 1847, but not before being swarmed with emoluments as he glided into gilded exile in Damascus with an annual stipend of 150,000 francs, sweetened with the *grand cordon de la Légion d'honneur*.[46]

Alas, Abd-el-Kader's departure failed to secure France's Algerian conquest. To put the problem in terms framed by Hannah Arendt, Bugeaud and his ilk confused tactical virtuosity and coercive violence with power, "this disastrous reduction of public affairs to the business of dominion."[47] Small wars prosecuted in the absence of a viable political end state acceptable to the governed was not a long-term remedy. Bugeaud realized that the tactical tradeoff of scorched-earth tactics was racial animosity. As he harbored no illusion that North African Muslims would ever willingly acquiesce to French occupation, perpetual repression became the price of domination. The Muslims were reduced by a settler population to the status of marginalized squatters and sharecroppers living in conditions of apartheid. The French continually suppressed rebellions somewhere in Algeria for the duration of French sovereignty into the twentieth century. For victorious National Liberation Front (*Front de libération national*, FLN) revolutionaries, the War of Algerian Independence did not suddenly ignite in 1954. Rather, it was part of a smoldering continuum of resistance they traced to Abd-el-Kader more than a century earlier.

This is not to say that French colonial soldiers behaved with less restraint than their counterparts from other nations. Nineteenth-century British military veteran of the Indian Mutiny, the Opium Wars, and at least two campaigns of conquest in Africa Sir Garnet Wolseley encouraged colonial commanders to seize what the enemy prized most. But in primitive societies and polities, there was often no army to defeat, nor capital to destroy, nor ruler to depose that would at a stroke break the back of resistance. Bugeaud's *razzias* were replicated by the Russians in the Caucasus, the British during the Indian Mutiny (1857) and the Second Anglo-Boer War (1899–1901), in the course of the Indian Wars in the United States (1865–1885), and by the Germans in Southwest and East Africa at the turn of the twentieth century. The French reprised them during the conquest of the Western Sudan in the late nineteenth century as well.

One problem with small wars in the opinion of Isabel V. Hull, expert on the evolution of German counterinsurgency techniques in the generation before 1914, is that the demoralization and destitution of the indigenous population becomes the objective when the absence of identifiable strategic targets combines with decentralized command and control to cause operational solutions to expand to fill a vacuum of civilian oversight and vague war aims. What begins as a narrow focus on the delegation of tactical initiative via mission orders transitions into a population-centric focus informed by racist assumptions that an "inferior, but cruel" enemy justifies reciprocal ruthlessness, of which hunger war tactics *à la* Bugeaud were standard.[48] And this small wars tradition is continued by *FM* 3–24, that views insurgents as beneath the respect accorded combatants by the laws of war.[49] At the very least, the notion however obliquely expressed that enemy combatants are the brainwashed offspring of a diabolical, fanaticized anti-civilization makes it more difficult to control the actions of troops on the ground and to insure that they conformed to civilized standards of warfare.[50]

The brutality of imperial conquest led to its racialization, as the enemy had to be stigmatized as infidels who opposed the spread of civilization. This racialization further widened the divide between conventional and small wars. Twentieth-century attempts to regulate the methods and means of warfare had their roots in the nineteenth century. The 1859 Franco-Austrian War signaled that conventional war had reached such dimensions that it invited supranational regulation. This led directly to the creation of the International Committee of the Red Cross in 1863, followed by the First Geneva Convention of 1864 which began a process of creating categories of protected persons – wounded and their care givers, prisoners, and civilians – in battle zones as a basis for International Humanitarian Law. The Hague Conferences of 1899 and 1907 were early attempts to create mechanisms to regulate international disputes, and to limit and control war through concepts such as distinction (between military and civilians), proportionality (in relation to the military advantage), and military necessity (targets must be of military value), the prohibition on the use of weapons that may cause excessive suffering, and to define war crimes.

These measures to regulate conventional warfare were dead letters in small wars where no one believed the indigenous populations or their civilizations were the equal of Western ones. Some have noted that "lesser breeds without the law" referred to in Rudyard Kipling's 1897 *Recessional* was directed at Germans "drunk with the sight of power," or perhaps even at Italians. Kipling's point may have been that the "white man's burden" required compassionate conquest. But small warriors claimed that the barbarous nature of their enemies exempted white men from the requirement to follow civilized standards of warfare in the empire. Imperial subjects might hope at best for a measure of protective consideration once they had ceased to resist, if for no other reason than their labor was required to make the colonies profitable and habitable.[51] But this was unlikely given the racial character of small wars. Even colonial soldiers conceded that conquest was purchased at the price of deplorable discipline in the units – officers were often power-less in the Algeria of the 1840s to protect the Muslim populations from the depredations of their own troops,[52] who viewed non-Western opponents as barbarians beyond the laws of civilized warfare.[53]

North Africa in the 1840s witnessed a war to the knife, with neither side asking nor offering quarter. Atrocities were justified as a requirement to avenge dead comrades and deter future rebellions, at a stroke institutionalizing generational conflict between the races. Bugeaud acknowledged Muslim hostility as the price of his methods, but rational-ized ruthlessness as the only mechanism to convince Arabs to "accept the yoke of conquest."[54] This attitude was generalized throughout imperial possessions. The central assumption correctly held that the European presence was fundamentally unwelcomed by indigenous majorities – although minority groups, upstarts, and weaker tribes might attempt to turn invasions to their advantage – so that the military became the pillar of empire, forced incessantly to police and pacify an aggrieved population encumbered by ignorance and religion. "Sovereignty operations" became continuous – "Imperialism *was* war."[55]

Feeble mechanisms of civilian control made it impossible to manage Bugeaud and the *armée d'Afrique*. In Paris, critics were quick to cite the costs of the Algerian conquest and occupation, as well as condemn its methods. Many believed the goal of the *razzia* was the enrichment of soldiers and trafficking in women, the least attractive of whom could be ransomed, traded for horses, or sold. The revelation in 1845 that, as part of its campaign to bring Abd-el-Kader to heel, the army had on at least two occasions asphyxiated hundreds of Muslims by building fires in the mouths of the caves where they sought refuge provoked outrage in France, and not just on the left. Bugeaud faulted Muslims who "refuse to accept our law" for the notorious *enfumades*, while castigating "stupid philanthropists" in France, whose humanitarian concerns only encouraged resistance and "eternalized" the war. He dared the War Minister and fellow Peninsular War veteran Marshal Soult to fire him – which, of course, Soult declined to do.[56]

The obvious option was simply to repatriate the troops from Algeria. But budget-busting invasions, once initiated, became virtually impossible to recall, according to colonial official Jules Harmand:

> *We remain because we are here, because we want to believe it is possible to continue the conquest without great effort, because we do not want to lose the benefits of the sacrifices already made, because we consider the interests of the nation and the natives who immediately attach themselves to this sort of enterprise, and finally because the honor of the army and prestige of the flag, sometimes the existence of governments, are at stake.*[57]

Although Harmand was writing in 1910, he had internalized a debate that began in Algiers in 1830, when the army and the colonial lobby intervened to adjourn talk of withdrawal even though the original goals of the putative expedition – to chastise the Dey of Algiers for insulting the French consul in 1827 and grab a military victory that would bolster the popularity of the Bourbon Restoration – were either achieved or overtaken by events.[58] But in the minds of colonial soldiers in both France and Britain, national interests were conflated with the political needs of the army, and the survival and governance of empire fused with military interests.[59] In any case, officers like Saint-Arnaud bridled at the ingratitude of Frenchmen who suggested that perpetual conquest was both a budget drain and a moral hazard: "Here we are in Africa, ruining our health, risking our lives, working for the glory of France, and the most uninformed observer can insult us and slander our intentions, imputing to us criminal feelings which are not of this century and which cannot belong to a soldier."[60] Sir Garnet Wolseley was similarly "disheartened" in the late nineteenth century that the British public and politicians failed adequately to value "the toil endured . . . all the fighting marches under a burning sun in the desert, and all the severe fighting [the soldiers] have had."[61] It signaled the beginning of a mutual civil-military mistrust, even contempt, that divided homelands and their praetorians abroad. After a tour of Algeria in 1846, Alexis de Tocqueville, no great admirer of Muslims, declared Bugeaud's project to govern Algeria as a military colony "imbecilic."[62] Algeria was run by the military into the 1870s, which even Saint-Arnaud admitted permitted a *tyrannie facile* – summary executions of Muslims based on "suspicions" that they were rebels or spies were commonplace because officers argued that humanitarian acts would be interpreted as a sign of weakness and fear.[63]

Therefore, small wars as a feature of colonial conquest were to have calamitous consequences for civil-military relations as soldiers on the colonial fringe deployed brutal tactics increasingly at odds with legal restraints organized for conventional conflict that sought to create protected categories of peoples in battle zones. Small warriors conspired to sabotage civilian oversight of military operations which they saw as unnecessarily meddlesome and an impertinent disrespect of military professionalism and soldierly sacrifice. Small wars seemed to serve no discernible national agenda, but instead came to be seen as self-perpetuating conflicts whose only justification appeared to be that military adventurers wanted to carry them out in the name of the honor of the army and the prestige of the flag. Governments fearful of the wrath of the military-imperialist alliance were often forced to acquiesce. And there lurked the threat that colonial violence would return to the homeland in times of civil unrest, or even as a normal means of civil control.

Knowing the country

Unlike conventional warfare that consists in the main of a confrontation of opposing armies that behave according to fairly predictable norms, followed by a peace treaty and withdrawal, imperialism required Western soldiers to adjust to a protracted rendezvous with exotic populations. "You conquered them by force of arms," Bugeaud barked at his Arab affairs officers, "you'll maintain them in subjugation by force of arms."[64] But conquest followed by the occupation and exploitation of non-European societies compelled cultural understanding as the codex of tactics and operations, not Clausewitz's metaphysics of war, a necessity that further distanced small wars in colonies from conventional conflict in continental Europe. Because the behavior of indigenous populations was believed to be racially determined, the task of the small warrior/administrator-cum-intelligence officer was to decipher local habits, customs, and what Lord Roberts of Kandahar called the "idiosyncrasies of the Natives" so as better to manipulate, fragment, defeat, and subsequently control enemies and eventually subjects.[65] Cultural understanding became an antiseptic term that in effect described a systematic process of cultural deconstruction wrought by the imperialist armies on the native population. Culture also became code for an anti-technological, anti-strategic, politically reactionary, even romantic escapism in imperial militaries that increasingly separated them from continental professionals and their home societies.

For the French in North Africa, the *bureaux arabes* provided a mechanism to weaponize language and culture for the benefit of conquest. Created in 1833 in each military district, the *bureaux arabes* gathered intelligence on the politics and personalities of the tribes to inform the expansion, administration, and policing of French-controlled territories through tribal chiefs willing to serve as intermediaries of foreign occupation.[66] The first director, Major Eugène Damas, a fluent Arabic speaker and avid student of North African custom, may be said to have pioneered militarized anthropology, which has transmogrified over the decades into such institutions as psychological warfare operations, Human Terrain Teams (HTTs), and even Female Engagement Teams (FETs) organized in Iraq and Afghanistan.[67] Central to French conquest and occupation, the *bureaux arabes* offered a trampoline to senior rank for many officers.

Language and culture became arms in the hands of these soldier administrators, who sought to understand the Muslims so as better to dominate them. Like contemporary combat advisers, *bureaux* officers deployed an arsenal of techniques that ran the gamut from diplomacy, persuasion, bribery, favors, and infrastructure projects to sanctions and violence – "No better friend. No worse enemy," in the vocabulary of contemporary COIN, cribbed from the Roman Emperor Sulla who knew a thing or two about the coercive dimensions of imperial warfare. However, effective management required linguistic ability, as well as an intimate knowledge of the tribes, their leaders, economy, laws, enemies, and allies – what in today's military advisory world is called enemy system theory. The hypothesis is that a group's identity is rooted in its narratives of conflicts with neighbors. Victories are celebrated while older defeats – traumas – linger to instill a sense of unresolved loss and vulnerability. In this way, contemporary grievances can be associated with the narrative of ancestral victimization as a basis for mobilization in tribal, ethnic, or sectarian conflict.

> "Chosen traumas and chosen glories provide, in other words, the linking objects for later generations to be rediscovered, reinterpreted and reused," writes Catarina Kinnvall "... A political leader may for instance reignite a dormant group memory by reactivating (or reinventing, reinterpreting) the original injury or glory."[68]

Enemy systems theory maps a group's unconscious narratives of chosen traumas and chosen glories as a way of understanding how the group rationalizes a conflict and develops an engagement plan to manage it.[69]

Applying a primitive version of this process, the *bureaux* both collected intelligence through agents, spies, and informants and acted upon it through the *goum* – irregular tribal levies commanded by *bureaux* officers mustered to carry out *razzias* to extend the conquest, punish the treacherous, terrorize neutrals, and incentivize the loyal. After Bugeaud rewarded his *goumiers* for every severed head they brought back, the *armée d'Afrique* adopted decapitation as standard practice.[70] Like scalping among native North Americans, French soldiers proliferated a practice that they then cited as evidence of Muslim inhumanity as a way to speed imperial conquest, enlist local collaborators, and bolster their case for occupation as necessary to curtail local barbarism.[71] It also handed Europeans an alibi for their "population-centric" savagery.[72] Likewise, Lyautey complained that *bureaux* officers unleashed *goums* that might number in the hundreds, no more than armed mobs perpetrating French-sanctioned mayhem.[73] But *goum*-led *razzias* offered valuable divide and rule mechanisms to shatter Muslim solidarity and win allies for the *bureaux*.

The Indian Political Service (IPS), a subdivision of the Indian Civil Service that recruited officers and civilian university graduates on the basis of fairly stiff university-level examinations in native languages, history, and law, offered a slightly upmarket British version of the *bureaux arabes*. Originally made up of civilian administrators, the IPS was significantly militarized from the 1830s as Soldier Sahibs conquered the Punjab and moved, toward the end of the century to secure the North-West Frontier of India. Unmarried, promotable line officers below the age of twenty-six could apply for a permanent transfer through their commanding officer. Preference was given to officers who possessed a university degree or exceptional linguistic ability, but connections and a family history of IPS service also helped – some Anglo-Indian families counted five generations of IPS officers. As the principal attraction was a considerable pay boost, as well as the opportunity to exercise "powers that were comparable with those of a general," applicants greatly exceeded openings.[74]

Seventy percent of IPS agents on the North-West Frontier were soldiers on "indefinite secondment" from their regiments to manage the "congeries of warlike and unorganized tribes" in frontier areas, act as diplomats, consular officers, and spymasters in the Princely States, and staff the Viceroy's secretariat in New Delhi that coordinated IPS activity – "lean and keen men on the Frontier," as one official noted, "and fat and good-natured men in the States."[75] Both of these institutions offered recognition in theory that an understanding of the values, practices, and behavior of indigenous societies against which colonial campaigns were fought benefited conquest and furnished a foundation for post-conquest stability. Such practices fused the tasks of security, intelligence collection, and governance into a single body, and pushed the politics of conquest and stabilization down to junior officer level. Both were key elements in a forward-leaning frontier policy with significant implications for military professionalism and civil-military relations in the small wars arena.

In this way, the French and British empires established a cadre of culturally informed and linguistically proficient administrators whose job was to control North African Muslims and Indians, particularly the restive tribal societies of the North-West Frontier with Afghanistan, not necessarily to make their life better. Indeed, as C. A. Bayly has noted, "the ideal of the lone colonial officer and sage, standing at the centre of a web of untainted knowledge, the man who 'knows the country'," formed a central myth of imperial governance.[76] However, these men suffered from at least three shortcomings: their local knowledge was imperfect; their mission as the link between the imperialists and the colonized was an ambiguous one; while the intelligence they collected as the basis for their enemy systems theory to inform and guide governance was corrupted by prejudice, suspicion, and outright ignorance.

First, critics complained that IPS reliance on a British officer corps legendary for its intellectual mediocrity deterred more gifted recruits, which translated into a "lethargic, anti-intellectual and slow thinking" organization.[77] In any case, even the most studious outsider was challenged to comprehend the internal dynamics of the amalgam of tribes, clans, and kinship groups on the North-West Frontier with their exotic social mores, complex cultural practices, and incomprehensible dialects. For this reason, despite linguistic training and area experience, the "cultural" understanding of those trained to manage the locals might barely rise above an anthology of clichés and stereotypes based on the alleged national characteristics of the group or tribe which shaped the approach to them.[78] One problem was language: an Arab Bureau chief trained in classical Arabic or an IPS officer top in his promotion in Persian (the language of the Mughal Empire) or Urdu had to rely on interpreters when dealing with local dialects and languages. This situation only worsened as the empires expanded and colonial officials and officers rotated among unfamiliar tribes and regions, and even continents. Therefore, a generalized "parachute expertise"[79] allowed them quickly to size up the natives in ways that did not actually depend on cultural fluency, but on the basis of imported imperial best practices, which consisted of bribery, euphemistically referred to in Service vernacular as "improve [the tribes'] circumstances," alternating with severe repression.[80] Not only did this failing open them to manipulation and misunderstanding, but it also accentuated the administrator's outsider status. While the British in particular convinced themselves that their impartiality and probity informed by cultural sensitivity gave them legitimacy both at home and in country, in fact it often meant imposing incomprehensible decisions on the locals behind an imaginary façade of cultural knowledge.

While there is no doubt that some administrators, like American soldiers in the West in more or less the same era, bonded with the local populations and tried to protect them from exploitation, indigenous peoples offered an indistinguishable assemblage of inscrutable brown faces whose actions were determined by arcane social codes and conventions. Therefore, "knowing the country" might translate into nothing more than superficial platitudes that more or less mirrored the racism and integral nationalism of the age: French administrators in Algeria viewed their charges as "a primitive mass made up of individuals who are liars, hypocrites, and cruel (and) who must be controlled by force."[81] The French *code de l'indigénat*, in force in North Africa until 1944, allowed Muslim civilians to be court-martialed, or simply administered justice through administrative fiat and collective punishments, because Western judicial practices anchored in evidence and sworn testimony were thought to be wasted on natives, considered to be congenital liars.[82] Similar sentiments informed the views of a district commissioner in Waziristan, who described the population as "[c]owardly, bigoted, of poor physique but of different types, all reduced to a harmonious whole by the tint of universal dirt."[83] Even shining paragons of cross-cultural understanding like Frederick Lord Lugard, whose name is associated with the preservation of the Fulani tribal structure of Northern Nigeria, spoke of Africans in terms that would have qualified him for a senior position in the Ku Klux Klan. T. E. Lawrence regarded the Arabs who provided the fodder for his famed exploits as "a limited, narrow-minded people, whose inert intellect lay fallow in incurious resignation."[84] The cultural knowledge of Gertrude Bell, who as a political officer, administrator, and alleged "expert" on Arab culture helped to shape British policy in the Middle East, was limited to unflattering stereotypes of Arabs as "vicious" and lacking morals: "You will very rarely find a Mohammedan who lives a decent existence! ... It's surprising, when you come to think of it, that we in Europe have found out that a reasonable minimum of virtue and honesty are essential concomitants of any successful society. They have not found it in Asia, no matter what religion they happen to belong to."[85]

The relative cultural ignorance of "politicals" was magnified by their doubly ambiguous position as soldier administrators able to overrule decisions of higher commanders, and as the hinge between the imperial state and its subjects. Indigenous governance required compromises that might include participation in social rituals, perhaps adopting aboriginal dress, as baby steps in a gentle slide into a cultural adaptation that led to accusations of going native. Even in a decentralized imperial military organization accustomed to small wars missions, political officers were accused of losing their military edge, preferring to talk when action was required, and going native to the point that their advice was thought to reflect "stubborn" or "corrupt" indigenous viewpoints.[86] And if truth be told, Jacques Frémeaux, French historian of the *bureaux arabes* in nineteenth-century North Africa, writes that, as a group, these men were not "distinguished by their integrity."[87] At the very least, an "advisory" posting proved a fortuitous assignment for an impecunious lieutenant or major with gambling debts to settle: Arab Bureau officers had the power to adjudicate local disputes, levy fines, collect and distribute the proceeds of *razzias*, or even to rent out the *goum* to settle private scores. Their power meant that their favor might be curried with gifts of Arabian horses, topped with a *marriage à l'indigène* with an adolescent provided by a local chief. At the low end, Arab Bureau officers were accused of abuse, inflicting "tortures worthy of the Inquisition," and even summary executions.[88] While every British officer "went to India to make his fortune," Hew Strachan points out that a monopoly of local contacts and knowledge meant that politicals were best placed to manipulate situations to their advantage.[89]

The prospect of loot motivated imperial soldiers while it kept subjects in line.[90] While Christian Tripodi reckons that the political officers, mainly former soldiers, on the North-West Frontier were a pretty upstanding, conscientious, and competent lot,[91] the same might not be said of those assigned as adviser to a Maharaja of one of the Princely States, which Sir Harcourt Butler, Secretary of the Foreign Department of the Government of India in 1907, called "a loose despotic system tempered by corruption." And as the person in charge of Maharaja relations for Delhi, Butler should know! Even if the commissioners and political agents were above reproach, many of the indigenous clerks and assistants who served them and adjudicated minor disputes may not have been.[92] In any case, the colonies offered a world where, in the words of one historian, "a heathen, ribald sensual class of Britons absolutely unbound by convention" were allowed to suspend probity in the interests of imperial stability.[93]

The autonomy and power of the politicals transformed them into a military sub-species who might develop a highly romanticized view of the people they administered, act as their spokesmen, and advocate policies that might put them at odds with the military hierarchy, not to mention other advisers, with their own psychological and emotional attachments to "their" tribe. Administrators who evinced "humanitarian fantasies" were denounced as being at best naïve, at worse as having gone native and so betrayed their mission, service, and race.[94] For their part, politicals complained that the military was dysfunctional, operationally focused, and unable to grasp the cultural, psychological, and political dimensions of the theater of operations – a view that persists to our own day.[95] But the bottom line was that success, and hence legitimacy, was defined as an absence of "organized violence against the state."[96] In short, so long as the political officer kept a lid on things, his mission was a success.[97]

Keeping a lid on things, however, required accurate intelligence. The robustness of the French conquest meant that, as far as North Africans were likely to cooperate, it was out of either fear or opportunism. In neither case was the political officer likely to collect accurate information. The British in India, however, arrived in the seventeenth century as a trading company that under Clive became a collection agency for the Mughal Empire. This allowed the East India Company (EIC) to annex well-developed Mughal commercial and political intelligence networks. However, as the nineteenth century progressed, the EIC's information superiority eroded. Racial segregation that increased with the arrival of evangelicals and English women in the nineteenth century reinforced fears that going native had undermined the company's moral fabric, to place well-informed Eurasian groups beyond the pale of social acceptability. British men abandoned Indian mistresses and so forfeited extensive female networks of information that at the turn of the nineteenth century could extend to centers of Indian power and influence. Salaried, literate Mughal "newswriters" were displaced by despised police *darogas*, considered "people of low character," paid principally to tip off the EIC to sources of taxable wealth and blow the whistle on those who continued outlawed practices, like sati. As the Raj grew, information became mangled, fragmented, dated, increasingly esoteric and useless as it passed through congealed layers of bureaucracy. While the Mughals had used information to inform power, exercise moral suasion, and increase legitimacy, the British operationalized it in the police and army.[98]

Cooperation and understanding facilitated by social interaction gave way to segregation and suspicion that corrupted the cultural approach. Denis Judd argued that colonial occupiers projected "all manner of delinquencies, inadequacies and barbarities" onto indigenous societies as a way to justify their exploitation and manipulation.[99] In his late nineteenth-century "classic text of military Orientalism,"[100] Callwell warned that "while in civilized warfare such a thing (as treachery) is almost unknown," colonial commanders must stay alert for it, especially when evaluating intelligence reports from natives.[101] In the absence of sound information on the ruled, however, imperialists evolved ill-informed attitudes toward their charges. On one hand, they viewed them as ignorant and credulous, if cunning, folk who could be awed by modernization and seduced by infrastructure projects like the creation of a school or market, or the digging of a well. But these characteristics left them vulnerable to schemers and fanatics. Knowledge gaps created "knowledge panics," the most infamous being Major William Sleeman's campaign in the 1830s to rid India of "Thuggee" – a secret religious network of ritual stranglers devoted to the Goddess Kali who preyed on travelers in early nineteenth-century India.

Sleeman has become the poster boy for what one scholar calls "military Orientalism" run amok, which occurs when cultural knowledge becomes a cover for imperial paranoia, racial stereotyping, and distrust of the other.[102] Many modern scholars insist that the Thuggees were a product of Sleeman's "information anxiety" and his controversial interrogation methods. Even Sleeman's defenders, who argue that murderous highwaymen had been a problem for at least twenty years and probably longer, admit that at the very least Sleeman fashioned the Thuggee crisis to enhance his own reputation, showcase the barbarity of Indian customs, and so expand the reach and legitimacy of the colonial state by projecting an image of good governance through the enforcement of security.[103]

The important point, however, is that Sleeman's Thuggee campaign confirmed the imperial trend that culture in its elite ramification rather than strategy in its nineteenth-century scientific form should inform the conduct of small wars, a Sun Tzuian dedication to "know your enemy," which has communicated itself to the campaigns of COIN and counter-terrorism in the twenty-first century.[104] The assumption that deception and trickery lurked behind a mask of indigenous inscrutability caused Sleeman to conjure up a 'Thuggee and Dacoitee Department," versions of which were replicated throughout the subcontinent. As a result, entire castes, communities, and tribes were registered under the Criminal Tribes Act of 1871 as "habitual offenders" requiring constant surveillance and control.[105] At the same time, the post-Mutiny Raj, chagrined at the disloyalty of high-caste Hindu sepoys, identified "martial races" to whom were ascribed racial characteristics desirable in soldiers. The fact that these so-called martial races – Punjabi Sikhs, Nepalese, and Gurkhas – were also often deracinated minorities, recruited among illiterate frontier populations, went a long way to explaining their attachment to the Raj.[106]

Indian nationalists argued that the so-called criminal tribes were merely groups who rejected the legitimacy of British rule, nursed their own grievances, and clung stubbornly to their own customs. However, rather than simply stigmatize groups as criminal, the modern-day anthropological soldier can treat "tribal social pathology" by working to alter the historical narrative that tribes utilize to consolidate collective identity. Groups employ "chosen traumas" and "chosen glories" in rituals that require accommodation, or revenge and resistance. The role of the engagement mission is to reduce the potential for conflict by deemphasizing memories of humiliation and harmonizing a tribe's historical narrative with the larger narrative of the political state.[107]

Critics like Patrick Porter and the anthropologist Anna Simons argue that there are at least three problems with this interpretation. First, it is based on a sort of yard-sale anthropology that views culture as a very static phenomenon, "a distinct and lasting set of beliefs and values," rather than, in Porter's words, "an ambiguous repertoire of competing ideas that can be selected, instrumentalised, and manipulated, instead of a clear script for action."[108] Anthropologist David H. Price complains that *FM 3–24* canabilizes a "mishmash of inconsistent social theory" into a "swampwater version of culture" with cues "on notions of 'status' [that] alerts COIN operators to specific roles that can be manipulated to COIN's advantage."[109] This offers a generalization that applies as much to Britain and France today as it does or has to Algeria, India, Iraq, and Afghanistan. Second, an outsider's perception of the narrative is probably ill-informed, or misinformed because, as Simons argues, "[n]atives – the locals – never tell the truth about the things that are of greatest importance or most value to them until they have taken the measure of the person asking."[110] So, the outsider's cultural observations probably say more about his own cultural perspectives and prejudices than those of the observed group. Third, the idea that culture mandates behavior denies the ability of the natives to make choices based on a rational calculation of their interests and options. Historian of Africa T. O. Ranger argued that the decision to resist imperial rule was made by leaders "adept at assessing European officers," who then calculated whether they had more to gain by resisting or accommodating the intruders. The decision to resist or cooperate was a fluid and dynamic process based on economic and political interests, in particular a reaction to the evolving sub-imperialisms as tribes leveraged cooperation with the Europeans for local advantage.

"Resistance on the part of an African people did not necessarily imply a romantic, reaction rejection of 'modernity,'" Ranger writes.

> *In certain instances, migratory military groups or societies organized for slave-raiding and looting, successfully accommodated themselves to the whites ... Some resisting societies desperately attempted to avoid the necessity of resistance. Some co-operating societies made it plain that they were ready to resist if their cherished privileges were attacked ... Many societies began in one camp and ended in the other. Virtually all African states made some attempt to find a basis on which to collaborate with the Europeans; virtually all of them had some interests or values which they were prepared to defend, if necessary, by hopeless resistance or revolt.*[111]

So, resistance and cooperation were impelled by strategic calculation reflective of reasonable and rational political and economic choice, not tribal instincts dictated by a "criminal" or confrontational trauma narrative. Culture, like the conduct of war, is an interactive, reciprocal process that contains evolving, competing codes so that leaders can selectively mobilize culture to support expediency.[112] Rejection of kinship with a distant colonially imposed community proved perfectly logical, especially if it led to coercion and exploitation through taxes, conscription, forced labor, and abolition of communal rights and privileges of a "modernizing" centralizing authority like the Raj.[113] But proliferating versions of Thuggee and Dacoitee Departments failed to detect a logical basis for resistance because their intelligence suffered from an overload of exotic information, social isolation, and political and racial bias. This fact made them vulnerable to "ideologically-generated 'knowledge panics'" because they continued to sift through irrelevant information.[114]

The road to Sedan

By the mid nineteenth century, few Western Europeans would quarrel with the proposition that empire held out the prospect of improvement for barbarous yet perfectible non-Western populations. On the other hand, Europeans also recognized the moral hazards of imperialism. The East India Company's rapacity in Bengal, the licentious reputation of its officials, and its corruption of the British political system with large inflows of cash to speed the elections of MPs favorable to EIC interests inspired serial parliamentary attempts at reform and stirred Adam Smith to write *Wealth of Nations*, a barely veiled critique of the EIC's monopoly on trade with the East. The 1857 Mutiny, which the US historian Timothy Parsons calls "one of the largest popular anti-imperial uprisings in the history of empire," was the last straw. The Mutiny showcased Indian rejection of Christian civilization and confirmed stereotypes of indigenous malice and ingratitude, while simultaneously exposing the ruthless underpinning of imperial rule.[115]

European populations focused on home defense grew impatient with interminable, expensive wars on the sidelines of civilization. Napoleon III abandoned Mexico in 1867, like his uncle had done in Spain, having failed to prove that small war tactics could surmount the absence of a viable political strategy. Because conquest was prosecuted in an atmosphere of fear, mistrust, racial animosity, and the "clash of civilizations," small wars aimed to induce submission through hunger-war tactics followed by divide-and-rule strategies of occupation. Even if European public opinion, which grew more sophisticated as the century wore on, believed that non-Europeans were representatives of inferior civilizations,[116] they objected to *enfumades* and similar tactics. Colonial soldiers increasingly found it prudent to practice their profession on the quiet, a policy assisted in France by the strict press censorship of the Second Empire (1852–1870).[117]

But no one had yet accused imperialists of being second-rate soldiers because for the moment small wars were perceived, at least to the general public, as professionally equal to continental warfare. French and British armies whose combat experience had been acquired in the colonies dominated their Russian opponent in the Crimea in 1854–1856, while in 1859 French soldiers outfought the Austrians in Italy. But that was about to change, when the Franco-Prussian War of 1870–1871 ignited a debate over whether small wars abroad offered adequate preparation for big war in Europe. Continental warfare appeared to have entered a new phase post-1870 that eclipsed its colonial counterpart in both complexity and lethality.

2 THE ROAD FROM SEDAN

Bugeaud cast a dark shadow over France's defeat in the Franco-Prussian War of 1870–1871. The surrender of Napoleon III and the major French army at Sedan on September 2, barely six weeks after war was declared, was a stunning reversal for French arms. Until this devastating loss, the French armed forces enjoyed the esteem of their countrymen and their counterparts in other national militaries alike. The army that had forged a fearsome reputation under Napoleon I, conquered Algeria, bested Russians in the Crimea, and trounced the Austrians in Italy while holding its own in Mexico produced what generally passed for the best soldiers in Europe. Many of its commanders fell into the savior general category so beloved of the right, while French colonial units like the Zouaves and the *Chasseurs d'Afrique* were regarded as the *nec plus ultra* of the military world – so much so that French uniforms were imitated in the US Army in the early nineteenth century while versions of French units were replicated in both Confederate and Union forces during the American Civil War.

Sedan produced a small wars backlash among makers of policy and military thinkers in France amid the general recrimination and soul searching of a Third Republic born of defeat. A big piece of the failure of small wars sprang from the dubious methods and motives associated with it. The problem wasn't just that irregular tactics failed to translate to the European continent or even that the leading lights of nineteenth-century colonial warfare proved to be, in fact, shockingly inept soldiers in combat. The whole colonial project that small wars supported proved untenable for sound political, moral, and military reasons. For a nation-state attempting post-1870 to integrate a mosaic of peoples, a quarter of whom did not even speak French as their first language, into a French nationalist project, overseas adventures that would eventually incorporate 3.5 million square miles with a heterogeneous population of 26 million souls offered at best a distraction, at worst a perilous incongruity.[1] Algeria seemed to be an army-outsourced racket anchored in race-based arrogance and exploitation that did nothing for the metropole beyond sullying France's international reputation with war crimes. Napoleon III's Mexican adventure came to be denounced as the product of a closed-door conspiracy of conservative Mexican exiles who had gained the ear of the Emperor's Spanish-born wife Eugénie in which a group of bondholders had profited handsomely.[2]

The collateral damage that post-Napoleonic colonial expansion had inflicted on the French military had been nothing short of catastrophic. The most obvious conclusion to draw in the shadow of Sedan was that the small wars, which stood at the core of France's post-1815 military experience, had proven a poor school of the soldier and command in the mid nineteenth century. Worse, they had distorted French defense priorities: Imperial victories had been purchased at the expense of continental collapse. The defeat at the Battle of Sedan became symbolic of a horribly mismanaged campaign that was blamed on such second-rate officers who, like Marshals Achille Bazaine and Patrice de Mac-Mahon, had forged their reputations fighting small wars. So, post-1870 France appeared ready to turn its back on small wars which was at odds with national consolidation, sullied France's self-image as the standard bearer of European civilization, diverted resources required for continental defense, and undermined the professionalism of the French army. Case closed.

Bismarck's Europe and the validation of continental war

The Wars of German Unification (1864–1871), which culminated in the humiliation of Sedan, proved a game-changer, for at least three reasons. First, it bonded the German states, minus Austria, into a powerful empire that, at a stroke, intensified the nature of European interstate competition. Second, it showcased the growing impact of the Industrial Revolution, which quickened the pace of technological change so as to make warfare both more expensive and more lethal. This development required European states to organize, plan, tax, and conscript on a scale hitherto unimaginable. Mobilization on a scale heretofore unseen was to be strategically decisive, with the result that the generations prior to August 1914 lived with the permanent prospect of war on the horizon. Finally, Louis-Napoleon's emblematic surrender at Sedan instilled the requirement for European states to establish a professional officer corps competent to mobilize, manage, lead, and maneuver large bodies of men. It escaped the attention of no one that the foundation for Prussian Chancellor Otto von Bismarck's unification of Germany had been laid by military reform directed from 1862 by War Minister Albrecht von Roon and General Helmut von Moltke, Prussian Chief of the General Staff. Henceforth, the Prussian/German Army and its vaunted General Staff became the gold standard of military proficiency against which governments and armies measured their chances of survival in a conflict with Berlin. By comparison, small wars came to be regarded in the military as small bore, quasi-professional tropical excursions by ragtag colonial mercenaries in which victory or defeat mattered hardly a jot in the wider scheme of national survival.

The Third Republic (1870–1940) did its best to learn from defeat and adapt its military posture in the age of mass armies. Living next door to a united, dynamic, populous, and increasingly industrialized Germany convinced Frenchmen to upgrade their forces and keep them on the Continent. Conscription aimed to create a "nation in arms" whose task was to train for conventional war against Germany.[3] The post-1870 metropolitan army was to become the "school of the nation" in imitation of the Germans whose mission was to transform "peasants into Frenchmen" by infusing citizens with a love of *la patrie*, create conditions of social mobility, and unite conservatives and progressives around a common symbol of youth, order, and national revival.

The foundation of the post-1871 French military renaissance rested on the assumption that metropolitan and colonial warfare constituted separate categories of conflict. With the French army now focused on *la Revanche* for 1870, skirmishes with Arabs, Africans, and Indochinese henceforth became a sideshow, not an overture to the main event.[4] Imperial defense was delegated to professional French marines and colonial mercenaries.

Yet, despite the focus of European armies on organizing for continental conflict, a shift in Europe's diplomatic alignment, as well as political and intellectual trends over time plucked small war from the abyss of its post-1870 discredit. One upshot of Bismarckian Europe that served to isolate France diplomatically was that continental confrontation rekindled colonial competition, one encouraged by the European worldview in the second half of the nineteenth century that was increasingly informed by integral nationalism, racism, social Darwinism and its political spinoff, geopolitics. In this context, colonial expansion was framed as an international, zero-sum *mêlée* for imperial *Lebensraum*, geostrategic advantage, economic resources, and colored cannon fodder. Success in the game of imperial expansion came to be viewed as a Darwinian test of national vitality especially among the leading social classes unnerved by the domestic politics of class friction. For them, imperialism offered a national mission that could override social and political divisions. Imperial apologists like French General Charles Mangin and British Foreign Secretary Lord Salisbury argued that black and brown legions of colonial troops would act as force multipliers in a continental war.

Then as now, peddlers of small wars required a concrete national threat to sell colonial projects to a skeptical public. Bugeaud had argued in the 1840s that he was fighting a Muslim jihad in Algeria that posed a global threat to French interests, a claim adopted by later generations of French soldiers in the Western Sudan. Now, however, the main impediment to imperialist schemes came from a deficit of national purpose and energy that would forfeit to European rivals lands as yet unclaimed in Africa and Asia. From the 1880s, therefore, imperial soldiering became a growth industry with more nations carving out and consolidating colonies in Africa and Asia. French soldiers set such a frenetic pace of conquest in the Western Sudan, North Africa, Indochina, and Madagascar that British, Germans, even Portuguese felt obliged to preempt colonial claim jumping with conquests of their own. In this way, small wars spokesmen marketed humble, back-of-beyond outposts as strategically vital pieces of real estate coveted by other European powers. Britain's army invaded Afghanistan twice in the nineteenth century to foil nonexistent Russians designs on that hapless land. Upper Burma, three Opium Wars in China, Southern Africa, the Sudan and elsewhere also received the attentions of Britain's imperial soldiers. "Imperial Germany's combat history from 1871 to 1914 was purely colonial," writes Isabel Hull; it included "countless 'punitive expeditions' in Germany's colonies" in the 1890s, the Boxer Uprising in China (1900–1901), the Herero revolt in Southwest Africa (1904–1907), and the Maji Maji Rebellion in German East Africa (1905–1907).[5]

However, imperialists faced two problems. First, by the mid 1890s, colonial collisions increasingly threatened to ignite continental conflict, so that Paris and London strained to rein in imperial expansion. In the two decades following the Franco-Prussian War, small wars remained a discrete, largely low-risk advance against poorly armed and organized primitives. Occasional military defeats like Custer's at the Little Big Horn (1876), Chelmsford at Isandlwana (1879), Bonnier near Timbuktu (1894), and Baratieri at Adowa (1896) were little more than fleeting humiliations that, because they were inflicted by an indigenous foe, failed to trigger a nationalist response, but instead heightened the sense of risk and hence the drama of imperial adventure. Gladstone refused to be blackmailed into action by Charles "Chinese" Gordon's "ambitious and vain" 1884 attempt to annex the Sudan by refusing to evacuate Khartoum, a gamble that Gordon paid for with his life.[6] Imperial nations kept to their lanes: Russia focused on consolidating Central Asia; the United States, on its frontier West. Japan had to modernize following the 1868 Meiji Restoration, while Germany under Bismarck seemed content with symbolic slices of the imperial pie in Africa and in Asia that never became the center of gravity in his statecraft.

This state of affairs began to change in the 1890s as diminishing acreage unclaimed by another European power threatened to escalate Franco-British imperial competition in Africa beyond the "small wars" category. Attempts by French diplomats, parliamentarians, and colonial administrators to hobble their imperial soldiers met with no more success than had attempts to cage Bugeaud a half-century earlier.[7] In 1898, French Major (later General) Jean-Baptist Marchand planted the tricolor on a desiccated sandbank in the upper Nile called Fashoda. One of the Third Republic's musical-chairs cabinets had approved Marchand's expedition that departed the mouth of the Congo River in 1896. But a successor government was suddenly confronted with a crisis provoked by a harebrained colonialist scheme – stake a claim to the Sudan and force the British to concede privileges in Egypt to the French. The subsequent war scare so overstretched the French that they were forced to ship 12,000 metropolitan conscripts to the colonies. "We have behaved like madmen in Africa," exclaimed French President Félix Faure, appalled that France had almost been lured into war with Britain over a remote and desolate place in Africa, "having been led astray by irresponsible people called colonialists."[8] Fashoda, however, proved merely a curtain raiser that would transform small wars into prolonged, expensive, and murderously large ones that challenged the international order.

Rebranding Bugeaud

A second problem faced by imperialists intent on expansion was the popular perception dating from Bugeaud and the Indian Mutiny that imperial expansion and occupation offered a low-skill, morally ambiguous enterprise anchored in destruction, intimidation, and exploitation. Even as Bugeaud brought Abd-el-Kader to heel in the 1840s, critics in the army like the future Generals Louis Jules Trochu and Jules Lewal, as well as Marshal Boniface de Castellane complained that what they called the "African Mutual Admiration Society" had gained a lock on the army's senior positions by touting their skirmishes against ill-armed Muslims and Mexicans as the next best thing to Austerlitz. The marginal battlefield skills of the *armée d'Afrique* had failed to decelerate the express-train promotion of its officers to the highest positions in the army. The fact that "Africans" seemed to believe that order and discipline like drill and impeccable uniforms were unimportant was particularly offensive to metropolitan soldiers who prized elegance and decorum as the embodiment of soldierly bearing. And while Sedan had not been a battle of etiquette, long-time critic of the colonial style of warfare, General Trochu, argued that the *armée d'Afrique*'s casual approach to soldiering overall extended to its "famous and traditional formula *débrouillez-vous*" (basically "muddle through"), which, when combined with its glorification of physical strength and violence, offered an inadequate dress rehearsal for battle with Bismarck and Moltke.[9]

British historian Richard Holmes argues that the "Africans" unfairly took the rap for the 1870 defeat, the consequence of multiple systemic and leadership problems in the French army. However, Frenchmen scavenging for scapegoats attributed their thrashing by the Germans to a decades-old legacy of raids and skirmishes in Algeria and Mexico that had left generals both complacent and ill-equipped to manage large, articulated, multi-arm forces equipped with modern weapons and led by modern forms of command. Campaign plans, precise orders, and sizable staffs to implement them, and logistics of the machine age adequate to sustain large armies in the field for months were mysteries into which colonial soldiers remained uninitiated. Badly outnumbered French infantrymen went to war in 1870 loaded like tinkers' donkeys and bivouacked in the open as in Algeria instead of billeting in civilian homes; they launched ragged bayonet charges against well-disciplined German troops armed with the legendary breech-loading rifles. Cavalry failed to scout and became tangled and out of position on the battlefield. French artillery, once Napoleon's pride and the foundation of many of his victories, was jettisoned as superfluous impedimenta on colonial battlefields. Composed of bronze, rifled muzzle-loaders, it proved hopelessly archaic, totally outranged, and appallingly organized. In short, Bugeaud's "swarmers" were clueless about how to fight a modern, industrial conflict.[10]

The problem was that this burst of colonial expansion – and, along with it, the pay, promotion, and early retirement inducements to attract young men into colonial service – failed to reverse the perception earned in 1870–1871 that imperial soldiers dealt in a devalued professional currency, so that most of the best officers preferred to prepare for continental service. There were exceptions: men bored with garrison routine, adventure seekers, those who sought to (re)make their fortunes, or men eager to escape European social or sexual constraints; Gallieni joined the Marines straight out of France's famed military academy, Saint-Cyr, in July 1870, while Joffre, a graduate of the elite *École polytechnique*, volunteered for colonial service in 1884 following the death of his wife. However, from the turn of the twentieth century as the imperial competition overseas reached its zenith, both men put imperial assignments and small wars behind them and focused on preparing the French army for life-or-death continental conflict. Lyautey's imperial vocation was initiated by his disillusionment with the failure of the metropolitan army to live up to the moralizing social mission that the Third Republic's founders envisaged for it. (Instead, he discovered that the officer corps he had joined in 1873 to revitalize France was filled with bureaucrats, exam takers, and careerists indifferent to their social mission.[11]) But even these exceptions confirm the rule that the colonies were a dumping ground that attracted the French army's bottom feeders – "bachi-bouzouks" forced abroad by poor professional prospects or personal scandal, to include gambling debts and paternity suits. Marine vacancies were filled from the bottom quarter of each year's class at Saint-Cyr. Imperial service was seen as a *pis aller* for the French army's remaindered men, the poorly connected, adventurers, and misfits like Hubert Lyautey.[12]

The same might be said for the imperial armies of Britain and Germany, whose attitude might be summed up in the Kipling couplet: "Ship me somewheres east of Suez where the best is like the worst, / Where there aren't no Ten Commandments, an' a man can raise a thirst." The British Army in India attracted the ambitious, the impecunious, and the Scots gentry, which combined all categories.[13] As Germany, a late convert to colonialism, created no separate imperial army, line units were combed for volunteers for expeditionary corps that were, at best, auxiliaries of the army and navy. While no sociological comparisons as yet exist on the German officer corps abroad, the anecdotal evidence suggests that imperial volunteers were frequently men fleeing scandal, who sought to redeem some misdemeanor in the cauldron of colonial combat, were "rough fighters" whom garrison commanders were eager to shed, or men recycled from other colonial forays, like the noteworthy Paul von Lettow-Vorbeck who became a national hero for his East African campaign in 1914–1918 and later a Nazi darling.[14] Colonial service offered a means for the pariahs of society to join the master race, a world where the gentleman and the criminal floated untouched above a world unqualified and disinclined to judge them.[15]

Not surprisingly given its imperial focus, the small wars backlash in the British Army was far more muted than that which infected post-1871 France. British reformers in the 1860s and 1870s concluded that Crimea and the Mutiny in the 1850s had discredited a system that maintained a separate army for use in India, while the Franco-Prussian War demonstrated the need to create a trustworthy reserve in the event of a continental emergency. The influence of the Prussian-German territorially based corps and replacement order of battle on a mass scale and the brains of the General Staff were evident in the 1871 Cardwell Reforms that instituted short-service enlistment and the "link-battalion" system whereby regiments maintained a battalion in Britain and one abroad. But the British Army's imperial focus and the Royal Navy's maritime shield obviated the requirement for a continental-style conscript army with a million-man end strength as became the norm elsewhere. The British Army's two senior generals in the 1870–1880s, Frederick Roberts and Garnet Wolseley and their respective "rings" of loyal subalterns and protégés, split bitterly over the Cardwell Reforms, a split that reflected their Conservative/India *vice* Liberal/Africa political views, patronage, and professional experience. This reluctance to professionalize on the continental model was reinforced by the attitudes of the British upper middle class from which most officers were drawn, and the educational philosophy of the "public schools" to which they sent their sons, where the romanticism of an amateur ideal trumped practical training.[16]

An army of long-service professional soldiers, together with "regimental exclusiveness and independence of command" masked the British Army's professional shortcomings. Until the Second Anglo-Boer War of 1899–1902, the largest British force deployed was 35,000 troops for the 1881 invasion of Egypt. London expanded the Indian army, paid for by taxes collected in India and not subject to parliamentary scrutiny, to operate both in India and elsewhere in the Far East. Therefore, British officers simply did not feel obliged to develop the same level of professional competence as their continental counterparts; they largely boycotted the staff college, remained ignorant of technological developments, and preferred what would later be called Colonel Blimpish improvisation to planning and standardization.[17] Reduced pressure to professionalize on a continental model forced British officers to play casualty-heavy catch-up well into two world wars. But in the interim, they managed to keep the Punjabis and the Pashtuns pacified before the balloon went up in 1914. Thereafter, however, the game changed, even in Africa where von Lettow-Vorbeck's success against British forces applied Zulu tactical concepts while exploiting the propensity of British troops to be "moved and led [with] clumsiness" – an observation that dated from von Lettow-Vorbeck's participation in the multi-national expedition to suppress the 1900 Boxer Rebellion.[18]

British Army soldiers in the colonies were just as politicized as their French imperial contemporaries. In his marvelous book *The Politics of the British Army*, Hew Strachan argues that, far from being an apolitical force, the British Army was a supremely political organization. This process was rooted in the imperial phenomenon itself, in which the state exported its machinery of violence – the police and the army – unaccompanied by institutional mechanisms of control.[19] Imperial service, where the army had long fused administration with warfare in the face of restive local peoples, and where the imperial administration was ultimately dependent on the army to enforce its authority, was a major impetus for its politicization. "The empire was therefore the most consistent and most continuous influence in shaping the army as an institution," Strachan writes. "It was the principal agent in the army's acquisition of professionalism."[20] Nor did professionalism provide a bulwark against the politicization of soldiers, but quite the contrary.

To allay this image and raise the status of colonial soldiering in the shadow of the Moltke-style General Staff and mass conscript army as well as that of modern high seas fleets, a modern "small wars school" began to emerge in the 1890s promoted principally by two men: British Colonel C. E. Callwell and future Resident General of Morocco and Marshal of France, Hubert Lyautey. Their goal was to emphasize not only the nobility of imperial soldiering, but also its unique requirements, in an attempt to demonstrate that "small wars" should be accorded a professional status equal, if not superior to, continental soldiering. Callwell, an artilleryman who saw action in Afghanistan in 1880 and subsequently in the Anglo-Boer War of 1881, was a soldier-scholar who assembled an impressively thorough compendium of tactical lessons of small wars, beginning with Hoche's suppression of the revolt in the Vendée during the French Revolution through the Second Boer War of 1899–1902. The first edition of Callwell's volume dates from 1896, and it remained a staff college staple into the 1920s.

Callwell can hardly claim to be the Clausewitz of colonial warfare, but that is precisely the point. From its earliest days, small wars were embraced as a refutation of modern, intellectual, more strategically sophisticated analytical and technological approaches to warfare. "The finest gimmicks of our newest theoreticians of war lose their magic power [in Africa]," declared Prussian General Paul von Decker after a visit to Algeria in the 1840s, clearly relieved to have found a combat category where "European ideas" like the "center of gravity" were dismissed as so much new-fangled theory.[21] From its earliest nineteenth-century origins, small wars were focused on tactics and, with the Arab Bureau and Indian Political Service, created primitive versions of human terrain teams dedicated to the manipulation of indigenous groups based on cultural and racial platitudes extracted from primitive anthropologized observation.

Callwell's title was itself deceptive marketing in an age when product promotion was becoming a feature of military and naval professionalism as it was in mass politics and mass society. There was nothing particularly "small" about small wars – most proved to be protracted, unlimited, murderous, expensive, total-war assaults on indigenous societies. They might also escalate beyond the bounds of "small," as in South Africa in 1899. In *Small Wars*, Callwell advanced the case that the tactical flexibility required of imperial warfare not only distinguished it from the "stereotyped system" prevalent in Europe, but also qualified it in prophetic words for the century to come as "an art by itself."[22] He identified three classes of colonial campaign: conquest and annexation; suppressing insurrection; and, finally, retaliation for an insult. He cautioned the commander first to decide what he wished to achieve, then carry out a thorough net assessment of his operational and tactical capabilities, as well as those of the resistance. Rapid advances by mounted men to seize an objective was his recommended method, largely because "irregular armies" were loose coalitions that "always count many waverers ... mere lookers-on" who would bolt for safety in the face of a resolute offensive. Forbearance was wasted on "uncivilized races who attribute leniency to timidity. Fanatics and savages must be thoroughly brought to book and cowed or they will rise again." He acknowledged that this required actions "which the laws of regular warfare do not sanction," the application of harsh measures that "shocks humanitarians" and makes reconciliation problematic.[23] So, in one small book, Callwell laid out in 1896 the contours of modern COIN as a distinct category of warfare whose success depended on speed and maneuver rather than mass and firepower, which would assure the psychological domination over a fanaticized but inferior enemy, and cause his biddable supporters to skulk away. He also concedes that the process will likely be inhumane, possibly criminal, certainly beyond the legal boundaries permitted by conventional warfare against a white opponent. As a consequence, the occupation will be delegitimized both in the eyes of the occupied and the sponsoring Homeland. Now that's a formula for victory!

If Callwell shared with Bugeaud the "positivist" belief that brutality formed an unavoidable spinoff of imperial conquest, Lyautey understood that small war must be repackaged for an age of mass politics to which imperialism was closely bound. Deeply influenced by social Catholicism, Lyautey believed colonialism's Achilles heel to be its failure to distinguish combatant from non-combatant in an unregulated total war assault on vulnerable indigenous populations. Bugeaud-style *razzias* formed a first step in a process that destroyed the economic livelihood of the indigenous populations, disaggregated their tribal structures, and left them vulnerable to exploitation. If Bugeaud may be seen to be the father of population-centric COIN, Lyautey became its impresario. A charmingly aristocratic if somewhat brittle cavalryman well networked with Parisian high society, Lyautey was ordered to Tonkin in 1894 under mysterious circumstances,[24] the initiation of an imperial excursion during which he updated, refined, and rebranded small wars as a patriotic and humanitarian enterprise and contoured it to France's self-image as the torchbearer of the *mission civilizatrice* and the wellspring of human dignity.

The colonial conversion befell Lyautey during his time as executive officer for Colonel Joseph Gallieni, who in October 1892 had taken command of Lang Son, the second of four military territories created in 1891 as part of a plan to pacify a mountainous region on the Chinese border. Lang Son contained a mixed population that included Chinese and Vietnamese, but consisted principally of what the French called *montagnards* – Nung, Thai, Meo, and Mung tribesmen. The *montagnards* were preyed on by both Chinese and Vietnamese, who had lairs in Tonkin's jagged mountains and who organized raids that captured *montagnard* water buffalo and women for sale in China. The French called these Chinese and Vietnamese predators "pirates," which they undoubtedly were. But banditry always had a political, anti-regime dimension in China and Vietnam. Many Chinese had established themselves in Tonkin following the suppression of the Taiping Rebellion (1850–1864), while the Vietnamese were survivors of the Can Vuong movement that for over a decade had resisted French colonization of Tonkin's Red River Delta until that insurgency was finally extinguished in 1889.

Gallieni's strategy was threefold. First, he began to clear each valley, after which he would plant a small outpost from which he expanded French influence through a *tâche d'huile* or "oil spot" tactic. The French would dig a well or establish a market to attract the local population, often through the purchase of local produce at above market prices. Intelligence officers worked the crowd on market day to build a picture of local relationships that would inform the second, more combat oriented, or as it is called today kinetic, dimension of his strategy – attacks on pirate lairs inside Tonkin with converging columns, one of which would fix the fortress while the others flanked it. Not much swarming occurred because the pirates, tipped off by their own intelligence networks and sometimes reinforced by Chinese soldiers from across the border, laid ambushes for the French, who were often steered into them by treacherous guides. Nor did the insurgents linger to *faire Camerone*, while the French were usually too exhausted after fighting their way for days through the hellish terrain to pursue. But smaller, more frequent columns launched from multiple posts established closer to the redoubts at least put the insurgents on the run because Chinese and Vietnamese bandits had no links to the *montagnard* population, which made it more difficult for them to settle. Gallieni encouraged this division by offering the *montagnards* twenty piasters for the head of each Chinese or Vietnamese, trophies which were placed on bamboo stakes as decoration around French posts. He also armed some of the *montagnards*, on the face of it a politically low-risk strategy because, unlike the Chinese and Vietnamese who might have turned the weapons on the French, they were judged to be too isolated geographically and ethnically, and too dependent on the French, to coordinate a concerted rebellion.[25]

But neither destroying Chinese networks nor creating his own solved Gallieni's fundamental strategic problem, which was the porous border. The border problem was complicated by the fact that the Chinese regarded the *montagnards* as objects of plunder: "China is an inexhaustible reservoir of bandits," Major Emmanuel Chabrol who served under Gallieni complained.[26] So the third arm of Gallieni's strategy became to eliminate the pirate safe haven. To do this, he must convince the warlord who controlled the Chinese side of the border, a Marshal Sou, to clamp down on cross-border raids. To this end, Gallieni settled an outstanding territorial dispute with the Chinese, mounted a raid into the warlord's territory to show that two could play this game, and patiently negotiated. Next, he convinced the French-Indochinese opium monopoly to sell the *montagnards* large quantities of opium at dumping prices so that the Chinese would have to deal with them on a commercial basis, rather than simply plunder them.[27] The French christened this *la politique des races* – a Tonkin Awakening that was a standard find and support the ethnic/ religious minority strategy put in motion by every clued-in imperial power.

Gallieni's oil spot and "combining politics with force" methods proved to be Lyautey's epiphany, for several reasons. Philosophically, they harmonized with his paternalistic, social Catholic outlook. Professionally, they promoted a method that enhanced the status of "colonials" within a French army that accorded colonial skirmishes little respect in the pantheon of military professionalism. Politically, Lyautey reconceptualized the tactics of Colonels Théophile Pennequin and Gallieni into a theory of soft conquest – "peaceful penetration" promoted by a cadre of officer-administrators – that he expounded in a 1900 article, "Le rôle colonial de l'officier" published, as had been his 1890 article, in the prestigious *Revue des deux mondes*. This time, however, he garnered praise, not censure. Peaceful penetration, a term associated with Lyautey, was in fact plagiarized from French traders who were critical of destructive military expeditions that alienated local populations, and who advocated expanding French influence exclusively through commerce.[28] Lyautey aligned his tactics with the commercial and cultural vision laid out by pro-colonialist Prime Minister Jules Ferry in 1885.[29] Henceforth, imperial conquest would advance in the guise of a population-friendly strategy more compatible with French values – "*C'est du meilleur Bugeaud*," Lyautey boasted, although it is difficult to imagine, given the absence of mustard gas and other weapons of mass destruction (WMDs) at the time, how one might have replicated a *pire* Bugeaud.[30] At a stroke, Callwell's racist, kinetic small wars transitioned into a modern, population-centric counterinsurgency method designed to bestow the benefits of Western civilization on non-Western peoples.

This conceptual leap has not been lost on contemporary COIN proponents who cite Gallieni's campaign in upper Tonkin as evidence for the applicability of "the need to understand how networks fight – and how to build networks of one's own."[31] However, in making Gallieni the father of network-centric warfare, they vastly oversimplify an extremely complex situation, and hand a victory to Gallieni that he did not achieve. This twisted interpretation occurs because they buy into Lyautey's promotion of Gallieni as the very soul of small war brilliance. Conveniently omitted from Lyautey's account was the fact that Gallieni's tactics failed to stabilize Tonkin. If pressed, pirates simply crossed the border, or migrated to other military territories in the region. This violence dipped temporarily in 1895 for two reasons. First, in September 1894, Gallieni's major enemy, Hoang Hoa Tham, better known as De Tham, the "Tiger of Yen The," shifted his strategy to attacking trains on the Lang Son (Yunnan–Vietnam) railway and kidnapping important colonists and their families, which forced the government to strike a temporary truce with him. Second, the Forbidden City, fearful that France would leverage the Sino-Japanese War that broke out in August 1894 to expand its influence in China, ordered its proconsuls in the south to cease raids into Tonkin. But fighting flared again in 1896, the year of Gallieni's departure. De Tham was reinforced by defectors from French-led Vietnamese units that he had purposely infiltrated to gather intelligence and recruits. French sweeps of Tonkin in 1897 were ineffective, which forced Hanoi to conclude yet another truce with De Tham that, according to historian of Vietnam David Marr, allowed the bandit/resistance leader "to continue for fifteen more years of plotting uprisings and assassinations and occasionally providing aid and comfort to a later generation of anti-colonial leaders."[32]

As a further irony, Lyautey's attempts to replicate Gallieni's networks in the sud-Oranais, the volatile border area between Algeria and southeastern Morocco that he commanded from 1903, also failed to dissolve the resistance, as theory predicted. On the contrary, Lyautey's peaceful penetration based on oil-spot expansion out of French posts proved a highly destabilizing enterprise because it dislocated trade patterns and alienated powerful economic interests. Finally, collective punishments for attacks or even robberies tended to fall on near-to-hand natives who "must have known." So, the impact of Lyautey's networks in southeastern Morocco was to mobilize Moroccan resistance, first as a boycott of French markets in 1906, which transitioned into a general insurrection two years later. Thus, in the final analysis, the benefit of Lyautey's networks was that they provoked an insurrection that forced the French to fall back on the *razzia* to shatter a poorly armed resistance.[33] Lyautey fumed that his oil spot, progressive penetration, and combination of politics with force prescriptions were deprecated as twaddle by metropolitan soldiers, peddled by "men [e.g. Lyautey] fearful of war."[34] But modern COIN advisers have recognized that the introduction of infrastructure improvements as part of hearts and minds strategies can unsettle local relations, advantage one group over another, and actually ignite conflict.[35]

There may be several lessons here for modern COIN tacticians. First, a network unsupported by a viable *politique des races* – that is, a reliable minority who allies with the occupier as a strategy of survival (see the twenty-first-century example of Iraq: "Anbar, the Surge") – is simply a yawning invitation to overthrow. Second, networks may easily develop their own agendas, especially if they become self-financing sectarian or warlord-run criminal enterprises, which may undermine the goals of COIN. Finally, the importance of networks, like information operations or swarming, as anything other than a tactic is overstated.[36]

But the facts mattered little. Where Callwell had offered a tactical manual for soldier-practitioners, Lyautey's *rôle colonial de l'officier* provided a sophisticated debut for an orchestrated lobbying campaign by small war devotees to redefine their craft in a way familiar to contemporary COIN proponents. First, small wars in its peaceful penetration dimension offered an inspirational activity distinct from its conventional counterpart with its own canon and professional ethos. Second, the *rôle colonial de l'officier* advanced small warriors to a status co-equal to that of metropolitan officers. Finally, Lyautey aimed to leverage the Third Republic's cockamamie political environment to secure more budgetary autonomy for imperial operations and so remove a layer of civilian oversight, and exclude conscripts whose presence in imperial operations attracted unwelcome parliamentary scrutiny.

The scandal of the Dreyfus affair, which hit its apogee in 1899 with Captain Alfred Dreyfus' return from Devil's Island for retrial and eventual presidential pardon, offered the small warriors a political opening. Lyautey's goal was to create a protected organizational realm for small warriors within a *fin de siècle* French army that was being battered by the domestic politics of the Dreyfus affair. Dreyfus offered small warriors an opportunity to avenge the blame heaped on them as the authors of 1870. The general argument went as follows: The colonial army contained in its ranks a dynamic corps of men of action with battlefield experience at a time when France's conventional army – buffeted by politics, sunk in routine, and manned by demoralized, half-trained conscripts – might prove unable to defend the country. Citizen-soldiers were abundant, but they were also soft, inefficient, and politicized. According to Lyautey, the metropolitan army was ruled by "mutual admiration coteries, lovers of clichés and formulas, ... good at book learning, carrying to the ministry and to the high command petty schoolboy jealousies, flattering the prefects, eager to please, shirking personality and freedom of spirit. This is why, when I set foot on the boat [for the colonies] four years ago, I felt as if I were escaping from jail."[37]

Jailbreak pitched Lyautey into a cauldron of audacity, valor, toughness, initiative, and the spirit of sacrifice. And the argument carried the day with the creation in 1900 of a separate, 70,000-strong *armée coloniale* that joined the *armée d'Afrique* stationed in North Africa to form a reservoir of professional French marines, foreign legionnaires, and colonial mercenaries as an imperial expeditionary force. Implicit in the separation was the assertion that France's two armies were worlds apart in spirit, the metropolitan army Prussianized, bureaucratized, "a citadel of every routine, of every stupidity," Lyautey proclaimed, which he contrasted with the initiative, creativity, and, for him, liberation and exhilaration of colonial service abroad.

The problem in the long term with the 1900 reorganization was that, while armies, war, and society became increasingly entwined on the

Continent, the Clausewitzian bond between state, society, and use of force was severed in the colonies. Loosed from Clausewitzian constraints and a sense of the army's interaction with a constellation of national and international priorities and pressures, colonial soldiers were free to characterize their brand of warfare in Jominian terms, *à la* Callwell. However, the expansion of France's empire confronted soldiers with the old dilemma of seeking to modernize societies versus respecting tradition and local particularities, a tension that remains at the heart of counterinsurgency today. In truth, small warriors tried to play it both ways. For instance, while slavery had been officially abolished in France and its colonies in 1848, Algeria was slow to implement abolition. French soldiers in the Western Sudan continued to tolerate slavery with the argument that the 1848 decree did not apply in territories conquered after that date. They also successfully auditioned the very contemporary argument that the so-called slaves were in fact enemy combatants under indefinite detention. Furthermore, French officers understood that abolition would alienate powerful local social and economic interests, as well as undermine the basis of French military efficiency, which hinged on giving their indigenous allies carte blanche to slave raid.[38] While slavery was only officially outlawed in the French colonies in 1905, it continued to be tolerated in the Sahel in particular. French-organized *villages de liberté*, ostensibly transitional establishments for liberated slaves, in fact became repositories of forced laborers for infrastructure improvement projects, women, and conscripts.[39]

"Peaceful penetration" and "hearts and minds" – a term in use on the North-West Frontier of India at least by 1891 – now became codified by proponents of small wars and imperialism as philosophies of governance, as well as tactics of conquest.[40] Indirect rule, a concept as old as empires, was merely an update of the methods of the Arab Bureau and the IPS practice to rule through sheiks, maharajas, and tribal chiefs. Advocates of indirect rule, like Lyautey and Sir Frederick (Lord) Lugard in Fulani (northern Nigeria), equated the modernization of non-Western cultures with contamination and destabilization– what today is denounced as social engineering that seeks to alter governance practices, the official economy, and legal codes that run counter to indigenous cultural norms and so court rejection.[41]

Lyautey and Lugard were determined that Morocco and Fulani should not replicate what they saw as the failed imperial projects in Algeria and India, where modernization in the name of development had shattered what they imagined to be a pristine antique hierarchy of rank and order. And they had a point – Lyautey decried the marginalization and impoverishment of Algerian Muslims whose lands had been expropriated by settlers, and whose sheiks had been reduced to day laborers under French administrators. Lugard correctly realized that progressively opening upper ranks of the Imperial Civil Service to indigenous recruitment in the second half of the nineteenth century and the Anglicization of the legal system in the wake of the 1857 Mutiny meant that a "baboo" class of largely Hindu lawyers and administrators educated in mission schools and Inns of Court had become the adjudicators of British rule in India, and would ultimately coalesce to seize the Indian subcontinent.[42]

However, as an antidote, indirect rule had its limitations, beginning with the fact that it was anchored in a romanticized, Orientalized Western vision of a timeless indigenous society – a view that had far more to do with the nostalgia of conservative imperial administrators and soldiers for an idealized *ancien régime* Europe of hierarchy and deference than with an accurate understanding of the social arrangements and values of native culture. The imperial view, one that has translated to contemporary COIN as a hearts and minds, good governance, state-building exercise, is that non-Western societies exist in a time-warp which the adoption of Western practices like democracy, rule of law, and capitalistic competition will allow them to overcome. And while embracing some or all of these institutions may, and indeed has, upgraded the quality of life of certain countries, it has caused small warriors and imperial state builders to view non-Western customs and institutions as primitive versions of Western ones. In this vein, Lyautey reimagined the Sultan of Morocco as a Bourbon monarch, when in fact his status as a descendant of the Prophet translated in Moroccan eyes to a venerable religious personage whose secular authority was strictly circumscribed. British imperialists conflated Bengali *nawabs* and *zamindars* with a hereditary English squirearchy that they could preempt to govern the peasantry. In reality, they were more like tax farmers and mafiosi with no connection to the soil, who directed small regiments of agents and gangsters to shake down artisans and peasants.[43] Likewise, contemporary COIN-dinistas who celebrate the Anbar Awakening as successfully breaking the code on the tribalized nature of Iraqi society, ignore the fact that they may be dealing with a ward boss or gang honcho who has emerged victorious in the latest power struggle to control territory and economic resources.

But these romantically inclined imperialists of the late nineteenth and early twentieth century strove to preserve indigenous society as if they were living out their Orientalized fantasy. Imperial service, like small wars, offered a deferment from the political and social modernization and leveling at home from which they felt increasingly estranged. The disproportionate number of Scots on India's North-West Frontier, called to supervise a Pathan rendering of Robert the Bruce's Caledonian clansmen, could dream that they were living a Sir Walter Scott novel.[44] The colonies became a test bed for Orientalized experimentation in governance. Lyautey, a recovering monarchist, hoped that the example of a stable Moroccan sultanate could inspire a secular, egalitarian France to regenerate itself along more traditionalist lines in the face of socialism and chaos.[45] The deeply conservative Lugard sought to institutionalize a Fulani gentry in Nigeria in the image of a fading English aristocracy.

Lyautey and Lugard's attempts to institutionalize feudalism and make it tolerable caused at least five problems that reverberate in the contemporary celebration of COIN. First, colonial administrators clung to a fundamentalist version of 1960s Development Theory that poverty was the root cause of indigenous rebellion, a condition that could be remedied by infrastructure improvements to facilitate trade and hence increase prosperity, as well as to allow for speedier troop deployments to troubled areas. However, when added to occupation overheads, infrastructure development of "deficit provinces" either had to be paid for by the exchequer or accomplished through forced labor. Needless to say, the latter tactic made these projects extremely unpopular with the locals, further undermined the legitimacy of imperial rule, and provoked insurrections that could double the price tag of occupation – and invite scrutiny from home. Second, many frontier areas did not have a well-developed tribal structure to serve as a vehicle for indirect rule, especially in more agriculturally developed or urbanized areas. In fact, it is quite possible that colonialist-imposed tribalized governance actually encouraged those on the wrong side of the political arrangement to emigrate. Third, imperial administrations disliked devolving tribal affairs to officers and had to be on guard against their own who went native and manipulated indirect rule to create fiefdoms, in a Kipling, "The Man Who Would Be King" scenario.[46]

Fourth, the hypocrisy and deliberate deception of the indirect rule theorists lay with the fact that many of the "traditional" hierarchies in which the indirect rule organizers of Morocco, the post-Mutiny Raj, and Fulani invested their authority were opportunistic creations, men selected for their willingness to serve the interests of the colonizers rather than leaders with a claim to status and legitimacy in local society. When in July 1912, the Sultan of Morocco, Moulai Hafid, resisted the imposition of a French protectorate, Lyautey did not hesitate to replace him with his brother Moulai Yousef. Lyautey's removal of Moulai Hafid for standing up for Moroccan independence, and the association of Moulai Yousef with the consolidation of French and Spanish control over Morocco meant that Moulai Yousef's reign, which ended on his death in 1927, was pockmarked by numerous rebellions against his legitimacy, the most notable being that of Abd el-Krim in the Riff (1919–1926).[47] Finally, indirect rule also meant that imperialists might turn a blind eye to kleptocratic misdemeanors and other abuses by their chosen proconsuls out of ignorance, as the price of peace, or because they could do little to thwart their abuses – Lyautey, for instance, appointed Madani and T'Hami Glaoui, complete upstarts and thugs, to run the region around Marrakech.[48] The British too discovered that abuses by their chosen native chiefs "caused a constant corrosive instability ... resulting in internecine strife," on the North-West Frontier.[49] So, placed in its historical context, the Anbar Awakening in Iraq or the reliance on warlord upstarts to control territory in Afghanistan, far from being the product of a brilliant anthropology-informed strategy, simply offer the latest installments of an opportunistic Orientalized reliance on compliant or unsavory local collaborators which only serves to thwart progress and undermine the legitimacy of the occupation.

Imperial recklessness and small wars in a changing international system

Just as imperialists began to codify their tactics and methods of governance at the dawn of a new century, and achieve a measure of autonomy by advertising their projects as cheap, low-risk ventures that captured trophy territories for the homeland and showered the benefits of Western civilization on primitive societies, colonial warfare escalated beyond small wars dimensions. There were two reasons for this shift in perception and prestige. First, Britain, France, and Russia were challenged in their global primacy by three rising powers, each with its own imperial ambitions – Japan, Germany, and the United States. Competition for imperial spoils in the years 1890 until 1914 became less manageable as escalating scrambles for colonial real estate sucked the Great Powers into areas where they had scant substantive interests. In the process, these escapades called into question the morality of the methods used to advance Western "civilization." Second, despite the heightened risks, even as small wars threatened to explode into large ones because of the ever more brittle alliance system and the ill effects of navalism, imperialists continued to behave as recklessly as ever. The British committed 440,000 men to the Second South African War, while the Italians shipped almost 100,000 troops to Tripolitania in 1911–1912 to wrest that parched province from the Ottoman Empire. Rome was even prepared to launch an amphibious invasion of the Turkish mainland had Russia not intervened to veto it; of all leaders, Kaiser Wilhelm eventually mediated an end to the war. The French poured almost 75,000 men into Morocco from 1911, in the process threatening to advance the Great War by at least three years by provoking a conflict that came dangerously close to embroiling all the European powers in a mutual war over prerogatives and profile in Africa. No longer could small wars be peddled as nontoxic byproducts of explorations, or short, glorious collisions with heathen potentates whose defeat liberated the conquered to receive the benefits of Western civilization.

In East Asia, for example, a combination of internal rebellions and punitive expeditions had so weakened the Qing (Manchu) dynasty that, by the 1890s, Japan and Russia competed to absorb Manchuria and Korea. Meiji Restoration modernizers promoted imperial expansion as a prerequisite for Japan's security and status. In August 1894, Japan successfully went to war to push China out of Korea. The Boxer Rebellion, in 1900, left Russia in possession of Manchuria, and Tokyo feeling ever more insecure about her grasp on the Korean peninsula. On the night of February 8–9, 1904, Admiral Togo Heihachiro launched a surprise torpedo-boat attack against the Russian Pacific squadron anchored at Port Arthur, on the Liaotung Peninsula of Manchuria. What followed was no small war but a monumental clash over Manchuria in 1904–1905 – a hint of things to come in the era of total war. Military defeats led to mutinies, strikes, and demonstrations that shook the very foundations of the Russian throne. Japan annexed Korea in 1910. The Qing dynasty collapsed in 1912, and the outbreak of the Great War two years later pulled the Western powers back to Europe, clearing the way for Japan's aggressive imperialism in the Far East. But Tokyo's quest for security in imperial expansion only fostered insecurity, isolation, alienation, and over-extension, a path that terminated in further gigantic adventures in China and finally at Hiroshima.

Washington discovered its colonial vocation in the Spanish-American War of 1898, one that prolonged and updated a small wars tradition in the US Army and Marine Corps into the twentieth century. This development was not particularly auspicious in a US army where a "modern warfare movement," which the brilliant but dyspeptic Emory Upton led until his 1881 death, viewed small wars as an unwelcome impediment to reform along the lines of the Prussian-German prototype. Military progressives advocated the creation of the institutions that would allow the US Army to modernize and professionalize on a European model. They envisaged an army anchored in industrialization, new weaponry, and a Prussian-like staff system peopled by select officers educated in military schools reformed to high standards that became the continental norm post-1870. Reformers like Upton saw small wars as an unwelcome obstacle to this progress. In the event, attempts to meld the dispersed batteries, battalions, and squadrons of the US Army into a command of brigades, divisions, and corps capable of fighting conventional war were slowed by the antiquated command structure such as it was, as well as bureaucratic infighting, the fundamental conservatism and divisions of opinion among the reformers, and the persistence of small wars missions – most notably those spun off at the turn of the twentieth century from the Spanish-American War in the Philippines and the Caribbean.[50]

"Civilize 'em with a Krag"[51]

For Americans, the Spanish–American War of 1898 propelled the moral ambiguity and brutal tactics of the recent Indian Wars onto the world stage. American anti-imperial activist Moorfield Storey argued in vain against the "annexation of new regions which, unfit to govern themselves, would govern us," and that territorial expansion accompanied by the enlargement "of standing armies and growing navies," would test the Republic's ability to control them.[52] Unfortunately it was easier to recognize the perils of colonialist initiatives than to sidestep them.

Washington's April 1898 declaration of war on Spain was precipitated in large part by popular anger over Spanish General Valeriano "Butcher" Weyler's use of *reconcentrado* tactics in Cuba, which English-speaking tacticians of the time called hamleting. One of Spain's savior generals already famous for his no-nonsense enforcement methods in the Carolinas, the Philippines, among Basque and Navarese separatists, and socialists and anarchists in Catalonia, Weyler was sent as governor to Cuba in 1896. Within a year, Spanish loyalists under Weyler had uprooted 300,000 Cuban peasants, burned their homes, and forced them to resettle around the cities in "reconcentration camps." But hamleting Weyler-style proved to have three disadvantages, all of which bedeviled subsequent counterinsurgency operations: the dubious strategic benefits of resettlement; the manpower-intensive requirement of offensive counterinsurgency operations; finally, the information operations catastrophe of population-centric tactics.

In Weyler's case, while reconcentration was meant to deprive the rebels of food and recruits, in fact it was the peasants forced into concentration slums inadequately supplied by Weyler who died by the thousands of starvation, dehydration, and disease. Meanwhile, a second defect of Weyler's approach was that his strategy contained no offensive component, in part because his garrison in Cuba was depleted to provide troops to suppress the independence movement that broke out in the Philippines in 1896. Untroubled by the Spanish who lacked sufficient forces to mount offensive operations, the Cuban rebels enjoyed the unmolested run of the countryside. Finally, Weyler's population-centric tactics stirred up a political ruckus both in Washington and Madrid. Cuban exiles in the United States enlisted newspaperman William Randolph Hearst to publicize the misery of the concentration camps, in the process giving Weyler his nickname of the Butcher. Liberal protests in Spain brought down the government and led to Weyler's recall in 1897. So, the irony was that when US troops landed in Cuba in 1898, Weyler was long gone.

The irony of events played out in the US Army's counterinsurgency campaign in the Philippines. The knock-on consequence of the Spanish–American War precipitated in large part by indignation over Spanish counterinsurgency practices, the American conquest of the Philippines from 1899 combined the misery of population concentration with scorched-earth offensives that the defensive-minded Weyler never managed to orchestrate.

The Americans intervened in a war for independence that had erupted against the Spaniards in 1896. Initially welcomed as liberators, relations between the Filipinos and the Americans turned sour once it was revealed that US forces had no intention of departing. A hastily improvised US force that numbered 70,000 troops secured Manila by December 1900 and fanned out over the archipelago. They did try to win over the population with a menu of amnesties, cash for guns, public works projects, and other hearts and minds outreach, to include dances where Filipinas were exposed to the gallantry of US officers. These same officers quickly concluded, however, that – in the words of one – "this business of fighting and civilizing and educating at the same time doesn't mix very well." In the absence of security, locals interpreted benevolence as an admission of weakness. Recipients of the benefits of US Army civic action often continued to support the insurgents as well. Once McKinley's re-election was assured in December 1900 – and even southerners began to speak nostalgically of Sherman's torching of Georgia as a model for Philippine consolidation – the Americans dropped all pretenses at peaceful penetration and resorted to violence. Most guerrilla hideouts were simply too inaccessible and the risk of casualties too high for swarming to be considered practical. So population concentration, port lockdowns, arbitrary arrests, liberal use of the "watercure" as waterboarding was called at the time and other inquisitorial intelligence-gathering methods, and Bugeaudesque *razzias* swept the archipelago in a series of "concentration/devastation campaigns on a massive scale" – with a ferocity that made Weyler seem like a pacifist. Indeed, the military governor of Taybas province complained to Congress in 1902 that abuses by US troops that included torture, rape, and literally working priests to death on road gangs had undermined the legitimacy of the US project in the eyes of both Filipinos and Americans.[53] Not surprisingly, these harsh tactics helped to deflate popular support for the war back in the United States and emboldened the American Anti-Imperialist League, whose membership included Mark Twain, former President Grover Cleveland, Ambrose Bierce, Samuel Gompers, Henry James, and Dale Carnegie, some of whom had united behind the unsuccessful presidential campaign of William Jennings Bryant against McKinley.

Might the Philippines have been fully pacified with less suffering? The leading historian of the insurrection, Brian McAllister Linn, thinks not. The independence movement suffered from many handicaps. It was concentrated in a narrow, Tagalog-speaking, *principale* oligarchy in south and central Luzon. Its leadership was corrupt and incompetent, while its soldiers, though tough, were undisciplined and indifferently armed. It managed neither to consolidate a secure base area, create a centralized command, nor constitute a titular government. It made many strategic mistakes, beginning with independence leader Aguinaldo's decision to engage US forces in conventional conflict in February 1899. "A remarkably competent cohort of (US) field commanders and post officers," combined with sea control isolated and fragmented the rebellion, writes Linn. But, like all small wars practitioners of the era whose worldview was informed by racial stereotypes, the Americans ultimately won by a "harsh but effective" swarming of the population, not the insurgents. The price in many areas was depopulation; destruction of farms, crops, and animals; food deprivation; the disruption of commerce lest the proceeds feed the rebels; and summary executions.[54]

While the independence force could never have won in any political sense, they might have prolonged the anarchy, banditry, and strife that had characterized the Spanish-ruled Philippines. Even after the capture of insurgent leader Aguinaldo in March 1901 and the end of the conflict in January 1902, US forces were obliged continually to put down insurrections with concentration strategies in Albay Province in 1903 and Samar in 1907–1908, to secure a base increasingly vulnerable to Japanese attack.[55] The good news was that the shortcomings of command and operations exposed in 1898 served as a catalyst for a series of reforms promoted by Secretary of War Elihu Root. The bad news was that, as Mark Twain predicted, "trampling upon the helpless abroad" threatened the health of democracy at home. And he was more correct than he imagined. The Spanish–American War and the invasion and occupation of the Philippines introduced the US Army to media manipulation, civil-military fusion, and the requirement for methods of social control abroad that ricocheted home. The requirement to sell controversial colonial adventures to a skeptical US public saw General Leonard Wood recruit his personal press agent in the form of an English aristocrat and Associated Press correspondent, Captain Edgar Bellairs. Bellairs' glowing dispatches praising the General as a far-sighted founder of America's new empire laid the groundwork in Washington for Wood's nomination as Military Governor of Cuba and later as commander of the Philippines Division. In Cuba, Wood paid reporters to write good stories about him, and excommunicated those critical of his policies. Alas, Bellairs was exposed as a con man and former Florida convict with a fake English accent named Charles Ballentine, in cahoots with Wood to discredit Governor of the Philippines William Howard Taft, and secure the Republican Party's 1908 presidential nomination. Indeed, Alfred McCoy concludes that the Bellairs–Wood episode demonstrates "how U.S. national politics became entwined with colonial intrigues in this imperial age, seamlessly weaving together Manila intrigues, Ohio machine politics, New York media, and Washington policy."[56]

Having parried Wood's attempts to unseat him, Taft as the first civil governor of the Philippines understood the importance of information dominance as a precondition of colonial rule. The Philippine administration was militarized as officers, active and retired, took over the police, the courts, and the civil administration. The Division of Military Information (DMI) imported, in 1900 to collect intelligence on the insurgency, was expanded by Captain, later General, Ralph Van Deman into a formidable machine with "the capacity to weave discrete strands of data into a dark tapestry of threat." This allowed the administration and its militarized constabulary to control the island elite, whose salient characteristic in the view of US intelligence was "the absence of integrity," through infiltration of nationalist political organizations, the blackmail of uncooperative activists on the basis of information provided by DMI or constabulary informants, and lawsuits based, in the words of one US Senator, on "the harshest [libel and sedition laws] . . . known to human statute books."[57]

This police state would have merely mocked the US democratic mission had it remained in the Philippines, where by a decision of the US Supreme Court, Filipinos enjoyed no constitutional rights, like freedom of expression. But the indefatigable Van Deman introduced both his internal security apparatus and his imperial mindset to the continental United States. From 1917, Van Deman transformed what became in 1918 the Military Intelligence Division into domestic spy agency staffed in part by veterans of the Philippines, whose job was to collect data on potential subversives to include anti-war activists and labor union militants, to underpin the Espionage Act of that year and the even more draconian Sedition Act of 1918. But the end of the war and a turf war with the Bureau of Investigation convinced the army to ditch the domestic surveillance business. Van Deman retired to San Diego, California in 1929. But he and his wife continued to collect information on subversives provided by "agents" and other walk-in sources, meticulously filed according to a colonial color and ideological code – Americans of Japanese and Italian descent, German Jewish émigrés in Hollywood, and union activists in the southern California aeronautical plants or in the agricultural industry.

Such single-minded devotion earned Van Deman the American Civil Liberties Union's classification as "a phobic nativist red hunter." With the approach of war, Van Deman returned to the US intelligence community as adviser to the War Department. After the war, the general put his knowledge and card file at the service of Hoover's FBI and right-wing Congressional attacks on alleged communist influence in Hollywood's Screen Writers' Guild and elsewhere, to the point that, in the opinion of McCoy, Van Deman might be called "father of the American blacklist." In this way, counterinsurgency techniques designed to strengthen the mechanisms of colonial rule were bounced to the homeland, whose citizens were deemed subversives simply because of their ethnicity or ideas.[58]

Small wars become large ones

The Second Anglo-Boer War of 1899–1902 lifted small wars to a whole new level of political and strategic costs, while showcasing their geopolitical hazards. What began as a conspiracy of imperialists became, in the words of British historian Thomas Pakenham, "the longest, the costliest, the bloodiest, and the most humiliating war for Britain between 1815 and 1914."[59] It forced London for the first time to acknowledge the problem of imperial overstretch, amid a vocal anti-war movement at home and condemnation abroad. The Boer image as sturdy farmers battling the might of the British Empire romanticized their insurgency to the point that it attracted a significant number of foreign freebooters into Boer ranks, in this way inaugurating a twentieth-century infatuation with the guerrilla.[60]

The British seizure of the Cape of Good Hope from the Dutch in 1806 was all about protecting the sea route to India. With the acquisition of the Cape, however, London also acquired a settler population of Dutch, French, and German Calvinists who called themselves "Afrikaners" – "the People of Africa." A subset of Afrikaners known as *trekboers*, shortened to Boers, drifted further inland in search of grazing lands. Following parliamentary passage of the 1833 Abolition of Slavery Act, *trekboers* were reinforced by a mass exodus of *voortrekkers* (pioneers), who left the Cape to stake out lands beyond British jurisdiction. Britain recognized the Transvaal and the Orange Free State as independent Boer Republics in 1852 and 1854, respectively. A subsequent attempt to annex the Transvaal in 1877 ignited the First Boer War, which led to the British defeat at Majuba Hill and confirmed Boer independence. London then opted to wait out the Boers until an expected influx of English immigration would strengthen the Cape Colony and marginalize the Boer Republics. However, the discovery of gold in the Rand in 1886 made the Transvaal the most powerful state in Southern Africa. Immigrants headed to the Rand instead of to the Cape, which, in the eyes of British imperialists, led by Cecil Rhodes and British High Commissioner for South Africa Sir Alfred Milner, posed a potential threat to British control of the strategically vital Cape Colony.

In 1895, Rhodes and gold and diamond magnate Alfred Beit financed a raid by L. S. "Doctor Jim" Jameson, a charismatic Edinburgh physician who had immigrated to Kimberly in the North Cape and, after becoming wealthy by successfully treating influential Boers and native chieftains, joined Rhodes in several ventures, the most daring of which came to be known as the Jameson Raid. At Rhodes' behest and with the knowledge of the British Colonial Office, Jameson assembled around 600 Rhodesian mounted police and volunteers from the Cape, whose goal was to seize Johannesburg and provoke an uprising of *Uitlanders* – mainly British "foreign workers" in the gold mines who were denied political rights by the Boers. The *coup d'état* failed ignominiously when Jameson and his men were intercepted by armed Boers twenty miles outside of Johannesburg and forced into a humiliating surrender. Rhodes, Milner, and the British Colonial Office had tipped their hand. Boers inside the Transvaal as well as in the Free State, Natal, and the Cape united to resist further British conspiracies against Boer independence. Transvaal President Paul Kruger invested more than £1 million to arm his Transvaal militia.

The Jameson Raid raised the curtain on a larger war that erupted in 1899, on the pretext of Boer repression of British *Uitlanders*. The British totally underestimated the Boers, whom they believed could field no more than a few thousand ill-trained riflemen. In the end, however, London was forced to dispatch around 450,000 men. It cost more than £200 million and 22,000 dead to subdue a *soupçon* of Boer insurgents between 1899 and 1902.

As the United States had discovered in the Philippines, with the defeat of the main Boer "armies" the conflict slipped toward insurgency – and the British response slithered toward harshness. Unable to bring Boer fighters to battle, British tactics escalated into a sustained campaign of farm burning; hostage taking; internment camps where an estimated

20,000 Boers and 12,000 Africans died; barbed wire; and blockhouses to serve as barriers for mounted infantry "drives." Such measures, telegraphed back to Europe for the mass-circulation press, provoked public protests and even had some of the war's enthusiasts complaining that British tactics were contrary to law and "international usage." In June 1901, the prominent social activist Emily Hobhouse delivered a report to Parliament outlining the appalling conditions in what Kitchener called camps of refuge, but which anti-war activists, in honor of Weyler, were already calling concentration camps. This Hobhouse report provoked the government to form the Fawcett Commission, a group of pro-war Tory ladies under Millicent Fawcett, dispatched to investigate conditions in the camps. In December 1901, Fawcett made a report that Pakenham calls damning in its fairness.

> Conditions in the camps were less than ideal. Tents were overcrowded. Reduced-scale army rations were provided. In fact there were two scales. Meat was not included in the rations issued to women and children whose menfolk were still fighting. There were little or no vegetables, no fresh milk for the babies and children, 3/4 lb of either mealie meal, rice or potatoes, 1 lb of meat twice weekly, 1 oz of coffee daily, sugar 2 oz daily, and salt 0,5 oz daily (this was for adults and children who had family members on commando). Children who were under six years of age received 0,5 lb of meal daily, 1/2 meat twice weekly, 1/4 tin of milk daily, 1 oz sugar daily and 1/2 oz of salt daily. This very poor diet led to the rapid spread of diseases such as whooping cough, measles, typhoid fever, diphtheria, diarrhea and dysentery, especially amongst the children.[61]

Boer women and children and Africans who perished in the concentration camps probably account for at least half of the estimated 75,000 deaths suffered in the Second South African War. The lesson was that population concentration run by the military was guaranteed to become a hearts and minds fiasco because such tactics invariably instigated a humanitarian disaster.[62] Indeed, Weyler's post-Spanish–American War defense was that he simply applied the same population concentration tactics that the British used in South Africa and the American Army in the Philippines. He just did it less effectively.[63]

But the most searing indictment against Kitchener was that his counterinsurgency tactics, for all the damage they caused to the Boer population and to British prestige abroad, did not work. His 60,000-man search and destroy "drives" on the Veldt failed to corner Boer commandos, who generally dodged the pursuit. And while the British dragnet did capture wagons and cattle on which the commandos depended, it proved a slow, attritional strategy. One reason that the Boers remained so elusive was that they shed the burden of their families, who were in British care in the camps. Concentration camps probably prolonged resistance in the Orange Free State because De Wet and his men felt – wrongly – that their women and children were safe in British custody. In fact, Kitchener belatedly realized this and so issued orders in 1901 to cease taking Boer women and children into the camps, but instead to leave them on the Veldt where they became encumbrances for the commandos.[64] This order speeded the surrender of Botha and the Transvaal commandos because they could not both fight the British and protect their families from the Africans who were increasingly being enlisted into the conflict by the British.

The South African counterinsurgency was not only costly to Britain's reputation. It also hit the Exchequer. Even Milner recognized that the Boer War was the most costly since the campaigns against Napoleon a century earlier, which had forced Westminster both to raise the income tax and to borrow heavily abroad. Yet he discovered that once a campaign had been launched, the army mobilized, and the population enlisted to support the war, civil-military relations became skewed as the generals held the whip hand. Government pressure for Kitchener to begin a drawdown were met with the General's prevarication, protests, delay, citing the "bag" – monthly figures of killed, captured, and surrendered Boers – as proof of progress, reporting minor skirmishes as evidence of "light at the end of the tunnel," all of which forced the cabinet "to go crawling to Parliament to ask for extra money."[65]

The Treaty of Vereeniging signed on May 31, 1902 that ended the war proved the value of attritional strategies in counterinsurgency warfare. But who had attrited whom was unclear. Although the Boer resistance was at the end of its tether, Whitehall also had run out of money, the British Army had been drained of men and morale, needed army reforms had been postponed, while the war had isolated Britain diplomatically at the very moment that Germany had begun to lay the foundation for a High Seas Fleet to challenge Britain's sea dominance. Both Briton and Boer feared that if the war were prolonged, Africans would increasingly assert themselves. British High Commissioner Sir Alfred Milner had wanted to destroy the Boers as a political force and refashion South Africa as an entirely Anglicized colony, like Australia or New Zealand.[66] However, the English immigrants never arrived, while the Boers had acquired in the course of the war another heroic myth to strengthen their sense of nationhood and their prominence in postwar South African politics. Peace came to South Africa behind a deceptive façade of white unity. Much money had been spent, many people had died, Britain had been diverted from more important national objectives, the international system had been roiled, and not much had changed in South Africa, which caused some British veterans to declare that they "never saw the point" of the war.[67]

Small wars as a race to the bottom

Warfare at the turn of the twentieth century was a highly imitative endeavor. As has been noted, following Sedan Europe tracked Germany's lead as armies increased in organizational complexity and technological sophistication, which required ever greater degrees of officer education and professional development. In the wake of South Africa, however, the otherwise vaunted German army followed that of Britain, even Spain and the United States, down a humanitarian rat hole. And if truth be told, from a professional perspective counterinsurgency boils down to the application of some fairly rudimentary principles – contain the space the insurgents have to operate with blockhouses and barriers; lock up the inhabitants who are reduced to minimal rations; organize mobile forces to sweep territory and hunt down insurgents; enlist indigenous allies by persuasion or force; collect and collate intelligence. But the true key to success was pitilessly to target anyone and anything that sustained the insurgency. In this way, colonial warfare simply boiled down to national displacement and ruining the countryside by making it unlivable.

Judged by that standard, the German army captured the prize on all counts in the first half of the twentieth century beginning with the Herero (1904–1907) and Maji Maji (1905–1907) wars. Lothar von Trota's order, following the August 1904 Battle of Waterberg in

German Southwest Africa, that male Hereros be executed and their families driven into the desert meant that perhaps as many as 100,000 Herero perished of hunger and thirst. A 1985 UN report classified von Trota's campaign against the Herero as the inaugural genocide of the twentieth century. The subsequent outcry forced the Germans to replicate population concentration as a humanitarian measure by comparison. But while concentration camps established by Weyler and Kitchener may rightly be accused of guilt by neglect born of indifference, the Germans in Southwest Africa were deliberately exterminationist. An estimated 17,000 Herero and Nama survivors of von Trota's massacres were confined to camps, where they were given only raw rice with no pots or water to cook it, whipped, and literally worked to death. Doctors traveled from Berlin to conduct medical experiments on the Africans that included sterilization, and injections of typhus, smallpox, and tuberculosis. A combination of overwork, starvation, general mistreatment, and medical experimentation combined to kill almost half of the inmates of German camps.[68] American historian of Germany Isabelle Hull writes that the 1905 uprising in German East Africa produced an even more barbarous response, if that were possible. German-led *askaris* systematically destroyed crops, livestock, and villages with the goal of producing a famine that resulted in the starvation deaths of as many as 300,000 native Africans.

Hull argues that German soldiers in Africa were particularly unrestrained for several reasons: first, the German army had no small wars tradition, with its panoply of native affairs officers to manage the population and publicity-savvy officers like Lyautey or Leonard Wood with their support team of press lackeys and legislative lobbyists to market massacre as the inescapable spinoff of the civilizing mission. The German army in the colonies was simply a European army that expected to achieve quick victory through the application of superior technology and organization. When that failed to happen, German soldiers initiated violence on the local population that spiraled upward. This pugnacious military reflex became impossible to modulate because there was no cabinet-style mechanism of civilian control over the military. As a consequence, the German military in Africa became a "juggernaut of military extremism" impossible to brake because it depended directly on the Emperor. Furthermore, the centrality of the army to the concept of German nationhood and to national security created a military populism that allowed the government to vilify protestors as traitors. As a consequence, Hull argues that unchecked by civilian constraints, the German army in the twentieth century pursued strategies of absolute destruction and annihilation which in the process elevated small wars and counterinsurgency into the stratosphere of mayhem.[69]

Hull's critics argue that barbarous tactics form the default position of all colonial armies because they abhorred guerrilla warfare, sought quick victory, felt isolated and insecure in the imperial environment, were often poorly trained, and ramped up the violence especially when they encountered unexpectedly strong resistance.[70] All governments blessed with overseas possessions found it difficult to rein in colonial soldiers in this era. Protests over Bugeaud's *enfumades* only elicited his defiance. British attempts to control its colonial soldiers were also muted by Liberal Party fears that they would be branded as unpatriotic. The British Cabinet fretted about Kitchener's tactics of internment and destruction, not because they were inhumane, but because they were slow. Attritional strategies that failed to show demonstrable progress allowed civilian busybodies like Hobhouse to join the strategic debate, and required cosmetic counters like Ladies' Commissions to diffuse opposition with the promise that missteps were being rectified. Even opponents of the war were not eager to prolong their protests, which had won them the nickname of "pro-Boers." So the concentration camp debate in Britain quickly fizzled and war protests were unable to speed the end of hostilities.[71]

Hull contrasts the outcry in Britain over Boer War population concentration with the comparatively muted response in Germany to more significant atrocities carried out by its soldiers in Africa. Hull may be correct that the idea of a "Ladies' Commission" organized in response to the British protests to inspect conditions in the concentration camps was unthinkable in Germany, where the investigation commission for Southwest Africa was composed exclusively of officers. The conclusions of the Fawcett Commission were no whitewash, and they certainly led to the amelioration of conditions in the camps containing Boer women and children. But the "ladies" were indifferent to the fate of Africans, whose camps they never visited, and were quick to declare mission accomplished without addressing the underlying issue of internment for Boers and Africans. Far from blowing the lid off British excesses in South Africa, the Fawcett Commission's efforts removed the protestors' major issue and allowed the war to continue to its dismal conclusion.

Similarly, popular protests and journalistic exposure of French excesses carried out during the Druze Revolt, the Riff War, and in Algeria in 1954–1962 invited only cosmetic adjustments to the counterinsurgency tactics that did nothing to curtail the prosecution of those wars.[72] Indeed, it is difficult to escape the conclusion that public and international protests against small wars tactics became a factor only when Britain fought other white Europeans, who could be plausibly portrayed as engaged in a justifiable struggle of national determination – in South Africa, Ireland 1919–1921, and post-World War II Palestine.

Berlin realized that the German government had to impose controls on counterinsurgency. Weber makes the point that, by the time news of the Herero and Nama atrocities reached Germany, they were already a *fait accompli*.[73] But exercising civilian control of small warriors was in fact very difficult to implement because Wilhelmene Germany's political culture was misshapen by "a pervasive sense of national insecurity," the fact that the imperial discourse was managed by experts and agitation groups like xenophobe geographic societies and naval leagues with their propaganda machines.[74] Disquiet over the brutal suppression of the Herero and Maji Maji rebellions did lead to reforms. Colonial scandals in 1905–1906 became a central issue in the so-called Hotentot elections of 1906, which the conservative government of Bernhard von Bülow barely survived. In the aftermath of these elections, colonial budgets came under the scrutiny of the Reichstag, rather than of the governor as was the case of the British colonies. Berlin created a colonial office, the first step in an attempt to replace officers with a more professional cadre of colonial administrators, because the Germans realized that rebellions destroyed precarious colonial finances, the economies of the colonies, and invited Reichstag scrutiny.[75]

German reform attempts were cut short by the Great War. But Germany's problems were replicated in France and Britain where colonial pressure groups, military interests, and jingoistic patriotism made it difficult for governments to set policy. Exploitation of the indigenous population to include massacres was simply accepted as normal and necessary at the turn of the twentieth century, a prerogative of a master race in the exercise of their Darwinian right to rule inferior folk. Civilian control of colonies was bound to be fragile because the homeland was far away, colonies and colonial armies generated their own revenue streams, civilian administrators were few, and their authority ultimately depended on a politicized and independence-minded corps of military officers. For all of these reasons, counterinsurgency operations were difficult to contain within the confines of national interests, legality, and compassion.

Imperial warfare as COIN prologue

Lyautey updated Bugeaud's operations, but tailored them for the increasingly tense international political environment that threatened increased scrutiny for imperial shenanigans from the press and Parliament. His solution: stealth advances from southern Algeria into Morocco by small units to grab a strategic town or oasis.[76] However, Lyautey's nibbling tactics became more difficult after March 31, 1905, when the Kaiser debarked at Tangier and pronounced Berlin's determination to stand behind Moroccan independence. Germany's goal was to smother the 1904 Entente Cordiale, which had resolved the Fashoda crisis when France dropped all claims in Egypt in return for a free hand in Morocco. Germany's reasons for challenging the Entente were complex, but the bottom line was that Berlin was now willing to see the Great Powers go to war with each other nominally over colonial competition in a war that would not remain confined to the colonies. Imperial expansion now became a powder keg that threatened to explode into a European conflict. The French risked it anyway in 1907, when they disembarked an expedition at Casablanca to avenge attacks by Moroccans on Europeans in that city. Lyautey seized on the Casablanca distraction to enter eastern Morocco and quell a rebellion there. The final French surge into Morocco came in 1911, in response to a rebellion of the Sultan's troops against their French military advisers in Fez. This French invasion touched off an international crisis which almost advanced the Great War by three years. Germany allowed France to consolidate a protectorate over Morocco only after it had received territorial compensation in Cameroon. But it illustrated once again how the reckless behavior of small warriors with their expansionist agendas destabilized the international system. They also jeopardized homeland defense: Politicians like Georges Clemenceau had complained for years that imperial expansion diverted French assets away from continental defense. Now, French Commander-in-Chief Joseph Joffre feared that the tens of thousands of French troops committed to stabilize Morocco might compromise mobilization against Germany in Europe. Small wars threatened to produce the calamity that caused the zero-sum international order of the day to implode.

Colonial encounters bequeathed a legacy of assumptions and attitudes that have shaped COIN into our own day, beginning with the claim advanced by Callwell and Lyautey that small wars constituted a distinct category of warfare whose practitioners deserved professional deference because their work required, in their own view, a range of professional skills seldom exhibited by their continental colleagues – among them initiative, diplomacy, cultural and linguistic knowledge, and an ability to manage civil society. In short, the complexity of the small wars mission, which combined diplomacy and governance, gave colonial warriors a professional status at least equal to that of conventional soldiers. In fact, linguistic skills were often inadequate, cultural knowledge came down to clichés about native behavior which in the end only responded to force, while diplomacy meant cutting deals with minority groups and outsourcing control to warlords. Small wars became the vehicle for the creation of fragile, under-administered territories that relied on the coercion and exploitation of the population to survive.

The colonial worldview, which infuses modern COIN, requires a global, inchoate threat that makes peripheral wars central, not marginal, to national security. Great game imperial competition among European powers supplied the threat to justify war and conquest in the decades surrounding the wars at the turn of the twentieth century. Colonialism's nineteenth-century "clash of civilizations" heritage holds that Islam or ignorance proliferated fanatics who blocked the spread of Western values, impeded trade and Christianity, and ultimately posed a threat to the homeland. This dogma also meant that, despite Lyautey's attempts to sanitize Bugeaud, the boundary between "small," "race," "hunger," and "dirty" wars remained porous and ill-defined. "Civilized" standards of warfare, even basic human rights and judicial procedures, were considered superfluous by Europeans in non-Western settings against an enemy viewed as culturally, racially, and morally inferior, and whose subjugation was approached in the spirit of total war. Imperial soldiers bristled at criticism by civilians who, in their view, failed to acknowledge the fanatical, irreconcilable character of the security environment, or the sacrifices made by their soldiers to subdue the West's irredeemable enemies.

The "clash of civilizations" mindset carried over into occupation – yet another legacy. The gift of civilization was all the legitimacy colonial governance required, so that coercion became the bedrock of empire, governed by a system of civil-military fusion. Soldier-administrators were required to master the tricks of political survival through intrigue, cultivation of influential political contacts, and information management. While Lyautey's peaceful penetration, like the British hearts and minds, sounded like a winning strategy to gain the consent of the ruled, in fact it served principally as a mechanism for intelligence collection. As diplomacy, hearts and minds boiled down to divide and rule tactics that served to keep the population fragmented and passive. Popular passivity was marketed by colonialists as proof of indigenous acquiescence and the legitimacy of imperial rule. Bad actors and criminal tribes had to be smited.

The risk that colonial military violence, racist attitudes, and brutal norms of behavior would be re-imported to the Continent, in conditions of civil war when applied against domestic political opponents who espoused subversive doctrines, was real. While Jacques Frémeaux fails to excuse the brutality of French soldiers toward the Muslim population during the conquest of Algeria, he notes that summary executions of French workers by soldiers was fairly common following revolutionary disturbances of the 1830s. However, contemporary commentators attributed soldierly outrages against French civilians in 1848 and 1871, including summary executions, to the brutalizing experience of colonial warfare.[77] Isabel Hull, like Hannah Arendt before her, argues that "the drift to extreme treatment of civilians" by German soldiers in Europe in two world wars was accelerated by imperial experience. German soldiers acquired a suspicion and fear of insurgency in occupied France in 1870–1871 that migrated through Boxer China and Southwest Africa to return home as race war. The freedom of action contained in mission orders that set an objective and gave subordinates a free hand to achieve it at the tactical level, a lack of supervision in a dispersed colonial combat environment, reliance on the "officers' military virtues or character traits" to curb excessive violence, lack of civilian control of the military, and absence of coherent policy in wartime all contributed to the evolution of a German military culture that became notorious for its mistreatment of civilians in occupied areas generally.[78] It followed, therefore, that in the colonies, the Germans developed no indirect rule practices, but subjected populations to the direct authority of soldiers who, as representatives of the German state, had a duty to crush opposition.[79] The thing is, Germany was no exception. Neighbors with a more established democratic political culture found that distrust of civilians was ingrained in their small warriors. French imperial officers had the disconcerting habit of comparing the Paris revolutionaries of

1848 and 1871 to Algerian insurgents, and to treating them that way.[80] As has been seen, US Army veterans of the Philippines pioneered techniques of domestic surveillance on their return home. "Actionism" – the requirement to act whatever the circumstances as the first step on an escalatory ladder – was a characteristic shared by all small warriors.

Finally, in the hands of its colonial protagonist, many of whom were outsized personalities backed by influential lobbying groups, "hearts and minds" became both a public relations exercise and a "tactic in a box" to market imperialism as social control as effortless and low-risk to those who feared that the costs would prove too high. Small wars offered as a win-win formula that would both propagate the influence of the homeland and benefit the local populations, who would welcome invasion as liberation. The goal of such soldiers was to secure status and influence within their military organizations, and insulate them against intrusiveness and criticism of their methods by stab-in-the-back civilian politicians who they came deeply to resent.

The scope, duration, and brutality that characterized wars in Cuba, South Africa, the Philippines, and the German colonies at the turn of the century, as well as public anxiety over imperialist eagerness to risk major war to absorb remote, revenue-draining regions into empire generated opposition at home. While too slight, unorganized, and tardy to impede them, such opposition invited the very public scrutiny that imperialists sought to avoid. Furthermore, the outbreak of the Great War in 1914, a long-anticipated social Darwinian battle of peoples, vindicated the centrality of conventional combat and seemed to relegate small wars to the periphery of military professionalism. But while small wars were eclipsed by the grand European conflagration, they refused to disappear entirely. Instead, they were kept alive by a new set of heroic actors operating on the imperial margins of the Great War to carry small wars forward into the interwar years.

3 THE PAROXYSMS OF IMPERIAL MIGHT IN THE SHADOW OF THE GREAT WAR

If the French defeat at Sedan had discredited small wars as an organizing principle for European armies after 1870, the battles of Verdun and the Somme in 1916 challenged the usefulness of conventional war as the continuation of politics by other means, and sent military theorists in search of alternatives to the industrialized attrition of trench combat in the age of total war. A postmodernist malaise emerged at the intersection of Lyautey's warnings about the bureaucratization of conventional war, which provided few opportunities for individual self-validation through heroic acts, and the irrelevance of such personal qualities as toughness, valor, and discipline in the age of machine warfare. Only fighter aces, U-boat commanders, storm troopers, and small warriors stood out from the unrelieved mechanization of slaughter as much needed heroes who represented soldierly values and as figures to return decision to warfare as master of the machine and not its servant. In these circumstances, the old wine of small war, if not in new bottles then at least with updated labels, reasserted its allure. Paul von Lettow-Vorbeck's campaign of harassment against the British in East Africa and T. E. Lawrence's alleged unraveling of the Ottoman Empire with a posse of Bedouin captured the public imagination much in need of reinforcement in the face of strategic ambiguity and growing domestic sacrifice. Theorists as varied as Basil Liddell Hart and Mao Tse-tung proffered insurgency as a strategy to achieve "victory without battle." In this way, insurgency and counterinsurgency could legitimize themselves as a Sun-Tzuian substitute for the conventional Jominian quest for the "decisive battle."[1]

The romanticism of insurgency clenched a small but loyal following on the right in the postmodern era in which Lost Generation writers like Hemingway nurtured nostalgia for a life of loyalty, comradeship, self-sacrifice, and honor that military bureaucrats, conscription, moralizing internationalists, and teetotalers had stripped out of conventional conflict.[2] Imperial traditionalists like Lugard and Lyautey captured this Beau Geste moment to reinvigorate the ideal of empire based on indirect rule as a way to preserve traditional indigenous societies from the ravages of modernity. The result has often been passed off as strategic insight, as, for instance, in the celebrated French doctrine of *guerre révolutionnaire*. In fact it is a mythology of inversion, in which the heroic guerrilla becomes the heroic white adventurer, residing among the natives; mastering their mentality, languages, and tactics; whipping them into an efficient military force; and leading them to a victory they could never achieve on their own. The idea took more than a page from the German Karl May, who had proclaimed the Native American resistor to white US expansionism as a new form of knighthood.

None of these fictions represents real learning, military or otherwise in army and society. On the contrary, such romanticization of the small warrior and his clandestine opponent has often stood in the way of a sound understanding of what success in the unforgiving arena of "war among the people" requires, tactically and politically. It is one more legacy of the ethos of paternalism that imperial small wars have bequeathed to contemporary COIN, the belief that the duty of the white Western man at arms is to assist primitive folk to a superior stage of civilization.[3] Only after these competing forms of nostalgia are set aside can the true costs of such fighting be recognized. The absence of battle does not rule out suffering on an epic scale, after all, while the idea of victory on today's new battlefields remains as elusive as on the old ones.

Small war on the periphery of the Great War: Paul von Lettow-Vorbeck and T. E. Lawrence

Von Lettow-Vorbeck and Lawrence were the latest of a celebrated lineage of soldiers with a journalistic following who had "gone native," whose number included Captain Richard "White Nigger" Burton, James Brooke, the White Rajah of Sarawak, Josiah Harlan, Prince of Ghor, and

Charles "Chinese" Gordon, all larger-than-life characters who seemed to have stepped out of a *Boys' Own* adventure. Their family tree also included fictional ancestors like Daniel Dravot and Peachey Carnehan from Kipling's *The Man Who Would Be King*, and even Mowgli and Tarzan, feral children who combined jungle cunning with a mastery of animal languages and extraordinary physical skills. Their descendants in films of the recent past would include Kevin "Dances with Wolves" Costner and Tom "The Last Samurai" Cruise. All contributed to the romanticism of the imperial adventurer that transferred through propaganda and popular culture in the twentieth century through the Special Operations Executive (SOE) and Office of Strategic Services (OSS) to the Green Berets and special operations. These hard, self-assured men of action embodied a muscular male subculture, which offered at once an anti-modernist rebellion against a pampered, effeminate, civil society, while they held out the promise of restoring decision to the battlefield in an era of political complexity and operational stalemate through heroic action.[4] In the view of John Arquilla, von Lettow-Vorbeck and T. E. Lawrence conquered this niche as "masters of irregular warfare who have shaped our era."[5]

Though described as "a Prussian of the old school," Paul von Lettow-Vorbeck embraced imperial warfare, first as a volunteer for the storied "Germans to the front!" contingent dispatched in 1900 to quash the Boxer Rebellion and subsequently as a participant in the Herero genocide 1904–1906, a campaign in which he lost his left eye. Commander of the *Schutztruppe* in German East Africa in 1914, the tall, blond 45-year-old colonel resolved to keep the German flag flying somewhere in Africa so as to tie down as many British-led troops as possible. Von Lettow-Vorbeck's low opinion of British troops, acquired while in China and an echo of the Frederickian tradition to fight outnumbered to victory, convinced him that he could pull off his audacious plan. And at first glance he seemed to have been proven correct – for four years he survived in guerrilla fashion by keeping his force mobile and refusing to defend conventional objectives. His admirers emphasize the inventiveness of his operational concepts, "not simply by reverting to hit-and-run guerrilla tactics from the beginning," writes John Arquilla. "No, his particular brilliance was in seeing how irregular concepts of operations could be used to engage the main conventional forces of the enemy." By some estimates, the British invested up to a million men to pursue a handful of von

3 Paul von Lettow-Vorbeck in 1919.

Lettow-Vorbeck-led *askaris* around East Africa: "Thus, in addition to the great diversion of military forces, the campaign against von Lettow-Vorbeck had caused a massive manpower shortage in several colonies, all of whose economic output suffered dramatically from this loss." Finally, Arquilla concludes, von Lettow-Vorbeck's heroic endurance against overwhelming odds helped to shore up German morale through a long, exhausting conventional war.[6]

While von Lettow-Vorbeck's campaign captured the popular imagination in Germany even as the Great War was being fought, and became mythologized after the war, at the time von Lettow-Vorbeck's peripatetic seemed hardly to merit a marginal note in the great flow of armies in Europe and the Near East, and with good reason. In 1914, the British focus in East Africa initially was to deny the Germans seaports for maritime raiders and to close down wireless stations. Successful in this, they then turned their attentions to the conquest of Southwest Africa, and subsequently to the Cameroon in 1915–1916, both because West

Africa was strategically more important and because the only troops available to deal with German East Africa were Indian B divisions whom von Lettow-Vorbeck had humiliated when they attempted to land at Tanga, just south of Mombasa in British East Africa in November 1914. The British spent most of 1915–1916 in successfully occupying East African coastal enclaves including Dar es Salaam, which von Lettow-Vorbeck did nothing to oppose. British pressure on von Lettow-Vorbeck only began seriously to organize with the arrival in March 1916 of famed Boer resistance leader turned British imperialist Jan Christiaan Smuts at the head of mainly Afrikaans forces. And even then, von Lettow-Vorbeck won a reprieve of several months because Smuts, with an eye on expanding a greater South Africa, was more interested in preempting Belgian encroachment into German East Africa, controlling the Great Lakes region, and securing territory that he could later barter with the Portuguese in return for land in Mozambique. A handful of von Lettow-Vorbeck-led *askaris* roaming the vast interior of East Africa far from the vital coastal regions and posing no threat to South or British East Africa hardly constituted a strategic challenge in Africa, much less to the outcome of the Great War in general.

When, however, Smuts did turn his attentions to tracking down the Germans in the summer of 1916, von Lettow-Vorbeck fled southward generally avoiding battle. Smuts soon discovered, however, that his South African forces, organized as if on the Veldt as fast-moving mounted infantry with pack mule and wagon logistics, were ill-adapted to campaigning in the monsoonal, malarial tropics. In early 1917 Smuts was called to London, leaving his successor J. L. van Deventer to reinforce his disease-depleted Afrikaans with King's African Rifle and West African Frontier Force Africans, upgrading his weaponry, and hiring tens of thousands of coolies. In October 1917, von Lettow-Vorbeck stood and fought van Deventer on the Mahiwa River in a battle that he, and Arquilla, declared to be a German victory because British casualties were higher. But the truth was that the Mahiwa River proved a strategic defeat because von Lettow-Vorbeck had expended his ammunition, lost too many troops to continue a static defense, and as a consequence was forced to flee into Mozambique, where his campaign henceforth became one of survival against a diminutive, largely inept Portuguese garrison. Von Lettow-Vorbeck remained in Mozambique until the end of the war, when he surrendered to the Rhodesian forces on November 25, 1918.

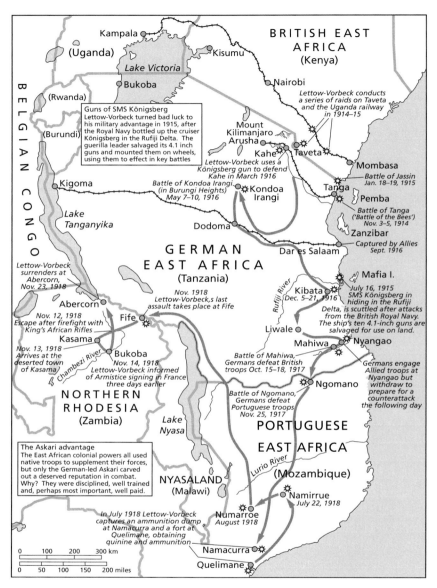

Map 1 Von Lettow-Vorbeck's meanderings

Arquilla and others see von Lettow-Vorbeck's resistance as a *tour de force* that proved the value of insurgents as a strategic diversion, highlighted the effectiveness of hit-and-run guerrilla tactics, and proved the value of peripheral campaigns as a morale booster for the main front.

However, on closer examination, von Lettow-Vorbeck's campaign diverted no British troops from the main front. The Allies' ration strength stood at slightly over 100,000 men in theater at the end of the war, almost all of them – Indian army reserves, Afrikaans, and African troops – not deployable to Europe in any case. The campaign against von Lettow-Vorbeck had effectively lasted eighteen months from March 1916 to November 1917, in which there was only one confrontation that might possibly count as a sizable skirmish. The best case for diversion lies with naval forces required to supply East Africa at the height of the U-boat campaign in 1917.[7]

Whether von Lettow-Vorbeck can be considered a successful guerrilla leader depends on how one defines guerrilla. His repertoire of hit-and-run tactics and raiding belongs more to the tradition of *kleiner krieg* rather than guerrilla warfare, a 1960s accretion to von Lettow-Vorbeck's reputation, that enjoyed the support of a significant portion of the population.[8] In fact, his campaign was a war against the people, not a people's war. He avoided the tribal areas of his *askaris* for fear that they would desert if they smelled home. Far from enjoying popular support, von Lettow-Vorbeck survived through the predatory exploitation of the African population, whose losses are reckoned to have exceeded even the death rate of the Maji Maji rebellion (1905–1907), estimated to have been between 200,000 and 300,000.[9] Indeed, Ludwig Deppe, the surgeon who accompanied von Lettow-Vorbeck's expedition, compared the passage of the German-led *askaris* to that of the marauding armies of the Thirty Years War (1618–1648).[10]

As for a morale boost for Germans, two questions: How does one measure morale? And second, how does the fact that von Lettow-Vorbeck and a diminutive group of Black *askaris* were busy plundering Mozambique while missing all the fun in Europe uplift morale at home in 1918 when more German civilians perished of famine than soldiers were dying at the front, when the desertion of German soldiers in transit through Germany from the Eastern to the Western fronts in the winter of 1917–1918 had reached epidemic proportions, when a million American reinforcements were pouring into Europe because *Kriegsmarine* assurances that the unrestricted U-boat campaign would knock Britain out of the war and sink US troopships had proven empty boasts, and the German armies were on the verge of collapse?

Arquilla inflates the strategic importance of von Lettow-Vorbeck's resistance against second-tier troops. The truth, however, is that von Lettow-Vorbeck's East African campaign constituted a minor incident in a strategically marginal theater that was mythologized as an episode of heroic resistance in a process of romantic escapism in the Great War's aftermath in a defeated nation desperate to salvage some shards of self-respect from their cataclysmic defeat. While von Lettow-Vorbeck's four-year maraud elevated him to heroic status in post-1918 Germany, it proved strategically useless. His force numbered a paltry 1,200 fighters on its surrender, armed mainly with antiquated 1871 Mauser rifles with black power cartridges, barely enough to disturb the peace of a medium-sized town, much less divert significant forces from the Western Front or shatter London's grip on Africa. The German's tactical *tour d'Afrique* remained more gangster than guerrilla, a four-year-long raid barren of strategic benefit because it was never anchored by a popular base in Africa and because the German army was finally defeated in Europe. Von Lettow-Vorbeck's postwar career saw him both saving the Weimar Republic from a communist uprising in Hamburg, and then joining the unsuccessful pro-monarchist Kapp Putsch in 1920 to overthrow the fissile German democracy, an action that cost him his commission. He joined the pantheon of Nazi heroes and retained his polish as a soldier into the 1950s. Small wars *à la* von Lettow-Vorbeck were never to form a center of gravity in German military practice either in the 100,000-man Reichswehr to say nothing of the Wehrmacht and Waffen-SS in national socialism. Von Lettow-Vorbeck's legacy to contemporary counterinsurgency was to amplify and perpetuate the myth of the heroic guerrilla leader and master tactician who with a handful of men operating on the periphery could impact the strategic dynamic and lift the morale of the main front through stubborn, prolonged resistance.

"An unfortunate charlatan"

In contrast to von Lettow-Vorbeck, T. E. Lawrence, impresario of the "Arab Revolt," at least helped to organize a movement that could plausibly be represented at the time and in subsequent years as an insurgency in the style of people's war with a viable political goal that attracted a large popular following, not a four-year buccaneer ransack that sustained itself on terror, plunder, and blood. In the process, the Arab Revolt was hailed by military intellectuals like Sir Basil Liddell Hart as the breakthrough transition from small wars to popular insurrection that carried the British to strategic success against the Ottoman Empire in the Middle East. Lawrence pioneered the vision that inspired the British and subsequently the Americans to encourage and supply World War II resistance movements as a militarily effective tool against Axis occupation, and as political movements to underpin the legitimacy of the Allied cause and lay the foundations for postwar governance.

Despite the hype, however, if anything, the Arab Revolt affected the course of the Great War even less than did von Lettow-Vorbeck's four years on the lam. For one thing, the Arab Revolt was a fiction of propaganda and public relations. There was no groundswell of Arab discontent with Ottoman rule before 1914, least of all in the Hijaz (Hejaz), the coastal region of the Arabian Peninsula bordering on the Red Sea that included Mecca and Medina. The Hijaz together with Yemen constituted the most backward provinces of the Ottoman Empire. In 1909, the Committee of Union and Progress, an umbrella reformist political coalition that included the Young Turks, fixed their sights on the region.[11] From 1912, the amir, Husayn ibn 'Ali, the Turkish-appointed Sharif of Mecca and guardian of Islam's holiest site, sought support from Arab nationalists concentrated principally in Beirut and Damascus, as well as from the British to resist the Committee's Ottomanization of the Hijaz. The idea of an independent Hijaz was attractive to Husayn for economic reasons and to prevent Istanbul from removing him as they had his predecessor following the Young Turk revolution of 1908. Arab nationalism held no appeal for the significant communities of non-Arab Muslim pilgrims who had settled in the Hijaz. Tribalism and religion, not Arab ethnicity, formed the basis of a pre-modern regional identity. Arab nationalism as such flourished in the postwar opposition to the Anglo-French mandates and the influx of Zionists into Palestine, not as an ideology of resistance to the Ottomans.[12]

In the closing weeks of 1914, British intelligence in Cairo began to explore sabotage projects in Istanbul's Arab domains, but received little encouragement from London until Husayn, together with his sons Abdullah and Faisal bin al-Husayn bin Ali al-Hashemi, proclaimed the Arab Revolt with a successful attack on the Turkish garrisons at Mecca and Jeddah in June 1916. The expected *levée en masse* failed to materialize, however – maybe a thousand ill-armed tribesmen assembled, described by Lawrence who first made contact with Faisal at Jeddah in October 1916 as:

> *continually shifting. A family will have a gun, and its sons will serve in turn, perhaps men drop off occasionally to see their wives, or a whole clan gets tired and takes a rest. For these*

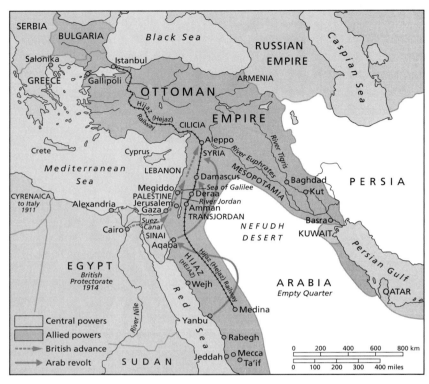

Map 2 Lawrence's campaign

> *reasons the paid forces are more than those serving, and this is*
> *necessary, since by tribal habit wars are always very brief, and*
> *the retention in the field of such numbers as the Sherif has*
> *actually kept together is unprecedented. Policy further often*
> *involves the payment to sheikhs of the wages of their*
> *contingency, and many such payments are little more than*
> *disguised bribes to important individuals.*[13]

Nor did the 28-year-old Lawrence appear chiseled in the image of a legendary guerrilla leader – scruffy, standing barely five foot six inches, Lawrence had first come to the Levant as an undergraduate to study Crusader castles, the subject of his Oxford thesis. After graduating with First Class Honors, he returned to eastern Syria to lead a series of archeological excavations, in the process acquiring a command of colloquial Arabic sufficient for dealing with laborers on the digs. He volunteered for the army in 1914 and was posted to a desk in the intelligence department in Cairo, with the rivetingly boring job of updating the Ottoman order of battle.

In October 1916, Husayn's call to arms appeared on the verge of collapse. The Turks had retaken Medina and appeared poised to march on Mecca 200 miles to the south. The Allies had no issues with the Turks' advances. For Paris, supporting a "nationalist" flare-up in the Hijaz would set a regrettable precedent should it enflame France's North African possessions. Stung by the failure of the Gallipoli campaign in 1915, Horatio Kitchener, Secretary of State for War until his June 1916 death, had opposed a diversion of yet more troops from the Western Front into a brawl with Istanbul. Lawrence's orders were to meet with the Hijaz rebels on the coast and report back that an infusion of British forces in Arabia would be wasteful. Sensing a chance to escape his Cairo office for good, Lawrence donned Arab robes and rode off into the interior to assess the situation with Husayn.[14]

While Lawrence found the "Beduin of the Hejaz" cheerful, hard, and recklessly brave, his catalogue of guerrilla shortcomings included a lack of camels and modern weapons; the reluctance of clans and tribes to cooperate or to venture far from home; "a living terror" of airplanes and artillery; an unwillingness to follow orders; fragile morale; and a predilection for plunder that caused discipline, such as it was, to dissolve at critical moments.[15] Nevertheless, Lawrence reported that modern weapons, British advisers, some aerial reconnaissance, and the substitution of Faisal for the aging Husayn, would turn their fortunes around. Lawrence's clincher, however, was that if Britain failed to prop up the revolt, the French, who had already installed a military mission in the Hijaz, would commandeer it for their purposes. The prospect of a French strategic coup energized the Fashoda veterans who staffed British intelligence's Cairo bureau.[16]

American historian David Fromkin believes that the Arab Revolt "had no material effect on the conduct or outcome of the war ... The Arab Revolt was supposed to rescue Britain, but instead Britain had to rescue it."[17] Faisal and Lawrence failed to take Medina, their principal objective, despite significant British logistical support. In fact, the Turks only abandoned Medina three months after war's end following a mutiny in the garrison.[18] Lawrence's first significant military accomplishment was to persuade a local Arab sheik to seize the small port of Aqaba, where the Turkish garrison surrendered on July 6, 1917, without a fight after the main outpost in the hills behind the port fell. This victory allowed Faisal and a few hundred followers to be sea-lifted out of the Hijaz. Their numbers inflated to around 3,500 by incorporating Arab deserters, many of whom were Syrians, from the Ottoman army, Faisal's force became even more factious.

Lawrence and Faisal joined the army of Edmund "The Bull" Allenby as it advanced through Palestine to Syria as part of Prime Minister Lloyd George's scheme to have Damascus liberated by Faisal to preempt French claims on the Levant. Even by incorporating Royal Engineers and Gurkhas into his force, Lawrence was unable to cut the branch of the Hijaz Railway that linked Damascus to Palestine to prevent the Turks from reinforcing Gaza. What British historian James Barr calls "the tactical climax" of the Arab Revolt came on September 16, 1918, when Lawrence's force, stiffened by British advisers and supported by armored cars, blew the tracks leading to the railway junction of Dara (Deraa), eighty miles south of Damascus. The Dara raid had three goals: support Allenby's advance on the city, and preempt French claims on Syria and Lebanon ceded by the 1916 Sykes–Picot agreement.[19] Third, Lawrence believed that the appearance of the raiding party would create a popular outpouring of support for his Bedouin that would lend credence to the claims of a popular revolt against the Ottomans.[20] But the speed of the Turkish collapse overtook events. Faisal was still three days' ride away on October 1, 1918, when Anzac cavalry and Damascenes occupied the city in the wake of the retreating Ottomans. (Allenby had cautioned Lawrence to prevent a premature Arab dash into the city.) The primary military benefit of the Arab Revolt was to disorganize the Turkish retreat in 1918, while forcing the Turks to devote a portion of a force already weakened by sickness, to railway security.[21]

T. E. Lawrence and the "great new truth in strategy": "victory without battle"

British officers of the era were in no doubt that Lawrence's contributions to the Ottoman defeat were purely cosmetic. Without British support the Arab Revolt was bound to collapse. The problem was that Husayn's, and subsequently Faisal's reliance on the British infidel for cash and weapons allowed the Turks to claim (correctly) that Husayn was a merely front for a British project to occupy the Holy Land and Syria, which helped to discredit him in the eyes of many tribes and limit the religious and political appeal of his rebellion. Because more overt naval and conventional military support for Husayn provoked opposition in the Hijaz, and because the failures of British expeditionary forces at Gallipoli, Kut, and Salonika stirred the fantasy, repeated after 1940, that a popular uprising in occupied territories could succeed where conventional forces had failed, the military headquarters in Cairo downsized military assistance into a small advisory mission of intelligence officers, of which Lawrence was a member. Even this adjustment proved insufficient as the presence of infidel advisers split the fragile tribal coalition: Lawrence's "guerrilla army" was judged to be "pretty useless" in January 1917. Six months later another adviser concluded that despite a fair amount of raiding, railway track demolition, and a generous distribution of rifles that had demoralized outlying Turkish garrisons and put them on the defensive, poor discipline and inter-tribal intrigue among the Bedouin meant that "all of us are wasting our time here, instead of getting on with the war."

The capture of Aqaba in July 1917 proved to be the transitional moment, because it allowed Faisal's militia to depart the Arabian Peninsula to join the right wing of Allenby's army advancing into Syria where Arab nationalists optimistically predicted that up to 65,000 Arabs were prepared to join a London-sponsored nationalist uprising.[22] In Syria, the British upgraded the Lawrence–Feisal rag-tag insurgent force into an all-arms mobile column in the small wars tradition that included 450 Egyptian Arab regulars, a British camel corps, an armored car troop, an artillery battery, and Gurkha and Egyptian demolition parties, with regular air support from January 1918. Nevertheless, many senior officers complained that Lawrence's *Bedu* served only for plunder and had constantly to be bribed to stay in the field. These same officers lamented the arms, munitions, and cash lavished on an Arab "army" that proved more of a "nuisance" for the British than for the Ottomans. Some of Lawrence's more prominent superiors alternately labeled him "a curse" and "an unfortunate charlatan."[23]

Given the poor opinion of the military value of the Arab Revolt among professional soldiers of the era and its inability to achieve significant military and political objectives, the insurgency's inflated postwar reputation can be explained by several factors rooted in propaganda, military particularism, and imperialist statecraft in the further evolution of the Eastern Question and Arab nationalism. First, it was compatible with the West's narrative of liberating oppressed Arabs as the first step in the creation of the Modern Middle East as spheres of influence of the victorious Entente powers. Second, the argument that the Arabs had simply seized control of events also gave London the excuse to renege on its commitment, laid out in the 1916 Sykes–Picot treaty, to partition the remnants of the Ottoman Empire with Paris. Third, the myth of an Arab-led liberation leveraged Hashemite ambitions. Husayn deliberately adopted the language of Arab nationalism in his negotiations with the British from 1915 because it was an idiom comprehensible to Cairo. It also allowed him to validate his rebellion against the world's major Muslim power and lent legitimacy to postwar Hashemite rule in the Transjordan and Iraq.[24] A first generation of Arab nationalists, loath to acknowledge that the British Army had smashed their Ottoman shackles, also embraced the fanciful narrative of self-liberation, bolstered by mock media events featuring bouncing Hijabis whipping their camels down Damascus boulevards, anonymous imaginative dispatches to *The Times*, and self-aggrandizing books subsequently written by Lawrence. The ardent Zionist Orde Wingate, whose irregular tactics carried out by Special Forces formations in pre-World War II Palestine, and subsequently in Ethiopia and Burma owed a debt to Lawrence's pioneering effort, complained nonetheless that the Lloyd George/Allenby/Lawrence choreographed conspiracy to create a myth of self-liberation gave Arabs an undue influence on British policy in the Middle East of the interwar years.[25] But the truth was that the fairly limited actions of Faisal's Arab irregulars in 1918 on the flanks of Allenby's army looked more like a cameo reprise of Wellesley's Iberian *guerrillera* than a Maoist "people's war" preview.

The myth of Lawrence of Arabia was a deliberate public relations fabrication of Lowell Thomas, an American showman who crossed the Atlantic in 1917 on a mission to identify and promote a war hero in keeping with the advertising spirit of the age. When the Western Front offered only acquiescent cannon fodder, Thomas drifted to Cairo. Lawrence, an Oxford scholar converted into an intelligence officer who, dressed in flowing robes, led primitive Bedouin in daring attacks on Turks, looked to have stepped right out of a John Buchan novel. At least one contemporary scholar argues that Lawrence became the insurgent commander and strategist of the Arab Revolt after he discovered a vacuum of policy and leadership upon arriving in the Hijaz.[26] Thomas made "Dances with Camels" Lawrence a celebrity with narrated lectures on the Arab Revolt using photos mounted on lantern slides that were attended by an estimated million people in London. It was a role that Lawrence, a consummate actor, was eager to play, and which he

4 T. E. Lawrence and Lowell Thomas circa 1917.

promoted in the *Seven Pillars of Wisdom* (1926) and the abridged version entitled *Revolt in the Desert* (1927), a highly fictionalized account of the desert war that appealed to interwar tastes for desert escapism. Lawrence also conformed to the intellectual turned armed protagonist model made modish in the 1920s by André Malraux and Ernest Hemingway. This fame catapulted him into the ranks of London's literati, where the poet and novelist Robert Graves was enlisted to write the first of many biographies. Lawrence's 1935 death in a motorbike accident preserved his youthful image and existential folk-hero status.[27]

     Another of Lawrence's biographers, none other than Sir Basil Liddell Hart, puffed him as a strategic genius whose exploits validated the military theorist's strategy of the indirect approach – avoiding the enemy's strength and winning through intelligence, guile, cultural knowledge, and by sowing psychological confusion. That Liddell Hart's theories of strategy and operations were anchored in fictionalized history, guerrilla mania, and a cowboys-and-Indians imagination mattered not a jot in a shaken island nation after 1918 where the search for victory without battle was full on in the aftermath of the horrific and costly-beyond-imagination bloodletting on the Western Front. While airpower – specifically terror bombing – was available only to advanced industrial societies, and insurgency seemed in the interwar years to have little applicability to the European continent, these alternative theories to counter the early twentieth-century search for decisive battles that had seemed so profligate in lives shared in their strategic essentials: each was anchored in a rejection of conventional warfare; each was population-centric in that they made no distinction between civilians and combatants; each promised victory without battle; and each emphasized a near magical employment in combat of politics and psychology by a handful of military geniuses to undo the suffocation of the age of the masses and the slaughter of total war.[28]

In like vein, Arquilla not only cites Lawrence as a pioneer of modern adviser-choreographed irregular warfare, the forerunner of the Green Berets. But also, in his view, the Lawrence–Liddell Hart tandem "unearthed a great new truth in strategy," namely that irregular warfare and technology had made concentration of force outmoded and would "enliven and expand irregular approaches to warfare far more than it will reenergize or improve upon traditional, conventional concepts of operations."[29]

Even though Lawrence agonized that Liddell Hart "carries his revulsion against Clausewitz too far,"[30] it was largely through the theorist's intervention in 1927 that Lawrence, rather than Callwell, was chosen to write the entry on guerrilla warfare for the 1929 edition of *Encyclopedia Britannica*:

> *Here is the thesis: granted mobility, security (in the form of denying targets to the enemy), time, and doctrine (the idea to convert every subject to friendliness), victory will rest with the insurgents, for the algebraical factors are in the end decisive, and against them the perfections of means and spirit struggle quite in vain.*[31]

Liddell Hart praised Lawrence for providing "a wider and more profound treatment" of guerrilla warfare than had Clausewitz, by demonstrating "its offensive value . . . both as a struggle for independence and as part of the Allied campaign against Turkey."[32]

So, two assertions have been made on the basis of Lawrence's experience and Liddell Hart's interpretation of it: First, Lawrence's "algebraical" calculation that sufficient popular support guaranteed victory because counterinsurgent forces would never command sufficient troops to stand against a people in arms basically denied the fundamental Clausewitzian principle of the interactive nature of war and the fundamental importance of strategy to victory. Clausewitz's goal in theory and practice, according to the *doyen* of modern Clausewitz studies Peter Paret, was to provide a methodical framework for analyzing events, not an "algebraic formula for action ... In short, the role of theory is to educate our judgment, not to press it into fixed channels."[33]

However, small wars practitioners were on a quest for a victory formula, not theoretical frameworks to refine their strategic analysis. The problem of the Great War was that decision in warfare had shifted away from the battlefield where armies seemed unable to produce a decision. Victory depended on the ability of the civilian population to endure great hardship, a requirement that proved to be beyond the capacities of the Russians by 1917 and, in the eyes of Ludendorff, Germans as well in 1918.[34] Soldiers became acutely aware that they had to regain control of warfare in the age of total war. One group sought to do this through a combination of technology and operational concepts that would deliver victory quickly and thereby minimize, if not eliminate, civilian influence. The other option was to regain control of war through popular mobilization. This was essentially a vision shared by Ludendorff and in the immediate postwar years by a minority in the General Staff who envisaged a popular war of liberation or *Volkskrieg*,[35] an idea replicated in its essential lines by Mao, the Bolsheviks, and the Nazis. The focus of strategy should be to act on popular culture to keep people in the fight. In this context, the modernity of Lawrence lies in his use of propaganda as "doctrine" to promote insurgency as a strategically decisive popular mobilization. As experience would soon demonstrate, however, popular support was far from sufficient to guarantee victory in people's war.

The second "great new truth in strategy," Arquilla's assertion that irregular warfare allied with technology had made concentration of force obsolete and demonstrated the applicability of irregular warfare to conventional operations, would have astonished most post-Great War military leaders. This was especially so after the mid 1920s in Germany when the idea of combining *Volkskrieg* with mobile warfare was discredited following the failure of popular German mobilization in the face of the 1923 Franco-Belgian occupation of the Ruhr, and subsequently abandoned by the General Staff. In any case, *Volkskrieg* like the French *levée en masse* was envisaged as a deterrent, not a practical blueprint for resistance. Each was based on mythologized histories of popular mobilizations against invasion during the wars of the French Revolution and Napoleon, not on the actions of von Lettow-Vorbeck and Lawrence. People's war was rejected by planners in Europe because society was considered too fissiparous to cohere, because the military would lose its autonomy and monopoly on strategy if it threw open its ranks to the *volk*, and because the idea of defense in depth would prove so destructive that victory would look identical to defeat. In the interwar years, therefore, mechanization separated from people's war in Europe.[36]

Despite Arquilla's contention, irregular warfare had absolutely no influence on the major strategic thinkers in the interwar years, like J. F. C. Fuller, Charles de Gaulle, Hans von Seeckt, Guilio Douhet, or Billy Mitchell. In the age of total war, all armies bought into the machine culture, so that in the words of Michael Geyer, "the 'strategist' became the supreme organizer of weapons – he turned into an engineer."[37] The Fall of France in May–June 1940 to a technologically advanced concentration of tanks and airpower, confirmed the centrality of technology and concentration of force to victory in World War II. A belief in the applicability of Lawrence's irregular operations in the Great War Middle East to warfare in World War II survived in the SOE, and in the pre-El Alamein British Army in the Western Desert Campaign in 1940–1942. Irregular operations were subsequently transferred by Orde Wingate and Archibald Wavell to Burma from 1943 as a sign of desperation, as a legacy of the lingering amateurism inherent in the British Army's small war heritage, and the Lawrencian quest for victory without battles, not as a harbinger of a new era in warfare.

Small war becomes people's war

The most charitable thing one can say about Lawrence and Liddell Hart is that they were ahead of their time, for neither algebraical factors nor the indirect approach seemed to be working too well for the actual insurgencies in the 1920s, versus those in newspaper serials and journals of military theory. The Great War had proven a transformative event in warfare, however, both because it witnessed the advent of the three-dimensional battlefield and because the outcome of wars was seen to hinge on the willingness of populations to support them. Lawrence and his handlers had identified through a haze of invention that small war was in the process of transitioning to people's war, as anti-imperialism and nascent nationalism among non-Western peoples nourished by the war and its aftermath took hold among the Muslims in North Africa and the Middle East, Indians, and Chinese. People's war combines a strategy of popular indoctrination around a shared vision of economic, social, and political transformation that imparts the stamina to allow a people, however defined, to apply tactics of mobile and guerrilla warfare over a prolonged period against a militarily superior enemy. In the Maoist vernacular, mobile warfare as a phenomenon in China in the 1920s and 1930s in the contest between the conventional forces of Chiang Kai-shek's Koumintang and Mao Tse-tung's communist guerrillas, meant essentially maneuvering to avoid positional battles against superior forces.

To be sure, while post-1918 colonial nationalism only slowly gained momentum,[38] the *Chouans*, Iberian *partidas*, Abd-el-Kader in the Maghreb, Samory in West Africa, and Shamil in the Caucasus, not to mention Smuts and de Wet, invoked race, religion, culture, or tribe to induce popular cohesion in the face of alien invasion. Some people bought into resistance, others opted out because they disagreed with the premise, or were skeptical of the prospects for success, belonged to a different class or tribe, did not feel up to the sacrifice, were bought off, or coerced into neutrality. Colonial-era resistors auditioned the Maoist tactic of drawing the enemy deep into the interior of one's territory to slash them with "mobile" and guerrilla warfare.

The bottom line was that people's war was hardly new. It simply repackaged and codified for the benefit of twentieth-century insurgents familiar tactical and operational methods. What had changed was not the tactics, but the strategic context in which insurgencies were fought in the wake of Leninist anti-imperialism and the civil war in China. Mao's concern was to increase the stamina of revolt for a new era, "put new flesh on the bones of Clausewitz's familiar proposition that war is a political instrument," and more closely articulate tactics with strategy.[39] The Great War and its immediate aftermath seemed to shift the momentum toward rebellion, for at least two reasons. First, the slaughter in the trenches followed by postwar economic and political chaos eroded confidence in the West's inalienable right to oversee Callwell's "inferior races."

"The 1930s began in August 1914," writes the historian of France, Eugen Weber.[40] Founded in 1921, the French Communist Party adopted as a matter of faith J. A. Hobson's (erroneous) accusation leveled in the wake of the Boer War that imperialism was a product of capitalist competition. Britain's Labour Party promised measured empire emancipation, although they often backtracked in the face of Conservative opposition. League of Nations mandates carried the obligation to transition the erstwhile inhabitants of the Ottoman and German empires to independence.

Diminished certainty in society and culture about the intrinsic superiority of Western civilization as the legitimizing principle of imperialism was matched by a new, if gradual, assertiveness among the ruled, a second post-Great War development. The Versailles peace sanctified the principle of self-determination that accompanied a wave of nationalist-inspired instability in Ireland, North Africa, the Near East, Indo-China, China, and India. The post-Great War settlements handed the moral high ground to independence movements, which framed the struggle for legitimacy between imperialism and people's war. Callwell had no doubt that small wars were a legitimate enterprise because native societies were unorganized, racially inferior, in the thrall of benighted practices and beliefs, and in desperate want of civilizing. An ability to orchestrate people's war, however, suggested a level of social self-affirmation, organization, and staying power on the part of the insurgents that challenged the legitimacy of the imperial occupier while exposing its prescriptive oil spot, progressive penetration, hearts and minds, and combination of politics with force formulae as imperialist clichés more likely to ignite insurgencies than appease them. The immediate post-Great War years led to crises in legitimacy as the major powers had to reach more deeply into their small wars bag of tricks in search of a victory, which discredited imperial occupations.

The great revolts as people's war, 1919–1926

The interwar years were times of turmoil in Europe, with the economic and social dislocations caused by the Great War expressed in the form of new radical ideologies of the left and right. Despite these developments – or rather because of them – imperialists in France and Britain clung fast to their colonies, deemed more than ever to be vital components of national survival. Empire in these years also served the cause of nostalgia, a retreat for traditionalists who found in the colonial abroad a sense of order, hierarchy, social deference, and racial superiority that had eroded at home. As conflicting ideological and cultural visions of legitimacy solidified and spread in the Great War's aftermath, hearts and minds tactics concocted in the nineteenth century to establish communities of interest between colonial conquerors and hitherto fragmented non-Western societies became less effective instruments of political and military control. Nor, increasingly, were colonies viewed as legitimate enterprises by Europeans, but as systems for racial exploitation, or refuges for relics of a prewar political order, Belle Époque or Edwardian social anachronisms uncompetitive and out of place at home. In this context, challenges to European dominion would become more intense, widespread, and tactically and strategically sophisticated, while the expense and legitimacy of enforcing imperial order became difficult to justify unless the cost of imperial development and policing could be passed on to the colonized. Politicized colonial military forces, and police forces mustered and militarized to confront an increasingly sophisticated panoply of seditious behaviors, adapted badly to imperialism's new world.

With the proclamation of the Independent Republic of the Rif, Abd el-Krim presided over a quasi-organized state that combined a central bureaucracy, a prison system, a standing army made up of both male and female conscripts backed by tribal militias, a flag, and even a diplomatic corps into an organization that far exceeded the scope of the localized tribal *jacqueries* that Lyautey's peaceful penetration was designed to smother. Control in the tribal areas of Morocco depended on the *Service de renseignement* (SR), the offspring of the *bureaux arabes* that Lyautey had resurrected for Morocco after 1912. The SR confidently predicted that the Rif Rebellion was anti-Spanish, not proto-nationalist, and so would remain confined to the Spanish zone, probably because that was the story Lyautey peddled to Paris. But it was also based on confidence that native affairs officers could use intelligence to control events, when in fact their intrusion into local affairs produced resentment and rebellion.[41] The Resident General proved to be the architect of his own demise when in 1924 he ordered French troops to occupy the Ouergha River valley (one of Morocco's most productive grain-producing regions north of Fez) and seal it off behind a barrier of blockhouses. The goal of this occupation was better to exert French influence over the tribes in both the Rif and the French zone through the manipulation of their food supply. What Lyautey and his SR had accomplished by this act was to unsettle the local tribes who postponed planting, which disrupted commerce and drove up food prices throughout Morocco, so that the unrest in the Rif began to contaminate Fez, Casablanca, and Marrakech. For their part, Abd el-Krim and his Riffians were forced to attack into the French zone or starve (the Spanish had already blockaded the coast). Lyautey became doubly culpable when he then ignored warnings of increased Riffian activity, while the SR failed to detect that supposedly pacified tribes in the French sector had also been persuaded to support the Rif Republic.[42] When on April 12, 1925 Abd el-Krim surged into the French zone, a system of colonial control-based intelligence collection, alleged cultural knowledge, and political manipulation failed catastrophically. Over forty French border posts were overrun, 20 percent of French forces in Morocco were killed, wounded, or missing, and Fez was threatened. Lyautey's meticulously constructed pacification strategy folded like a house of cards as an estimated 20,000 French-armed tribesmen defected to Abd el-Krim, exposing, in the view of American historian and Lyautey biographer William A. Hoisington, Jr., "the defects of his methods of conquest and rule," and demonstrating "that French economic and political pacification among the tribes ... mattered little when there was an alternative." Claiming that he faced a an unprecedented Muslim jihad, a clearly rattled Lyautey begged French Prime Minister Paul Painlevé for permission to deploy the quintessential horror product of industrialized warfare – mustard gas – against his one-time collaborators,[43] a request that accelerated his replacement by Philippe Pétain, the master of conventional warfare, who broke the Rif advance with conventional tactics and established heavily fortified positions in the north, acts which convinced many of the tribes that the insurgency had passed the culminating point of victory.

Hoisington concluded that the Rif Rebellion demonstrated that culture, religion, and tribal solidarity trumped the French promise of peace, progress, and prosperity as a reward for loyalty to the imperial system. Lyautey's peaceful penetration, which advanced by recognizing customary Berber law and tribal governance, pushed the Sultan, who correctly saw it as a transparent attempt to weaken his authority, into a collaboration with the nationalists and failed to curtail rebellion. It was also expensive as Lyautey either lavished cash on tribal leaders or took female hostages to reimpose loyalty. The left seized upon Lyautey's setbacks to attack him in Parliament, and to organize anti-war protests and

5 Lyautey greets World War I hero Marshal Philippe Pétain in Casablanca in 1925. Pétain arrived to direct the Riff War following the collapse of Lyautey's tribal engagement strategy.

dockers' strikes that aimed to halt military shipments to Morocco. And while this was hardly enough to force a rethink of France's civilizing mission, it showcased the political risks created by fantasist theories of colonial conquest peddled as cheap and effortless by a mastery of cultural knowledge and oil spot tactics. The rebellion also shattered Lyautey's dream that the colonies could serve as the vehicle to regenerate what he saw as a decadent French homeland.[44]

Lyautey's "combination of politics with force" fared little better when imported by his disciples into Syria, and further challenged the Gallic conceit that Frenchmen were uniquely gifted Muslim managers. Initially, at least, the French could plausibly claim to have arrived in the Levant as popular liberators. Faisal bin al-Husayn bin Ali al-Hashemi, leader of the so-called Arab Revolt, had appeared in Damascus in 1918 at the head of a group of young Arabs, many of whom were rural, middle-class Syrian graduates of Ottoman military schools, whom he subsequently rewarded with posts in his government. On September 15, 1919, the British agreed to hand over Greater Syria to French troops. Deprived of British subsidies by what was called the "Evacuation Crisis," Faisal's government raised taxes on everything, often demanding payment in gold from merchants. This sent an already war-ravaged economy into a nosedive. Peasants crowded into cities in search of work, civil servants and soldiers went unpaid, while insecurity increased around Damascus and other cities as Bedouin, brigands, and armed gangs ambushed travelers, shook down merchants, and fought running gun battles with police in the towns. Strikes, food riots, and inter-communal tensions pockmarked Syria by the spring of 1920. On March 8, 1920, Faisal declared Syria independent, an initiative rejected by the Allies meeting at San Remo to divvy up Ottoman spoils in May. Headed for a showdown with the French, Faisal instituted conscription in an attempt to raise a force to insure internal order and protect against invasion. This was the last straw for many Syrians, as desertion and evasion of military service became endemic. When the French army shot its way into Damascus in July 1920 to extend the mandate from the coast to the interior, they were welcomed by the old Ottoman elite who looked upon Faisal's followers as a collection of incompetent upstarts and embraced the French as saviors who would restore Syria's natural order.[45]

The French would have been better off to exercise a little benign neglect. However, the mandate had to pay for itself. It also had to be "civilized" in keeping with the imperial mission, which required some pretty aggressive social engineering. The Syrian mandate's human terrain was as complex as the post-1920 political situation was volatile. Unfortunately for them, French native affairs officers who arrived from Morocco prideful of their cultural understanding to join the newly constituted Levant Administrative Service expected to slip effortlessly into formerly Ottoman administrative posts. They transferred their Orientalized Moroccan conceptual framework to Syria, which they interpreted as a static, changeless, feudal society, rather than recognize the dynamic social and economic forces unleashed by the Great War and the collapse of the Ottoman Empire. They sized up Syria as a collection of communities coexisting in simmering hostility, and they probably found plenty of locals – especially Christians – willing to reinforce their preconceptions. The ethno-religious make-up of Greater Syria (Syria and Lebanon) was so diverse that the French referred to the mandate as a "mosaic of minorities."[46] Indeed, the French conviction that Syrians were incapable of cooperating – and that without resolute management, the mandate would disintegrate into anarchy and bloodletting – supplied the moral justification for the occupation and the application of the so-called "Moroccan formula of government" which consisted of breaking Syria into federal entities to prevent the majority Sunnis from consolidating power. While this Orientalist viewpoint caused the French fundamentally to misinterpret a complex set of inter-communal relationships, in the long run it proved to be a successful strategy of governance, because Paris found Syrian allies – especially Christians, the old Ottoman aristocracy of service, and even moderate nationalists, Alawites, Druze, and Turkish minorities in Alexandretta – prepared to leverage the mandate to hold and extend their own power.[47]

"At the base of the conception of colonial rule was a romantic notion of timeless and changeless 'Oriental' society, best governed with fatherly 'love' for the colonial citizens," writes American historian of the Great Revolt Michael Provence. "Combined with paternalistic love was an emphasis on the material and economic advantages of colonial rule."[48] The French administration believed that an aggressive program of public improvements would demonstrate the benefits of French rule in both Damascus and Paris, and shatter what it saw as the iron grip of the feudal elite. This presented several problems, beginning with the fact that the Ottoman Empire had been an economic as well as a political unit, whose breakup severed suppliers from traditional markets, as happened in the case of the other vanquished central powers with destabilizing results. The situation was made worse by the 1924 nosedive of the French franc, which took the Syrian currency down with it. Broke, the French sought to slash mandate expenses, to the point that they could not even restore basic services, much less trade and transportation networks common under the Ottomans. However, lack of cash could not be allowed to stand in the way of hearts and minds. French officers forced community leaders and shaikhs to boost taxes and mobilize corvée labor to finance public works projects, a practice that undermined their authority and prestige by making them appear powerless to resist French demands. "They thought to make it a second Morocco," a contemporary British observer concluded of the French project in Syria. "They have succeeded in making it a second Rif."[49]

By 1925, even the most ardent imperialist would have been hard pressed to identify the benefits of the mandate. The economy was in a tailspin, the value of the currency was in free fall, the French partition of Syria into five states and its separation from Lebanon substituted familiar mechanisms of Ottoman rule with a proliferation of corrupt, redundant, and inefficient French-sponsored political entities, while convincing the population that French divide and rule policies had contributed to economic stagnation. Deprived of their trade with southern Turkey, once thriving population centers in the north, especially, became ghost towns, and brigandage, even attacks on French forces, soared. The strategic circumstances under which the French invaded and occupied Syria combined with bureaucratic mismanagement and lack of mandate legitimacy in the eyes of the population to create conditions that led to the Great Syrian Revolt of 1925–1927.[50]

On the surface, the fact that the spark for the Great Revolt was supplied by the Druze might come as something of a surprise. After all, they stood to benefit from a French policy imported from Lyautey's Morocco that sought to protect minority, rural, and clan-centric Berbers from the allegedly nefarious influences of dominant Sunni Arab culture. The French equated the Druze to Moroccan Berbers – a "primitive and inorganic" warlike Muslim sect living in a state of quasi-anarchy, exploited by tribal chiefs. In truth, although Druze society was far from democratic, the class warfare approach promoted by native affairs officers who sought to gain the favor of the peasantry by liberating them from the exploitation of a feudal elite *à la Révolution française* led to serious missteps. In the 1860s following clashes with Maronite Christians in southern Lebanon, of whom the French were the self-appointed protectors, the Druze had been resettled at Paris' insistence in Djebal Hawrân – a mountainous region south and east of Damascus, clothed by oak forests, and sliced by deep valleys. The area became known as the Djebal al-Druze, where the 86,000 Druze lived in 123 villages, many of them accessible only on foot. Since the 1860s, the Druze had transformed the Djebel Hawrân into a dynamic frontier society of largely autonomous villages whose lucrative grain trade attracted immigrants and whose farmers established commercial and social links with Damascene merchants, among whom nationalist sentiment was strong. They also tended their links to the approximately 3,500 Druze living in Damascus.[51]

As in the other four states of Greater Syria, the treaty of March 4, 1921 that established the state of Djebel Druz allowed the Druze their own governor and representative council, or *majlis*, in return for recognition of the mandate and freedom to station French advisers and troops at the Druze "capital" Suwayda (Soueida). In this way, in return for guaranteeing Druze independence, the French gained legitimacy for their mandate and the right to reorder the Djebel Druze.[52] However, this attempt at indirect rule backfired in a Druze society deeply divided between veterans and opponents of the Arab Revolt.

On January 1, 1924 the French named an officer of the SR, Major Gabriel Carbillet, as governor of the Hawrân. Carbillet's energy appears remarkable and drawn from the best years of Third Republic modernization in France. In two years he opened thirty schools, drove roads into the Djebal's remote backwoods, and created a water system for Suwayda. He abolished the village taxes collected by the chiefs as part of an anti-corruption campaign (the chiefs took their cut), stopped the monthly pensions paid to the former governor's supporters, and distributed communal lands to the peasantry, a prerogative hitherto reserved for the leading families as a way to build up and reward their client networks. Whatever benefits accrued to the Druze, this French exercise in hearts and minds backfired badly because it was socially divisive, coercive, and humiliating for the tribal leaders and large landowners. Furthermore, it created a vacuum of political authority and social control, as a foreigner who had no local legitimacy stripped Druze leaders of many of the traditional resources and prerogatives that had cemented their client networks together.

Infrastructure improvements failed as a hearts and minds strategy largely because they were accomplished by unpopular corvée labor. Even mild opposition to French-led modernization and unpaid labor was punished by internment, collective fines, and house demolitions. Men who could no longer provide for their families were disenfranchized and disgraced. Also, a significant faction of Druze regarded Carbillet's assumption of the governorship as a breach of the treaty, and protested the Frenchman's meddling in the election of the *majlis*. Yet, when a delegation of Druze notables traveled to Damascus to petition the High Commissioner for Carbillet's recall, they were arrested and imprisoned, an act that ignited the Djebel Druze and sparked rebellion in other cities, regions, and groups.

The Great Syrian Revolt succeeded initially because it synthesized local grievances shared by confessional or ethnic groups who otherwise were deeply distrustful of each other. The French blamed "feudalists, bandits, extremists, anti-Christians, and opportunists looking for plunder," when in fact the Great Syrian Revolt was a tribute to French policy that managed to unite urban and rural elements across the social and religious spectrum against their unpopular mandate.

The rebellion enjoyed initial military success because Paris was focused on the Rif. Once reinforcements began to arrive, however, the rebels lacked the skills or adaptability to respond to the firepower of French colonial units, supplemented by local Circassian and Kurdish irregulars whose low military proficiency and poor discipline caused them to act against the rebellion's base rather than against Druze fighters, which further sharpened ethnic and confessional tensions and created an atmosphere conducive to human rights violations and war crimes.

Damascus amnestied mercantile urban nationalists frightened by the violence, bought Turkish neutrality with territorial concessions in the north, and persuaded the British to seal the Palestine border and deny asylum to rebels. Having isolated the theater and crumbled the insurgency with a combination of concessions and force, the French fell back on collective punishment of villages that harbored rebels, wholesale summary executions, detentions, hostage taking, buying the neutrality of Bedouin tribes, deportations and population transfers, and indiscriminant artillery and air bombardment of Damascus neighborhoods that were not in revolt and other population centers to regain control.[53] This approach induced fence-sitters, opportunists, or those who had simply suffered enough, to seek accommodation.

In the end, crushing the Great Revolt bought the French another nineteen years in Syria because Paris was able to manipulate an elite that was seriously divided over their vision for Syria, indeed over what "Syria" actually meant, and who retained strong residual loyalties to their sub-national groups. But France's Syrian mandate from the beginning came to be seen as a failure of the civilizing mission. The bombardment of Damascus was denounced internationally and produced a hot debate in France over the nature and moral foundation of imperialism, which cost the High Commissioner Maurice Sarrail his job in November 1925. Even with the end of the Druze Revolt in 1927, the mandate persisted as a nation-crushing, rather than a nation-building project. It proved neither cheap nor efficient. French indirect rule allowed Damascus to seek out compliant collaborators on both the national and the local levels, who employed their extended families and clans and enriched themselves with bribes and insider deals that created a costly, redundant, and corrupt administration to preside over a stagnant economy. Syria remained a focus of Franco-British intrigues that intensified into open conflict in 1941 after Syria became a stronghold of support for the collaborationist Vichy regime. Two decades of the French mandate allowed moderate nationalists to consolidate their position under a policy of "honorable cooperation." Continued counterinsurgency campaigns against Druze and Kurd rebels that featured the familiar village destructions, livestock confiscations and aerial bombardments, urban unrest, strikes, and rancorous Syrian politics and short-lived governments in the decade of the 1930s created a country woefully unprepared for independence when it came in 1946.[54]

In the final analysis, neither people's war, nor Lawrence's algebraical formula, nor Liddell Hart's indirect approach could produce success for the insurgencies in the Rif or Syria. Each revolt was a sub-national rebellion able to capitalize on discontent with French rule in other communities, but as yet lacking a unifying nationalist vision to sustain a prolonged conflict, a political structure able to impose social order and discipline, or a military organization that held out hope of strategic success. The French were able to peel away support for the revolts with combinations of military pressure and political concessions. On the other hand, French promises of modernization and infrastructure improvements had proven destabilizing. So, the occupiers fell back on divide and rule strategies and the toleration of corruption and inefficiencies as the price of governance.

Britain and imperial defense in the 1920s and 1930s

The challenge to patriarchal colonial rule in Morocco and Syria was duplicated in the resistance of subject peoples to British imperial governance. Harsh countermeasures taken in reaction to Gandhi's postwar *satyagraha* ("force of truth") campaign of passive resistance culminated in the April 13, 1919 Amritsar Massacre, when Indian army troops under the command of Brigadier Reginald Dyer opened fire on a political meeting, killing 379 and wounding over 1,000. In the mind of many, Amritsar exposed the hypocrisy of a policy of "combining coercion with kindness."[55] Once Ottoman forces in Mesopotamia surrendered to the British in November 1918, British political officers invaded the provinces to sack the Arabs who had run the country for the Ottomans and imposed their own arbitrary exactions. When London was awarded the mandate for Iraq in April 1920, little time elapsed before a revolt broke out in the Shi'a regions of the mid-Euphrates in June 1920 and spread down river. Southern Kurdistan seized on the confusion to rebel. The British lost 2,300 mainly Indian soldiers and Churchill authorized the RAF to contemplate using mustard gas against "recalcitrant natives." But Mesopotamia was too splintered by tribe and religion; and the rebellion, too localized to form a common front against the mandatory power. By October 1920, Britain had regained control by promoting Faisal as a façade of Arab self-government and empowering the Sunnis who had dominated the Ottoman administration and served in Istanbul's army to work for them.[56]

But if the British faced revolt in India and Iraq, in Ireland, London encountered what American historian Tom Mockaitis has called the first true people's war, of which the 1916 Easter Rising was the opening salvo. If anything, the challenges to civil-military relations and policy formulation over Ireland from 1919–1921 proved even more intense than typical of counterinsurgency operations generally because Ireland was considered an integral part of the United Kingdom and the actions of the security services were more visible, in large part because the Irish Republican Army (IRA) created an effective IO strategy. That said, why Mockaitis qualifies the struggle for Irish independence as a people's war is unclear. The level of violence remained remarkably low – numbers vary, but final estimates say 624 members of the British security forces, mostly policemen from the overwhelmingly Catholic Royal Irish Constabulary (RIC) died, along with similar numbers of insurgents, mainly in the first six months of 1921. This tally was fewer than the number of troops killed in Iraq in 1920, similar to the average "wastage" of 1,500 men on a quiet day on the Western Front, and far fewer than the 22,000 sacrificed to annex the Boer Republics into a larger South African project barely twenty years earlier.

While there was no doubt a common sense of Irish identity, a folk memory of previous uprisings against English occupation, and discontent with rule from London had steadily increased since the 1880s, whether this tipped the Troubles into a people's war is questionable. Neither the economy nor sacrosanct "race meetings" were disrupted. London enjoyed solid support among minority but significant Protestant "tribes" in Ireland, not dissimilar, one can say, to the percentage of Sunnis in Mesopotamia on which both the Ottomans and British based their rule. Great swaths of Ireland remained quiet – violence was concentrated in Cork, Dublin, Tipperary, Kerry, and Limerick, so that a watered-down version of martial law which required neither the issuance of identity cards nor press censorship, much less calorie control, was declared in only a fraction of the twenty-six counties.

This quiescence worried the IRA, who feared that a relatively peaceful countryside and a preference for many Irish to emigrate rather than fight for independence undermined the plausibility of people's war and freed British forces to concentrate against the most active fronts.[57] The IRA, which answered to its own executive, did not enjoy the support of a majority of the independence party Sinn Féin, who disliked its methods and distrusted its independence, much less the Irish people or the Church hierarchy, who questioned whether violence was necessary at all as British reform from the late nineteenth century had removed the most salient grievances and whose major desire was for an end to hostilities.[58] The unpopular IRA courts; prohibition of emigration which the IRA equated with desertion; IRA patrols that entered houses to confiscate weapons, food, or money, sometimes for private gain; and excessive violence that included the murders of informants or RIC officers on the way to or from mass savaged popular support. In fact, the high level of IRA intimidation suggested a lack of faith in Irish patriotism. In 1920, Dublin Castle deemed the IRA to be "a handful of revolutionaries, badly armed and only partly supported by the people."[59]

Like Lawrence's Arab Revolt, the IRA probably numbered no more than 3,000 active combatants at any one time (although the military estimated their numbers to be considerably greater) – more-or-less one guerrilla for every twenty-four members of the security services. Their military accomplishments were confined mostly to assassinating informants and burning abandoned rural police stations. Attempts to carry out larger operations to demonstrate that it was a true army and not mere congeries of terrorists were quickly countered by British sweeps and counter-ambushes.[60] Indeed, terms like people's war, insurrection, or revolution seem so wildly disproportionate to what Irish activist C. S. Andrews labeled a surge of "terror and tyranny tempered by assassination" – directed by Michael Collins and executed by a fringe of IRA gunmen – that the population adopted the Troubles as the most descriptive term for the events that led to independence.[61]

The victory of the Irish independence movement did not come about as the result of Lawrence's algebraical factors that deliver victory automatically to the insurgent, or because it was an irresistible people's war, nor because British security forces, taken by surprise, were slow to adjust their tactics and build up their intelligence on the IRA, although it was all of that.[62] In places like Ulster it was a civil, sectarian war. Elsewhere, D. M. Leeson describes what degenerated into gang warfare between the RIC and the IRA. The sheer cost of holding on to Ireland in Britain's straitened post-Great War budget circumstances combined with imperial overstretch certainly weighed on policymakers. Indeed, Lloyd George apparently balked at the 100,000-troop, £100 million estimated price tag for Ireland while 370,000 British troops were simultaneously deployed in Burma, Afghanistan, and Iraq, as well as policing a coalminers' strike in Britain.[63] But, as William Fuller argues, cost was not the determinant factor, especially given the compelling counter-arguments that Irish secession would compromise the security of the British Isles and telegraph London's brittle imperial resolve to a restive empire. Nor did American pressure play a critical role, despite Sinn Féin President and Dáil Prime Minister Eamon De Valera's attempts to harness the political muscle of 20 million Irish-Americans to force Westminster into negotiations.[64]

Colonial violence comes home

D. C. Boyce argues that Ireland was granted independence because elite public opinion in Britain was shocked by the government's counter-insurgency tactics, which it felt mocked Britain's ideals of justice and fair play, and undermined its good name abroad, especially in the United States.[65] While it is tempting to see public reaction to the Irish counter-insurgency campaign as an escalation and intensification of anti-Boer War sentiment from twenty years earlier, the analogies are limited. To be sure, there are some meaningful similarities. In both South Africa and Ireland, for example, civilian leaders lost faith in military promises that an escalation of punitive military measures could quell rebellion at a reasonable cost in public opinion and diplomatic credibility.[66] The Second Boer War kicked off as an immensely popular enterprise, unlike Ireland where repression of the Troubles enjoyed the support of a narrow band of Tories and Ulster Unionists. The Boer War ended fairly quickly as Boer resistors split and the offer of dominion status provided the fig leaf of Boer autonomy behind which peace could be concluded.

Although the Anglo-Irish confrontation was centuries in the making, Ireland in 1920 shared some commonalities with France's relationship with Algeria in 1954, more than with South Africa in 1900. Both unions were like hasty marriages, consummated between nations of starkly different religions, cultures, languages, and levels of economic development, that gave voice to the feeling that Irish, like Algerians, were an inferior race that answered to a foreign faith. The 1801 Act of Union, voted practically without debate in a Westminster preoccupied with the French wars, imported into British politics a panoply of political issues to include Catholic emancipation, "the Famine," Fenian subversion, peasant exploitation by absentee landlords, and bitter Home Rule squabbles from 1886 that transmogrified into Sinn Féin demands for independence by the turn of the twentieth century. Despite the insurmountable incompatibility that made it impossible to integrate Ireland or Algeria into a coherent national project, the prospect of divorce was decried by nationalists as an attempt to break up the nation. Both Ireland and Algeria had been colonized by a vocal loyalist minority – Ulster Protestants and *pieds noirs* respectively – who at first elicited sympathy but who over time came to be perceived as a bigoted and intolerant stumbling block to a solution. Indeed, the requirement to use the army against one's own population was a clear indication of weak internal legitimacy.

The brilliance of the IRA's information strategy, which integrated politics, warfare, and publicity and enlisted people like the best-selling author Erskine Childers to plant stories in neutral newspapers, surely encouraged the growing perception among an attentive public that British policy in Ireland was morally compromised. *The Irish Bulletin* began in November 1919 as an IRA broadsheet that, despite its Republican bias, came to be treated as a reliable source for the mainstream British press.[67] Reports of British atrocities especially resonated because pacification in Ireland from 1919 was observed in a context created by wartime propaganda that had been shaped by German atrocities against subject populations from 1914 onwards. However ambiguous British or French people weary of war might feel about their colonial enterprise, no longer could they take scant comfort in the confidence that German generals and admirals held a monopoly on barbarism. Analogies between British reprisals against the Irish population in the wake of IRA attacks and German war crimes in occupied Belgium were frequent. For instance, the *Guardian* described the "sack" of Balbriggan in September 1920 by RIC policemen following the assassination of two of their number as "an Irish Louvain."[68] Riots by British security services that laid waste to Tuam, Galway, or Cork caused British progressives to wonder how the behavior of their Great War heroes had come to resemble that of Germans in Belgium or the Turks in Armenia.[69]

In 1912, Ireland appeared to be headed toward a civil war, as Irish and Ulster Volunteer organizations armed and squared off over Home Rule, a crisis that was postponed by the outbreak of war in 1914. Easter week in 1916 witnessed an attack organized by the Irish Republican Brotherhood on key locations in Dublin. This was suppressed by the British who court-martialed and executed fifteen leaders, which earned them a sympathy they had not met from the Irish public during the Rising. The British further antagonized Irish public opinion in 1918 by threatening to impose conscription in Ireland. This created a backlash that benefited Sinn Féin, which won 75 of 105 Irish seats at Westminster in the 1918 elections. In January of the following year, these MPs formed a Dáil or parliament, and declared an Irish Republic. The Irish Volunteers reconstituted themselves as the IRA and initiated hostilities by assassinating RIC policemen, burning RIC barracks and tax offices, and raiding arms depots.

Those who see tactics as the problem in Ireland of the 1920s have noted how poorly prepared the British were to confront the Irish insurgency, despite their centuries of presence in Ireland. But London's tactical failures were the product of deeper institutional distortions typical of the small wars environment of colonial occupation – a militarized police force and a politicized military – together with the after effects of the Great War on legions of its participants. When these factors were combined, the campaign scenario in Ireland – surprise, followed by a brutal crackdown on the population – was fairly typical of post-Great War responses to colonial unrest as was the pattern in the Rif and Syria in the 1920s. What proved most shocking for the British public was to observe the toxicities of colonial warfare repatriated to the Homeland.

The blurring of missions and institutions in constabulary forces became characteristic of the RIC from the moment that Sir Robert Peel, Chief Secretary for Ireland between 1812 and 1818, established it as an armed, quasi-military force that drilled, lived in barracks, carried arms, and served as an adjunct to the military. The principal tasks of "the Peelers" were to keep order and operate as the eyes and ears of Dublin Castle through intelligence collection, not to ensure the liberty of the subject and the sanctity of property through consent and public cooperation as was the Bobbie model in England.[70]

As for the army: "It was in Ireland that the security of the empire and the army's politicization through its imperial experience came together," writes Hew Strachan.[71] Colonial service had increasingly politicized the British Army and distorted civil-military relations. The famous British formula of "Duties in Aid of the Civil [Power]" suggested that British rule rested on civilian governance and the application of minimum force through the police. The army was to intervene only in emergencies. In fact, colonial police forces were essentially thinly deployed intelligence collection agencies, one of whose primary purposes was to warn of impending trouble, not always successfully. Imperial rule ultimately resided in military force, which gave the army the whip hand in the colonies.[72] In November 1905, the British Viceroy Lord Curzon resigned complaining that a "military autocracy" and a "military despotism" led by General Horatio Kitchener had conspired to undermine civil primacy in India. Curzon's departure cleared the way for the centralization of military authority in India under Kitchener as commander-in-chief.

In the decade leading up to war, the army was politically engaged in the issues of the day, most notably conscription and especially Irish Home Rule, through the National Service League, a pressure group under Lord Roberts of Kandahar formed to advance the cause of conscription, and the cultivation of contacts in the press and the Conservative Party. However, the corrosion of the democratic political culture in Britain came to a head over the issue of Home Rule in Ireland. Since Sir Arthur Wellesley, Anglo-Irishmen had been well represented in the upper ranks of the army and included such notables as Roberts, Kitchener, and Wolseley. But the principal concern of army leaders, apart from the prospect that civil war in Ireland might split the army, was the fear that Home Rule would set a precedent that would reverberate in India. Therefore, they conspired against Home Rule. In 1912 as talk of Home Rule progressed, Roberts founded the Ulster Volunteers which was staffed by many retired Indian officers and armed by gunrunners who vowed to launch a civil war should Home Rule be enacted. The civil-military crisis came to a head with the Curragh incident, or Curragh mutiny, named after the military camp in Ireland where, on March 20, 1914, many officers, with the support of some senior generals, vowed to resign their commissions rather than obey lawful orders to combat Ulster Protestants in arms opposed to Home Rule. As Strachan writes:

The Curragh incident was therefore the denouement to the army's politicization in the course of the nineteenth century through its involvement in the empire. Imperial soldiering was the basis on which ambitious officers built their careers. The context in which they developed their political skills and convictions was consequently professional ... Moreover, Curragh was not just a culmination. Its significance lay also as a pointer to the future. It emphasized that the British army entered the First World War deeply politicized and versed in the arts of political intrigue ... Its consequences were to be

played out against the background of a war that was
primarily a war for Europe, but was also of course a war for
the defense of empire.[73]

Though fought in part as a "war for defense of empire," the Great War
had loosened Britain's grip on Ireland. Disappointment over London's
failure to enact Home Rule in 1914 matured almost imperceptibly over
the course of the next four years into a movement for outright separation
led by Sinn Féin. W. B. Yeats' "terrible beauty" of Irish independence
had been given a boost when the British martyred the leaders of the 1916
Easter Rising – including John McBride who had fought against the
British at the head of an Irish Transvaal Brigade in the Boer War.
London answered opposition to 1918 attempts to implement conscription in Ireland with arrests and internment. After Sinn Féin swept the
December 1918 elections, its MPs organized a secessionist Dáil in Dublin
rather than occupy their seats at Westminster.

London's security services were poorly positioned to deal with
growing Irish unrest and the first incipient signs of insurgency which
began with the collection of weapons and cash and the creation of
parallel government structures. By 1919 when the murders of RIC constables began, the Peelers had declined into an aging, ill-armed rural
constabulary of roughly 9,200 men which, despite its military appearance and organization, was more accustomed to administrative respon-
sibilities than crime fighting. Irish Volunteer violence against the RIC,
pro-independence propaganda that labeled RIC constables "England's
janissaries" (surely an insult to janissaries), and the prospect of fighting a
brutal guerrilla war for which many felt unprepared further hollowed
out the ranks. By the summer of 1920, the RIC counted 1,300 vacancies.
IRA violence caused the consolidation of about a third of the smaller
rural outposts in the first six months of 1920 into larger, more defensible
barracks. This defensive crouch made the RIC safer, but less effective and
less informed. For the purposes of understanding the strategic environment through cultural and linguistic awareness, the mostly young
40,000 British soldiers, scattered in remote outposts, might as well
have been in Nepal.

London's response, over the protests of the RIC inspector general, was to top up depleted police ranks through the incorporation of
unemployed English veterans of the Great War, the vast majority
recruited in London and the Home Counties. The infamous "Black and

6 British Auxies, a Peeler, and a Tommy in Ireland 1921. The British reflex to fuse police and army roles into a paramilitary, even a special operations approach to order, undermined routine police work and discipline.

Tans" earned their nickname because a uniform shortage caused them to be kitted out in a mix of army khaki and various RIC accoutrements that included black coats and hats. In fact, the Black and Tans were not a separate force, but merely English latecomers who shared barracks and missions with veteran Irish Peelers. The same could not be said for the Auxiliary Division, however, an Emergency Gendarmerie – another of Winston Churchill's bad ideas –first proposed in May 1920. Recruited among veteran officers most of whom had been promoted through the ranks in 1917–1918 and enlisted as "temporary cadets" to camouflage their military antecedents, the roughly 3,200 "Auxies" were conceived as an offensive, mobile force separate from the RIC. Major General Henry Tudor, the Police Adviser to Dublin Castle and leader of the war party in the Irish government, colonialized the upper echelons of what quickly came to be nicknamed "Tudor's toughs" with small wars veterans from

India and Africa who were ordered to "crush the present campaign of outrage."[74]

That proved difficult to do for a variety of reasons beginning with the fact that the British government was slow to formulate a clear policy to guide a coherent counterinsurgency response: Westminster was focused on the myriad of post-Great War problems while the British population suffered from an acute case of war-weariness alloyed with Irish fatigue. Civil-military clashes during the Great War left Lloyd George desperately allergic to generals, so that he neglected to establish coherent mechanisms to coordinate strategy. The Prime Minister insisted that the disturbances in Ireland were primarily a police problem, which was correct insofar as the police – the RIC with its Black and Tan upgrades and the Auxies – quickly became a problem. For its part, the army led by General Sir Neville Macready, the commander-in-chief in Ireland, was horrified at the excesses of the RIC and Auxis and so reduced contact with them to a minimum.[75] Together, these factors help to explain the strategic and operational context of London's fumbled counterinsurgency response in Ireland.

Although Viscount French's request to establish concentration camps in Ireland was denied and martial law was never imposed in all of Ireland because Lloyd George feared that this would surrender primacy in Ireland to the military, the Restoration of Order in Ireland Act of August 1920 allowed for indefinite detention and courts-martial of suspects. Some 4,500 men were eventually detained,[76] which certainly helped to decapitate IRA leadership, deplete insurgent manpower, and force many survivors to flee to the countryside, where they organized "flying columns" from the autumn of 1920. From September of that year, the word "reprisals" appeared with disturbing frequency in reports as the RIC lashed out with house and crop burnings, beatings of "Shinners," hair bobbing of wives, daughters, and girlfriends of Republicans, and recreational pillage. On November 21, 1920, on what became known as Bloody Sunday, RIC constables opened fire on a football crowd in Dublin. The assault came in retaliation for Collins' coordinated attack on British intelligence that day that had killed four-teen British officers, many of whom had no links with intelligence.[77] The next month, on December 11, 1920, two square blocks of Cork were torched by Auxies. In December 1920, martial law was declared in four of the twenty-six counties, later extended to eight, which among other refinements allowed authorities to confiscate all bicycles in an attempt to deny the IRA mobility. "Organized retaliation" was legalized from January 1921.[78]

Police reprisals in Cork and elsewhere rescued the IRA from a popular backlash against their campaign of assassinations of RIC police-men and snitches.[79] Most "British" reprisals were orchestrated by Irish constables in the RIC precisely because police violence, even death squads, was unofficially tolerated, even encouraged as policy in Westminster, so long as known Sinn Féin leaders and Republican sym-pathizers were targeted. Critics of this counter-terror were informed that rules of war did not apply to an irregular enemy, and that stern measures opened a floodgate of intelligence and saved lives. Indeed, RIC, Auxie, and army reprisals were viewed as a form of "due process" against a cowardly army of Fenian assassins. Because police and soldiers refused to give evidence against each other in courts-martial, and because officers strictly followed Tudor's instructions to restore order and do nothing to undermine police morale, verdicts of "justifiable homicide" or murder "by persons unknown" were common. Meanwhile, rather than admit that the Troubles had become, in many places, a civil war, even a gang war, between Irishmen in the RIC and the IRA, Republican propagand-ists like Erskine Childers shifted blame onto the English Black and Tans and Auxies. D. M. Leeson argues that a misinformed British public attributed Black and Tans and Auxie violence to the fact that these units assembled the scum of the London's East End, men whose unstable personalities had been further traumatized by years of trench warfare. In fact, violence in Ireland was an artifact of a climate of lawlessness common to small wars, one encouraged at the highest levels of govern-ment in the name of national security.[80]

By the spring of 1921, these measures of mayhem and state power unfettered tipped the tactical initiative toward the British. Dublin Castle had reestablished and strengthened intelligence networks disrupted by the IRA although army-police intelligence cooperation still left much to be desired.[81] More flexible platoon-sized drives, often scouted by aircraft and assisted by bloodhounds, took back Republican safe havens. Village males were organized into Civil Guards and forced to accompany convoys to deter IRA ambushes, a form of hostage taking much criticized by the British press. The army began increasingly to communicate by wireless, so that postal workers sympathetic to the Republicans could not intercept letters and phone calls. Curfews, requirements for vehicle permits, and confiscation of bicycles immobilized the population. By 1921, the British boasted that they could capture, interrogate, judge, and execute an unarmed IRA suspect within forty-eight hours. Those captured with arms could be summarily executed.[82] These classic counterinsurgency measures registered increasing success against an IRA desperately short of arms and ammunition. Summary justice also obviated the need for extracurricular retaliation, in keeping with Tudor's desire to bolster police and army morale, reassert discipline, and obviate the need for reprisals that attracted embarrassing publicity.

In fact, from a political perspective, the British position appeared recoverable. Tories deployed the domino theory to warn that Irish independence would mean the sunset of empire, even of Britain itself. Independence would set a precedent that would lead to India's departure from the empire and allow Ireland to become a base for hostile foreign powers – a theme underscored by British psyops that linked Sinn Féin with Germany until 1918 and Soviet Russia thereafter. British propaganda came late to the conflict, but it shifted into high gear with assertions that the typical Irish Volunteer was characterized by "ignorance, emotionalism, credulity and unquestioning obedience to the Roman Catholic Church,"[83] a claim rather undermined by the fact that the Church condemned IRA violence. With traditional domino-theory hyperbole, small wars protagonists asserted that a Republican victory in Ireland would delegitimize the monarchy and invite imitation from Welsh and Scots separatists. Irish land redistribution would lead to a confiscation of Loyalist property, a step in a disenfranchisement of Old Ascendency Anglicans and Ulster Presbyterians. In short, a Republican victory would ignite the implosion of Britain.

On the other hand, the case of Ireland in the 1920s proved that, while tactics cannot rescue defective policy, they can certainly accentuate policy/strategy disconnects in command and civil-military relations. Internment, martial law, collective reprisals, and house burnings undermined a government IO campaign to spotlight the "barbaric cruelty" of the IRA. Newspapers filled with stories of Black and Tans and Auxie excesses, which deepened the feeling that London had lost control of its own forces. US and Commonwealth public opinion condemned British actions and caused Lloyd George to fear the unraveling of empire. Although nationalist legend reinforced by historical interpretation attributed Britain's exit from Eire as a victory for guerrilla tactics and people's war, Michael Collins confessed that the British counterinsurgency campaign had rendered the IRA "dead beat" by the summer of 1921. Insurgent tactics had been downgraded from flying columns to terrorist attacks.[84] London threw in the towel because the political objective had been delegitimized by the tactics used to achieve it.[85] British intelligence admitted by early 1921 that "the bulk of the population was in a state of open rebellion or was in sympathy with such rebellion,"[86] a conclusion confirmed in May when Sinn Féin took all but four of 128 parliamentary seats in the May 1921 elections for the Parliament of Southern Ireland created by the December 23, 1920 Government of Ireland Act, and then refused to take their seats. Westminster could now choose between escalation or negotiation. Lloyd George, who somewhat ironically had made his name as a rabble-rousing "pro-Boer" in 1900, proved reluctant to terminate "a mean and unnecessary war," until informed in the spring of 1921 that growing anti-war sentiment had put his Caernarvon constituency in jeopardy.[87] The groundwork for negotiation had been laid by the Government of Ireland Act which allowed the Protestant Unionists, the main stumbling block to Home Rule, to fence off a separate fiefdom in the North. Conservative leadership had mellowed under Austen Chamberlain. In this way, London arranged a truce on July 11, 1921 which led to the Anglo-Irish Treaty of December 1921 that traded Dominion status for Southern Ireland in exchange for Ulster autonomy.[88]

The British campaign, in particular the behavior of its militarized police forces, had severely damaged Britain's image abroad, especially in the United States, roiled the political landscape at home, wasted resources, and caused even ardent imperialists like Churchill to conclude that the moral costs of counterinsurgency proved a price too high to pay for an ephemeral tactical success. In a portent of Algeria in the 1950s and 1960s, Churchill justified cutting Ireland loose: "What was the alternative? It was to plunge one small corner of the empire into an iron repression, which could not be carried out without an admixture of murder and counter-murder ... Only national self-preservation could have excused such a policy, and no reasonable man could allege that self-preservation was involved."[89] Of course, the British, including Churchill, did not hesitate to clamp iron repression on other corners of the empire, an enterprise that the future Prime Minister considered central to British self-preservation. To apply Isabel Hull's framework, counterinsurgent violence expands to fill a vacuum of civilian constraints until forced to fight war "humanely."[90]

Conclusion

British historian John Keegan concluded that the flutter of post-1918 insurgencies was stilled by 1925 for three reasons: "the unity of interest between the victorious powers; the continuing strength of the imperial idea; and the underdevelopment of what today is called the Third World."[91] It was also true that middle-class nationalists in European colonies like Morocco, Syria, and India often preferred to adopt the long view, pressure the imperial powers for political concessions, and thus close the door to violent elements whose visions for post-colonial governance might prove more radical or at least radically traditional. The French completed their conquest of the Middle Atlas of Morocco, and stamped out with characteristic brutality a communist-led insurrection in Annam in 1930–1932.[92] Britain kept nationalist agitation in India and the Middle East at bay by intelligence surveillance and repression, and by slow-rolling reform. More kinetic methods were required to deal with perpetual turmoil on the North-West Frontier, especially in Waziristan, which the British attempted to attenuate with a program of road building, the creation of a frontier force, and the forward positioning of thirty battalions.[93] Chief of the Air Staff Sir Hugh Trenchard argued vehemently that a combination of airpower and expanded police forces would allow a reduction in imperial army garrisons. But airpower was too indiscriminate a weapon to employ in urban areas where much interwar colonial strife occurred. Colonial officials instead put their faith in early intelligence-generated warnings of impending unrest combined with security force mobility and declarations of martial law to quell disturbances before they turned into rebellion.[94]

Nevertheless, in the 1920s, the Great Powers experienced the last paroxysms of largely unfettered imperial might. In the process, they suffered significant political and practical blowback for their trouble when their legitimacy was challenged, not only by indigenous peoples, but also at home. The Morocco and the Great Syrian Revolt hoisted France on its petard of *liberté* by showcasing the pretense of the civilizing mission and exposing supposedly persuasive small wars methods like oil spot and peaceful penetration as a public relations veneer for what in effect was a menu of cultural misunderstanding, intelligence failures, social engineering, and political meddling that had to be rescued by armed coercion. The Troubles exposed Ireland's colonial subordination behind a façade of monarchical harmony. Ireland also provided Britain's least happy ending in no small part because of the discredit that counter-insurgency repression, spearheaded by an ill-disciplined paramilitary police force, brought on London.

British staff colleges in the 1920s and 1930s refocused on small wars, in part because no sooner had the Great War ended than British soldiers declared it an aberration. The professional assumption that Britain would never against dispatch an Expeditionary Force to the Continent prompted a relapse into a pre-1914 imperial mindset, beginning with the reinstatement of the nineteenth-century home/colonial link-battalion system in the regiments.[95] The General Staff of the Irish Command wrote a lengthy assessment of British shortcomings in the Troubles, especially those of intelligence. But while the historical verdict is that counterinsurgency lessons from Ireland became a mere after-thought in the Staff College curriculum,[96] in fact, Ireland did not have to be combed for special lessons learned because, in the minds of British officers, insurgencies were defined by the national characteristics of the people who fomented and supported them. The Irish fell into an already established category known from long imperial service outside of Europe, the Oriental, whose leaders "are recruited from a low and degenerate type," who elicited support from local police and postal workers, and benefited from the apathy, when not the outright support, of the Catholic hierarchy. In the shadow of the stab in the back, soldiers concluded that militants were undeterred by the prospect of penal servi-tude "because everyone was certain that, sooner or later, an amnesty would occur, his release would be secured, and, as a reward, he would wear the martyr's crown."[97]

The Great War and the years immediately surrounding it were pivotal in the transition in thought and practice of criminal tribes into communist-tinged nationalist movements, imperial rebellions into peo-ple's war, and small wars into imperial policing and counterinsurgency. It would also intensify the growing crisis in civil-military relations. For French and British soldiers of empire and small wars, disloyal popula-tions, criminal leaders, and procrastinating, appeasing colonial admin-istrations composed a trinity of familiar insurgent challenges to imperial conquest and governance. This accentuated the feelings of estrangement among soldiers who felt that the importance of empire to imperial defense, the nobility of the imperial mission, and the vicissitudes of colonial service went unrecognized, and in fact were even denigrated at home. They alone stood tall against terrorism in defense of national sovereignty.[98] This distance and alienation from the homeland joined the weakness of political mechanisms of control of the army in the colonies further to politicize soldiers. Paramilitary police forces strengthened and became more ubiquitous in the wake of the Great War. Civil-military fusion, combined with the inherent racism of colonial soldiering that justified the implementation of barbarous methods of population control, conspired to politicize colonial soldiers beyond limits that might be tolerated at home.

These trends, apparent before 1914, were to intensify in the following decades. As colonial warfare became more ideological, ramped up in operational intensity, and sharpened civil-military stress, colonial soldiers embraced tactical solutions to the political problems of insurgency and deepened their faith in the ability of heroic soldiers with a handful of loyal indigenous followers to alter the course of history. Ironically, their soon-to-be adversaries were moving in a similar direction.

4 FROM TIPPERARY TO TEL AVIV: BRITISH COUNTERINSURGENCY IN THE WORLD WAR II ERA

Thomas R. Mockaitis argues that the foundation for British success in post-World War II counterinsurgency was laid in the in the decades following the debacles at Amritsar in 1919 and Ireland between 1919 and 1921. The interwar period, rife as it was with much military innovation, he argues, saw a transition from the racist attitudes and scorched-earth tactics of nineteenth-century small wars, to the rigors of imperial policing, and with the Arab Revolt (1936–1939) in Palestine to the theory and practice of modern counterinsurgency. This change was the product of three factors: first, violence against civilians in South Africa and Ireland had appalled British and international opinion and undercut popular support for those wars. Second, there was a belated realization that in Ireland, the ferocity of Royal Irish Constabulary and Auxiliary reprisals had driven moderate Irish nationalists and IRA extremists together in a common cause against the British occupation. Finally, in the post-Great War era, tribal rebellions had been supplanted by sophisticated nationalist and communist mass political movements deploying an array of techniques that ran the gamut from strikes and protests to terrorism and insurgency.[1]

British-style imperial policing was anchored in three fundamental principles. First, English common law dictated that disturbances must be constrained within a legal framework, which required the application of minimum force. This, in Mockaitis' view, elevated the British counterinsurgency approach over that of the Americans who have placed great faith in the use of force. Second, confronting growing colonial unrest required the cooperation of civilian officials, the police, and soldiers to pass laws and ordinances, gather intelligence, and cooperate to apply force selectively. The reliance on a "whole of government" approach avoided the "state of siege" trap that impelled the French military to absorb most civil functions in Algeria, placed the army in the counterinsurgency vanguard, and removed civil constraints on the use of force. Finally, the British Army's storied regimental system, versus a continental general staff hierarchy, was perfectly suited to the decentralized, flexible, small-unit organizational structure required of imperial settings. While occasional excesses invariably occurred, the diffusion of these principles in manuals and staff college studies, as well as during the disturbances of the interwar years explains how, in Mockaitis' view, the "most successful counterinsurgency school was built" by the British. Therefore, Britain's "impressive victory" in the Malayan Emergency (1947–1960) could not be attributed to contingent circumstances in the strategic environment – namely, the fact that the insurgents, overwhelmingly Chinese immigrants, composed a geographically isolated racial minority. Rather, the critical factor in British counterinsurgency successes in Malaya and elsewhere lay in Britain's doctrine and its experience in imperial policing evolved following Britain's departure from Eire.[2]

Mockaitis' sanguine assessment of the success of British counterinsurgency methods reinforced the claims previously advanced in 1966 by Sir Robert Thompson's *Defeating Communist Insurgencies*, and in the recent past echoed in academic studies by John Nagl and Richard Duncan Downie, who contend that, unlike the US Army, the British Army was indeed a "learning organization" able to achieve institutional consensus around a set of effective counterinsurgency techniques and bequeath them to subsequent generations.[3] Other scholars have cast doubt on Mockaitis' conclusions, beginning with Hew Strachan who attributed British success in counterinsurgency operations to timely political concessions, not the excellence of British tactics. John Newsinger noted that post-World War II British counterinsurgency campaigns failed more often than not, while those that succeeded, as in Malaya and Kenya, were hardly models of "the comparative restraint" that purported to distinguish British counterinsurgency campaigns from those of the French and Americans, a conclusion subsequently confirmed by other scholars. David French argues that many contingent factors – Clausewitz's "fog and friction of war" – intervened to unsettle the smooth application of British counterinsurgency doctrine advanced as a coherent program of minimum force, civil-military cooperation, and decentralized, flexible command response.[4] Finally, David Cesarani and Simon Anglim trace the melding of military special operations and imperial policing in Palestine before and following World War II in police special squads whose actions there and in subsequent British counterinsurgency operations in Malaya, Kenya, and Northern Ireland present paradigms of official heavy-handedness rather than restraint.[5]

This chapter will argue that British counterinsurgents learned little from their defeat in Ireland in the 1920s. The twisted path of small wars through imperial policing to counterinsurgency identified by Mockaitis went unaccompanied by an imposition of legal and institutional restraints on the repression of small wars anywhere, especially in the British Empire, which witnessed an expansion of repressive powers, the further racialization of counterinsurgency, an increase in civil-military fusion, and the further militarization of imperial police forces that expanded their intelligence collection functions and acquired a special operations character that targeted the civilian population. World War II linked counterinsurgency more closely with special operations, which favored "kill or capture" decapitation strategies and dramatic coups as quixotic solutions to intractable political or strategic problems. So, the post-Great War years did indeed lay a foundation for the evolution of British counterinsurgency in theory and practice. They simply did not, however, contribute to its humanization, nor to smooth civil-military relations.

That imperial Britain's small wars retained their dirty, violent, racist character meant that they were simply conforming to a type well identified in this work and others. Indeed, two trends were at work in the interwar years to expand the scope, stakes, and hence the violence of small wars. The first was the fear that what Brian Linn calls "the confusion, violence, and moral ambiguity" of small wars might soon be revisiting a country near you.[6] This return homeward of insurgents was the case during World War II when, with active Allied encouragement, resistance to Axis occupation spawned insurgencies throughout occupied Europe and Asia, further strengthening the doctrinal and operational link between special operations and insurgency/counterinsurgency. That the German response to subject populations in the New Order was nothing short of frightful is hardly surprising given the racialization of counterinsurgency that was native to fascism and especially to National Socialism. German hysteria over the use of North

African and Senegalese troops in the trenches of the Great War and subsequently as part of the post-1918 occupation caused Germans to argue within the rampant racism in the wake of war that, by employing Africans to occupy the Rhineland, the French had turned their back on Western civilization and were using black *Untermenschen* to corrupt the German race with syphilis and mixed-race bastards.[7] This screed subsequently became a staple of Nazi propaganda and contributed to the massacres of African prisoners of war (POWs) in 1940 France.[8]

As it happens, German counterinsurgency in Southern, Eastern, and Western Europe, of which the Holocaust can be said to have been a central part, set the benchmark for barbarity in World War II. Although the links between colonial small wars and the Holocaust are disputed, many scholars of Germany accept as commonplace and a truism that the German massacres and concentration camps in Africa at the beginning of the twentieth century as well as German technical assistance to the Turks with the Armenian massacre added further virulence to Nazi anti-Semitism and to the system of state terror symbolized by Dachau. This school detects a direct line running from von Trota's obsession with "blood cleansing" of the Herero as the precondition to racial renewal in Africa, via the Armenian genocide, to Auschwitz.[9] Although Germany forfeited its African and Asian colonies in 1918, the fusion of a Darwinian competition of nation-states, the precedents of ethnic cleansing in Africa and Armenia, Hitler's faith in Aryan racial superiority, and the German army's "*hantise* (obsession) *du franc-tireur*" that dated from the Franco-Prussian War converted war crimes into a normal mode of operations against enemy civilians.[10]

The post-Great War years also saw the emergence of nationalist, communist, and fascist ideologies that espoused total war and people's war, a second factor that accelerated a trend to broaden the definition of security in the twentieth century in extravagant and fateful ways, as a means to justify extraordinary methods of repression, not least in the British Empire. Even Gandhi's *satyagraha* campaigns, which sought to exploit legal loopholes to short-circuit armed insurgency and expose the hypocrisy of Western values, caused British imperial soldiers to expand the definition of subversion to incorporate the broader political process. Counterinsurgency theorists began to consider terrorism and armed insurgency as the top end of a sliding scale of "sub-war" that also embraced civil disobedience, labor unrest, and political protests, all of which required an armed response.

This shift was reflected in British doctrine. Camberley Staff College Commandant Major General Sir Charles Gwynn excluded Ireland as "inadvisable" when he compiled his cases for his 1934 manual on *Imperial Policing*, for unspecified, but nevertheless redolent reasons. Hew Strachan suggests that Gwynn "did not develop the political aspects of his subject in the way that either Ireland or Palestine suggested was necessary," in part because "the idea that the army enabled Britain to hold Ireland was inimical to the concept of the United Kingdom."[11] But the real reason was that imperial soldiers and policemen resisted the suggestion that policy, let alone morality or ethics, should constrain their ability to apply extreme operations and tactics to quell insurgency, which is why Kitchener defended scorched-earth tactics in South Africa, and Sir John French wanted to import concentration camps into Ireland in 1920.[12] Gwynn's goal was to offer a tactical treatise on army aid to the civilian power "whose organizing principle," he said, should be minimum force.[13] However, like peaceful penetration and hearts and minds, "Duties in Aid to the Civil" in practice surrendered the initiative in imperial defense, especially in times of crisis, to soldiers and policemen, whose hostility to political constraints left them immense latitude to fill the political vacuum with the operations and tactics of small wars and counterinsurgency. Strong-armed methods to deal with legitimate civil dissent also threatened, as Hannah Arendt pointed out, to boomerang to the Homeland.

One of the alleged strengths of the British aid to the civil approach to counterinsurgency is that it dictated close cooperation between the police and the army, both in law enforcement and intelligence collection. The police were often depicted as the face of "Britishness" in the colonies that differed from the militarized French gendarme model, a symbol of legitimacy and testimony to the fact that British imperialism rested on the principle of government by consent.[14] The reality, however, was that imperial practice was to fuse police and army roles into a paramilitary, even a special operations in the case of the Auxiliaries approach to order, a trend accelerated by decolonization and by the fact that, like the French colonies, the British Empire was a "bluff" – no more than a collection of woefully under-policed, under-administered, fragile states.[15] Although both the Royal Irish Constabulary (RIC) and the Metropolitan police claim the paternity of Sir Robert Peel, they were conceived with different mothers. The RIC was a stratified, militarized force whose mainly Catholic constables lived in barracks under the command of Protestant officers, and patrolled with arms to teach London's Irish subjects to respect the law rather than to guarantee their liberty or the sanctity of property. One of the RIC's primary duties was intelligence collection on the population. And although disbanded in 1922, the RIC model with its significant contingent of Black and Tan and Auxiliary veterans, not the unarmed, community-policing English "Bobbie," was transferred to the empire following the Troubles through the Royal Ulster Constabulary (RUC) and the Palestine Gendarmerie/Police. The RIC's intelligence collection functions reappeared in police Special Branches and Criminal Investigation Departments (CID) that proliferated in colonial police forces after 1945.[16]

Decolonization conflicts put police in the front lines against subversion, reinforced their military posture and recruitment, and upgraded their armaments to infantry standards. They also acquired enhanced authority to arrest, declare curfews, and set up roadblocks in "disturbed" areas without recourse to higher authority. And that was the benign part. Settlers, headmen, and ethnic groups were permitted to proliferate their own police auxiliaries as cost-effective security enhancements. Mockaitis concedes that these ad hoc formations occasionally got out of hand, especially in Kenya (1952–1959).[17] But this ignores the fact that vigilante police formations were a requirement to the maintenance of order in the colonies, not the least because, as in Ireland in 1920–1921, they became a form of hostage taking. Indigenous civil guards accompanied patrols and convoys and guarded settlements to insure against attacks, and could be held accountable should things go wrong. Traveling under names like Home Guard, Police Reserve, Auxiliary, Mobile Force, Kenya Cowboys, CID, "strike force," "special force," or Native Authority Police, these minimally supervised, special operationalized, counter-terror, law enforcement formations engaged in private vendettas and in general instituted a "rule of fear" on estates, in *kampongs*, or "new villages." The Malayan Special Constabulary recruited some "rough types and adventurers" out of the Palestine Police who contributed little to hearts and minds, but essentially created their own army-style "pseudo-guerrilla units," Police Field Forces, and Ferret Forces for jungle patrols. Police-spearheaded food denial operations succeeded more in alienating the population than cutting insurgent logistics. "Snatch squads ... became a law unto themselves" in Palestine and Kenya writes historian of the British imperial police Georgina Sinclair. "Pseudo gangs" disguised as Mau Mau dealt harshly with anyone who befriended them, while the settler-dominated Kenya Police Reserve went on "killing sprees" against the locals and shot suspects just to collect the £5 bounty, a practice that the British Commander, General George Erskin, found difficult to control. In Cyprus (1955–1973), as elsewhere, police and army missions were fused to the point that, as in French Algeria, the two forces became indistinguishable.[18]

A central function of imperial police forces was to collect timely intelligence. As the "eyes and ears" of the colonial authority, police CIDs and Special Branches were expected to collect, collate, assess, and disseminate intelligence that affected public order, as well as protect their own organizations from infiltration. Yet, despite years of occupation and the brilliant exploits of British intelligence in World War II, they were ill placed to carry out these functions for a variety of reasons, beginning with the fact that intelligence was considered a dead end – even dangerous – division in a colonial police force that required "the barest of educational qualifications" followed by a six-month training course offered in Britain or Northern Ireland which apparently not all colonies could afford.[19] The fact that colonial law enforcement drew no distinction between a political and a criminal act, nor could determine when political activity tipped over into a security threat, translated into poorly defined oversight of multiple activities from infiltrating political groups and press censorship to smuggling and immigration. Police forces throughout the empire depended on local revenues, which kept them relatively small, poorly paid career options that forced police intelligence officers to shoulder other duties, like traffic control.

Few British police officers spoke indigenous languages, and so they relied on local recruits to keep an ear to the ground, translate documents, and carry out interrogations. So Special Branches often remained in the dark about the strength, armaments, or tactics of insurgent groups, all the more so because indigenous junior policemen would often retail café gossip as solid intelligence or exaggerate the importance of inconsequential information to curry favor with superiors and so inflate their career prospects. In times of crisis, police intelligence found their human resources ill tailored for the mission – Jewish police in post-World War II Palestine were in short supply, as were Chinese in Malaya, Greeks on Cyprus, Arabs in Aden, because service with British intelligence offered both an unpopular and potentially terminal career choice. Indigenous police agents and informers might survive only by offering information to anti-colonialist forces. It also made CID/Special Branches vulnerable to surprise, infiltration, and misdirection, which was one reason why the army often refused to share information with the police.

Aid to the civil authority was also compromised by divergent viewpoints. For while the army viewed the insurgent as a military adversary to be "bagged," for the police he was just a thief, extortionist, or murderer operating on a grander scale to be stalked and, if possible, arrested. Special Branch had to cultivate agents for the long term, to detect trends, disassemble plots, and build cases that would stand up in court, while the army just wanted "actionable intelligence" to eliminate terrorists and insurgents. Intelligence-coordinating committees, cross-posted liaison officers, joint operations rooms, and intelligence training and coordination courses run by Scotland Yard and MI5 were slow to sort out conflicting priorities or improve the abysmal level of threat analysis until fairly late in the Malayan Emergency, and even less so in Kenya, Cyprus, and Aden.[20] The intelligence breakthrough in Kenya came not with progressive improvements in the organization, but with Operation Anvil, the massive April 1954 detention and screening of Kikuyu in Nairobi. Detentions offered the opportunity to recruit inform-ants, and to bargain for release against information. But mass detentions joined cordon-and-search, collective punishments, or property destruc-tion as sledgehammer intelligence collection tactics guaranteed to alien-ate the population whatever its information benefits.[21] And there always remained the suspicion that Special Branches, like Latin American police death squads, too often operationalized the information they collected to disappear suspects rather than share it with the army.[22]

This deployment of armed strength mocked the whole concept of minimum force as a bedrock principle of British colonial policing. General Frank Kitson's *Low Intensity Operations*, published in 1971, followed the trend set by Gwynn and Simson that saw civil disorder as part of a continuum of defiance that escalates through peaceful protests to war.[23] Kitson shared with David Galula the conviction that, "inwardly you must consider (every civilian) as a rebel ally until you have positive proof to the contrary."[24] An attitude that placed the onus on civilians to prove that they accepted the legitimacy of the occupation was a mindset that contributed to the institutionalization of collective punishment, torture, resettlement, internment, special night squads/fer-ret forces/counter-gangs, and RAF terror bombing for imperial policing. The key to success was to rebrand these kinetic methods as hearts and minds and prosecute it out of public view. Because once international opinion became involved, as in South Africa in 1900, Ireland (twice), postwar Palestine, Algeria, Vietnam, and Nicaragua, then the counter-insurgents ran smack into a PR problem.

Well into the post-World War II era, British counterinsurgency methods more often replicated those of Bugeaud's *razzias* minus the rape than adhere to any concept of minimum force, much less aid to the civil power – villages might be bombed from the air, shelled, burned, or simply knocked down, wells poisoned, crops fumigated or destroyed, livestock slaughtered, the wounded executed, and the population displaced. Twice the weight of bombs was dropped in Radfan (Yemen) in the last six months of 1958 than the Luftwaffe had managed to unload on Coventry in November 1940. Suspect ethnic groups were driven out, some to resettlement camps in Malaya and Kenya where their land became free-fire zones. But in Oman and Yemen they wandered as malnourished refugees. And as had been the case in post-Great War Afghanistan and Iraq, airpower proved to be no substitute for troops on the ground.[25]

The paramilitary posture of imperial police forces rather made a mockery of Lloyd George's insistence in 1920 that suppression of the Troubles "was a policeman's job supported by the military and not *vice versa*. So long as it becomes a military job only it will fail."[26] In the event, military and police functions, armaments, and recruitment became practically indistinguishable, which helped to expose counterinsurgency formulae like aid to the civil power, minimum force, legal constraints on operations, and so on as just so many COIN clichés. Failure to distinguish between criminal and political misdemeanors increasingly drew imperial police forces into intelligence-gathering and special operations aspects of counterinsurgency operations made more problematic by the politics of the interwar years with economic and social strife overlaid by ideological confrontation. Gwynn's preferred method for confining operations within legal boundaries was martial law under which "actions not normally offences can be made criminal," "the scale of punishment for crimes can be raised," while "judicial procedure can be speeded up to ensure that a maximum deterrent and moral effect will be produced by punishment." Indeed, Gwynn's endorsement of martial law and indefinite internment, which had produced such baleful consequences in Ireland, the salutary value of collective fines and communal punishments imposed in the wake of "sabotage," and his assertion that light howitzers and "machine guns can be usefully employed (in crowd control) without any suspicion of ruthlessness" in effect describes a doctrine of escalating force, known as the "defense climb,"[27] to muffle political expression, the bedrock principle of Western values and institutions. But democratic notions were overwhelmed by the conviction that "boldness, aggression and severity" formed the pillars of imperial policing, because leniency would be interpreted by unsophisticated and excitable natives led by "a militant, organized minority pursuing a radical nationalist agenda" as evidence of a lack of resolve among those in charge.[28] In short, the doctrine of British imperial policing put forward by Gwynn, Simson, and later Kitson offered a temporary tactical solution to a strategic problem. In Northern Ireland in the 1970s, it proved a formula for transforming a civil rights campaign that sought to change the law into an armed insurrection dedicated to the overthrow of the state. But in doing so, they were merely doctrinizing the attitudes of British soldiers and policemen, and no doubt their civilian superiors as well.

In another respect, however, Gwynn was simply codifying an imperial attitude that conflated political and criminal misdemeanors, as well as the means through which each was to be controlled. "Crime and political subversion appeared as much the same to a colonial government," writes Sinclair.[29] Such attitudes reflected the belief in the rectitude and legitimacy of the imperial enterprise and the absolute confidence that the vast majority of natives were content with British rule – a handful of troublemakers could not possibly have genuine grievances. (Denouncing dissenters as rabble, bandits, thugs, and the like made for reassuring propaganda.[30] Such a mindset explains why British officers saw Reginald Dyer's dismissal in the wake of the 1919 Amritsar massacre as an injustice.) And like any military man worth his salt, Gwynn was also in search of a mission for the British Army in the wake of "the war to end all wars," the "no war for ten years" budget strictures, and the Geneva Disarmament Conference where, in 1932, the same year that Chief of Staff Douglas MacArthur flouted civilian control to torch the Bonus Marchers' camp in the nation's capital, US President Herbert Hoover proposed that all armies create a "police component, bearing the same ratio to the population as has the German Army under the terms of the Treaty of Versailles."[31]

The idea of civil-military fusion under martial law was vigorously seconded by H. J. Simson's 1938 *British Rule and Rebellion*, a grumpy, frequently anecdotal rant published for staff college use in response to the Arab Revolt in Palestine in 1936 in the face of Zionist immigration from Europe in the shadow of the swastika. This episode, after Ireland in the 1920s, represented a further escalation of theory and practice in the British experience of counterinsurgency and its effects on strategic and political culture. In this doctrinal tract, Simson conflated levels of defiance into a category he labeled "sub-war," an amalgamation of subversion and criminality, against which aid to the civil power was an exercise in futility – makers of policy in London were whiplashed by indecision; concessions and amnesties offered by misguided mandate administrators simply inflamed violence; insistence on legality encouraged delinquency; court-imposed standards of evidence sabotaged law and order; and, as in Ireland, native police and indigenous government employees abetted bad actors.[32] Sub-war was a political act that required a political response that included martial law, extensive use of the death penalty, even powers of summary execution, with the army, not civilian administrators and police in the lead. Simson assumed that the legitimacy of the imperial power removed the requirement to behave within the framework of the law, or even ethically; instead, he advised acting as "one dog in a dog-fight, no better, and perhaps no worse, than the other dog."[33] Woof!

And that is precisely what occurred in Palestine from 1936, where Gwynn's "minimum force" slithered over into martial law enforced by two divisions that combined 80,000 troops and four bomber squadrons shipped to Palestine to deal with the insurrection. Courts-martial for Arab civilians, collective fines, the shooting of prisoners, torture, hangings, village destruction, the assembling of "hostage corps," the recruiting of a 19,000-strong Zionist Supernumerary Police known as the "legal *Haganah*," and the use of frontier barriers and forts were mustered as part of an offensive strategy to fragment and isolate the Arab population. Aggressive counter-terror tactics by Orde Wingate's Special Night Squads and Wingate-trained Zionist murder squads, and egregious "Black and Tan tendencies" displayed by British police and military units included requiring Arab hostages to walk ahead of military convoys on mined roads as an early counter-improvised explosive device (IED) tactic. Simon Anglim argues that even though Wingate's party piece was to force captured Arabs to swallow oil-soaked sand, both his actions and those of his Special Night Squads fell within the behavioral norms of other British-led units in Palestine, and in fact may even have been mild in comparison with the savage retribution inflicted on villages

7 British soldiers of the Royal Engineers mark a Palestinian house for demolition, a measure taken to clamp down on Arab dissidence during the Great Uprising (1936–1939).

by out-of-control British troops.[34] The point being that, even if Ireland was not explicitly studied in the staff college as a cautionary tale, the British responded to the Arab Revolt as if Palestine were Limerick in the Levant, in the process proving that Amritsar and RIC and Auxiliary ruthlessness had been no fluke, but rather constituted a Callwellian response catapulted into the 1930s.[35]

Gwynn's *Imperial Policing* and Simpson's *British Rule and Rebellion* both argued the benefits of martial law in the face of insurgency because police tactics were insufficiently aggressive. (Martial law also served to preempt imperial administrators too quick to offer political concessions, in this view.) Both insist that the civil power should back the military, not vice versa.[36] However, British soldiers discarded martial law after 1948, not out of deference to the supremacy of civil authority or because the Gallic concept of "state of siege" was alien to British common law,[37] but because by mid-century martial law had proven career-threatening, counterproductive, and superfluous. Reginald Dyer's 1919 destitution following Amritsar served as a cautionary tale for soldiers eager to avoid the legal responsibility of defining acceptable levels of violence for which they might later be held accountable. Finally, martial law was superfluous because the 1939 Emergency Powers Order-in-Council, with supporting local statutes, handed soldiers wide coercive powers to criminalize political activity, allow for preventative detention, limit freedom of movement, impose curfews, issue identity cards, deport troublemakers, and force millions of people into concentration camps. British imperial soldiers could obey Thompson's admonition to keep their campaigns within legal limits precisely because legality was such an elastic concept that it permitted most forms of unlimited, extra-judicial coercion. Definitions of terrorism were so broad that courts incarcerated and executed suspects at rates unprecedented since the Indian Mutiny.[38] Kitchener would have been jealous!

The Arab Revolt dwindled following the success of the May 1939 British White Paper that promised Arab self-government within a decade. But this vow in turn enraged Zionists who, after 1945, fortified by an influx of postwar Holocaust survivors and US support for a Jewish national state, would successfully expose, once again, that minimum force and aid to the civil power were absent from the British counterinsurgency repertoire. What's more, repressive counterinsurgency tactics actually inflamed popular opposition to colonial occupation both inside and outside the theater that might produce an unfavorable impact on the strategic environment.[39]

World War II and insurgency

The character of the British waging of small wars, as well as the aspects of doctrine and strategic purpose, entered a vital, new phase with the withdrawal of the British Expeditionary Force from Dunkerque in June 1940, when the Wehrmacht had apparently demonstrated the hegemony of conventional battle in Belgium and Northern France. In the face of the German air offensive in the summer and autumn of 1940, Spitfire pilots became the instant symbol of heroic resistance, in contrast to the serial incompetence of Britain's conventional army symbolized by Colonel Blimp. That incompetence was the fruit of the persistence of a small wars mentality in an army that failed to embrace a unified operational and tactical doctrine, to impose a common template on the conduct of war at the strategic and operational level, or even enforce common training standards on battalion and regimental commanders. Generals whose command experience topped out at leading a division to quell uprisings of ungrateful colonial miscreants cut an amateurish figure against the Wehrmacht.[40]

8 Orde Wingate, a pioneer of Special Operations Forces, in Burma late 1942.

Allied Special Forces and deep reconnaissance units that prolif-erated in all theaters followed either the Orde Wingate special operations or the T. E. Lawrence popular insurrection model. Wingate rejected the Lawrence *levée en masse* as inefficient and argued that small units of specially trained soldiers could disrupt enemy supply and communica-tions and so prevent them from concentrating. The distinction between the two approaches was somewhat artificial, however. Lawrence had been forced to rely on a limited popular mobilization of Bedouin because attempts to introduce trained British, even Egyptian soldiers, into the Hijaz in 1916 had met violent religious objections that threatened to split Faisal's coalition. By the time Lawrence reached Damascus, his Bedouin insurrectionary army more resembled an all-arms mobile column that incorporated Egyptian regulars, a camel corps, an armored car troop, an artillery battery, and Gurkha and Egyptian demolition parties.[41] In its essential operational and tactical characteristics, therefore, the "Arab Revolt" foreshadowed Gideon Force and Long Range Patrol Groups rather than differed from them. Nor was Lawrence a military amateur;

he was an experienced intelligence officer who carried out thorough reconnaissance and topographical studies, and carefully planned each operation on the basis of intelligence gleaned from POW interrogations and elsewhere. He also pioneered air support to insurgent forces, which foreshadowed Wingate's logistical and support innovations in Burma from 1943. Nor was Wingate totally opposed to "scallywagging," as irregular warfare was termed in the interwar British Army, so long as insurgents brought intelligence.[42] Service on Allenby's staff in World War I left General Sir Archibald Wavell with a fascination for special operations forces, which he encouraged in the Western Desert and later in Burma in the form of Wingate's Third Indian Infantry Division, better known by their nickname of Chindits. The complaint was that the small wars heritage combined with the predilection of conventional force commanders like Wavell to "maneuver" with ad hoc tactical concoctions like Long Range Patrol Groups, SAS formations, Jock Columns, and other light cavalry razzle-dazzle combos and T. E. Lawrence Bedouin mobile column updates in the Western Desert into 1942 instilled a "tip and run" mentality in the officer corps. Before General Bernard Montgomery instilled a controlled battle concept prior to El Alamein, the Eighth Army's fighting style consisted of raids hyped into doctrine were mere mosquito bites against a desperately over-extended but nevertheless operationally competent Afrika Korps.[43]

The idea of using airborne troops as an adjunct to conventional operations in the best petty war traditions was not radical per se. It was just that the delivery systems of parachutes and gliders were so inefficient and dangerous that the Anglo-Americans failed to transition a promising operational idea into a tactical success. Over and over again in Sicily, Salerno, Normandy, Southern France, and Arnhem, paratroop divisions recruited, trained, and equipped at great expense were dispersed, drowned, crash landed, or marooned when not shot down by their own forces as in Sicily, so that they made no significant contributions to operational success. The amazing thing is that Allied commanders continued to fritter away many of their best troops in this failed experiment. Even Adolph Hitler, a man not usually celebrated for his military sagacity – or any sagacity at all, for that matter – recognized the operational limitations of paratroops following their successful but casualty-heavy May 1941 deployment in Crete and subsequently grounded them.

World War II special operations flourished in inverse proportion to the fortunes of conventional forces. Italian special operations incorporated the Italian navy's Tenth Light Flotilla which combined an array of weapons, including midget submarines, explosive motorboats (EMBs), frogmen, and manned torpedoes called *maiale* (pigs). An EMB sunk the British cruiser *York* off Crete in March 1941, while an attack on Alexandria in December by three pigs sank a pair of battleships and a tanker. German special operations units, quite small and superfluous when the Wehrmacht stormed through Europe in the early years of the war, began to proliferate in the Brandenburg Division and especially in the Waffen-SS as the war's momentum shifted against the fatherland. The highlight of German special operations was *Obersturmbannführer* (Lieutenant Colonel) Otto Skorzeny's September 1943 rescue of Benito Mussolini, who had been arrested in July and imprisoned at Gran Sasso in the Abruzzi Mountains by the Italian government. Other such operations were infiltration of SS special operations units in US uniform to disorient the broken US Ardennes front in December 1944.

The second Lawrence-inspired special operations model involved the organization and supply of guerrilla bands. Churchill's orders in 1940 to his Special Operations Executive (SOE) to "set Europe ablaze" by sparking and sustaining resistance movements in Axis-occupied countries was inspired by the needs of propaganda; Lawrencian romanticism, which created a constituency for "scallywagging"; Liddell Hart's indirect approach, "victory without battles" escapism;[44] and sheer desperation born of another conventional war near defeat, as well as the limitations of British sea and airpower in the year 1940. Despite the weakness of Britain's strategic position in 1940 – or rather, because of it – Churchill turned to special operations to create an illusion of offensive momentum. The SOE was formed in July 1940 under Minister of Economic Warfare Hugh Dalton with the mission to carry out espionage, sabotage, and reconnaissance behind enemy lines, mainly by making contact with local resistance forces in Europe. SOE agents were first dropped into France in May 1941, Yugoslavia in September, and Greece from November 1942. In June 1942, the United States established the Office of Strategic Services to replicate the SOE in its essential organization and missions. Thus, the Gallic beret superseded the symbolic Lawrencian *keffiyeh* to perpetuate the romanticism of revolt among decision-makers.

The value of insurgents in World War II, British or otherwise, was a subject of debate at the time and into the present. As in the Peninsular Wars of the Napoleonic era and the trans-Jordan in 1916–1918, guerrillas

9 Tito and Yugoslav partisans circa 1943. Encouraging resistance groups did little to advance Allied strategic goals, made non-combatants the targets of retaliation, and created post-conflict problems of disorder and political control.

and special operators might play a useful, if minor, role as adjuncts to main force units, saboteurs, and intelligence collectors, although the tendency of special operators to call attention to their presence by dramatic violence often undermined their value as collectors of intelligence. Special operations advised and supplied resistance groups were also serviceable, up to a point, as a political symbol of popular resistance to the Nazi occupation of continental Europe. But German commanders seldom had to practice aid to the civil authority in Western and Mediterranean Europe, where collaborationist governments like the Vichy regime in France used the cover of occupation to prosecute a civil war against what they believed to be Bolshevik subversion masquerading as patriotic resistance. Further, the Axis side was expert in the organization of local counterinsurgency forces of special brutality and striking power in all parts of Europe.

The myth of the Resistance as a militarily effective phenomenon was propagated by those eager to publicize their wartime exploits and puffed by SOE and OSS propagandists who exaggerated the effects of Resistance sabotage on German defenses and morale.[45] The truth was that Resistance movements in Hitler's Europe remained small, factious, poorly armed, easily contained, and fixated on seizing power at war's end. When British economic historian Alan Milward questioned Albert Speer, Reichminister for War Production, on the impact of the French Resistance on German war production, Speer replied, "What French Resistance?"[46] Resistance groups survived best in remote areas far from Axis or collaborationist-controlled population centers or axes of communication, as in Yugoslavia, where they were noteworthy. An Italian resistance mushroomed after the invasion of the Italian peninsula in September 1943 because Allied offensives meant that the Germans had few troops to spare for counterinsurgency operations. However, once General Harold Alexander suspended conventional operations for the winter and in November 1944 called on Italian partisans to "save munitions and materiel until further orders," German commander Albert Kesselring slaughtered – in their thousands – the resistance and anyone thought to support them.[47] A search for martyrdom in reckless shootouts with well-armed Axis forces and their local collaborators elicited savage reprisals that, with the possible exception of portions of Yugoslavia,[48] usually made the local population resistance shy. Ultimately, the bottom line was that for resistance guerrillas, victory without battles translated into avoiding hostile contact with the Axis occupiers, positioning one's group to grasp power at war's end even if this meant making a temporary alliance with the Germans, as was Tito's case in 1943, and hanging on until conventional forces could win the war.

As a strategy for Axis defeat, "setting Europe ablaze" also qualified as morally reckless because it put the populations of occupied Europe, whom the Allies could not protect, in the crosshairs of Nazi reprisals. In all fairness, the Germans were not the only predators on the peninsula: "French colonial troops are on the rampage again," Norman Lewis, a British military intelligence officer in Italy, recorded in May 1944. "Whenever they take a town or a village, a wholesale rape of the population follows."[49] Muslim *tirailleurs* constituted Bugeaud's little *cadeau* to the Italian peasantry to reap the small warriors' reward of rape and *razzia*, inescapable accoutrements of the civilizing mission and the preamble to liberation. Of course, it may be countered that resistance constituted a spontaneous reaction to German exactions, persecution by and waning support for collaborationist regimes, the political ambitions and conspiratorial reflexes of left-wing groups led by the communists, and the requirement to assemble a foundation for postwar governance and legitimacy. The belief that, through resistance, occupied populations played a part in their own liberation became a necessary postwar myth, even though an infinitesimal percentage of the occupied populations actively participated in resistance activity. Charles de Gaulle in particular based his legitimacy on the assertion that the French Resistance, of which he was the titular head, represented the acclamation of the French people. There was also certainly something to be said for organizing intelligence networks as a basis for inserting sabotage teams to hit strategic targets at times when these attacks would best further conventional operations. However, Orde Wingate believed that parachuting SOE and OSS "peddlers of war material and cash" behind enemy lines to produce a people's war "rush of tribesmen, the peasants with billhooks, is hugaboo."[50] And he had a point. Encouraging resistance groups did little to advance Allied strategic goals, resulted in the slaughter of legions of non-combatants, and created post-conflict problems of disorder and factiousness normally associated with poorly disciplined militias who harbor their own political and personal agendas.

Setting Europe ablaze also set the stage for betrayal once the war wound down. Indeed, by late 1944 as Tito bolted from British control and communist partisans seized Athens in the wake of the German retreat, the concerns of the Western Allies transitioned to containing the politically unpredictable actions of partisans in France and Italy.[51] Charles de Gaulle ordered French resistors to go home or join the French army upon the liberation of mainland France by conventional Allied armies in the autumn of 1944. Stalin quashed the aspirations to power of communist-dominated Italian partisans at war's end, to ensure that the Western Allies would not contest his occupation of Poland. In Greece, British, and subsequently US support allowed the erstwhile Axis collaborators to crush the resistance movement that the Allies had nurtured from 1942. Wartime OSS/SOE-resistance alliances in Southeast Asia did not long survive Hiroshima. Only in Yugoslavia was Tito, with huge Soviet assistance, able to utilize his partisan movement as a trampoline to postwar power. Most partisans were accidental rather than ideological resistors – deserters; escaped POWs; young, single men forced from their homes by destruction, persecution, hunger, or to evade deportation to work in German factories – who were regarded as a nuisance, and even a survival threat, by locals. But in the postwar era, the myth of *la Résistance* became Lawrence's Arab Revolt on steroids. And like the Great War Arab Revolt, the contribution of resistance movements lay primarily in their political and propaganda value – far more than in any damage they managed to inflict on the Axis occupation.

In postwar Europe, however, the myth of widespread popular participation in resistance to Axis occupation offered a face-saver for countries whose populations had acquiesced to Axis occupation in 1940–1941, and a vehicle for discrediting wartime collaborationist regimes.[52] Because participation in the resistance might offer a ticket to a political career, access to government employment, or a coveted decoration, postwar resistance veterans exceeded actual wartime combatants – indeed Harold Macmillan discovered that already in April 1945 "certificates of merit" issued in resistance stand-down parades in Italy fetched high prices on the black market.[53] In this way, special operations-sponsored resistance movements truly produced victory without battles when they were promoted in the postwar years for reasons of national self-esteem, to discredit wartime collaborators, and to assemble political constituencies, as well as to acknowledge the genuine courage and sacrifice of a very few.

Although special operations actions in support of local resistors sometimes made for spectacular theater, their strategic and operational contribution to victory was minimal. These operations then took on a self-serving doctrinal aspect, especially in hindsight in the years after. The sinking of two British battleships in Alexandria harbor already mentioned did wound the Royal Navy in 1941 as it attempted to maintain supply convoys to Malta and interdict Axis shipping between Italy and North Africa. But a special forces raid, no matter how daring and spectacular, could not even in the short run rescue the Italian navy that was indifferently led, devoid of organic air support or radar, and stocked with an inventory of poorly designed and fragile ships. Otto Skorzeny's Gran Sasso raid utilized nine gliders and a light plane to liberate and evacuate Mussolini. As *Il Duce*'s Italian jailers put up no resistance, however – indeed, the colonel in charge of Mussolini's incarceration hospitably offered Skorzeny a bottle of wine to see him on his way – one can conclude that the SS could just as well have arrived at the Gran Sasso in a Fiat Topolino, bundled the defunct dictator into the back seat, and sped off; they would have enjoyed the same success with minimal risk and at a fraction of the cost. In any case, Mussolini was a spent force without even symbolic importance, who exercised no influence during the remaining two years of war except to execute those Fascists who he believed had betrayed him, including his son-in-law and former foreign minister Galeazzo Ciano. Skorzeny's subsequent special operations plans designed to redress Germany's deteriorating position – assassinate Churchill, Roosevelt, and Stalin at the 1943 Tehran Conference, capture Tito alive in 1944, make contact with mountain tribes in Iran to sever Allied supplies to Russia, and set up an SS Werewolf resistance to Allied occupation of Germany, among them – were complete failures. And even had these operations succeeded, what difference would they have made to the outcome of the war?

Special operations enthusiasts count Orde Wingate's Chindits that formed air-supplied, long-range penetration groups to operate behind Japanese lines in Burma from 1943 as among the more celebrated special forces units of World War II. John Arquilla tendentiously argues that the advantages of the Chindits resided in their (unquantifiable) psychological impact on the enemy, and the fact that isolated *faits d'armes* tendered a testosterone-laced display of machismo to buck up the home front.[54] Supporters, mainly those who served under him like Sir Robert Thompson, also claim that the Chindits disrupted Japanese offensives against India by diverting troops and attacking lines of supply. While William Slim, British Fourteenth Army Commander and Wingate's superior, commended the spirit and courage of the Chindits, he found the investment in special operations wasteful in men, resources, and time. In Slim's view, the Chindits assumed tasks that could be carried out just as well by better-equipped conventional units with a more balanced force structure. The Chindits lacked punch because they were basically light infantry unsupported by heavier elements like artillery, deficient in logistics, which limited their operational stamina, and subject to heavy casualties both because they succumbed to tropical diseases and because casualties were difficult to evacuate from remote jungle sites. They also proved difficult to support, competed with other special operations formations in the region, such as Force 136, and depleted line units of the best men, which "lower[ed] the quality of the rest of the Army." In short and with great insight, Slim concluded that British special operations had become a cult, whose doctrinal proponents in mass persuasion evangelized their tactics as the path to strategic salvation, when in fact their modest achievements were bought at great cost to the rest of the army.[55]

But like the resistance, the special operations legend of the Chindits has been exaggerated. Arquilla sees Churchill's "impulse" to take Wingate to the 1943 Quebec Conference as testimony to the Chindits', and Wingate's, importance to the British war effort. Simon Anglim notes that Wingate, together with Wing Commander Guy Gibson of Dam Buster fame, accompanied the Prime Minister to Quebec "for cosmetic purposes" to demonstrate Britain's resolve to defeat the Axis and to harness the propaganda illusion of special operations success to mask the systemic shortcomings of British conventional forces on glorious display in France in 1940, Greece and Crete in 1941, and Tobruk and Singapore in 1942. Wingate embodied the strategic promise of special operations, the T. E. Lawrence of the tropics, whose diminutive frame, signature solar topee, full beard, and evangelical fervor symbolized in Wingate's singular eccentricity British determination and combat skill to a US ally skeptical that British soldiers were willing or even capable of putting up a fight.

Wingate used the opportunity presented by *Quadrant* to sell the Combined Chiefs of Staff on his concept of creating "strongholds" – basically fortified air bases – in the Japanese rear. And to his credit, Wingate did divert Japanese troops up to a point in Northern Burma. Anglim argues that the postwar debate between Slim and Wingate's supporters is somewhat artificial, however, because Wingate's culminating Operation Thursday, launched in February 1944, featured an amalgamation of conventional and special operations forces and tactics. "Strongholds" or "boxes" minus their air supply feature, as yet undeveloped in 1942, were used most notably in the Battle of Gazala in May–June of that year in the Western Desert. Wingate's Long Range Patrol forces in Burma had ballooned beyond special operations proportions, many of its members were conventionally trained soldiers, and Wingate used them in conventional infantry missions. Air support, both tactical and logistical, had become so ubiquitous by 1944, that it no longer served only special operations forces. Nor was there any indigenous resistance in Burma for the Chindit Long Range Patrol Groups to support. "There is no more need for Chindits," Montbatten declared at Thursday's end. "We're all Chindits now." Wingate was also fortunate as Japanese forces were divided, operationally spent, and too malaria ridden at war's end to concentrate against his vulnerable "boxes." Post-Thursday analysis concluded that long-range penetration formations were too light to achieve anything more than a diversionary effect and worked best when they coordinated closely with conventional forces.[56]

Therefore, even though special operations and resistance action through intelligence collection, sabotage, disruption, diversion, and popular mobilization had played at best a minimum, even a morally ambiguous, role in the Axis defeat, World War II propelled the myth of the military effectiveness of Wingate-inspired Special Operations Forces (SOF), Lawrencian people's war, and paratroops into the postwar. Faith in the military efficacy of the French Resistance combined with Wingate's fortified air bases proved a seductive but particularly toxic operational cocktail for the French in Indochina. The resistance myth also boomeranged on Paris in Algeria from 1954, where in information warfare terms the FLN cast themselves as patriotic *maquisards* pitted against a French army in the role of Nazi oppressors. But British and Americans too would find ample opportunity to test the theories and refine the practices of SOF as the war had laid the groundwork for insurgent-fueled upheaval in an arch running from the Mediterranean, through the Middle East, India, and Southeast Asia to China.

"A world in which there are no obstacles": British counterinsurgency in Palestine

The first test of post-World War II British counterinsurgency came in Palestine, a territory seen as the linchpin of British presence in the strategically crucial Middle East and the Eastern Mediterranean. A British military presence would defend the region in case of another war and bolster friendly Arab governments who would keep the oil flowing and the Suez Canal open. Britain's problems began with the 1917 Balfour Declaration that opened Palestine to Jewish settlement. Zionists allied with the British to suppress the Arab Intifada of 1936–1939. Despite the concessions of the 1939 White Paper that promised to limit Jewish immigration and grant independence to an Arab Palestine within a decade, or rather because of them, Chaim Weizmann, president of the Zionist Organization, and the Jewish Agency, the settler government in Palestine, encouraged 32,000 Zionists to enlist in the British Army in World War II. SOE organized an elite Zionist force, the Palmach, to launch an insurgency should Rommel's army in the Western Desert break through British defenses in Egypt and overrun Palestine. Weizmann and the Jewish Agency expected this commitment to the survival of the British Empire to pay off in the repudiation by London of the 1939 White Paper. Nor did this aspiration appear fanciful, as both Churchill and the British Labour Party favored the creation of a Zionist state in Palestine.

Not all in the settler community, known as the Yishuv, trusted the British, among them two small terrorist organizations: the Irgun Zvei Leumi (IZL) and the Lohamei Herut Israel (Lehi), a small conspiracy of Jewish zealots that, even though its leader Abraham Stern was killed in January 1942 while in British police custody, continued to be called the Stern Gang by the British. From March 1944, the IZL, many of whose members had served in the British forces, reorganized under the leadership of a right-wing Polish refugee, Menachem Begin. Together with the Lehi whose leadership troika included Yitzhak Shamir, the IZL launched a campaign of bombings and attacks on police stations designed to drive the British from Palestine, a campaign that culminated in the November 1944 assassination in Cairo of Lord Moyne, the British Minister Resident in the Middle East, by Lehi gunmen. Initially, the extremists, who numbered barely one thousand, gained little traction in the Zionist community, so that David Ben Gurion, the Jewish Agency and its Haganah military, which included the elite Palmach strike force, cooperated with the British to turn over the names of members of Begin's IZL to the CID. Although Begin escaped, the IZL was driven deep underground and the Zionist movement split.

But support for the Jewish Agency's policy of cooperation with the British began to erode. As the war drew to a close and the true dimensions of the Holocaust became apparent, London's refusal to allow more Jewish refugees into Palestine during the war made the British complicit, in the eyes of many Jews, in the Holocaust. The Yishuv had ballooned from a mere 66,472 in 1935 to 560,000 people by 1946 with its own government, military force in the Haganah which included an intelligence service, the Shai, and special forces in the Palmach, not to mention two terrorist organizations. This presented a significant security problem from the autumn of 1945 when the Agency ceased to cooperate with the British. On the night of October 31, 1945, the Lehi and the IZL joined in the United Resistance Movement to launch a series of bombing and attacks against oil refineries that expanded over the next months to include barracks, government buildings, and airfields. This Zionist Revolt soon contaminated the British-trained Palmach, which turned on its tutors to sabotage railway tracks and police patrol vessels in Haifa and Jaffa meant to intercept shiploads of Jewish immigrants organized by French intelligence operatives in Marseilles. This turn of events incensed British Foreign Secretary and Labour politician Ernest Bevin, who on November 13, 1945 made public his hostility to Zionism and vowed to oppose further Jewish immigration to Palestine. Bevin's comments triggered a general strike in Tel Aviv the following day, which provided an opportunity for the British Army to showcase their colonial crowd control techniques by sniping "ringleaders." The spectacle of British troops targeting Jews in this and other increasingly frequent confrontations shocked public opinion, especially in the United States. In response to increasing terrorist attacks, by early 1946, the British had flooded the Mandate with troops and police, established Defense Regulations for Palestine, a resurrection of the 1920 Restoration of Order in Ireland Act that created a system of military courts with the ability to hold suspects indefinitely without trial and to impose capital sentences despite vague rules of procedure and the fact that neither legal expertise nor experience were required of judges. Military commanders were handed extensive powers including the ability to seize and destroy property.[57] But this worked even less well against the Jewish insurgency than it had against that of the Irish in 1920–1921 for two reasons, according to Newsinger: an intelligence drought and inappropriate tactics.

British intelligence in Palestine consisted of an overlapping patchwork of CID, military intelligence, MI5, and the Special Intelligence Service (SIS), that lacked Hebrew language skills and whose members were targeted for assassination by the Zionists. Better organization of intelligence services would have had a marginal impact on the campaign in any case, because the Yishuv proved unwilling to rat out fellow Jews, even right-wing terrorists, once heavy-handed British counterinsurgency tactics alienated moderates. "This intelligence failure is without any doubt the key to the security forces' inability to defeat the Zionist underground," Newsinger concludes.[58] Without intelligence, massive cordon and search operations, the primary counterinsurgency tactic in Palestine, seldom produced weapons or suspects and only served further to aggravate the Jewish community.

Given the fact that Britain's basic problem was that no political compromise acceptable to both Arab and Zionist existed, short of enlisting Arabs in the fight against the Zionist Revolt, no configuration of counterinsurgency tactics was likely to succeed. Arab allies must be purchased with political concessions, which presented monumental conundrums. Nor could the British apply the same menu of racialized tactics that had squelched the Arab Revolt of 1936–1939 – shooting prisoners, collective punishment, torture, and hangings – against European Jews, for fear of alienating Washington in the incipient Cold War, not to mention the British population twice squeamish after the British Army had terrorized Boer and Irish. "This inability to use the hostility of the majority of the population of Palestine against the Zionist was without doubt one of the major reasons for the British defeat," concludes Newsinger.[59] In short, the failure to apply counterinsurgency tactics within a divide-and-rule, civil war, ethno-religious context severely constrained London's ability to pacify Palestine.

The army seemed to have no answer as attacks on military installations continued into the early months of 1946 beyond invading homes to round up military-age males for screening. But because the British did not know who they were looking for, this only succeeded in frustrating the counterinsurgency while further alienating the Jewish community. As in Ireland, the deaths of soldiers at terrorist hands provoked reprisals that officers were hard-pressed to restrain. Claiming that their troops were on the verge of mutiny, army commanders demanded even more extensive powers from Westminster. In June, the Haganah carried out large-scale infrastructure attacks and kidnapped five British officers as they dined in the Tel Aviv officer's club. This uptick in violence coincided with the visit to Palestine of the new Chief of the Imperial General Staff, Field Marshal Bernard Montgomery. On his return to London, Montgomery successfully persuaded the British Cabinet to approve Operation Agatha, his plan to transform "the Mandate into a prison"[60] through the application of ever more extensive cordon and search operations, curfews, arrests, and internments.

In reply, on July 22, 1946 the Irgun dynamited a wing of Jerusalem's King David Hotel that housed the offices of the Military Command Headquarters, killing ninety-one people. The army retaliated with a massive 17,000-strong four-day cordon and search operation in Tel Aviv. A few arms were discovered and 787 people were detained. The repression served to convince the Jewish Agency, fearful that the Haganah would be depleted by the British crackdown and hence unable to protect the Yishuv from the Arabs, to curb the Lehi and the IZL. But the Agency proved reluctant to take more than tepid measures to discourage Zionist extremists, whose terrorist attacks became increasingly spectacular, brazen, and costly for the British. Meanwhile, the Haganah contracted with French authorities seeking payback for Britain's 1941 invasion of Lebanon and Syria, to engage in a full-out campaign to import Jewish refugees to Palestine. Concluding that he had gained the cooperation of the Jewish Agency, and that Montgomery's sledgehammer tactics had failed to wound the terrorists, the High Commissioner for Palestine, General Sir Alan Cunningham, called off repressive measures and, backed by the Cabinet, ordered the release of several of the interned Jewish leaders, despite the violent protests of Montgomery and the generals.[61]

The bombing of Britain's Rome embassy on October 31, 1946 by the Irgun and rumors that high-level British officials had become targets for Zionist assassination squads "triggered something close to hysteria in Fleet Street." The police reinforced the atmosphere of panic in a spasm of largely ineffective countermeasures in Britain that included stepped-up security in government buildings, at state events and concerts, and intensified immigration checks that included stopping incoming ocean liners to strip-search Jewish passengers. While this importation of colonial security measures and religious profiling to the homeland failed to produce a single arrest, the publicity surrounding them raised the level of anti-Semitism in Britain while it elevated the heroic profile of Begin and the Irgun in Palestine.[62]

Montgomery exploited this counter-terrorist, xenophobic overreaction in early 1947 to extract a "blank cheque" from the Cabinet to go after Zionist terrorist groups. However, the application of martial law in Tel Aviv and Jewish neighborhoods in Jerusalem in March 1947 failed to wound the Irgun and the IZL. Martial law shuttered economic activity, curtailed tax revenues on which repression depended, alienated those whose cooperation the British sought, and handed a propaganda victory to the Zionist extremists. This measure also proved to be a highly manpower-intensive process that left the terrorist networks unmolested and so failed to curtail terrorist attacks, which continued, often in spectacular fashion in March and April 1947.

As had been the case with the Black and Tans and the Auxiliaries in Ireland in 1920 and would subsequently be applied in Malaya and Kenya in the 1950s, the British reflex in Palestine, anchored in wartime propaganda extolling the efficacy of special operations, was to top up the understrength Palestinian Police Force with soldiers. In February 1947, a blandly worded "Secondment of Army Officers to Palestinian Police" memo created police "special squads" composed of soldiers with SOE experience to kill or arrest terrorists. At a stroke, the SOF "world in which there are no obstacles"[63] ethos was integrated into the police with the implication that extra-judicial killings would now be tolerated. As during the Arab Revolt of 1936–1939, small patrols, ambushes, undercover observers, and snatch squads reappeared in the British tactical repertoire. Experienced policemen protested "this sort of commando campaign which merely intensifies the hatred and increases the risks to decent policemen in uniform."[64] And they were correct – some of these SOE veterans, like Major Roy Farran, may have been genuine war heroes. But they made sloppy, even murderous cops, as became apparent when Farran's squad disappeared a seventeen-year-old Lehi suspect, Alexander Rubowitz, whom they apprehended as he put up pro-Lehi posters. As D. M. Leeson argues for Ireland in 1920–1921, police murder squads may have been tolerated in Palestine by the military, colonial civil service, and government as a deliberate policy of targeted retaliation, a counterinsurgency version of due process in reaction to illegitimate acts of war by Zionist terrorists, and as a way to preserve military morale.[65] If so, as in Ireland, it proved strategically disastrous because the inevitable court-martial whitewash of Roy Farran, freed because the body of Rubowitz was never found,[66] proved highly damaging to the British cause. In the wake of the Rubowitz case, even Monty was forced to recognize the dangers of mixing police functions and special operations. David Cesarani concludes that, in the Farran affair, the British reaped the bitter rewards of the militarization of the Palestinian police, the culmination of a trend that had begun there in the 1930s.[67]

Several factors in the conflict are generally credited with convincing the British to abandon the fight in 1947, despite the fact that Palestine was considered strategically vital for the maintenance of Britain's empire: First, given the political constraints and the absence of intelligence, the British had simply found no effective counterinsurgency strategy in Palestine, so that the war continued to escalate with no end in sight. This was symbolized by the hanging of two kidnapped British sergeants by Begin's IZL in retaliation for the execution of three IZL captives in July 1947, which provoked anti-Semitic riots in Britain and reprisals by British security forces against Jewish settlers, as a campaign of Zionist terrorism appeared in Britain. Second was the public relations fiasco of expediting the *Exodus* intercepted off the coast of Palestine, to Hamburg where Holocaust survivors, fire-hosed by German police and British soldiers, exposed to public view in the inauspicious political context of the concentration camps and other British counterinsurgency

10 The *Exodus* in Haifa July 1947.

tactics, that London could concoct no viable policy for Palestine. Third, there was the growing fear that the counterinsurgency was radicalizing British security forces to the point that their discipline was in danger of collapsing, although this threat may simply have been an army ploy to pressure the government to authorize more repressive measures.[68] Fourth, 1947 found the British in severe economic straits, which put their ability to finance operations in Greece and Palestine, not to mention India, in jeopardy.

In sum, the British counterinsurgency campaign in Palestine in the years 1946–1947 offered anything other than a doctrinal case study of the minimum force, civil-military cooperation/aid to the civil power, tactically flexible campaign based on decentralized decision-making prosecuted within the bounds of legality. British tactics against the Zionists had certainly proved faulty, in part because they were carried out in an intelligence vacuum, one created when the high-handedness of a militarized British police force and travesties of colonial justice alienated moderates in the Yishuv. But even in the unlikely event that the British might have acquired better intelligence and introduced earlier more flexible small-unit tactics, counter-gangs, snatch squads, massive detention camps, and so on that were to become a feature of subsequent campaigns, what difference would it have made to the outcome in Palestine in its dimensions of policy, strategy, and domestic politics as well as the international system in the Cold War? Their ability to crush the revolt with sheer repression was constrained by public opinion, especially that of London's major American ally with its own domestic political dynamic of Jewish Americans intent on the creation of Israel and the centrality of the US–UK relationship for the Cold War. Enlisting Arabs against Turks T. E. Lawrence fashion had been one thing in a different era of Britain's place in the world. Arming Arabs to fight European Jews, fresh from surviving the Final Solution, was an invitation to political disaster. The real lesson of Palestine was that even the best tactics – that is, even the finest grand tactics – were powerless to rescue a politically compromised enterprise in the face of vastly more powerful political and strategic realities. But in true stab-in-the-back fashion, British counterinsurgents claimed that the anti-Zionist campaign had failed because of spineless political leadership, and that the special squads were on the verge of victory against the Zionists when the politicians decided to abandon Palestine. Therefore, despite its disastrous consequences, Palestine impelled the British tradition of police militarization in small wars, with its concomitant brutalization of counterinsurgency policy and tactics, forward into British operations in Malaya, Kenya, and Northern Ireland.[69]

5 FROM SMALL WARS TO *LA GUERRE SUBVERSIVE*: THE RADICALIZATION AND COLLAPSE OF FRENCH COUNTERINSURGENCY

France's adjustment to the post-World War II counterinsurgency challenges proved more traumatic than for the British for several reasons. First, France's defeat in 1940, followed by the bitter struggle between Vichy and Free French forces had seriously undermined Paris' legitimacy in its imperial possessions. Second, two world wars had sharpened the debate in France over the value of the empire. In 1914–1918, the million or so imperial conscripts and workers who flowed into France made a critical contribution to national survival through four years of war. In World War II, empire provided the strategic depth and a springboard for the return of Charles de Gaulle and the Western allies to the European continent. The post-1945 colonial wars in Indochina and Algeria also found French soldiers determined to redeem on colonial battlefields France's honor and military reputation forfeited in Europe. These debates proved particularly caustic in France's bifurcated metropolitan/colonial army, where separate traditions, perspectives, and mentalities were eventually to produce insoluble tensions of organization, manpower, and resource allocation. The War for Algerian Independence also revived the civil war dimensions of the occupation, as Vichy loyalists ostracized after the liberation of 1944 sought rehabilitation via imperial nostalgia and the resistance against Charles de Gaulle of the *Organisation armée sécrète* (OAS).[1] By 1958 if not before, rival political outlooks and strategic choices had created serious rifts within the military that eventually drove a portion of the army into open rebellion against the French government.

Third, in post-World War II Indochina and Algeria, the French army faced operational, strategic, and political challenges that, with the possible exception of the much smaller scale Zionist revolt in Palestine, proved to be larger and far more complex and difficult to resolve than those faced by Britain in the same period. Fourth, France, and ironically its insurgent adversaries, emerged from World War II firmly in the thrall of the Resistance myth, which would lead to serious strategic and operational miscalculations on both sides. Finally, France was encumbered in the fourteen years following the end of World War II with weak, factious governments that essentially ceded control of colonial policy, strategy, and operations to the military and its imperialist supporters. This resulted in an increase in civil-military fusion and hence the politicization of a portion of the French army. The debate that came to a head in the army and the larger political community by 1958 was in fact the resurrection of a question asked since 1830 – what is the value of Algeria to France? On one hand, the prosecution of small wars abroad into the Cold War era was offered as evidence of national resolve and proof that France was not in terminal decline, but rather assuming the burden in the fight against international communism, Pan-Arabism, and other anti-Western movements. Others who eventually coalesced under Charles de Gaulle after 1958 insisted that the dogged persistence in neo-imperial expeditions locked the military into an antiquated organizational model and mindset, expended precious political capital and scarce national resources in areas of marginal strategic value, put France at odds with her principal allies, and hence actually contributed to national decline.

If World War II had proven the pivot of irregular warfare because it transitioned popular resistance and special operations from small wars experiments via permanent military organizations and the folding of ever more grand, elaborate, and ambitious operational concepts into the calculations of global strategists, the valorization of the irregular warrior had its most far-reaching consequences on the left, where the persistence of imperialism did much to discredit Western liberal values and institutions as models for modernizing non-European societies. Indigenous resistance had not fared well against Western armies before 1914, and continued to prove ineffective in the interwar years. This was about to change, however, as the Soviet triumph in Russia gave revolutionaries a strategic vision for which the idea of people's war, whose contours were defined by Mao Tse-tung in China in the 1930s, would combine an ideological dimension with new tactical principles that were supposed to be far superior to those that had animated the peasant militias of the past. The myth of the guerrilla thus blended seamlessly with the ideal of the nation in arms as promoted by advocates of total war on the right and of the masses as a self-organizing, morally unimpeachable, and ultimately unconquerable force against which the machine armies of the bourgeoisie and the ruling classes were immobilized.

The 1949 victory of Mao's communists in China had enormous repercussions for counterinsurgency. First, it was good for business – Mao's triumph proved contagious, an inspiration to revolutionaries in Southeast and South Asia and Latin America who set out to organize their own copycat national liberation movements, albeit with mixed results. Second, as the Soviet Union slipped out of the World War II Allied camp, and with China, the world's most densely inhabited country now in the clutches of communists dedicated to fomenting permanent revolution, even if only rhetorically, counterinsurgency now acquired the globalized threat that had eluded it in the interwar years, against which they could plausibly rally home country support. Anti-colonial uprisings were cast as functions of an international communist conspiracy, a zero-sum contest that required France, the United States, and Britain to defend their clients and values abroad or risk being politically neutered and culturally marginalized.

Third, Mao's doctrine of protracted people's war that combined military action with social reform as the basis for popular mobilization – now consecrated as the Holy Grail of insurgency – required counter-insurgents to respond with similar hearts and minds formulae. Small wars doctrine *à la* Callwell was updated to modern, population-centric COIN, which combined civic and psychological action programs to capture the hearts and minds of indigenous populations, with petty war tactics and special operations to saturate insurgent areas, organize self-defense forces, and decapitate insurgent organizations.

The consequences of this counterinsurgency adaptation to a Cold War context were baleful in all respects. First, elevating COIN into a national security mission coequal to conventional conflict resurrected and embittered the rivalries between colonial and conventional soldiers that had been masked, if not totally effaced, by the world wars. These rivalries have persisted in the US military into the twenty-first century, where they have been a drain on resources, distorted force structures, and confused the national debate over strategic priorities.

Second, counterinsurgents proved to be particularly inept at popular mobilization, both of indigenous peoples and of metropolitan populations unconvinced of the centrality of counterinsurgency to homeland security. In fact, the first impacted the second, as frustration at indigenous reluctance to embrace salvation orchestrated by the West out of fear or conviction triggered ever harsher counterinsurgency tactics. This, in turn, helped to convince an already skeptical public opinion at home that, in the words of sixteenth-century French essayist Michel de Montaigne: *Le jeu ne vaut pas la chandelle.*

A final consequence of the reinvention of small wars doctrine as COIN and its upgrading into a major national security mission is that it intensified the politicization of counterinsurgents for at least three reasons. First, convinced that they faced a coherent ideological attack on the West, counterinsurgents became the storm troopers of the anti-communist crusades. Second, COIN doctrine with its focus on popular mobilization accelerated the process of civil-military fusion, by which soldiers took over police, judicial, and administrative functions in theaters of operations. COIN also required the proliferation of military specializations, particularly psychological and information operations, grassroots intelligence collection, and what was broadly termed civic action, which were highly political by their nature. Last, protracted war which invited press scrutiny and the intervention of politicians into the operational sphere, and tested the stamina of home populations impatient for results, placed increasing strains on civil-military relations, which in France erupted into mutiny during the Algerian War (1954–1962).

Mao and the triumph of "people's war"

Mao Tse-tung is credited with transforming pre-World War I anti-colonial uprisings into a modern, ideologically coherent, and tactically proficient people's war challenge to a Western political, economic, and cultural domination. Mao's 1949 triumph in China over Chiang Kai-shek's Kuomintang (KMT) appeared to validate Lawrence's 1929 *Encyclopedia Britannica* assertion that a small nucleus of insurgents armed with no more than a vision and a design for success can indoctrinate, mobilize, and guide the peasant masses to achieve strategic decision in warfare. Mao was important to insurgency, and by inversion to counterinsurgency, on three levels: first as a theoretician of Marxist revolution; second as the originator of insurgency doctrine; and third as a strategist and architect of victory in China. In all three aspects, his reputation far exceeds his actual accomplishments.

Mao's major theoretical contribution to established Marxist theory was that the peasantry as a social class, rather than the industrial proletariat, comprised China's true revolutionary base. Aghast that French peasants had voted en masse for Louis-Napoleon Bonaparte in 1848, Karl Marx dismissed this "class" as irretrievably traditionalist, a viewpoint that passed intact into Soviet ideology and placed Mao's disciples at odds with orthodox communist movements. Mao's alternative vision of the insurrectionary mobilization of the peasantry freed up subsequent generations of revolutionaries to dispense with the classic Marxist bourgeois phase of development and decline and the Soviet tutelage that accompanied it. The Chinese communists did indeed enjoy some success in mobilizing China's peasantry by combining coercion with grassroots social action – forcible land redistribution, organizing self-defense groups against brigands, collecting the harvest, dyke and road repair, and so on – in a sort of self-help, revolutionary oil spot approach that in its essential aspects would have been familiar to Gallieni and Lyautey. But this was accomplished in the exceptional circumstances of the Japanese invasion of China from 1937 that swept away the KMT presence in much of northeast and central China. With Japanese forces concentrated in the cities and along major road axes and in Manchuria to oppose a potential Soviet invasion, vast areas containing millions of Chinese remained in effect ungoverned space. The communists infiltrated these areas to extend their political control, build up the People's Liberation Army (PLA), and burnish their patriotic bona fides as an anti-Japanese resistance. Revolutionaries who subsequently attempted to operationalize Mao's peasant-centric vision in other areas like Latin America found that rural folk often made reluctant revolutionaries so that organizing them against an even moderately competent regime seldom met with success.

Second, Mao's *On Guerrilla Warfare* was hailed as the insurgent's Bible, its main doctrinal contribution residing in a protracted revolutionary process that consisted of three distinct stages: in the first defensive phase, revolutionaries indoctrinate the civilian population, recruit and train revolutionary cadres, and carry out acts of violence to discredit and undermine the regime. A second phase basically consists of an oil spot of territorial expansion with ever larger, more sophisticated, and better-armed forces able to isolate and defeat government contingents. Finally, the incumbent will become so physically and psychologically weakened that he will succumb to defeat by large, conventionally organized revolutionary forces.[2]

In reality, however, *On Guerrilla Warfare* offered fragmentary reflections on the state of Mao's conflict with Chiang Kai-shek rather than a recipe book for the successful pursuit of victory through the sequencing of a three-stage insurrection, a strategic process that his counterinsurgent opponents attribute to him.[3] Some scholars detect ghost-written or plagiarized passages that lack the verbose, histrionic style of Mao's political writings. He had scant military experience or knowledge before the late 1930s. Chiang, in contrast, had decades of combat experience both in fighting campaigns of consolidation against warlords and communist insurgents in the 1920s and 1930s, and against conventional Japanese forces in World War II. Chiang's Fourth and Fifth Encirclement campaigns of 1932–1934, which combined blockhouses and military colonization with mobilization of the gentry and peasantry, mocked Mao's theories of peasant-based insurrection and precipitated Mao's Long March to Yenan, during which the peasants proved reluctant to support the fleeing communists.[4] (Typically Mao blamed his subordinates for communist failures, in particular Soviet advisers for encouraging the defense of fixed positions rather than entrusting survival to mobility and surprise, during Chiang's campaigns of 1930–1934.)[5] The Long March winnowed the Chinese Communist Party (CCP) down to a hard core dominated by Mao that sought refuge in Yenan, a remote province in north-central China. Mao began to lay out his revolutionary concepts which centered upon protracted, three-stage struggle. American historian William Fuller speculates that Mao's articles "may be regarded as a specimen of disinformation ... more to buck up the spirits of the demoralized Communist veterans of the Long March, than in the expectation that he was making a profoundly original contribution of Marxist thought."[6]

Finally, Mao's reputation as the Clausewitz of modern insurgency[7] due to his victory over Chiang was constructed in the wake of a series of contingent events that resulted in the 1949 communist victory in China, not because he realized a three-stage revolutionary grand vision. In fact, Mao might have finished as a minor footnote to China's turbulent interwar history had Chiang not been kidnapped in December 1936 by his own men, who correctly feared that the KMT leader planned to divert troops facing Japanese forces in Manchuria to Yenan. Instead of eradicating the CCP as Chiang planned, he was forced into a tactical alliance with Mao as a condition for his release. Barely seven months later in July 1937, a minor incident at the Marco Polo Bridge near Beijing sparked World War II in Asia. Within less than a month, fifty of Chiang's divisions were at grips with the Japanese and so were in no position to eliminate their communist rivals.

The war years proved devastating to the KMT, while Mao used them to leverage the CCP into a major player in China and position the PLA to make a bid for power in 1945. The KMT bore the brunt of the fighting against the Japanese, in which Chiang sacrificed most of his best divisions and their leaders. The Japanese advance occupied the eastern seaboard and lower Yangsi Valley, the KMT's center of its political power and source of its wealth. This helped further to fragment Chiang's political base, already riven by warlord rivalries, corruption, and rampant inflation. Rather than present Chiang with a triumph, the Japanese surrender in August 1945 found his nationalist regime devastated, divided, and demoralized. Nor was the KMT, which had been pushed back to the south and west of China, as well positioned as were the communists to fill the political void in the northeast left by the Japanese surrender and the Soviet invasion of Manchuria required by the Yalta agreement. The CCP collected Japanese arms sufficient to equip 600,000 troops, while CCP cadres and the PLA occupied Manchuria with Soviet support. This meant that when the United States assisted Chiang to occupy Manchuria's major cities, KMT soldiers became overextended along a thousand-mile-long rail corridor, their garrisons isolated and gradually asphyxiated. By early 1948, the KMT's position in the north had begun to disintegrate, as its soldiers increasingly defected to communist forces moving south. In early 1949, Mao brushed aside attempts by Chiang, now in possession only of Beijing and Tientsin in the north, to negotiate. The proclamation of the People's Republic of China in October 1949 found Chiang and what was left of the KMT in exile in Taiwan.[8]

In short, the communist victory in China was far more dependent on contingent circumstances that flowed out of the disorder, dislocation, and defeat of the Japanese invasion of the 1930s than on the smooth unfolding of a revolutionary doctrine anchored in peasant mobilization. Mao's post-1949 reputation leveraged the Chinese tradition of showering military and civic accolades on the leader, and willingly took credit for the accomplishments of others to construct his "great man" cult of personality. In a desperate search for a "victory without battles" liberation blueprint, strategic theorists of the indirect approach and the left-wing ideologues elevated Mao into the stratosphere of major strategists.[9]

While Mao's victory was dramatic, it formed part of an evolving trend, rather than a sudden reversal of Western fortunes. The challenge to nineteenth-century liberalism did not abruptly emerge at the end of World War II. Nor was it a phenomenon unique to states and nations seeking to decolonize in the formal sense. However, in a Cold War ideological context, Mao's success in China and the doctrine of revolution it spawned seemed to transform the inchoate post-1918 nationalist rebellions into a coordinated communist threat to "a wider and permanent system of general security" based on Western liberal principles laid out in the August 1941 Atlantic Charter, the guiding documents of the Nuremberg tribunal and the United Nations, the free-trade ideology of Bretton Woods, and the Marshall Plan.[10]

Daniel Moran lists some of the modern or even postmodern advantages enjoyed by post-1945 insurgencies available only in embryonic form to their pre-World War II predecessors. First he cites "asymmetrical motives" in the form of a desire for revolutionary political change and the political will and sagacity to follow the task to completion that put the West at a psychological disadvantage despite superior material means. Second, postwar revolutionary movements could mobilize global public opinion to garner diplomatic, economic, and military support, and even to undermine the civilian support of the counterinsurgents. Communism and Arab nationalism, to take but two examples, might muster resources and diplomatic pressure through international organizations like the United Nations to bolster insurgent movements. Publicizing the brutality of counterinsurgent tactics that might include torture, resettlement camps, or massacres of indigenous civilians raised doubts in Western populations about the moral costs of small wars fought to maintain outmoded imperial realms. "Although such assistance does not guarantee success, its absence is virtually synonymous with failure," Moran writes. In other words, revolutions that lacked outside support might be isolated and smothered, like those in the Philippines, Malaya, and Kenya post-1945. The victory of the Viet Minh/Viet Cong in Indochina, meanwhile, would have been far more problematical absent serious assistance from China and eventually the Soviet Union.

Third, successful insurgencies evolve resiliency through ideological commitment that rises above clan or tribe and the organizational capacity and popular stamina to engage in protracted war. Ideology could be mustered to explain the community of interests among diverse groups and arm them against divide-and-rule counterinsurgency tactics. Because revolutionaries recognize that war is a political act, they use protraction to raise the costs of a conflict to counterinsurgents in time and resources, consolidate their base though grassroots political, economic, and social action, and deny the counterinsurgent victory by relying on mobility and surprise rather than seeking to inflict military defeat. In this way, the insurgent can make time work for him to undermine the will of the counterinsurgent population to persist in a prolonged, costly, demoralizing, and ultimately futile conflict.[11]

The fact that few post-World War II insurgencies were communist, much less Maoist, either in ideological inspiration or strategic design mattered little.[12] The important point was that ideology provided the overarching rationale for a coherent strategic and tactical doctrine of insurgency that made mid-century people's war thoroughly modern or even postmodern, and sent small wars tacticians in search of a doctrine of counter-mobilization. *La guerre révolutionnaire* was basically neo-imperialism disguised as an anti-communist or anti-Jihadist crusade against, in the words of *FM 3–24*, an

> insurgent group [that] channels anti-Western anger and
> provides members with identity, purpose, and community, in
> addition to physical, economic, and psychological security.
> The movement's ideology explains its followers' difficulties
> and provides a means to remedy those ills. The most powerful
> ideologies tap latent, emotional concerns of the populace . . .
> Ideology provides a prism, including a vocabulary and
> analytical categories, through which followers perceive their
> situation.[13]

The ideological competition required that small wars doctrine be upgraded to modern counterinsurgency or COIN, to embrace the social, economic, and propaganda techniques utilized by Maoist or post-Maoist-inspired insurgents to assemble a popular following.

A doctrine for lost wars part I: France's colonial wars in Indochina and Algeria 1946–1962

One of the great ironies of the post-2006 rage for COIN is that it is a doctrine spawned in the shadow of two lost wars – a two-act contest in Southeast Asia whose intensity and longevity was the direct result of Mao's victory in China, and one in North Africa inspired, however indirectly, by a doctrine of prolonged people's war. Indeed, it is a fundamental assumption of counterinsurgency proponents that COIN doctrine properly applied would have won those wars for France and the United States. This argument should be highly suspect if for no other reason than that it celebrates a COIN-dinista pantheon filled with losers and sometimes war criminals who claimed that they were winning on their front and could have won the whole enchilada but for a government/people/conventional military establishment that knifed them in the back. The simple assertion that had proper tactics been applied in Indochina/Vietnam and Algeria, these conflicts would have slipped into the counterinsurgency win column is tantalizing but unconvincing. Both, or all three wars depending on how one counts them, were lost because the strategic context in which the wars were fought defied a tactical remedy.

These French and American counterinsurgency experiences share similarities other than the stab-in-the-back myth. Both witnessed a civil-military relations meltdown, although true to form the Gallic version proved far more spectacular. French counterinsurgents dug their own grave in Indochina and Algeria with their open defiance of the French government, fruit of the slow corrosion beginning with Bugeaud of Franco-colonial civil-military relations. By 1946, the French mainland was focused on post-World War II economic recovery, itself at odds with redirecting Marshall Plan aid into Indochinese bogs and forests, and torn between fear of the USSR and trepidation over German rearmament. This put them increasingly at odds with France's colonial officer corps, politicized by civil-military fusion, obsessed with chasing disrespectful, poorly clad dissidents through the imperial hinterland, and by a nostalgic attachment to the grandeur of France's imperial past as an indicator for the future. While initially supportive, neither population could sustain their enthusiasm for seemingly endless long wars. French ambivalence was compounded by repressive methods deployed against Muslims in Algeria, as well as the boomerang effect in the metropole against Muslim workers and French anti-war activists which looked uncomfortably similar to those applied in France during the four-year Vichy/Nazi condominium in World War II.

A final point is that the French and US small wars experiences are directly linked through doctrine. Following their 1962 defeat in Algeria, French officers evangelized their discredited methods in US staff colleges, at the Rand Corporation, Harvard University, and in several Latin American countries where military juntas like that of Argentina deployed brutal Battle of Algiers methods against its own population. Despite defeat in Vietnam and the questionable success of the French-inspired Phoenix assassination program in Vietnam, contemporary US COIN-dinistas have revived the French experience in the War for Algerian Independence through the writings of a French participant of that war, David Galula, whose ideas inspired the 2006 *FM 3–24: Counterinsurgency*.

Indochina: colonial mythology promoted as strategy

Nowhere was the search for a canon to underpin the ideological unity of counterinsurgency more intense than France. Barely had Paris emerged from the nightmare of defeat and occupation when it was engulfed by two "small wars" in Indochina and Algeria. In retrospect, it required extraordinary hubris and self-deception for a country emerging from four years of defeat and occupation to reoccupy an indefensible, revenue-draining dependency, with a shredded and humiliated army. However, as Daniel Moran has noted, retention of the colonies was regarded as an exercise in France's moral rearmament in the wake of the ignominy of World War II.[14]

The French army returned to Indochina in October 1945 courtesy of the British, only to discover Ho Chi Minh and his forces encamped in the north of the country. One historian believes that the Truman administration missed an opportunity to exercise its considerable leverage to force Paris to compromise with Ho.[15] Unfortunately, the problem was that although Paris was willing to come to a political compromise with the Viet Minh, the French military appeared determined to carry on in Indochina as if the French defeat, the Japanese occupation, and the Vietnamese resistance had never occurred. On March 6, 1946, the French government agreed to recognize Ho Chi Minh's Provisional Republic of Vietnam as a free state within the

French Union. But in a spasm of civil-military fusion, the governance of Indochina had fallen entirely into the hands of a French military that had no intention of honoring that agreement. Specifically, cohabiting with Vietnamese nationalists did not suit former Carmelite monk and hard-line colonialist High Commissioner Admiral Thierry d'Argenlieu. Fearing that Paris would sell out to Ho, d'Argenlieu purposely refused to negotiate the details of the agreement recognizing the Vietnamese Republic, and orchestrated other unpleasantness. Military confrontations between French and Viet Minh forces escalated until they tipped into full-blown war by December 1946.

Having provoked the war, the French military discovered that it was poorly positioned to fight it. Hostilities exposed some serious French debilities, beginning with Paris' priority to rebuild the conventional army for metropolitan defense and the occupation of Germany. The French army had begun to reconstitute itself with US assistance from 1943, but it was woefully short of officers and NCOs, to say nothing of mechanics, logisticians, and modern weaponry. As French conscripts were by law exempt from colonial service, the war was to be fought with a hybrid of French marines, Foreign Legionnaires, Senegalese, and North Africans – some 235,000 troops by war's end, joined by 261,000 ill-trained and poorly motivated recruits from the "Associated States" of Vietnam, Laos, and Cambodia.[16]

Paris' problem, however, was that it laid no political foundation for a counterinsurgency campaign. The Viet Minh political and military leadership proved to be both able and patient, especially after narrowly eluding capture in October 1947 when French paratroopers dropped in on their headquarters and logistical center at Bac Kan in the Tonkin highlands, scattering the Viet Minh leadership. Though the French decapitation strategy failed, the army held the main population centers, patrolled the major roads, and controlled the vital rice-growing areas in Cochinchina and the Red River Delta of Tonkin. The roughly 30,000 poorly armed Viet Minh troops were dispersed. However, the French failed to transform this tactical stalemate into a political advantage that would make time work for them. In 1949, Paris installed the former emperor Bao Dai as head of state. But he had no constituency, and to appeal to Vietnamese nationalists, he declared neutrality in the war between the French and the Viet Minh and promptly decamped to the Côte d'Azure. This left the French to replicate a nineteenth-century-era campaign of colonial consolidation.

While the French had a robust small wars tradition dating from Bugeaud, Gallieni, and Lyautey, putting together the building blocks of a successful counterinsurgency strategy in Indochina eluded them, although they tried. Despite having arrived in Saigon in 1858, the French had never created the equivalent of an Arab Bureau for Indochina. When they returned in 1945 following the Japanese occupation, they found that the situation had been transformed. Not only did Ho's forces control most of the territory north of the sixteenth parallel, but the old Indochina hands upon whom they might have counted for local knowledge had died in Japanese POW camps or had been dismissed from service by de Gaulle, irked that Indochina had remained staunchly pro-Vichy during World War II. This meant that the young conquistadors of the Free French movement – d'Argenlieu, Leclerc, and Salan – disembarked in Saigon in the fall of 1945 into an unfamiliar land.

They had to build a colonial infrastructure from scratch, beginning with an intelligence system, the building block for any successful counterinsurgency campaign. Denied in the Maoist vernacular the capacity to separate the fish from the sea, the French fell back on torture to obtain information. When units were ambushed, sniped, and mined, soldiers responded with collective punishments.[17] Population concentration offered a familiar tactic used by the French since Bugeaud's "villages de fellahs" established between 1846–1855, and by the British in Malaya at the time. Strategic hamlets claimed to have had some success in Cambodia as a counterinsurgency tactic, ostensibly because they were organized by Cambodian troops under the auspices of the King and met minimum standards of employment, hygiene, and defense, although success such as it was may have been due to political factors.[18] Neither the French nor the Americans were able to make strategic hamlets work as a pacification tactic in Vietnam.[19] Although the French committed Boer War-size expeditionary forces to Indochina, they lacked sufficient troops to blockade enemy areas, or systemically to carry out what they called *quadrillage d'auto-defense* – basically partitioning a zone to search for insurgents.[20]

With insufficient troops to control the countryside, the French resorted in colonialist fashion to striking tactical alliances with minority groups like the Cao Dai in Cochinchina, Catholics in Tonkin's Red River Delta, some *montagnard* tribes in upper Tonkin, and the Bình Xuyên, a dissident nationalist group turned criminal syndicate that controlled much of the prostitution, gambling, and opium smuggling in Saigon.

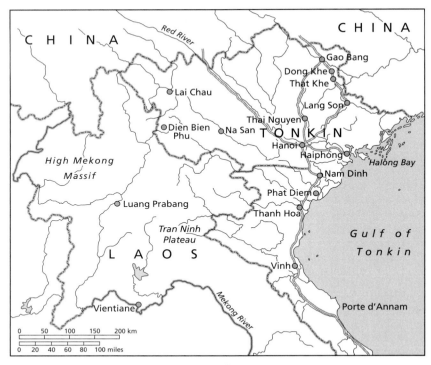

Map 3 Indochina

However, these groups were small, localized, and often struck non-aggression pacts with the Viet Minh as well as with the French.

French counterinsurgents probably congratulated themselves on New Year's Day 1950 that they had managed to stabilize the situation in Vietnam. But the momentum of the war would turn decidedly against them in that year. Barely had Mao conquered Chiang in 1949 than Viet Minh units began to travel north to be trained. They returned to Tonkin equipped with mortars, artillery, and radios and began to pressure the network of oil spots that Gallieni among others had created in the 1890s, outposts linked by the Route Coloniale (RC) 4 that twisted through the limestone peaks along the TonkinChina border. When the French opted to evacuate in October 1950, their retreat down the tortuous RC 4 turned into a rout. French troops careened out of the mountains toward the Red River Delta and Hanoi, leaving thousands of dead behind in what Bernard Fall called the worst French imperial defeat since Wolfe captured Quebec in 1759. Paris rushed in World War II hero Jean de

Lattre de Tassigny, who erected a ring of blockhouses around the Red River Delta backed by mobile infantry reserves, gun support from riverine craft, and airpower to blunt Vo Nguyen Giap's "third phase" assaults against Hanoi in the first six months of 1951.

De Lattre appeared to have again achieved a temporary stalemate. And although the French had largely surrendered the Chinese border, and had been forced back on the Red River Delta, the outbreak of the Korean War in June 1950 had caused Washington to view the French war in Indochina as an anti-communist, rather than a colonial struggle, and to pour in significant aid. The French also retained some potent military assets in the form of specialized commando, paratroop, and mechanized units.

French colonial soldiers contemplating defeat in Indochina in May 1954 concluded that they had lost because conventional soldiers failed to understand how to fight a counterinsurgency war, and because they had been "forgotten in the rice paddies" by a French government and people unmindful of the baleful repercussions of imperial retreat for national honor and influence.[21] Indeed, one of those military men turned historian, Jules Roy, explained the logic of Dien Bien Phu as, "the search for a classic, set-piece battle in which the French hoped to bring the destructive power of modern technology to bear on the elusive communist enemy and smash him with an iron fist."[22] This revisionism is hardly surprising – after all, stab in the back had been their refrain since Bugeaud. What they failed to concede was that growing counterinsurgent influence on French strategy in Indochina had laid the groundwork from 1951 for the debacle at Dien Bien Phu three years later. The French decision to occupy Dien Bien Phu in November 1953 was not a search for a climactic conventional Austerlitz in the jungle, but rather a desperate grasp at the straw of persistence and survival of France's Indochina enterprise through irregular warfare. Like the Germans in World War II, the more they were forced on the defensive, the more they turned to SOF to restore the strategic initiative. To French officers incarcerated in the Red River Delta, the idea that they could combine their offensive operational capabilities with an oil spot tactic to create pockets of resistance in the Viet Minh "rear" was the product of four myths of their own making.

The first was a lingering ancestral memory of Gallieni's oil spot tactic carried out in the 1890s among Tonkin's minority *montagnard* population. The belief in the tactical efficacy of oil spot formed an article of faith in a French army that never considered its context, nor realized that in fact oil spot had failed to stabilize the Tonkin frontier which continued to be a remote, turbulent, lawless region long after Gallieni's departure in 1896. Oil spot success was merely a colonialist myth propagated by Lyautey to promote the genius of his patron Gallieni and secure the creation of a separate colonial army in 1900. Gallieni's oil spot came down to introducing the opium poppy into the Tonkin highlands to redirect Chinese and Vietnamese attentions from rustling *montagnard* buffalo and women, and pitting *montagnard* tribes against each other for control of the opium trade.

The second factor that propelled French forces toward Dien Bien Phu was the Lawrencian myth of the white Special Operator assisting bands of simple mountain tribes to victory over the evil, cruel lowlanders, in this case the same, now communized, cocktail of Chinese and Vietnamese interlopers who had oppressed them in Gallieni's day. The French retained a romanticized conception of the *montagnards* as a simple folk whose loyalty could be won with a continuation of the *politique des races* that protected them from predatory Vietnamese and Chinese. "[The *montagnard*] deserve our nurturance and protection," French commander Raoul Salan wrote in his memoirs. "It loves us, it places its confidence in us. We do not have the right to abandon it."[23] In this way, the French proved willing to mortgage their entire future in Vietnam to a nineteenth-century racist sentimentality and to a belief in the strategic potential of SOF.

The third factor that propelled the French toward defeat at Dien Bien Phu was the myth that the World War II French Resistance had created what they called a "climate of insecurity" in German-occupied France, by which they presumably meant the diversion of German troops by Resistance attacks that allowed the June 1944 Allied invasion of Normandy to succeed. Teaming insurgents with main forces in World War II merely offered an updating of Wellington's use of *partidas* in the Peninsula and the interface of Allenby's expeditionary army with Lawrence's Arab Revolt. The belief in the strategic value of the World War II French Resistance was accepted as an article of faith in France and especially in an army desperate to conjure up any face-saving folklore to disguise its ignominious 1940 collapse. The transferability of this Resistance strategy to Indochina in 1951 lay in the calculation that significant Viet Minh forces could be diverted from their siege of the strategically vital Red River Delta that contained Hanoi and Tonkin's port city Haiphong by a French-organized "resistance" behind their "lines."

Faith in the sustainability of this resistance was bolstered by a fourth special operations myth – the invincibility of fortified airheads or "boxes" as evolved by Wingate during Operation Thursday in Burma in 1944. These air-supplied bases served both as "mooring points" for mobile operations to disrupt Japanese base areas and as sanctuaries that could withstand a siege. Never mind that the Japanese were at the end of their tether in 1944 and that post-Thursday analysis concluded that long-range penetration formations were too light to achieve anything more than a diversionary effect, and that "medium range penetration operations in conjunction with main forces for limited periods" was preferable to creating "boxes" distant from the main bases that could not be lavishly supported by air.[24] Instead, the French commander in Indochina at the time of Dien Bien Phu, General Henri Navarre, elected to defend low ground too distant from his Red River Delta base, chose the wrong commanders, underestimated the offensive power of the Viet Minh who, supported by the Chinese, were growing ever stronger, and ignored the political context of the Geneva conference that began in April 1954 to resolve outstanding issues in Korea and Indochina, which gave the communists the incentive to turn the tables on the French.

To operationalize these myths, in 1951, Major, later Colonel, Roger Trinquier inspired the creation of the *groupements des commandos mixtes aéroportée* (GCMA) whose goal was to create an anti-Viet Minh *maquis*. Trinquier would fly over the Tonkin highlands in the hope of eliciting a positive reaction from the groups of *montagnard* tribesmen who peopled the region. If so, he would land and convince the village headman to volunteer recruits who were flown to the special forces camp at Cap Saint-Jacques near Saigon for training in counterinsurgency tactics. Then they were to be reinserted with arms, radios, cash, and a special operations cadre of French officers and NCOs into the mountains. This nucleus would then form "hundreds," so called because each insurgent commando was to number around a hundred *montagnards*. So constituted, French-led *montagnard* tribesmen would attack Viet Minh forces from behind, collect intelligence, and interdict their supply routes, forcing their commander Vo Nguyen Giap to divert significant numbers of troops from the Red River Delta.

The experiment proved a disaster. Although initially taken by surprise, the Viet Minh quickly regrouped and moved against the dispersed pockets of French-led *montagnard* resisters in the latter half of 1952, and put them to flight. To rescue his dispersed bands of fleeing *maquis* and their French cadres, in October 1952 French commander Raoul Salan hastily constructed what he baptized a *base aéroterrestre* at a place called Na San. Salan's air/land "hedgehog" consisted of barbed wire, trenches, and mutually supporting strong points on high ground into which he airlifted 15,000 men with artillery support. Na San came too late to rescue most of Trinquier's *maquis* and their French cadres, who perished outside the wire. But when Giap tried to overwhelm Na San in late November 1952, French defensive fire repelled him until he exhausted his ammunition and had to adjourn the attack.

Therefore, while a tactical success insofar as the hastily constructed "hedgehog" had resisted Giap's attacks, as a "mooring point" for a French-led T'ai *maquis*, Na San had proved a strategic bust. Shorn of strategic value, Na San was abandoned by the French in 1953. That they proved willing to risk the *base aéroterrestre* gambit once again, following a year that had witnessed both further attrition of French forces and the end of the Korean War can only be explained by the fact that an obsession with special operations and its attendant myths had come to dominate French strategy. With every incentive further to clear its frontiers of capitalist powers, Beijing mobilized the Geneva conference, which Ho Chi Minh agreed to attend in October 1953. In fact, Operation Castor was nothing less than an updated oil spot – that is, the gradual expansion of a zone of pacification out of a secure base area through coordinated military, intelligence-gathering, economic, and political methods. And like most irregular warfare inspired scenarios, it spoke to the desperation, sense of strategic vulnerability, and capacity for self-deception of French counterinsurgents, who found a silver lining in the Na San disaster despite the fact that its primary *maquis* protection purpose had failed. Despite protests from paratroop officers that scarce resources were being squandered on Special Forces schemes to create an ephemeral resistance, by early 1954, the French claimed that they were on their way to creating "an immense guerrilla zone" in northern Tonkin which would become a second front. Henri Navarre boasted that the *maquis* was his "artillery" and laid plans to train 40,000 *montagnards*.[25]

The thing of it was, Giap was not distracted by French *maquis* fantasies and the expanding oil spot of French influence in the remote highlands. In September 1953, he was busy preparing to launch a "third phase" offensive against the Red River Delta to take Hanoi and Haiphong, which he saw as the center of gravity for the control of Tonkin and the beginning of a strategy to unravel the entire French position in Indochina. His Chinese advisers intervened to reorient Giap toward the T'ai *maquis* the French had created in northwestern Tonkin around Lai Chau. Their reasoning was that Giap still lacked the strength to take on the French in conventional operations against their Red River base. Beijing calculated that, having created their *maquis* at Lai Chau, the French would have to defend it, not the least because it was a major opium-producing area the profits of which partially financed French special operations. When, in early November 1953, French intelligence detected "the imminence of a rebel action against our *maquis* in T'ai country," the French command took the bait. Navarre launched an airborne operation to convert the broadest valley in the Tonkin highlands into a *base aéroterrestre* and shifted the T'ais from the indefensible Lai Chau to Dien Bien Phu. But Dien Bien Phu would prove to be no Na San, because the Chinese made certain that Giap had the resources to overwhelm the isolated French garrison.

In this way, a strategy driven by a belief in the efficacy of oil spot inculcated by Lyautey's propaganda, a sentimental attachment to the *montagnards* in the fashion of Lawrencian romanticism, the World War II myth of the *maquis* and an overreliance on special operations to reverse the strategic dynamic of the war, and a desire to retain control of an important segment of the opium trade set the stage for a disaster from which French fortunes in Indochina could not recover.[26]

Almost inevitably, proponents of *la guerre subversive* argued that soldiers trained in conventional war had forfeited prospects for victory because they had tried to fight a conventional battle at Dien Bien Phu too far from their support base and with inadequate air cover. However, French counterinsurgents failed to acknowledge the futility of counterinsurgency tactics as a path to victory in the absence of a viable political strategy. The more obvious it became that their COIN tactics were not working, the more desperate the French became to operationalize special operations fantasies to reverse the strategic momentum of the war. At Dien Bien Phu, the fascination with creating *montagnard maquis* over-extended the French and led directly to the climactic battle that put the exclamation mark on the French chapter of the Indochina War. All these problems would resurface in Algeria where, once again, the corrosive effects of civil-military fusion combined with the Gallic proclivity for the grand gesture to transition the usual COIN menu from tactical disappointment to strategic catastrophe.

L'armée pour l'armée: COIN, civil-military fusion, and mutiny in Algeria

While historically *la politique du faite accomplie* established the French colonial military's role as a political actor,[27] in Algeria tactics were deliberately calibrated to undermine any prospect, however improbable, that Paris might negotiate a political compromise that could transfer power to moderate nationalists. In the process, French counterinsurgents succeeded in uniting much of Algeria's Muslim population behind the *Front de libération national* (FLN) by the war's end. Furthermore, the basic tenets of French counterinsurgency doctrine combined with weak French administrative and police presence in North Africa to require the French military increasingly from 1955 to fuse administrative, police, judicial, and combat roles. It also began to take operational decisions that had far-reaching political consequences,[28] all of which helped further to politicize a significant portion of French officer corps. By attempting to direct French policy in Algeria, French counterinsurgents alienated the French population and transformed the French government's goal in Algeria from the defeat of the FLN and the perpetuation of *Algérie française*, into a battle to reestablish the authority of the state over a renegade military.[29]

The success of the Algerian FLN, a tiny intrigue of poorly armed revolutionaries whose theory of victory rested on the naïve assumption that a few terrorist acts would precipitate a Muslim uprising against the French occupation of the Maghreb, seemed a long shot in November 1954. The would-be liberators had far more powerful in-house rivals in Ferhat Abbas' *Union démocratique du Manifeste algérien* (UDMA), the body of Muslim clerics known collectively as the *ulema*; the Algerian Communist Party (PCA); and the *Mouvement national algérien* (MNA), against whom they battled constantly. Algeria contained an extremely diverse and notoriously fissiparous population, on which the FLN sometimes imposed itself in brutal ways. Still, even though the FLN contained some gifted leaders who made critical strategic choices and who managed to concoct a brilliant psyops campaign, it eventually emerged victorious largely because French counterinsurgency tactics managed in a few short years to discredit reformers, convince even moderate

Algerian Muslims that a radical break with France offered the only viable future, alienate the French population, and refocus Paris' goal from the defeat of the FLN and the perpetuation of *Algérie française* to a battle to reestablish the authority of the state over renegade counterinsurgency proponents.

Already in Indochina, the violence of French counterinsurgency tactics had driven many Vietnamese into the arms of the communists.[30] Rather than acknowledge that COIN tactics, whose lineage stretched back to Bugeaud, Gallieni, and Lyautey, failed to work as advertised, French counterinsurgents began to refine, codify, and transfer Indochina's operational "lessons" into Algeria in the belief that they simply had to perfect their COIN methods. Like Lyautey, Colonel Charles Lacheroy believed that his vision of social Catholicism could both unite the French army and forge a sense of national purpose in the French people through the imperial mission. Lacheroy insisted that communist-inspired subversive war was the conflict scenario of the future. For that reason, the entire army should transform into a counterinsurgency force on the grounds that conventional or nuclear contingencies were unlikely.[31] From 1953, as Director of Paris' *Centre d'études africaines et asiatiques* (CEAA), he led a select group of officers in the study of Mao, Liddell Hart, and T. E. Lawrence with the goal of "transforming the mentality of the political-military apparatus" to conduct a counterinsurgency struggle for the French Empire.[32] In order to defeat Mao's people's war, the French must uproot and resettle much of the population in order to protect them, create a psychological operations program guided by anthropologists, and a propaganda campaign that aimed to dehumanize the FLN and convince both Muslims and Frenchmen that the conflict in Algeria was about fighting communism and pan-Arabism, not perpetuating colonialism.[33] It was a recipe for failure that helped to eliminate the middle ground, straitjacketed imaginative political solutions more beneficial to French and Algerian interests, and ruptured both French civil-military and inter-military relations. But whatever influence Lacheroy and his disciples had on the mentality of French counterinsurgents, French population-centric tactics left a Muslim population not automatically inclined toward revolution with little choice but to coalesce behind the FLN by war's end. It is not going too far to argue that French COIN condemned the very cause of *Algérie française* that it was concocted to rescue, while it insured that defeat would prove politically, socially, psychologically, and morally traumatic for both countries.

COIN requires a global threat to justify the expenditure of so much blood and treasure in remote areas over long periods to a skeptical public that has other concerns. In 1954, the threat was configured in the form of the assertion that in Algeria, France faced a "revolutionary war" challenge manipulated by Moscow. This tendentious claim prompted French counterinsurgents to categorize Algeria as a domino in the great Cold War game, and the retention of Algeria as a zero-sum test for France's, and the West's, stamina, resolution, toughness, and moral fiber. In this way, the cause of *Algérie française* was cast as challenge in the best tradition of Lyautey by France's army to the French people, as a vehicle to recover France's self-respect and self-confidence in the wake of the humiliation of 1940, and a test of French moral rearmament and worthiness to play a global power role.[34] The communist threat scenario also incorporated a convenient alibi for defeat that could be transferred to a French population and government lacking the requisite qualities to prevail. The fact that the war in Algeria was pitched by counterinsurgents and their supporters as an ideological clash between Western democracy and communist barbarism, as well as redemption for World War II, made it more difficult for Paris to acknowledge the limits of French power and interests in North Africa.

Because counterinsurgency was seen as a test of national stamina and martial redemption, and because those returning from Indochinese POW camps had been impressed by communist brainwashing, French officers made psychological operations the central pillar of a campaign to control the war's narrative in both Algeria and France, but also internationally. The fundamental tenet of their operational approach was that the population, rather than the enemy's weapons systems, constituted the war's center of gravity. French counterinsurgents concluded that the Viet Minh had won because they had penetrated, propagandized, and psychologically manipulated the Vietnamese population. The effort to turn the psychological warfare tables in Algeria was not only an abject failure. It also brought the army directly into war politics via civil-military fusion, which occurred when special administrative and repressive powers delegated by the French Assembly to the Algerian Minister in 1956 were devolved upon the army. The assumption of wide governance, administrative, and police powers allowed the army to reconvert Algeria into "a military province" as in the days of Bugeaud.[35]

Given these circumstances, it may be a particular cause for concern that the French experience in Algeria has helped to shape

FM 3–24 through the works of David Galula, a French army major whose books *Pacification in Algeria 1956–1958* and *Counterinsurgency Warfare* made him the conduit to transfer France's Algerian experience into contemporary US doctrine: "'Of the many books that were influential in the writing of Field Manual 3–24,' say its coauthors, 'perhaps none was more important as David Galula's *Counterinsurgency Warfare*'," writes Galula biographer Ann Marlowe. Marlowe believes that Galula's "rigor, analytical sophistication, and capacity for self-criticism" as well as stylistic clarity explains why two tracts written in the early 1960s by an obscure French major with limited operational experience caught the eye of the authors of *FM 3–24*. "To American military intellectuals, Galula's practices were a revelation," Marlowe asserts; among them the importance of defending the population, of information operations, the requirement to "deal with root causes" of insurgency, and the benefits of civil-military fusion with the military assuming many governance and police functions.[36]

Why these standard counterinsurgency practices came as a "revelation" is unclear, as they had been on the books at least since the late nineteenth century and available to even a moderately assiduous student of military history. More likely Galula was attractive to the authors of *FM 3–24* for at least three other reasons. First, he stands firmly in the small wars tradition of viewing counterinsurgency with its overwhelmingly tactical focus, its studied ignorance of Clausewitz's warnings about the irrational influences that escalate war's intensity, and the intense politicization of its practitioners as a category distinct from conventional warfare. For counterinsurgents, tactics became the end-all, a formula that if properly applied would win such contests, irrespective of the strategic environment, just so long as governments have the stamina to see the enterprise through to a successful conclusion. Second, Galula allowed the authors of *FM 3–24* to isolate the French army's frequently innovative tactical adaptations in Algeria from its context of racism, brutality, and the implosion of French civil-military relations. Galula is acceptable to modern COIN-dinistas because he sanitized his account of the Algerian war into a description of how from August 1956 to October 1957 he sought to "reassure, support and control the population" of the Djebel Aïssa Mimoun in the Kabylia region of Algeria.[37] He does not actually admit that he tortured suspects picked up at random in the streets, although it is implied in his narrative.

Finally, he apparently phoned in sick during the April 1961 putsch against de Gaulle, an act of prudence that allowed him to avoid charges of treason. Galula's description of French COIN as "armed social work" among grateful Muslims is far less forthcoming than is General Paul Aussaresses' 2001 *The Battle of the Casbah* with his descriptions of the torture and disappearance of Muslims by the French army, collective reprisals and summary executions integral to French COIN that Aussaresses claimed correctly were condoned in the highest circles of the French government and covered by the Special Decree of July 1, 1955.[38] Aussaresses became military attaché in Washington, taught counterinsurgency tactics at the US Army Special Warfare School at Fort Bragg, North Carolina in the run-up to Vietnam in the early 1960s, and in the 1970s instructed officers in the Brazilian and Chilean forces on the finer points of "subversive warfare," which they applied against their own populations.[39] But that was then. Today, Galula fits the purposes for COIN enthusiasts in search of an obscure saint ostensibly unaffiliated with the inquisitorial unpleasantness and military mutiny of *Algérie française*, as the patriarch of their new monastic order.[40]

In his forward to Galula's *Pacification in Algeria 1956–1958*, American counter-terrorism expert Bruce Hoffmann explains that Galula's methods were so successful in his sector of the Kabylia in 1956–1957 that "the rebel's higher echelons abandoned the Aissa Mimoun range as a lost cause."[41] However, French researcher Grégor Mathias, who has compared Galula's claims with the archival record of operations in the Djebel Aïssa Mimoun during Galula's tenure there, found that while Galula's methods did account for some short-term successes, the French colonel exaggerated his accomplishments in the Kabylia. In 1956–1957, Galula was participating in a localized experiment in which the French saturated an area which in fact already had a low instance of FLN activity, with troops and resources.[42] But the point is that the French could neither sustain a high operational intensity nor commit that level of resources throughout Algeria for an extended period of time. Therefore, while some of his methods like stationing platoons of soldiers in the villages, issuing ID cards, requiring passes to travel, and so on caused the local *Armée de libération nationale* (ALN) contingent to shift to a neighboring region or simply go to ground, he never managed to eliminate the FLN in the Djebel Aïssa Mimoun, which continued to rebuild its cadres, collect taxes, distribute propaganda, assassinate collaborationist Muslims so as to intimidate the local population, and undermine Galula's attempts to consolidate a solid Muslim constituency for the French. Nor did sewing classes, schools, and random sweeps to collect young men for interrogation solve the fundamental political problem which led to rebellion in the first place – the system of apartheid under which Algerian Muslims lived in a society dominated by a minority of white settlers, the *pieds noirs*. Indeed, Mathias recognizes that in the absence of any viable pan-Algerian movement of Muslims favorable to *Algérie française*, those who chose to collaborate with the French on the local level usually did so at the sufferance of the FLN.[43]

But Galula's message is that, had the French applied these counterinsurgent tactics throughout Algeria, they would have emerged victorious. This is music to COIN-dinista ears because it reinforces the Jominian license to ignore the strategic context in which counterinsurgencies are fought. The COIN-dinista mantra is that the counterinsurgency formula invariably succeeds if it is not hijacked by conventional soldiers or sabotaged by impatient governments and peoples. The inevitable perils of COIN – the limits of military intervention's transformative impact on regional and in-country dynamics; the inexplicable ingratitude shown by populations liberated and reformed at the muzzle of foreign rifles; the politicization of the military through civil-military fusion and fear of the stab in the back; the militarization of security at home in the face of political dissent and the alleged globalized threat; the high risk of human rights violations in a racialized, frequently sectarian combat environment; the dissipation of national resources in hopelessly utopian social engineering projects; the diversion of the nation's strategic focus from more important concerns; the high potential for damage to diplomatic credibility and national reputation; the degradation of the military's conventional warfare skills; and so on – remain unspoken.

Taking Galula at his word, how did he win on his front while French soldiers elsewhere in Algeria stumbled toward defeat? Galula's answer is that the French never really applied COIN tactics in Algeria, because if one applies the tactical formula correctly, COIN cannot fail. However, the truth is that, contrary to Galula's claims, the French did obey most of his tactical prescriptions in Algeria. In doing so, they not only lost, but failed catastrophically. In fact, French COIN tactics helped to transform the FLN from a minor conspiracy into the vanguard of a people's war. In the process, by pushing the COIN principle of civil-military fusion over the precipice of politicization, French COIN-dinistas refocused Paris' objective from the defeat of the indigenous insurgency to mastering the mutiny of its rebellious soldiers. At the same time, almost single-handedly, Galula and his COIN-dinista colleagues actually handed the FLN a victory they might otherwise have been hard-pressed to achieve and challenged the very Western democratic principles they claimed to be defending.

David Galula's top ten prescriptions for counterinsurgency success

Galula's prescriptions are disordered and somewhat overlapping, but can be distilled to ten basic rules beginning with his assertion that successful counterinsurgency requires a doctrine. Galula complained that the French army lacked a doctrine at the beginning of the Algerian conflict. "In my zone, as everywhere in Algeria, the order was to 'pacify.' But exactly how? The sad truth was that, in spite of all our past experience, we had no single, official doctrine for counterinsurgency warfare."[44] Galula is certainly correct that French counterinsurgency practices were evolving as the army transitioned from Indochina to Algeria in 1954–1955. Professional units like the Foreign Legion were demoralized and under strength following Dien Bien Phu.[45] The army in

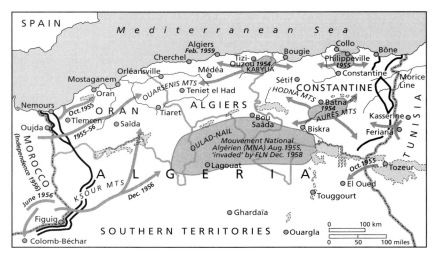

Map 4 Algeria

Algeria had been topped up with French conscripts sent from Germany with no counterinsurgency training, and who initially were out of sync with Indochina veterans.

Nevertheless, Galula's assertion that the French army was counterinsurgency clueless in the early months of the Algerian War is not only disingenuous, but also untrue. Galula writes in the opening pages of *Pacification in Algeria* that after eleven years spent studying insurgency in China, Indochina, and Greece, "I wanted to test certain theories I had formed on counterinsurgency warfare."[46] He was assigned to the 45th Colonial Infantry Battalion, whose job was to maintain French sovereignty in the colonies, in a specially designated "experimental" area to test counterinsurgency methods.[47] These local counterinsurgency experiments, begun quietly in 1955 in places like the Kabylia, went public during the 1957 Battle of Algiers before being generalized throughout Algeria in the Challe offensive of 1959.[48]

So, from the very beginning of the Algerian conflict, the French army established a thoroughly systematic approach to developing and then generalizing counterinsurgency doctrine and practice throughout the army. Doctrine is a trailing indicator of inherited practices and a receptive intellectual environment, combined with tactical and operational routines developed by units to meet current contingencies. In practice, the French colonial army in which Galula served, where Lyautey's peaceful penetration and his insistence on indirect rule as the foundation of imperial governance enjoyed iconic status, counted more than a century of experience with colonial pacification. More recently, the French army had just emerged from the Indochina War armed with the doctrine of *la guerre révolutionnaire*, the belief that the French Empire was targeted by an international communist conspiracy and that the French army should reorganize and redoctrinize to fight it. This threat to the empire justified a highly political and proactive role for the military.[49] Finally, counterinsurgency experimentation had been the order of the day in the latter stages of the Indochina conflict. So inherited practice, a receptive intellectual environment, and tactical and operational experimentation quickly translated into formalized doctrine. Because from the first months of the war support for counterinsurgency was strong in the French General Staff, the French War College, and in the highest political levels, the French army quickly wrote doctrinal manuals for small-unit tactics, psychological warfare, and helicopter and air support to counterinsurgency operations, and also produced a continuous stream of war college studies on regional adaptations to counterinsurgency in Algeria.[50] So, Galula to the contrary, by 1956 if not before, the French army had plenty of small wars experience as well as formalized counter-insurgency doctrine to draw on. Indeed, Mathias speculates that because Galula's two postwar works for which he is celebrated in counterinsurgency circles are so poorly sourced, surprisingly after stints at Harvard and RAND, he may have been totally ignorant of the vast literature, official and unofficial, on COIN.[51]

One of the lessons repatriated from Indochina and for which a doctrine was quickly established was the importance of psychological operations. Under the influence of Raoul Salan and Charles Lacheroy, psychological operations were to become an independent arm, in their view far more central than yesterday's weapons, like tanks or artillery, to success in *la guerre subversive*. Lacheroy laid out three rules for victory over *la guerre révolutionnaire*: don't fight it with an army organized in divisions (i.e. a conventional force); with a peacetime administrative structure (thus the requirement for civil-military fusion with its subsequent politicization of the military); or under the Napoleonic Code. (i.e. within a legal framework).[52] When added to his strong social Catholic sentiments about the requirement to indoctrinate the French population, his open contempt for democracy which he saw as weak compared to the superior social and psychological mobilization capacities of communist regimes, Lacheroy and his psyops disciples were a military *pronunciamento* in the making.[53]

Led by Lacheroy and future *golpista* General Raoul Salan, the French army's counterinsurgency mafia rapidly seized direction of the war through the *Service d'action psychologique et d'information* (SAPI) in April 1956 that became the *5e* (psychological operations) *bureau* the following year. A *Centre d'instruction et de preparation à la contre-guerrilla* was created in June 1956 to instruct officers and NCOs on "Muslim society and psychology" followed by a *Centre d'entrainement à la guerre subversive* and a *Centre d'instruction à la pacification et à la contre-guérilla* (CIPCG) in 1958, where 8,000 officers and NCOs were taught "interrogation" techniques using water and electric shock.[54]

The French army found its stride as it rapidly adopted population-centric *quadrillage, regroupement* of the Muslim population, expansion of the *sections administratives specialisées* – an updated version of the Arab Bureau – creation of auto-defense groups, oil spot reclamation of territory, inter-arm cooperation of infantry, artillery, and air support, and the harmonization of operations between mobile and sector troops that featured mobile "tactical groups" spearheaded by the *groupement parachutiste d'intervention* that pioneered the use of helicopters for mobility, and so on.[55] In fact, the French army's swift tactical adaptation caused the ALN serious embarrassment by 1958. The problem was not, as Galula asserts, that the French army lacked a doctrine for Algeria. The real issue is that the more the army appeared to gain the tactical upper hand, the more they became convinced that victory lay within their grasp, the more they feared that they would be stabbed in the back by a treacherous government or pusillanimous people, the more that the army and its *pied noir* constituency resisted political compromises and defied government policies to contain or end the war. Therefore, the irony of Algeria was that tactical proficiency made ultimate victory less, not more likely as French counterinsurgents persisted in their pursuit of total victory over the FLN and its armed wing the ALN.

A second irony about French tactical proficiency was that it was a wasting asset, because it consolidated support behind the FLN, undermined patience in the French population, shamed and demoralized French conscripts who recognized that they replicated Oradour-sur-Glane, the signature 1944 SS massacre of civilians in France, on a daily basis in Algeria, and radicalized a colonial military willing to sacrifice fundamental standards of human rights and professional restraint written into the laws of conventional conflict in the name of victory.[56] The French had a doctrine. The problem was that their notions of colonial control were anchored in impatience, racism, and brutality. Small wars were also considered unlimited ones, especially for officers of the *5e bureau* who believed that they were waging a *guerre totale* against a communist-orchestrated insurgency, in which it was difficult to distinguish friend from foe. For this reason, torture, a tactic used in Indochina, quickly appeared in Algeria as "an unlimited weapon deployed in a total war to dominate the population," writes French historian Raphaëlle Branche. It functioned as "a warning to everyone. Even the rumor (of torture) served to propagate its terrorizing dimension throughout the population ... (as) a constant reminder of French power." Torture was not merely a tactic, but "the unilateral expression of a political conflict."[57] Galula, a Tunisian Jew raised in Casablanca who had witnessed at close quarters how the French managed a protectorate, surely understood that. Nevertheless, Galula insisted on the importance of humane treatment to captured insurgents. "Throughout the war our prisoner camps were open for unannounced inspection by the International Red Cross, the reports of which were made public ." The truth however, was that captured men – insurgents or otherwise – were routinely tortured to elicit the intelligence the French failed to obtain by more subtle methods. One hundred and ninety-eight FLN supporters were guillotined with escalatory consequences for violence that led directly to the Battle of Algiers largely because the army insisted that the FLN were criminals who deserved execution and the political leaders of the Fourth Republic proved too gutless to face them down. Countless others, like Ben M'Hidi, simply disappeared. Proportionally, the number of Muslim dead during the eight-year undeclared war in Algeria equaled that of France in World War I, although not all deaths are attributable to French-initiated violence.[58] Needless to say, Galula's methods, especially when applied on a large scale as during the so-called "Battle of Algiers" in 1956–1957, caused many young men and women to flee into the arms of the FLN precisely to avoid French arrest, interrogation, and execution, and turned Muslim survivors into bitter enemies of the French army.[59]

If an army had a counterinsurgency doctrine in place, then it was better placed to smother an insurgency in the cradle. Galula's second prescription required the early recognition of insurgency as the starting point for proactive action. He complained that the French failed to recognize the budding insurgency in Algeria until it had already begun to gain momentum. "By the time the insurrection was finally recognized for what it was, only drastic political and military action would have reversed the tide, and slowly in any case."[60] The assumption here seems to be that an early demonstration of force will intimidate the population into neutrality. This was certainly consistent with how the French ran Algeria, as an occupation based on force. But there were two reasons why Paris may have failed immediately to recognize that it faced a popular insurgency, beginning with the fact that there *was* no popular insurgency in Algeria, at least until France created one by 1956 when all Algerian nationalist groups with the exception of FLN rival *Mouvement national algérien* had been closed down, their leaders and adherents arrested, or rallied to the FLN. The FLN, an organization formed by nine men in October 1954, claimed a minuscule popular following among Algeria's 9 million Muslims and practically no weapons in the first two years of the war. Moderate Algerian nationalists at first denounced the FLN as "adventurers" inspired by the myth of Abd-el-Kader and a popular folklore that romanticized bandits. FLN actions in the first year of the war were limited to isolated farm burnings and assassinations of moderate Muslim leaders, mainly in the eastern region of the country, in the lightly policed Aurès mountains in the southeast, and among Berbers in the mountainous Kabylia east of Algiers where rebellion had sparked in 1947. Only with the coordinated FLN attacks on August 20, 1955 in the Nord-Constantinois did French Resident Minister Jacques Soustelle abandon liberal reform measures designed to preempt Muslim discontent and opt for a more vigorous policy of repression, the first step in turning a minority mutiny into an insurrection. Until then, Algeria seemed to be quiet. French attentions were focused on more serious nationalist agitation in Madagascar, Morocco, and Tunisia, not to mention Indochina.[61]

Galula's contention that the insurrection must be recognized early and that the incumbent forces must "learn" to configure themselves quickly into a COIN-centric force if they were to have any hope of success is a frequent one among COIN proponents. The assumption is that there is a brief window of opportunity to pounce on the insurgency while it is small, relatively undeveloped, and has yet to spread its tentacles into the population. A failure to move early means that blame can be shifted onto politicians and civilian administrators eager to avoid trouble on their watch. Slow learning because, as Galula claimed, the French military had no counterinsurgency doctrine in place, allows blame for defeat to be shifted to unimaginative, conventionally minded soldiers.

There are several fallacies in Galula's argument, but let's begin with the more interesting question: What would the French have done had they somehow divined the problem earlier? After failure to secure Palestine in 1948, and as a direct consequence of the high costs in monetary and moral terms of the counterinsurgency campaign against the Kikuyu in Kenya, London recognized that what Prime Minister Harold Macmillan called "the wind of change" in 1960 required a policy of handing off power in the colonies to moderates.[62] France should have moved from the interwar years to integrate moderate Muslim groups in Algeria into the political process. There were several warning signs beginning with the Sétif uprising in 1945, after which General Raymond Duval warned that repression had bought Algeria perhaps a decade of peace, and the realization that nationalist agitation in Tunisia and Morocco would sooner or later infect Algerian Muslims, that should have prodded France to substitute their policy of racial and religious apartheid for either full integration or some version of Algerian self-determination. But the army and militant *pied noir* settlers who had combined to put down Sétif with exemplary ferocity would have sabotaged that, just as the military had deliberately scuppered negotiations with Ho Chi Minh in 1946. Indeed, Marie-Monique Robin argues that the whole point of *la guerre subversive* doctrine with its concomitant tactics of psychological action, population concentration, and torture was to sabotage a political solution.[63]

All the harbingers of trouble were swept under the political carpet.[64] But to be fair to the Fourth Republic, only gradually did it become apparent that the November 1, 1954 bomb blasts had inaugurated a War for Algerian Independence. From early 1955, it created a legal framework for repression capped by the March 1956 Special Powers Act, initiated some reformist measures to increase Muslim participation in political life, and called some *pied noir* reservists back to active duty. Only the Philippeville massacres of August 1955, initiated by the FLN to jump-start a stalled insurrection and assert its primacy over other Muslim political organizations, convinced Paris that it faced a significant crisis in North Africa and not isolated pockets of lawlessness. And it reacted with dispatch to expand the reserve call-up and retain conscripts in their units beyond their mandatory period of national service, both extremely unpopular measures that led to riots and protests. This was part of a plan to surge troop strength in Algeria to 450,000 by 1957 based on the view that this would demonstrate French resolve and overwhelm the insurrection with a *levée en masse*.[65] But repression combined with tepid reforms would not work, because, despite the fact that in the government's view the role of the army was to arbitrate a communal bloodletting by assuming a neutral position, both sides targeted moderates, the settler community was racist and intractable, and the army remained intent on scoring a victory against an insurgency it believed was inspired by Cairo and Moscow. The government's fundamental dilemma was that it had no good policy options: either France would have to integrate 9 million Algerian Muslims – roughly one-fifth of the population of greater France – into the national community with full rights of citizenship and a significant package of economic development to alleviate Algeria's grinding poverty and 85 percent illiteracy rate; or continue to repress Algerian Muslims and deny their rights, a path to financial ruin and diplomatic isolation; or some sort of interim solution with Franco-Muslim cohabitation as a stepping stone to partition into Muslim and *pied noir*-dominated enclaves or association under a moderate, pro-French Algerian government. In short, if the problem in Algeria was indeed one of learning, it was on the political, not the tactical, level where the lessons remained to be discovered.

Quick victory through early detection and action against an insurgency would minimize the impact of the media on public opinion. Galula's third prescription evoked the stab in the back by the media when he argued that the FLN realized the "greatest psychological effect on the French and on world opinion at the cheapest price by stepping up terrorism in the main cities, notably in Algiers, which served as head-quarters to most French and foreign correspondents and thus acted as a natural amplifier."[66] The first thing to note is that press stories about the violence in Algeria were not all one-sided – FLN terror in the form of bombings, assassinations, and massacres directed mainly against its MNA rival but also against Europeans in North Africa was extensively reported, which elicited condemnations from left-wing intellectuals and reinforced the stay-the-course arguments of *Algérie française* hard-liners in the government.[67] But it was neither the FLN nor the press that turned the Battle of Algiers into a French defeat. In fact, the FLN decision to take their insurrection into the heartland of settler Algeria where 300,000 *pieds noirs* lived with a series of high-profile bombings of targets in the European quarters of Algiers on September 30, 1956 was the product of an escalation of violence that began with the beheading by the French of FLN POWs, which prompted the FLN to attack European civilians, which in turn provoked an over-extended police force to counter-terrorize Muslim neighborhoods with bombs, the most notorious being that of August 10, 1956 in the Casbah's rue de Thèbes that killed an estimated seventy Muslims. It was also based on a faulty FLN net assessment. France, the FLN believed, was nearly bank-rupt and diplomatically isolated, while the government of Prime Minister Guy Mollet was increasingly unpopular. A surge into Algiers would produce an "Algerian Dien Bien Phu," as the French army would be forced to fall back to defend European neighborhoods against a tidal wave of Muslims, or so imagined the strategy's main architect Larbi Ben M'hidi.[68]

On the tactical level, it was the FLN who was delivered a Dien Bien Phu by the 10th Paratroop Division under General Jacques Massu, accorded full powers in January 1957 to clear the FLN out of Algiers. Massu accomplished his task with grim efficiency selecting his techniques from the usual COIN menu that included the *ratonade* ("mouse-hunt," an army sweep of Muslim areas to arrest "suspects"), heavy psyops saturation of Muslim neighborhoods with loud-speaker teams and pamphlets, and population lockdown with curfews, *quadrillage* (segmenting) of the Kasbah, informants, internment, torture, and "suicides" of high-profile FLN prisoners like Ben M'Hidi, unconvincingly choreographed by Paul Aussaresses.

The Battle of Algiers should have been a defeat for the FLN because their main objectives – take pressure off ALN units in the countryside, provoke a popular Muslim insurrection in Algiers, and convince the French to depart – had been defeated by the French reaction. Much of the senior FLN leadership fled Algiers to the disgust of grassroots fighters. Turned former FLN operatives fingered many mid-level commanders who remained. But by October 1957, the French army had transformed a tactical victory over the FLN into a strategic defeat.[69] The Battle of Algiers, launched in a period when French public opinion firmly supported *Algérie française*, exposed to public view the violence of the French counter-terror methods that the mainland press had been reporting since January 1955, and even earlier, to no avail. Now both international and French public opinion increasingly questioned the legitimacy of a rule that relied on such extra-legal methods. The press was simply one voice in a growing chorus of protest from 1957 against COIN methods that included priests, but also conscripts, reservists, and even senior military figures like General Jacques Pâris de la Bollardière, shocked that torture had become standard operating practice in their army. This and the growing number of disappearances reported by the press were condemned by the President of the Paris bar and other high-profile jurists as contrary to French law. But this did nothing to diminish government support for Massu's decapitation campaign. Mollet's government was brought down with a vote of no confidence in May 1957, not over the brutality of its campaign in Algeria, but because COIN costs threatened national solvency sending the franc into a tailspin.[70]

Psyops companies created in June 1956 in each division, whose goal was to "reestablish a climate of confidence" by explaining French goals in Algeria, were forced instead six months later to justify French counterinsurgency methods as a legitimate response to FLN terrorism,[71] all of which demonstrated the futility of psyops when the message lacks credibility. Like the 1948 repatriation to Germany of the passengers of the *Exodus* or the 1968 Tet offensive in Vietnam, 1957 and the Battle of Algiers proved to be the turning point that began to shift popular opinion toward a negotiated outcome to the war.[72] While popular pessimism about the prospects for a military victory did not end the war in Algeria, it helped over time to isolate the army politically and accorded Charles de Gaulle the leeway to bury *Algérie française* after 132 years.

If Galula believed that French public opinion should be spared the details of COIN methods as a requirement for maintaining popular support for a counterinsurgency, it was surely because even bedrock COIN techniques inflicted such misery on the people they are meant to save. Galula's fourth prescription was the familiar COIN adage that one must separate the population from the rebels, taking care not to antagonize the former. This population-centric strategy required population concentration, the issuing of identity papers, food rationing, house searches, curfews, and the creation of self-defense groups among other things. Mathias points out that these measures, implemented by Galula who based them on his observations of Chinese communists methods, were not entirely successful, because people had no surnames, birthdays were unrecorded, women objected to being photographed, and it was impossible to control influxes of people on market days. Those fined, put under house arrest, or beaten for infractions of the rules saw the entire counterinsurgency system as unfair, illegal, and without appeal, a product of the army assuming responsibility for justice from 1956. Self-defense groups had to be disarmed because their members deserted, failed to act, or were otherwise infiltrated by the FLN. In fact, Galula's attempts to enlist Muslims in self-defense groups produced at best ambiguous results – a Muslim's agreement to serve as a *harki* was not simply a sign of loyalty to France.[73]

Because the French could not stabilize the villages where the Muslim population lived, they transported them to camps where they could better control them. As concentration had acquired horrendous connotations during World War II, the French replaced it with *regroupement*, which was first instituted in the Aurès Mountains of southeastern Algeria in 1955. By 1957, resettlement was in full swing, as literally hundreds of thousands of Muslims were rounded up in their villages and deposited into camps where "the greatest anarchy" reigned. Separated from their land, the inmates sold their farm animals to eat, and then starved in conditions of deprivation and a hygienic Armageddon that provoked popular furor when revealed in a series of scathing articles by the French daily *Le Monde* in April 1959. The mismanagement of the Algerian resettlement camps by the French army created an uproar in France similar to that experienced in Britain during the Boer War.[74] By October 1960, fully 1.7 million Algerian Muslims – almost 19 percent of the Muslim population – had been crammed into these camps. Vincent Joly concludes that, more than any other counterinsurgency tactic applied in Algeria, *"regroupement* forged a popular consensus among Muslims for independence."[75] Furthermore, resettlement failed to separate the population from the insurgents, who continued to infiltrate the French-supervised camps.[76] Despite the abject failure of this tactic, the alienation of both French and Muslim opinion, and direct orders from the government after 1958, the army refused to abandon *regroupement*, because counterinsurgency dogma required it, not the least because it cleared the countryside to create "white" or free-fire zones where any human being found roaming there could be blasted as an insurgent.

While classic COIN doctrine requires winning the hearts and minds of the indigenous population, French counterinsurgents seemed to view all Algerian Muslims as potential traitors which justified concentrating them in fetid camps. Therefore, Galula's fifth prescription of counterinsurgency success follows logically that one must "distinguish between the people and the rebels . . . Outwardly treat every civilian as a friend; inwardly you must consider him as a rebel ally until you have positive proof to the contrary." In other words, the assumption was that Algerian Muslims had been won over by the FLN, which they definitely had not been in the period that Galula refers to (1956–1957). French COIN tactics, based on these erroneous assumptions of disloyalty, required Muslim males to be arrested, interrogated, tortured, concentrated, organized into auto-defense groups, and bombarded with propaganda.[77] The onus was on the locals to prove that they did not even passively support the insurgency. Galula executed *ratonades* in Muslim neighborhoods and markets to make indiscriminate arrests of local men in groups of no fewer than four; he would hold them in separate cells and interrogate them until one ratted out the others. Then he was "kind" to the person who spilled the beans on his compatriots by impressing him into a French-led self-defense group, which was no guarantee of survival.[78] Many Muslims compromised in this way had no choice but to flee to France. The others were sent to jail, their families deprived of the breadwinner; all likely became dedicated FLN converts at this point.

11 Algerian women like this ALN insurgent became "the lifeblood of the maquis." Despite claiming inspiration from French COIN theorist David Galula, who emphasized the importance of appealing to women, the 2006 edition of *FM* 3–24 contains no entry for women or female in its index.

Curiously among all this distrust and violence, Galula's sixth prescription for success in Algeria called for the promotion of women's rights: "I thought that the Kabyle women, given their subjugated condition, would naturally be on our side if we emancipated them."[79] In strategic terms, a campaign to win over Muslim women to the French cause made sense. Some Muslim women in Algiers burned their veils during the May 1958 settler-Muslim fraternization that accompanied the fall of the Fourth Republic and the arrival of Charles de Gaulle, although this was most probably coerced by French psyops officers like Trinquier. The French also recognized that bringing Muslim women into the political and social mainstream supported their contention that they were the progressive forces in Algeria, not the FLN. French psyops produced films like *The Falling Veil, Arab Women of the Bled* and *Women, Blessing of God* largely intended for foreign audiences. In September 1958, de Gaulle forcefully appealed to Muslim women to vote for the first time, telling them: "this enshrines your equality with men." In like vein, women's education was expanded, professional opportunities were opened for them in the public sector, and laws were introduced liberalizing marriage and divorce.[80]

The French also recognized that Muslim women were vital to the success of the insurgency. About 2,000 women were serving in ALN ranks by 1956 as nurses, couriers, and in other non-combatant, largely logistical duties. Women had played a vital role during the Battle of Algiers, to enforce boycotts and strikes, organize demonstrations, smuggle weapons and supplies, plant bombs, disseminate propaganda, as intelligence gathers, and so on, to the point that they became "the lifeblood of the maquis." As soon as the ALN secured an area, they appealed to the women for practical support. Recognizing this, the French had created 223 mobile medical units by 1961 whose purpose was to encourage "Muslim women to participate in public life."[81]

While embarking upon a program of women's liberation in the 1950s ironically placed French counterinsurgents, along with Simone de Beauvoir, in the feminist vanguard, Galula's divide-and-rule gender strategy did little to offset the fact that France had invested little in Muslim development. This was especially true of women, only one in sixteen of whom had received any formal schooling. French repression in the aftermath of Sétif seemed to betray the promise of liberation, which drove both women and Muslim veterans of the French army toward Algerian nationalism. Rural hatred for the French was strong in 1954 and only increased as Muslim women and their families were uprooted and "regrouped" in insanitary camps, where their houses were continually searched by soldiers using racist language, their families starved and children died while their menfolk were arrested and tortured.[82] A minimalist interpretation of Galula's prescription would translate into girls' schools, clinics, and army-sponsored sewing circles, which might prompt women to put in a good word for the French at the dinner table. But this model presumes both the dinner and the table.[83] At best, these measures allowed the insurgency to claim that the French only offered improvements because their legitimacy was being challenged. It was also a non-starter because, to paraphrase Henry Kissinger, there is simply too much fraternization with the enemy for a "battle of the sexes" COIN strategy to work.[84]

Lugard and Lyautey would have cautioned that tinkering with indigenous gender relationships offers a formula for cultural catastrophe. Women are central to a man's honor in a patriarchal Muslim society where they provide domestic labor and male heirs and solidify social relationships through arranged marriages and clan and family ties. In the imperial context, outreach to females allowed the insurgency to claim that the occupier was waging a cultural and religious war against the indigenous population, assaulting male honor by taking his land and seducing his female family members with Western mores and fantasies of gender equality, and by turning Muslim women into harlots – an accusation given credibility by the fact that since Bugeaud the French had used rape as an instrument of conquest.[85]

Finally, to paraphrase Andrew Bacevitch, what does dabbling in social engineering experiments have to do with soldiering and war?[86] Quite apart from its questionable assumptions anchored in development theory that populations are biddable if promised security and a higher standard of living, for soldiers COIN is a sub-professional category that at best requires petty war skills.[87] At worst, in the view of its proponents like Lacheroy, Galula, and Aussaresses, COIN requires a professional makeover so that its practitioners convert into policemen, administrators, and social workers, violate the laws of war and humanity as a condition for victory, and become politically *engagé*. Moreover, COIN is simply updated imperialism: Bacevich quotes an American officer in Iraq who argued that, "With a heavy dose of fear and violence, and a lot of money for projects, I think we can convince these people that we are here to help them," expressing a view that would have been understood by a nineteenth-century British officer.[88]

The requirement to abandon the military's core professional tasks is required by Galula's seventh prescription, that the army must turn to policing as its central mission. This blurring of missions and definitions was necessary in Algeria because there was a dearth of police to keep the peace, particularly once the unrest began in earnest. *Pieds noirs* also resisted the importation of police from the mainland, preferring those recruited from their own community. From the moment that the *état d'urgence* was decreed on March 18, 1955, the army began to replace the police in many areas. The army took over the police functions in January 1957 in Algiers and integrated policemen into military units, where they became fronts for extra-legal methods.

The assumption of civil enforcement duties enticed the military to overstep the bounds of legality in part because soldiers make lousy cops. They have no experience in solving crimes, apprehending suspects based on probable cause, or collecting evidence that will stand up in court. Few spoke Arabic or one of the Berber dialects. Their goal was to collect actionable intelligence to ferret out terrorists hiding in the population to intern, torture, and disappear them. These acts did not make the Muslim population feel more secure – *au contraire*! In the view of the military, every Muslim was a suspect. For instance, although the 10th Paratroop Division inherited police intelligence files in Algiers in 1956, paratroopers proved to be totally incompetent as policemen, capable only of imposing repressive and arbitrary curfews, lockdowns, house invasions, and mass arrests on a people who, as Galula admonished, "you must consider . . . as a rebel ally until you have positive proof to the contrary." In fact, the army acting in a police role translated into "the militarization of legality" and an exercise in counter-terror justified in the army's mind since Bugeaud by the conviction that it was fighting a ruthless, immoral, fanaticized enemy.[89] Turning soldiers into policemen offers yet another example of how COIN diverts soldiers from their core mission, undermines military professionalism, fosters civil-military fusion, and hence politicization of the military. It acted as the fulfillment of Lacheroy's admonition that one cannot fight a counterinsurgency while respecting the tenets of the Code Napoléon. Therefore, "justice" seems arbitrary and ruthless to the subject population on the receiving end and serves to delegitimize the counterinsurgency.

The policeman's focus on apprehending the criminal rather than on devising a strategy that encompasses the political and military dimensions of the battle space, tempts COIN into decapitation strategies anchored in the certainty that a basically apolitical and contented population has been led astray or terrorized by a handful of criminals, whose removal will return things to normal. In his eighth point, Galula wisely cautions that this may not be so. In Algeria, the decapitation strategy followed by the French "had little effect on the direction of the rebellion, because the movement was too loosely organized to crumble under such a blow."[90] Here Galula is both right for the wrong reason and flat wrong. Treating the insurgency as a criminal tribe may provide psychological and moral certainty to the counterinsurgent. However, it denies the political character of unrest and allowed the FLN to define the political narrative.[91] The FLN was also too balkanized an organization to be vulnerable to a decapitation strategy, although the French certainly tried with their tactic of *raillements collectives ou individuelles*. In another sense, however, French decapitation tactics had a huge effect on the direction of the rebellion by further radicalizing it. French authorities reacted to the outbreak of violence in November 1954 by arresting reformist Muslim leaders because their names were in the police files. In October 1956, the French army, acting on an intelligence tip and without permission from Paris, forced a plane owned by the Sultan of Morocco which was carrying five leaders of the FLN, including the relatively moderate Mohamed Ahmed Ben Bella, to land in Algiers. Ben Bella and his like were replaced by more intransigent men from the military wing like Houari Boumédienne. As the lines hardened on both sides, Muslim Algerians were forced to choose between the continuation of the *pied noir* apartheid regime backed by military repression or uniting behind the FLN.

Ninth, Galula emphasizes the importance of an effective information operations campaign: "If there was a field in which we were definitely and infinitely more stupid than our opponents, it was propaganda."[92] This may have been true, but it was not because the French had failed to recognize the importance of infowar. It was just that they had no sellable message, at least to Muslims. The *5e bureau* was created in 1945 and re-formed into a *bureau de guerre psychologique* by 1953 as Lacheroy and Salan prepared to inculcate the military with the principles of *la guerre subversive*. In Algeria, psyops was the particular focus of Colonel Roger Trinquier, who leveraged the Battle of Algiers to expand pamphlet and loud-speaker companies, as well as cinema teams whose goals were "to uphold the morale of French troops and keep the rural masses from being contaminated." Officers and NCOs were formed in the *Centre d'entrainement de la guerre subversive*. In August 1957 in the wake of the Suez expedition, the *5e bureau* was tasked with shaping operations so that they would achieve the maximum psychological and human impact through the creation of an ideology of *Algérie française* to counter the *Algérie algérienne* vision of the FLN. It was to "re-establish a climate of confidence" and "convince (French forces) of the realities of *la guerre révolutionnaire*."[93]

Galula fails to note two things: first, the psyops campaign run in the Djebel Aïssa Mimoun under his watch, which consisted of showing

World War II films of French glories and organizing political meetings, came close to farcical.[94] And while the French campaign became more sophisticated over time by appealing to Muslim women and vilifying the FLN as a gang of thugs, the chief architect of FLN psyops Abbane Ramdane ran circles around the *guerre subversive* crowd by creating symbols of Algerian independence like a flag and a national anthem, organized boycotts of French cafés, cinemas, and products like cigarettes, orchestrated the defection of Muslim players from the French national team on the eve of the World Cup, and propagated the FLN message of Muslim unity through declarations published in a clandestine press which isolated those moderates willing to compromise with the French, as well as the FLN's major rival, the MNA.[95]

Galula also fails to recognize that if French psyops enjoyed little success with Muslims, it proved very influential among French counter-insurgents and played a central role in the politicization of the French army, largely because it was directed at France as much as Algeria. French soldiers led by Charles Lacheroy inherited in full measure the colonialist belief that the greatest impediment to victory was defeatism at home. Defeatism constituted the inescapable spinoff of democratic values and a multi-party system that failed to impart the ideological cohesion and social and moral discipline required to confront a monolithic revolutionary enemy. This mindset was long established in the French colonial army, at least since Bugeaud and his acolytes had railed against the ingratitude of French humanitarians. Lyautey reinforced this sense of alienation when he combined social Catholicism with the imperial mission to argue that imperialism would preserve traditional tribal social structures and guarantee justice for imperial subjects thus insulating them against nationalist movements.[96] This attitude helps to explain why during World War II the colonial army remained stubbornly loyal to Vichy whose leader Philippe Pétain represented the paternalistic, Catholic values spurned by the secular Third Republic. At the same time, the civilizing mission of imperialism would revivify a decadent republic while it inspired and moralized its citizens. In this tradition, French proponents of *la guerre révolutionnaire* promoted the war in Algeria as "a crusade for the spiritual and national future of France," and for the honor of an army that – beyond corraling half-armed Druze and starving Rifs – had not scored a significant victory since 1918.[97]

So if Galula complained that French psyops campaigns were purely reactive,[98] it was because the premise on which they were based was 130 years out of date in Algeria, and out of sync with the citizens of a modern, secular French Republic, a majority of whom had concluded by May 1959 that France was enduring an imperial crucifixion in Algeria at the army's behest.[99] De Gaulle bested French psyops specialists as effort-lessly as had Abbane Ramdane with the simple message that imperial counterinsurgency adventures were actually undermining French great-ness, not contributing to it, and were an impediment to modernization. So, French psychological operations failed on both the Algerian and the home fronts. In the judgment of one French historian of that conflict, the army's psyops program was "a mediocre PR campaign cobbled together by amateurs" who spoke neither Arabic nor Berber, who, at best, had confused and contradictory notions about the nature of Muslim society, and who "applied their Indochina nostalgia to the Algerian problem."[100] Ultimately, the message matters, even in information warfare. The final French commander in Algeria concluded that French psychological action failed "because it was incapable of finding a sentiment to exploit" that could match that of "the desire to see the departure of Europeans and achieve independence."[101] Psyops could offer the Muslim popula-tion no vision for a bright future in a French-dominated Algeria – just a reiteration of Bugeaud's *razzias* followed by subjugation.

If the French were not going to improve the life of Muslims within Algeria, at least they could keep the bad guys out. Galula's final point is that safe havens must be denied the insurgent, so that the borders must be sealed to prevent infiltration. Sealing Algeria's borders was probably the single French tactical triumph of the War for Algerian Independence in that it isolated the battlefield, severed FLN logistics and reinforcements, and divided the movement between interior and external leadersip, but it failed to win the war. Completed in September 1957, the Morice Line – an electrified, heavily mined barrier backed by a railway and mobile forces – ran 460 kilometers from the Mediterranean to the sand dunes of the Sahara along the Tunisian frontier. A similar system of defensive barriers sealed Algeria's frontier with Morocco, effectively depriving the FLN of safe havens from which they could infiltrate. The elimination of outside resupply combined with vigorous sweeps inside Algeria, beginning with the Challe offensive of 1959, certainly stressed ALN units inside Algeria, which probably lost one-half of their strength. However, it failed to defeat them because the FLN could win by not losing – they simply hid their heavy weapons, broke into smaller groups, blended into the population, and awaited events. French repression of the Muslim population put time on their side, as did the increasing restiveness of the *pieds noirs* that forced the army to redeploy troops to the cities from 1960.[102] Ironically, by reducing the potency of the ALN, French counterinsurgents made it easier for de Gaulle to begin to roll back civil-military fusion from 1959 by recivilianizing many administrative, judicial, and police functions assumed by the army since 1956, thus weakening the military's control over policy. As a strategy for victory in Algeria, however, reimagining a Maginot Line along Algeria's frontiers was to seek an engineering remedy to more fundamental strategic problems. While the French army was busy isolating the battlefield tactically in a successful attempt to hurt the ALN, the FLN acted strategically and progressively to isolate the theater by eliminating nationalist rivals, consolidating support among the Muslim population, and advertising the human, monetary, and diplomatic costs of repressive French policies in the United Nations, the Arab world, and in France.

Bottom line: The French followed Galula's tactical prescriptions, and still today we are unable to locate *Algérie française* on a map. COIN apologists refuse to fault French tactics, but instead they argue that they were not applied properly, were applied too late, or shift the blame for defeat onto the French government. Galula claimed that his tactics had pacified his region by 1957. That claim is now shown to have been demonstrably exaggerated, when not downright falsified. That should have come as no surprise, because Peter Paret pointed out in the 1960s that there was no way that the French could sustain a comprehensive hearts and minds program throughout Algeria that required at a minimum issuing identity papers, identifying and dismantling FLN cells often using "turned" guerrillas, comprehensive psyops programs, youth counselors who created sports teams, women's groups, "medio-social teams" put at the disposition of unit commanders, public works projects to build roads, schools, clinics, and improve housing, the creation of self-defense units in the *douars*, and so on. But rather than submit Galula's assumptions to serious scrutiny before they set the doctrine that was to guide coalition forces in Iraq, Afghanistan, and future counterinsurgency operations, the authors of *FM 3–24* took Galula's claims at face value because he told them what they wanted to hear. It had been the same in April 1962 when the gurus of COIN congregated under the auspices of RAND to discuss counterinsurgency doctrine. According to American COIN specialist Joseph Hosmer who attended the seminar:

*Although we came from such wildly divergent backgrounds,
it was as if we had all been brought up together from youth.
We all spoke the same language. Probably all of us had
worked out theories of counterinsurgency procedures at
one time or another, which we thought were unique and
original. But when we came to air them, all our ideas were
essentially the same. We had another thing in common.
Although we had no difficulty in making our views
understood to each other, we had mostly been unable to
get our respective armies to hoist in the message.*[103]

Unfortunately, a half-century on, Hosmer's belief in the disinclination of "respective armies" to be seduced by the exaggerated claims for success of a French COIN-dinista trying to parlay his Algeria experiences into a steady job in a country whose faith in the universality of its values requires it to formulate a doctrine to operationalize its vision appears exaggerated. At least the torturer Paul Aussaresses was more forthright.

While French commanders praised the tactical benefits of these hearts and minds efforts, at the same time they admitted that they were a drop in the bucket and simply unsustainable. The Constantine Plan announced in October 1958, which envisioned a huge infusion of cash into Algeria to create 400,000 jobs, never got off the ground.[104] There were never enough troops or resources, the regions were simply too large to organize comprehensively, and FLN pushed out of one district would simply decamp next door and wait to move back in as soon as a region was stabilized and the French troops redeployed to pacify another location. "The fact is that even such a sizable force as the 800,000 who were serving in Algeria by 1959 could only contain – not roll back – an insurgent movement operating among 9 million Moslems," in a coastal area almost as large as France, Paret concluded of the French counter-insurgency effort.[105]

The second alibi for defeat is that the army was stabbed in the back by the government. Bruce Hoffman asserted that the French lost in Indochina and Algeria because a lack of firmness in Paris created continual uncertainty that "set definite limits to what a local pacification effort could achieve."[106] But Hoffman stands reality on its head – Paris was not "firm" in the colonial wars because it had never managed, since Bugeaud, to rein in an out-of-control French colonial military which tortured, hijacked the Sultan of Morocco's plane, bombed Tunisia, forced the government to guillotine FLN POWs out of fear of a backlash if they did not, and continued a disastrous resettlement policy in the face of government orders to suspend it. Prime Minister Pierre Mendès-France used the catastrophic performance of French soldiers at Dien Bien Phu to extricate France from Indochina. However, subsequently the refusal of French officers, convinced that they faced a communist-orchestrated *guerre révolutionnaire* in Algeria and seduced by their belief in "the magical qualities of (COIN) theory,"[107] to follow orders from Paris contributed to the downfall of six French governments from 1956 before finally collapsing the Fourth Republic in May 1958. One can only conclude that Hoffman has fallen for the romantic myth of the heroic combat soldier propagated by French COIN-dinistas, men who in their own estimation sacrificed themselves for France and retained their moral integrity in the face of vacillating and duplicitous politicians. In fact, the soldiers formed the main impediment that prevented successive governments from taking policy decisions in the interests of France until outmaneuvered by de Gaulle.

Charles de Gaulle and the de-fusion of the French military

Historians offer several explanations as to why Charles de Gaulle decided to vacate Algeria in 1962. The French voted for de Gaulle and approved the strong presidential constitution of the Fifth Republic in 1958 because they concluded that he was the only man who could manage a claque of out-of-control counterinsurgents and Vichy revivalists who were holding the country to ransom with their *guerre subversive* obsessions and threats to invade the mainland to overthrow the Republic. French public opinion had turned against the war by early 1959, and there were strong international pressures to leave, although neither was critical in the General's mind. For de Gaulle, the *guerre subversive* fraternity was the heir of the Third Republic's colonialists and the Vichy old guard whose obsession with communist treason had caused France to fold rather than fight on in 1940, and whose focus on a fantasy communist grand strategic conspiracy on the imperial periphery distracted from the main theater in Europe. War in Algeria had undermined French economic recovery, rekindled the metropolitan/colonial debate over France's defense center of gravity that dated from Bugeaud, and compromised French influence in Europe.

Jean Lacouture, de Gaulle's principal biographer, argues that de Gaulle knew that Algeria must be given independence sooner or later. His problem was to do it in a way to "save his boat from being wrecked on the rocks" of a COIN-dinista *pronunciamento*. Sylvie Thénault notes that de Gaulle's principal concern was to reestablish the authority of the French state over a renegade military politicized by civil-military fusion. He used growing public opposition to the war gradually to isolate his colonial military through referenda and plebiscites, and transfer or retire *la guerre subversive* ringleaders who had dictated policy to successive governments.[108]

The final irony was that, in their eagerness to combat *la guerre subversive*, France's small warriors transformed themselves into subversives, who lost sight of the fact that, as de Gaulle had to remind them, the army fights for the state, not for its own sake – *l'armée pour l'armeé*. De Gaulle discovered that he could take the army out of small wars, but to take the small wars out of the army he had first to de-COINify it by dismantling the *Centre d'entrainement à la guerre subversive* in 1958. This was followed in 1959 with a security assistance pact signed with Argentina to exile some of the more fanatical counter-terrorism proponents to South America's southern cone with ultimately disastrous results for that region. The long-overdue abolition of the *5e bureau* occurred in 1960, an important step in extracting the army from politics, although *5e bureau* alumni played an important role in the April 1961 Generals' revolt and subsequently in OAS assassination plots.[109] The most politicized officers were recalled to Europe, while military prefects, sub-prefects, and chiefs of police were replaced by civilians from 1960. In an attempt to end a situation in which suspects were interned indefinitely without being charged with a crime, civilian jurists replaced soldiers on internment commissions, and, after the army proved reluctant to turn suspects over to the civilian courts, reserve lawyers and judges were called up to run military tribunals. The *détachements opérationnels de protection* (DOP) famous for beating confessions out of Muslims and hotbeds of *Algérie française* sentiment in the army were dissolved in May 1960, part of a quiet campaign to eliminate torture begun by Paris the preceding year. Shifting populations to resettlement camps was restricted in 1960, while the following year the process of closing them down began. The army resisted these demilitarization steps, sometimes sabotaged them – the numbers of prisoners "shot while trying to escape" skyrocketed, while Muslims continued to be resettled right up to independence in 1962. But the message that the army must submit to civil control was clear. Discontent with demilitarization contributed to the attempted putsch of April 1961.[110] Three paratroop regiments were disbanded for their actions in the attempted coup, others were mixed to shatter a spirit of insurrection, two hundred officers were arrested, and special uniforms for elite units were abolished.[111] As a replay of Vichy versus Free France, the Algerian crisis allowed a conservative General de Gaulle, once again, to pose as the savior of French democracy against a group of military reactionaries and hence use the putsch to legitimize himself and the Fifth Republic.[112]

France lost in Indochina and Algeria because the French COIN-dinistas filled a political vacuum of their own making with tactics designed to defend a colonial project anchored in minority rule, military occupation, and economic dependency – a project that enjoyed ever-diminishing legitimacy in the eyes of the French population, not to mention in those of France's imperial subjects, as well as the international community. French colonial advocates failed to recognize that Mao's writings were inspired by Clausewitz, while the French counter-insurgent response consisted of a grab-bag of Jominian tactical reactions, one more counterproductive than the next. French officers believed that by promoting the moral superiority of their Western moral code, psyops would become the (unlikely) vehicle to retain the loyalties of Indochinese and consolidate a Muslim constituency for *Algérie française*.[113] The analogies between the British in Ireland and the French in Algeria have already been made. The difference was that the British Army followed the orders of Lloyd George, under intense domestic and international pressure, to grant independence to Eire. French small warriors, on the other hand, convinced that at last they had fine-tuned the tactical formula for success, toppled one republic and tried repeatedly to dictate the foreign policy of another until undercut by a conventional soldier skeptical of their methods and convinced that France's priorities lay in Europe, not in antiquated ideas of French *grandeur* evangelized through small wars tactics. So, it was *adieux* for French small wars which had plagued the nation and France's unfortunate dependencies since Bugeaud. Unfortunately, Britain and the United States would be forced to learn France's lesson the hard way.

6 VIETNAM, COUNTERINSURGENCY, AND THE AMERICAN WAY OF WAR

If Galula and the Algerian War have enjoyed an improbable early twenty-first-century resurrection, it is because this tragic episode serves as the preamble for the true unfinished business that inspires the counterinsurgency revivalists: the US defeat in Vietnam. Galula's "we won on my front" arguments underpin COIN-dinista assertions that victory is sabotaged by silent anti-COIN conspiracies struck among unimaginative conventional soldiers wedded to their big war bureaucratic interests, cowardly politicians, and a general public whose stamina for the sacrifices required for national greatness has gone soft under the influence of democratic institutions that corrode popular will.

The American military is allergic to COIN, or so conventional wisdom dictates. This theme, established in the immediate post-Vietnam era as a mechanism to assign US commander in Vietnam from 1964–1968 William Westmoreland and his coterie of conventionally minded officers blame for defeat in Southeast Asia, was taken up by organizational learning specialists in the 1990s. Led by Richard Duncan Downie, organizational learners argue that US security assistance continues to repeat the mistakes of Vietnam, in that it aims to bequeath a conventional military structure and a big war fighting style to third nation militaries that they cannot possibly afford, and that is entirely unsuited to their mission set.[1] No surprise, then, that in Iraq a conventionally minded US military had to be bailed out by a new generation of small wars officers who revived COIN doctrine in 2006 and "surged" just in the nick of time the following year to save the US military from defeat.[2]

This chapter will argue that this is a total distortion of the historical record: first, far from being learning-averse, the US military was defeated in Vietnam because by the mid 1960s the strategic environment had deteriorated beyond a point that any COIN tactical configuration could have redeemed. Second, that organizational learning specialists underestimate conventional soldiers' capacity to adapt to unconventional situations. Furthermore, the ability to "learn" is totally overrated as a predictor of success in security assistance missions. This is because, as in Vietnam, learning specialists focus on the organization to the neglect of the environment in which the learning takes place and is applied. Finally, a subsequent chapter will assert that the success of the so-called 2007 "surge" in Iraq had more to do with the evolution of the strategic environment there than with the arrival of a new general with a COIN-focused plan, and that conventional soldiers were steps ahead of the COIN-dinistas in sizing up the situation on the ground and adjusting their tactics to deal with it.

Vietnam: the USA rides to the rescue

French historian Vincent Joly argues that the French were defeated in Indochina because they never understood the kind of war they were fighting there.[3] Southeast Asia offered challenges on practically every level – political, demographic, geographic, strategic, operational, and tactical. But rather than looking at the fate of France as a cautionary tale, Washington seemed to believe that it could succeed where Paris had failed in Southeast Asia because it was not a colonial power, had an abundance of resources, and possessed a more competent, air-mobile military.

The new Kennedy administration, which replaced that of Dwight Eisenhower on January 20, 1961, inherited a deteriorating situation in Southeast Asia, especially Laos and Vietnam where Ngo Dinh Diem, a Catholic nationalist who enjoyed strong support from Francis Cardinal Spellman of New York, Senator Mike Mansfield, the US Senate's authority on Asia, and Secretary of State John Foster Dulles, had been installed as President of the Republic of Vietnam in 1955 on the heels of the French withdrawal. Unfortunately, Diem proceeded to alienate his local support in the Cao Dai and Hoa Hao religious sects around Saigon and the urban Bình Xuyên, a criminal network with tentacles in the police, whom the French had enlisted to contain the Viet Minh in the south. The two non-communist political parties Dai Viet and VNQDD became estranged by Diem's predilection for rigged elections, jailing political opponents, and appointing Tonkinese Catholic Diaspora cronies to choice political positions in an overwhelmingly Buddhist Cochinchina and Annam. One of Diem's first acts on taking power was to launch an "Anti-Communist Denunciation Campaign" that targeted former Viet Minh. Nevertheless, communists retained their networks and hence a great deal of political control in some of the most heavily populated areas of the Mekong Delta, north and south of Saigon, along the border with Cambodia, and in Phuoc Thanh province, northeast of Saigon.[4]

Although – or perhaps because – the 150,000-strong Army of the Republic of Vietnam (ARVN) had been raised and equipped with American aid, and advised by the Military Assistance Advisory Group (MAAG) which had disembarked in 1950, it seriously underperformed from 1959 when the Central Committee of the Vietnamese Communist Party formed the National Liberation Front and launched a campaign to overthrow the Diem government. In 1962, Mao Tse-tung agreed to

12 Green Beret with *montagnards* of Vietnam's Central Highlands in 1969. Reshaped by the Kennedy administration, SOF revived a Lawrencian nostalgia for the tough, self-confident man of action leading natives to a victory they could never win on their own.

support the Vietnamese war against the American-backed Diem regime, much as he had bolstered the Viet Minh anti-French fight. The question for the Americans was what to do about it.

Despite the warning of history and learned observers, the United States was in a receptive mood for COIN adventures in the early 1960s. COIN rapidly commandeered the Zeitgeist in Camelot. David Hogan of the US Army Center of Military History has argued that Special Forces were seen as a reaction against "modernist insecurities" about the capacity of Americans, emasculated by prosperity, indecisive about the nation's postwar leadership role, and fearful of the prospect of nuclear Armageddon, to engage in permanent conflict against a potent, amoral but seductive ideological foe in remote corners of the globe. Much as in the stalemate of the Great War, Special Forces and COIN offered an antidote, beginning, it seems, with some hearts and minds games at home. At the outset of the 1960s, concludes Hogan, "popular culture . . . glorified the manly virtues of toughness and courage, and worshiped the hard, self-confident man of action."[5] John F. Kennedy (JFK) was a young, activist president whose wartime record qualified him for heroic status, and under whose name a book appeared profiling eight courageous US senators. Robin Moore's 1965 novel *The Green Berets* appeared amidst a swirl of Westerns in which John Wayne and his ilk cleansed towns of bad guys. It was as if T. E. Lawrence had surged into Saigon just in the nick of time to rescue a faltering war effort.

An age primed by Hollywood into heroic mode required a rationale and a roadmap to guide the evangelization of liberty to huddled masses who yearned to breathe free. Kennedy's Deputy Special Assistant for National Security Affairs, Harvard economics professor and modernization theorist Walt Rostow came to the rescue with the argument that the Soviets stoked discontent caused by underdevelopment to foment revolution. Thus, American power must shield Third World regimes as they evolved through "stages" – a concept with an eerily Marxian echo – of economic development toward viable capitalist economic structures from being subverted by anti-capitalist insurgents.[6] Thus, the United States must nurture and protect nascent democracies or risk seeing them smothered in the crib by communists. For his part, Defense Secretary Robert McNamara aspired to transform Vietnam into a sub-national war experiment although, in the view of American historian David Kaiser, Body Bag Bob was no John Wayne. Rather, he "seems never to have acquired any real understanding of insurgency and counter-insurgency" and instead dedicated himself to "implementing other men's plans."[7] At its inception, counterinsurgency was imagined in the entrails of Washington as a collective effort in which conventional military units teamed with indigenous auxiliaries to kill insurgents, while civilian agencies would propel the political, social and economic reforms that would allow client governments to legitimize themselves in the eyes of their own peoples. Integrated, military-directed civic action programs were not envisaged by US planners at the outset of the American phase of the Indochina War.

Although the US Army had maintained a large mission in Indochina since April 1950, the complexity of the combat environment there went underappreciated in the quest for an "algebraical" formula to thwart what was perceived as a communist "sub-war" challenge to Western democracy. The United States persisted in the belief that it could reshape Vietnamese politics through persuasion and the manipulation of resources,[8] when, in fact, it was the South Vietnamese client who wielded the influence over its American patron who had invested too much blood, treasure, and political credibility to allow the Government of Vietnam (GVN) to fail. While armed nation-building pretended to be a modern Western response to the ideological challenges of Cold War communist subversion, in reality it simply fused questionable modernization theory, hearts and minds nostrums of the turn of the twentieth century, and punitive population concentration with a firm dose of Callwellian chastisement.

Vietnam and the ossification of "flexible response"

Fundamental to the COIN-dinista narrative is that the US Army's alleged institutional aversion to counterinsurgency offered the primary impediment to operational success. The "Green Berets" had begun the decade of the 1960s as the symbol of the Kennedy administration's culture of virility in the face of Che Guevara challenges in Latin America and communist wars of national liberation in the wake of decolonization. Celebrated in Robin Moore's 1965 novel, and subsequently with a "ballad" that topped the pop charts, followed by a 1968 John Wayne film, "Green Berets" embodied America's moral rearmament and crusade to rid the world of communist evil that manifested itself not with an H Bomb under the hammer and sickle, but with an AK 47 assault rifle in some tropical clime – Special Forces pallbearers had carried the slain President to his grave in 1963 and placed their celebrated headgear on his casket. In Vietnam, their small wars adventures at the side of *montagnard* tribesmen took up in the 1960s the battle the French had abandoned in the 1950s, down to *marriages à l'indigène*. Their adventures seem lifted straight out of *Boy's Own* and stood in stark contrast to the industrialized chemical (napalm and Agent Orange) + high explosive = body count victory of search and destroy formula followed by the conventional army and air force.

When JFK sought to expand Special Forces in the US Army, whose mission was to act as advisers to indigenous militaries fighting guerrilla insurgencies in preparation for what he anticipated would be a "below the threshold of war" challenge by Moscow, he met resistance from Army Chief of Staff General George Decker, who argued that "any good soldier can handle guerrillas." Decker's statement is frequently cited as an example of how profoundly out of touch the US military leadership was with COIN on the verge of intervention in Vietnam.[9] For Richard Duncan Downie, the conventional warfare mindset of the US Army's leadership meant that it proved unable to develop an organizational consensus that allowed it to react effectively to the challenges of counterinsurgency warfare in Vietnam, even as officers realized that their methods were not working. However, for men of Decker's generation, for whom Churchill's promise to "set Europe ablaze" with an army of resistance fighters constituted the biggest strategic bust of World War II, Special Forces were meant to sow disorder behind enemy lines as an adjunct to conventional warfare in Europe, the same purpose they had served during the Korean War.[10] In other words, Decker argued, as did Clausewitz, that "war is war," "more than a true chameleon that slightly adapts its characteristics to the given case."[11] Soldiers must therefore be prepared to fight wars in its whole host of guises.

The COIN argument holds that, given the fact that the US Army command never really understood Mao's strategic vision for people's war, it came as no surprise that General William Westmoreland failed to factor the political, social, economic, and psychological dimensions of counterinsurgency into US strategy, protect the population by expanding territorial forces, equip the ARVN with modern arms, and prioritize their training. Instead, the argument goes, he wanted to win the war with US troops applying big war concepts to defeat the enemy in open battle.[12] The MAAG replicated the conventional US force structure in the ARVN equipped with heavy weapons and helicopter support. Therefore, US and ARVN forces persisted in search and destroy, firepower-intensive operations executed by units structured for conventional operations. Suggestions from the field that ran counter to "policies and viewpoints rooted deep in the organizational culture of the U.S. Army" were rejected.[13] Promising initiatives like the multi-agency Civil Operations and Revolutionary Development Support (CORDS) launched in May 1967, expansion of Regional Forces and Popular Forces (RF/PF) from 1967 to back the People's Self-Defense Force, or the USMC Combined Action Program (CAP) platoons were limited,[14] underresourced, and developed too late to alter fundamentally the strategic momentum of the war. Even as officers on the ground reported that conventional search and destroy operations were not working, the US Army lacked a mindset and institutional structure to "learn" and adjust its doctrine and tactics to achieve success.

This argument continues that General Creighton Abrams, an armor officer and Westmoreland's deputy who succeeded his boss as Military Assistance Command, Vietnam (MACV) chief on July 1, 1968, understood the problems but was unable, or unwilling, to confront the US Army's organizational culture to challenge the prevailing conventional war mindset.[15] As with Galula in Algeria, the argument is that COIN doctrine would have won the Vietnam War for the United States and the GVN had it been applied earlier. But by the time institutional learning had begun to shift the tactical emphasis to counterinsurgency, it was too late. The Vietnam War eroded the Cold War consensus around the need to confront the ideological enemy, while it exposed the complexity of applying COIN formulae in foreign cultures.[16] Once the Tét offensive of 1968 collapsed the prospect of total victory and tilted American public opinion against the war, allegations that Special Forces soldiers working with the CIA had assassinated a Vietnamese "agent" focused attention on the controversial Phoenix Program, modeled on failed French decapitation tactics in Algeria, launched in July 1967 to "neutralize" the Viet Cong leadership. The "Green Beret Affair" encapsulated the moral ambiguity of unconventional warfare, while it solidified the image of Special Forces as a Legion of Misfits, a Dirty Dozen of uniformed nonconformists, the US Army's criminal tribe.[17]

The Watergate scandal undermined President Richard Nixon, paving the way for a Congressionally mandated withdrawal of US forces in August 1972. A conventional North Vietnamese army (NVA) invasion in March 1972 was turned back largely due to the intervention of US airpower. When air support was no longer available in 1975, an ARVN overly dependent on US equipment, logistics, and airpower designed for a big war folded, which flung open the door to Saigon, which fell to the communists on April 30, 1975.[18] The primary villain of this sorry and perfectly avoidable debacle, in the view of the COIN-dinistas, was William Westmoreland, an uninspiring, out-of-touch, conventionally minded theater commander, who reflected the institutional torpor of the US military's conventional, big war thinking, and whose dawdling embrace of counterinsurgency warfare squandered the opportunity for victory.

People close to the time said this was nonsense,[19] a verdict that has been upheld by more recent research that challenges, once again, this fairly standard COIN-dinista explanation of defeat in counterinsurgency as the result of tactical ineptitude that springs from a failure of organizational learning, rather than the strategic environment in which the war is fought. First, far from being locked into a rigid conventional warfare doctrine, the US Army was well aware of counterinsurgency developments at the outset of the Vietnam War and was prepared progressively to integrate them into US strategy as the war evolved. The 1958 bestseller *The Ugly American*, written by two US military officers, introduced America to Mao and counterinsurgency and activated an avalanche of popular and professional treatises on COIN. In that same year, the Command and Staff College at Leavenworth initiated a course on counterinsurgency, soon followed by the US Military Academy at West Point, and in the Army's Infantry and Armor schools.[20] While it still retained colonial small wars roots, by 1962, "counterrevolutionary warfare" had been modernized, refined, and rebranded as "counterinsurgency," in part to eliminate the heroic "revolutionary" subtext. COIN was defined as a war waged "amongst the people" by governments against non-state "national liberation movements." The keys to countering an insurgency were considered to be sufficient political will; winning "the battle for hearts and minds" through good governance and constructing a national identity, psychological operations, and the application of "minimum force"; and the operational primacy of police or indigenous forces. Finally, victory required the centralized coordination of all the resources of the state on all fronts to win over the population with a comprehensive civil-military program of nation-building.[21] US Army doctrine was continually adapted in the 1960s to integrate more counterinsurgency tactics as well as re-emphasize civic action projects that had been used in Cuba and the

Philippines at the turn of the twentieth century, such as building roads and schools, instituting medical clinics, programs to boost agricultural output, and so on.[22] Therefore, COIN was in the kitbag of US forces deployed to Vietnam who were prepared to incorporate pacification programs into their operations as they gradually got a handle on a military situation that had become fairly dire by 1965.

Second, US officers understood that Vietnam was more than a simple conventional war fought in the jungle. They proved quite willing to learn and adapt. The problem was that, in the words of Colonel Gregory Daddis, learning is not the same thing as winning. To equate the two is to fall into the fallacy noted by Clausewitz as "judgment by results."[23] According to this view, Westmoreland never envisioned his options as a stark choice between aggressive kinetic operations and a more defensive population-centric "pacification," but, with an eye on the strategic evolution of the war, saw kinetic and pacification tactics as working in tandem. Viet Cong areas had first to be cleared before the "hold and build" portion of the strategy could kick in, an appreciation of the required sequencing of clear-hold-build operations shared by his successor.

That said, population-centric pacification – that is, protecting the population and winning their loyalty with civic action, hearts and minds programs – as a stand-alone operational and tactical approach never offered a war-winning strategy in Vietnam, in part because the enemy there combined conventional and insurgent forces with international support and a sophisticated political infrastructure.[24] To spread US and ARVN troops too thinly over the countryside, as Galula was able to do in the Djebel Aïssa Mimoun because the Algerian rebels in his sector never numbered more than an ill-armed platoon, made them vulnerable to attacks by well-armed Viet Cong (VC) and NVA soldiers in superior numbers and often guided by locals against isolated outposts.[25] Furthermore, even as part of a comprehensive approach, pacification was fraught with problems, some of them structural and organizational – constant turnover of personnel, lack of cultural and linguistic knowledge, lack of intelligence, inability to eliminate insurgent presence in occupied villages, and the enormous consumption of troops and resources that such an approach required among them. But more importantly hearts and minds tactics were unlikely to win over a Vietnamese population for whom the corrupt Diem government enjoyed no legitimacy, any more than Algerian Muslims were likely to embrace the racial and religious apartheid of *Algérie française* as an alluring prospect, given the history of past repression and disenfranchisement. The so-called Strategic Hamlets Program in particular proved vulnerable to VC infiltration, intimidation, sabotage, and attacks. So, like French resettlement camps in Algeria, pacification often made the problem worse in the view of the population, because it uprooted them from their homes and placed them in the bull's-eye of the war.

Finally, far from failing to learn as the war progressed, US forces and the US government were constantly experimenting, adjusting, and reorganizing in an attempt to discover formulas for success. One problem was that, in a land as diverse as Vietnam, local success in one part of the country might not transfer to a region with a different geography or demographic composition. To take but one example, the Strategic Hamlets Program, instituted in 1961 on the advice of Sir Robert Thompson based on his Malayan experience, was poorly adapted to the Vietnamese situation for many reasons, beginning with the fact that it was designed to protect the population from being attacked or intimidated by relatively small insurgent detachments. And that might work well enough in areas where the population was favorable to the government, for instance in minority Catholic or Bao Dai communities. However, in many areas where the VC/NVA were militarily strong and well integrated into the population, they could simply infiltrate and disorganize them, make the area around the hamlets insecure, or assemble large units with substantial firepower to overrun them.[26] The US forces were constantly adjusting and adapting their methods. They just were not winning,[27] because the strategic environment was inauspicious, beginning with the fact that the ARVN proved to be inept even when well equipped because its soldiers for the most part lacked motivation. Meanwhile, the enemy was determined, resourceful, and well supplied, able to draw on a practically inexhaustible reserve of manpower.

Establishing the COIN narrative

The Kennedy administration kicked off the decade of US COIN infatuation – a somewhat ironic development, as the Senator from Massachusetts had been a leading critic of France's war in Algeria from 1957.[28] It was also surprising, given the French lack of success in Indochina and Algeria and the widespread violation of human rights and the laws of war by the French military, that the Kennedy administration played midwife to COIN in the United States. That a COIN surge in the American military was promoted at the very moment that JFK's French counterpart was dodging assassination attempts by *guerre subversive* renegades whose *golpista* tendencies and hostility to democratic values were on prominent display may even count as stunning.

That France's agonized colonial closeout failed to serve as warning to Washington can be explained in part by an apparent accretion of revolutionary momentum in China (1949), Indochina (1954), Cuba (1959), and Algeria (1962). Insurgency appeared to be on the march because, Sir Basil Liddell Hart and other defense intellectuals argued, insurgency and subversion offered the obligatory communist response to the escalatory risks of conventional warfare in an era of the hydrogen bomb and the Eisenhower-era doctrine of "massive retaliation." This view had a profound influence on the Kennedy administration, especially in the wake of the Cuban revolution and insurrectionary instability in Southeast Asia. Kennedy ordered McNamara to orient US forces toward "non-nuclear war, paramilitary operations, and sub-limited, or unconventional, wars." In this way, Liddell Hart noted in 1961, the Cold War was becoming "camouflaged war" in Southeast Asia, Africa, Cyprus, and Latin America.[29]

The Kennedy administration's "flexible response" aimed to counter communist aggression on any level of conflict, including operations that counted as COIN. This strategic pronouncement was controversial even as it was made, because some considered it too formulaic, just another seductive recipe for victory that would prove a disappointment. At the time, two very prominent US historians, Peter Paret and John Shy, attempted to restrain the "uncritical enthusiasm for the newest miracle weapon," by which they meant COIN. Paret pointed out that COIN doctrine had actually short-circuited learning in a French army because it eliminated the requirement to grasp the complexities of the strategic environment. He also noted that *la guerre subversive* had served as a military code for a hostility to democratic values and institutions in France.[30] Paret and Shy pointed out the confusion and disagreements over how COIN doctrine and policy were to be formulated and implemented, either by the direct intervention of US forces or through advisers to in-country security forces. If the latter, they asked how security assistance could be applied to produce operationally efficient COIN forces abroad "without throw(ing) doubt on the patriotism and independence of the regime they are trying to help." More urgently, they questioned whether the regimes under threat were capable of making the "profound social, economic, and political reforms" that must underpin any sound COIN strategy. For instance, upon taking power, Diem restored land distributed to the peasants in Viet Minh-controlled areas prior to 1954 to the landlords, who promptly demanded back rent and imposed exorbitant land-lease rates. Eric Bergerud concludes that the land issue was critical in turning Vietnam peasants against the GVN:[31]

> *In a traditional agrarian society, even one like Vietnam where much was changing quickly, the individual's relationship to the land is central to economic and social existence. Just as land was fundamental in determining wealth and status, it was fundamental in defining political position. Indeed, more than anything else, it was the land issue that ultimately brought Diem to ruin.*

No amount of convincing Westmoreland to apply COIN doctrine, strategic hamlets, Phoenix assassinations, USMC Combined Action Programs, distributing candy in orphanages, and the like could restore legitimacy to a corrupt regime. Paret and Shy also emphasized Clausewitz's warning that "of all forms of warfare, irregular operations are most difficult to calculate and to control." Prophetically, they predicted that, "once involved, the United States might easily find that its prior estimates of the situation were mistaken, and that it was facing an unpleasant choice between abandoning friends or raising the stakes to an unintended level." In agreement with Decker, Paret and Shy concluded that: "Despite their shortcomings, conventional forces, operating from a legal base and trained for unconventional warfare, still seem to provide the best military answer to the guerrilla problem."[32] These warnings failed to staunch the flood of French COIN-dinistas like Galula and Paul Aussaresses into US military schools, universities, and think tanks to pedal their dishonored, delusional, and bankrupt tactical formulae for success.

And given the fact that the main mission of the US forces in these years was to deter conventional attacks in Europe and on the Korean peninsula, a further commitment of military resources to defend Southeast Asia was at best a questionable strategic decision, all the more so if it meant reconfiguring the US Army as light infantry and Special Forces.

Strategic choices in Vietnam

David Kaiser notes in his brilliant book on the origins of the Vietnam War that three strategies initially competed in Vietnam: the first, put forward by the "GI generation" of senior American military leaders in late 1961, offered a hybrid of conventional attacks on VC sanctuaries in remote regions combined with clear-and-hold operations and COIN-inspired resettlement in more populated areas. Its strength was that it would concentrate ARVN units that hitherto had been scattered around the country in isolated posts easily intimidated and overwhelmed by the VC, into more offensively capable formations. It hedged against the possibility of a conventional, Korea-style invasion from the north. Finally, the ARVN, not US forces, would bear the brunt of the fighting.

This plan contained several weaknesses, beginning with the fact that it desperately underestimated VC strength, which it set at around 20,000 active guerrillas. It was based on a total misunderstanding of guerrilla tactics, which were thought to consist of attacks out of secure sanctuaries, rather than the infiltration of populated areas. It called for the heavy use of defoliants, which destroyed crops and so deprived the peasants whose support one required for victory from earning a livelihood. Conventional, big unit sweeps of the guerrilla-infested "sanctuaries" seldom made contact with the enemy because ARVN lacked adequate intelligence to pinpoint VC units, which broke into smaller elements in the face of increased ARVN firepower. Finally, relying on undisciplined ARVN units more adept at looting than combat, whose sweeps were backed by artillery and airpower that blistered the countryside and caused significant collateral damage, was hardly a formula to kill VC, much less win hearts and minds.

Most importantly, Diem opposed ARVN concentration because he feared a coup, and with good reason. Diem's strategic preference was to disperse his army in small, vulnerable posts around the country under the authority of trusted provincial governors rather than politically unreliable generals. But while this neutered the army politically, its drawback was that it also made the ARVN militarily ineffective.[33] The Vietnamese President's second nightmare was that ARVN concentration combined with a MAAG quest for "decisive battle" would invite a casualty-heavy military setback that would undermine his political standing. For this reason, he micromanaged operations and denied repeated US adviser requests for more operational autonomy for ARVN commanders. Diem played a double game, on the one hand complaining that the presence of US advisers sapped the authority of his commanders, while also seeking to convince Washington to commit US forces directly to the fight to counterbalance ARVN weaknesses.[34]

A third rival COIN-centric plan was presented in early 1962 by a younger "silent generation" led by Roger Hilsman, Director of the Bureau of Intelligence and Research (INR) in the State Department. An OSS veteran who had served in the China-Burma-India (CBI) theater, Hilsman more correctly understood that the Viet Cong lived in the villages, not in sanctuaries, so that the struggle would become for control of the populated areas, not search and destroy operations conducted in free-fire zones emptied of inhabitants. Based on his experience operating against the Japanese, he predicted that conventional sweeps, and locate, fix, and destroy operations would prove ineffective against elusive guerrillas. He was seconded by Sir Robert Thompson, hired as an adviser to Diem in 1962, who proposed in the classic "protect the population" COIN approach, the proliferation of "strategic villages" – dubbed "strategic hamlets" – in populated areas protected by civil guards and self-defense forces of the sort that had been featured in Malaya and Kenya to incarcerate minority populations whom the British were more interested in segregating than seducing.[35] "Strategic hamlets" would spread oil spots of government control through the countryside.

Operation Sunrise, launched on March 22, 1962 in Binh Duong province thirty-five miles from Saigon, initiated the Strategic Hamlets Program that Diem had approved in February 1962 as a way to separate the population from the communists and provide the Diem regime a captive audience to consolidate power.[36] In the classic approach to counterinsurgency based on the coercive techniques running from Weyler in Cuba, through the Boer War, Malaya, Kenya, and Algeria, strategic hamlets aimed to corral populations in VC-controlled areas in a series of fortified villages where, protected from the VC and under the watchful eye of the government, they could be persuaded by civic action and propaganda teams with a mix of security, economic incentives, and political indoctrination to support the government, which would in turn reap the rewards of intelligence, manpower, and legitimacy.

John Nagl, who tries to put a happy face on all COIN-inspired endeavors, insists that strategic hamlets kept the VC off balance,[37] while Andrew Krepinevich, in true Galula fashion of blaming the implementation, not the suitability of the COIN tactic, attributes the unpopularity and the eventual rollback of the hamlet program in the wake of Diem's overthrow to mismanagement.[38] The truth, however, is that population concentration in Vietnam as elsewhere offered a sure-fire COIN tactical recipe for a hearts and minds PR disaster. Sunrise displayed the generic drawbacks of population concentration from South Africa to Algeria, beginning with the fact that incarceration proved so unpopular that designated inmates fled ARVN advances rather than risk being corraled in camps. Those imprisoned under protest discovered that, as in Algeria, they were deprived of a livelihood because the "hamlets" were positioned too far from their fields, which search and destroy operations made too dangerous to farm in any case. As in Algeria, the true purpose of population concentration in Vietnam was to empty the countryside, Weyler-fashion, as a hunger-war strategy and to create free-fire zones. Building and maintenance requirements inflicted weeks of unpopular forced labor. Meanwhile, hamlets were either infiltrated by guerrillas, became a reservoir of VC sympathizers and combatants, or safe havens where VC, like Boer commandos, simply deposited their women and children, freeing themselves up for offensive operations. Many hamlets were poorly designed and hence vulnerable to attack; civic action teams were either absent or ineffective, as was GVN propaganda. Finally, strategic hamlets enjoyed little success in the most populated areas and were more likely to be attacked there by the VC than were non-fortified villages.[39]

William Westmoreland and the "loss" of Vietnam

When he became US commander in Vietnam in 1965, Westmoreland had to collect the shards of political instability, strategic confusion, operational and tactical ineptitude, and popular alienation into a plan for victory. Lewis Sorley may indeed be correct that Westmoreland was a shallow, self-promoting overachiever whose competency level probably topped out at division command, maybe even at Eagle Scout.[40] But whether Napoleon himself could have avoided "losing" Vietnam is doubtful. Westmoreland envisaged a three-phase strategy which, on the face of it, seemed logical. First, he meant to secure his base areas and population centers with US troops who began to arrive in 1965; second, he wanted to resume the offensive in early 1966 in conjunction with "rural construction activities." Finally, he wanted to clear the remaining enemy forces from their base areas. There was nothing wrong with Westmoreland's pacification concept per se. It was not larded with false dichotomies that subsequent COIN-dinista authors have ascribed to it. It combined oil spot with offensive operations. It attempted to use the strengths of his forces – firepower and mobility – to buy time to clear and build. It was merely difficult to implement.[41]

American historian Martin Clemis argues that counterinsurgency proponents have posed a false dilemma between search and destroy and pacification, because the purpose of sweeps was to clear the ground so that pacification could commence. As Galula discovered in Algeria, so long as insurgent forces lurked in an area even in small numbers, they could collect taxes, intimidate, and assassinate. Unfortunately, the ARVN was not particularly proficient at clearing operations. This deficiency had become evident on January 2, 1963, when a battalion of the 7th ARVN Division, backed by two battalions of Civil Guards and a company of M-113 armored personnel carriers, were fought to a standstill by a group of VC they had encircled in the village of Ap Bac, despite the superior ARVN firepower and helicopter support. Ap Bac cast into doubt the ability of the ARVN to master firepower and helicopter-borne strategic mobility.[42] The ARVN had most problems one would expect to encounter in a force in which risk-averse officers led soldiers utterly lacking in motivation and discipline: "[The officer] doesn't want to fight, because, if he does, he may spoil his record, and his Saigon chances; and he may be killed," read a contemporary report, which confirmed the common wisdom that the communists attracted the disciplined "Prussians" of North Vietnam, while the GVN recruited the mellow "Bavarians" of Cochinchina. In 1964 on the eve of US intervention, VC attacks had actually diminished. This paradox could be explained by the fact that GVN presence had been eliminated in much of the countryside while the ARVN seemed on the verge of meltdown.[43]

When US forces took over, the conventional wisdom holds that they concluded that a combination of firepower and air mobility would allow them to gain the upper hand against communist forces.[44] It is true that in 1966 Westmoreland preferred to operate in strength to avoid tactical setbacks, however minor, that the press would inevitably liken to Dien Bien Phu.[45] He also needed to reverse the momentum of communist forces and stabilize a rapidly deteriorating situation. However, kinetic operations did not exempt combat forces from COIN-focused "rural construction activities." From 1966, the United States began to emphasize what was euphemistically called "the other war" or "the village war," because officials concluded that US intervention had secured the GVN from a main force threat. It was also supposed to demonstrate to US and world opinion that American intervention could stabilize the GVN's political foundation. In May 1967, Westmoreland fused the competitive military and civilian agency programs into what became the Office of CORDS whose boss, Robert W. Kromer, reported directly to Westmoreland. A CORDS staff of 5,550 coordinated rural development and village and hamlet administrative training, and oversaw agriculture and public works projects over South Vietnam's forty-four provinces. With Saigon now behind pacification, an Accelerated Pacification Campaign was put in place in the autumn of 1968. As American historian Eric Bergerud makes clear in what must be the best, if generally overlooked, book on the American phase of the Indochina War, the 25th Division in the Mekong Delta's Hau Nghia Province threw itself with great enthusiasm into "the village war."[46]

But for US actors, mastering COIN was like learning to drive on a busy thoroughfare, an exercise that mingled lurches, bumps, sideswipes, and the screeching of brakes with frequent collateral casualties. The village war encountered a myriad of problems, beginning with the fact that definitions of pacification ran the gamut from infrastructure improvement, through calorie counting, to arbitrary detentions and targeted assassinations. Corruption, inefficiency, and US–Vietnamese misunderstandings plagued the program. Even alleged successes like the Chieu Hoi ("Open Arms") program that aimed to entice VC defectors out of the jungle only netted low-level guerrillas for whom search and destroy missions sent already Spartan service conditions to intolerable levels, rather than communist honchos seduced by psyops propaganda. Many GVN officers recruited to lead the RF/PF and the Rural Development Cadres meant to organize the villages were untrained, or came from urban areas where peasants were disdained as lower life forms. RF/PF forces lacked aggression and usually abandoned the night to the entirely local VC. This made them especially vulnerable to surprise ambushes. In any case, as in many civil wars and insurgencies, families hedged their bets by placing sons on both sides.[47]

In fact, hearts and minds was very difficult to sustain, and extremely vulnerable to provocation. The view that the GVN was illegitimate influenced not only the population. US forces, who perceived that a lack of government commitment translated on the tactical level to a half-hearted performance by ARVN, RF/PF, and police forces that put US lives at risk reacted, as had British forces in Ireland, by resorting to vigilantism, of which the My Lai massacre forms the most notorious example. US forces proved to be a blunt instrument whose "clear" phase of clear-hold-build too often leveled villages, blackened the countryside with artillery, napalm, and defoliants, and on occasion pacified the population by killing those who failed to flee on time. And while it is easy in retrospect to criticize the overreliance of US forces on firepower, in Bergerud's view it was unrealistic to expect different behavior from conscripts who arrived as liberators, only to discover that they were in fact prisoners:

> *Critics maintained that American forces should have employed more discriminating small-unit tactics during combat in populated areas. Theoretically, perhaps, they were right. However, the fact remains that a casualty-conscious, conscript force like the U.S. Army in Vietnam was bound to use the maximum amount of force within reason. In Vietnam, as in any other war, it was true that "fire kills," and it would have been disastrous for American morale to have asked "grunts in the grass" to use ground assaults when more effective means were available to deal with the enemy.*[48]

The enemy usually managed to avoid contact, but remained in the area to enforce their authority and attack supply convoys and ARVN units, assassinate local officials, recapture and hold pacified hamlets for a while just to show they could, or simply lay mines and booby traps that provoked inevitable retaliation. Dawn *ratonades* by US units that arrested military-aged males, followed by a hearts and minds distribution of food and medical care, and even band concerts were described as "ham-handed and clumsy attempts to win over the people." GIs came to despise and distrust Vietnamese civilians who, with some reason, they conflated with the enemy. Fear of indiscriminate violence by GIs caused peasants to abandon their fields. Relations between GIs and ARVN were fraught with tensions and mistrust, which made it very difficult to evolve a successful coalition effort and demoralized, even angered, GIs who felt as if they were missionaries trying to convert a population who did not want to be saved.[49]

When Creighton Abrams relieved Westmoreland in June 1968, he did not so much change the strategic approach, as inherit a war which had entered a new phase, with post-Têt communists relying more on conventional forces from the North and US strategy shifting to a Vietnamization of the war. The Accelerated Pacification Program kicked into high gear after the 1968 Têt offensive but outran the resources allocated to it. While both Washington and the GVN claimed increasing success for strategic hamlets and pacification generally, a decrease in violence post-Têt may have been more apparent than real, or due to other factors, including the decimation of VC cadres in 1968 and by the French-inspired Phoenix Program that sought to "neutralize" VC cadres, the flight of many peasants to the cities to escape the war, and a growing neutrality of a population that supported neither side, but who nevertheless regarded the GVN as "remote, arbitrary, and often abusive."[50]

Other sources suggest that by the latter phases of the war, the VC had become particularly adept at infiltration, identifying those cooperating with South Vietnamese and US authorities, and killing them. Pro-government rallies were attacked in a campaign of targeted violence that successfully intimidated village and hamlet security personnel and encouraged political neutrality even in supposedly "secure" hamlets. "The situation was such that, over a period of time, many village cadres and – according to intelligence reports – even some RF and PF outposts assumed a neutral position and merely gave a perfunctory performance."[51] US attempts to create *montagnard* militias in the highlands met opposition from Saigon whose goal was "their destruction as an ethnic entity, and the incorporation of the *montagnard* people and the *montagnard* land in an integrated Vietnamese community."[52] Successful tactical methods evolved in one area might not transfer, because the war looked different depending on the area of the country, so it was difficult to evolve a "one-size-fits-all" approach.[53] There is no evidence that Washington could have won in Vietnam with a more COIN-focused strategy from the beginning, not least because the GVN was slow to embrace the political and economic reforms required to translate counterinsurgency tactics into positive political results.[54] "Put another way," concludes Bergerud, "the GVN, even with massive American support, could never create the essential foundation for a strong and resilient morale – the perception that it could win. The collapse in 1975 is very intelligible in this light."[55]

The post-Vietnam verdict

Barely had the war ended when critics began to assign blame for: "Who lost Vietnam?" Hogan points out that this debate took place during a period of drift and demoralization in the United States in the aftermath of a Vietnam debacle that called into question the "American way of war" with its emphasis on firepower and technology, the utility of force in support of Wilsonian principles, the ability of the government to modulate combat intensity to achieve limited strategic goals, and the moral compromises required to deal with calculating, corrupt, feckless non-Western regimes. Defeat also placed the US military in the spotlight, characterized as an organization that was at once racist, careerist, and professionally inept.[56] It was in this atmosphere that Andrew Krepinevich penned his influential 1986 book, *The Army and Vietnam*. According to Krepinevich, in Vietnam the US military confronted a communist insurgency, which it totally misread and mishandled because its institutional culture required a conventional operational response. The US Army lumped COIN with air rescue, ranger operations, underwater demolition, and long-range reconnaissance as an "exotic" mission. In Vietnam, Krepinevich concluded, Westmoreland had adopted an attritional strategy more appropriate to a

> *mid-intensity conflict environment [rather than] defeating*
> *the enemy through denial of his access to the population.*
> *[Westmoreland's] strategy of attrition calling for*
> *the intentional creation of refugees, defoliation and*
> *crop-destruction programs, and a higher priority for body*
> *counts than for population security sabotaged progress*
> *in the campaign against the insurgents and failed to serve the*
> *objectives of U.S. policy.*[57]

Not only was the US military under the sway of cold warriors contemplating the expected titanic clash with the Red Army in Germany's Fulda Gap, he argued. But more urgently, the congenital inability of the US military leaders to learn from defeat had been reinforced by Harry Summers' 1982 book *On Strategy*,[58] which short-circuited "institutional learning" with the argument that the US Army had taken a "direct approach" in Vietnam by trying to defeat the insurgency, rather than isolating the battlefield by sealing the border with North Vietnam to free up the South Vietnamese to deal with the guerrillas.[59] Could such a line of attack logically aspire to any outcome but failure?

There were many contentious assertions in the books of both men, but they shared the belief that, had the operational solution been selected that best responded to the nature of the threat – conventional or unconventional depending on one's perspective – then the United States and its South Vietnamese ally could have handled the challenge. Critics have argued that army doctrine was only one of many problems in Vietnam, and not the most important one. James Lebovic concludes that there is no evidence that the United States could have won in Vietnam with a counterinsurgency strategy from the get-go; even assuming a willingness to carry out practically the World War II scale mobilization of men and resources this would have required in 1965, cajoled GVN cooperation, and assumed that the communists would not have shifted to a more conventional challenge in response. The "arch villain" Westmoreland pursued pacification vigorously, while counterinsurgency theory was well known and implemented within the limits of conditions on the ground by the US military. Pacification could be applied only sparingly before 1967 because the GVN controlled too little terrain and South Vietnamese society was less malleable than COIN theory assumes, as the desperate unpopularity of the Strategic Hamlet Program proves.[60]

Lebovic echoes Bergerud's 1990 conclusion that the population in the Mekong Delta evinced no enthusiasm for the GVN; American-forced political reforms only vindicated communist accusations of a "puppet" GVN; that more people were willing to die for the communists than for the GVN; and finally that attrition was the only viable strategy Westmoreland could employ because winning hearts and minds was dead on arrival because an outside power like the United States could not create the political conditions that allowed COIN to succeed. In fact, there is a strong case to be made that the US/ARVN had contained the counterinsurgency war. Unfortunately, the ARVN's commitment to COIN actually made it more vulnerable in 1975 when its forces dispersed in securing the countryside were unable to react quickly enough to an offensive by main force NVA units.[61]

The Vietnam experience inoculated the US military against counterinsurgency operations and reinforced its preference for big battalions as "the American way of war." What became known as the Weinberger–Powell Doctrine, refined from 1984 and ostensibly based on the lessons of Vietnam, essentially sought to circumvent conditions that had forfeited US public confidence there: vital US interests had not been at stake in Vietnam; Washington had not been fully committed to winning; the political and military objectives in Vietnam had not been clearly defined; the military lacked a reasonable assurance that US opinion supported the war; all non-military solutions had not been exhausted before US.troops had been committed. The underlying assumption of the policymakers and their apologists was that the Vietnam War was lost because the military was stabbed in the back by US public opinion.[62] The rejection of COIN as a strategy meant that US forces were completely unprepared to deal with the insurgency in Iraq that came close to defeating it, until saved in the nick of time by "the surge" led by the iconoclastic General David Petraeus and a clutch of maverick junior commanders able to adapt conventional US forces to the requirements of counterinsurgency.

But this version of events invites skepticism. The US military did not lose in Vietnam because it was too firepower focused, doctrinally inoculated against COIN, was led by an incompetent commander, and because it failed as a "learning organization." "Indeed, the 'other war' argument is based upon a major historical distortion and fundamentally wrong assumptions on the nature of U.S. forces available and the nature of revolutionary war in Vietnam," Eric Bergerud opined in a 1990 verdict that has been largely overlooked in the current revival of the "who lost Vietnam?" debate.[63] Tactics were not the problem. Rather Bergerud concluded that:

> *The errors made were on a much higher level. The American military seriously underestimated the difficulties involved in dealing with enemy forces. And the civilian leadership, particularly under Johnson, underestimated the strength and tenacity of the enemy and overestimated the willingness of its own people and soldiers to continue the struggle indefinitely. In short, American leaders, both civilian and military, committed a strategic blunder that has brought many a general to grief: They chose the wrong battlefield. Tragically, this error brought violent consequences that Americans must contemplate for a very long time indeed.*[64]

The United States failed because, like France, it inherited a strategic framework that made victory an uphill struggle, even had the opponents been less skilled and resilient than those it faced in Indochina. James

Lebovic believes that Vietnam demonstrated the limits of military power to influence the behavior of an indigenous ally, and that public opinion will quickly detect when excessive ambitions lead to rising costs in areas of marginal interest to the United States and the West.[65] In Vietnam a deliberate policy of optimistic progress reports anchored in unverifiable measures of effectiveness, like inflated body counts of insurgents killed, did little to court public confidence. Nor did the gloomy predictions, similar to claims offered by stay-the-course proponents of wars in places like Ireland, Palestine, Malaya, Kenya, Indochina, or Algeria, that a loss in Vietnam would undermine America's influence and encourage the spread of global communist insurgency come to pass.[66]

7 "A CONSPIRACY OF HEROES": REVOLUTION AND COUNTERINSURGENCY IN LATIN AMERICA

In the last half of the twentieth century, Latin America proved to be a particularly propitious laboratory for counterinsurgency because a combination of economic and social inequality and historically weak states made it a target for revolutionary activists, especially in the wake of the triumph of Castro's 1959 revolution in Cuba. The question for counterinsurgents became how to react? Precisely because large-scale interventions by Western armies in Malaya, Indochina (twice), Kenya, and Algeria with the goal of "protecting the population" and defeating insurgent armies either had not worked, or had achieved success at high monetary, political, and moral costs, little political will existed in the United States in particular for a large-scale intervention to stabilize states under insurrectionary threat in the Southern Hemisphere. Therefore, the answer seemed to lie in some form of security assistance – that is, small teams of advisers would deploy to boost the military capabilities of threatened Latin American governments either through what might be called low- or high-option counterinsurgency strategies. The low-option approach, focused on eliminating radical activists and their supporters, was imported into Argentina by French veterans of Indochina and Algeria and subsequently with US assistance spread throughout the Southern Cone in the 1970s and 1980s through Operation Condor. A second, high-option approach that focused on conversion through winning the hearts and minds of the population via what was called civic action found more favor further north. That approach, too, was criticized for at least three reasons, beginning with the fact that it was anchored in the flawed contention that revolution was the product of poverty and a democratic deficit. An alternative view argues that whether a traditional community opts for insurrection depends on the state of its "moral economy." For instance, if power brokers fail to respect community behavioral norms, rules of reciprocity and mutual obligations, and ignore constraints on their power, then a community is more likely, at least initially, to welcome guerrillas as a means to impose justice and rebalance culturally mandated social relationships. Communities might also attempt to enlist armed groups to gain the upper hand in inter-communal feuds. Indeed, attempts to modernize or radically transform those historic relationships by either side are likely to encounter popular resistance.[1] Second, the frontier between death squad and torture elimi-nationist and conversion via civic action approaches was ill defined. Finally, learning specialists asserted that conventionally minded US advis-ers were incapable of crafting appropriate counterinsurgent forces and instead smuggled conventional warfare approaches into Latin American counterinsurgency environments.

This chapter will make several arguments. First, that Latin American revolutionaries like their COIN-dinista counterparts were basically romantics whose strategies for promoting revolution in the region were based on flawed analysis compounded by incompetent tactics. Therefore, other than in a few places like Cuba, Nicaragua, and perhaps El Salvador where regimes were brutal, corrupt, and universally unpopular, Latin American stability was seldom seriously threatened by insurgency. The second argument follows from the first, that the form that security assistance took was immaterial to the success or failure of counterinsurgency. Third, that both low- and high-option counterinsur-gency techniques applied in Latin America demonstrated there as else-where that war among the people translated into war against the people. Low option turned some Latin American militaries into killing machines unleashed upon their own populations, while civic action approaches were naïve and inadequate remedies based on flawed theories of revolu-tionary upheaval, which on occasion produced crises in civil-military relations. Fourth, the social composition, deficient organization, fragile morale, and meager logistical capabilities of most Latin American armies make them poor candidates for successful conversion into the decentral-ized organizations that learning theorists believe are optimal for COIN-centric armies. Upgrades of forces afflicted with a deficit of leadership, organization, and initiative are best achieved through a centralization of command, a tightening of administrative and control functions, and a mastery of basic soldierly skills that US advisers were correct to emphasize. Finally, as elsewhere, most COIN victories in Latin America were achieved at a high moral cost.

A revolutionary continent?

Some would argue that endemic political violence in Latin America is a historical artifact of a rapacious Spanish conquest, race and class friction, and a weak culture of political compromise. Historically, many Latin American regimes resembled fragile colonial states, ruled by oligarchies whose low levels of legitimacy and tenuous territorial control made them vulnerable to coups, conspiracies, and civil wars. The counter-argument is that the regional unrest that rocked much of Latin America in the last half of the twentieth century was a contemporary phenomenon, the offspring of economic modernization and demands for land reform beginning in the 1950s, and waves of political and social activism of the 1960s which strengthened communist parties throughout the region. This occurred against a backdrop of examples of successful revolution elsewhere beginning with but not limited to that of Cuba in 1959. Finally, Liberation Theology which mobilized a common Catholic vocabulary against injustice created an intellectual climate conducive to change.

Modern challenges required updated state responses. Counterterrorist and counterinsurgency campaigns carried out in several Latin American states in the 1960s–1990s and beyond were institutional reactions to unrest in its modern guises. Therefore, the direct importation of French and US counterinsurgency methods in the aftermath of the wars in Indochina and Algeria via security assistance is also cited as a major contributor to the surge in political violence in the region in the last decades of the twentieth century.[2] While French and German military missions had been a permanent feature of many Latin American countries since the late nineteenth century, the Mexican-American War of 1846–1848 aside, modern US involvement in the region began with the Spanish-American War of 1898 and the subsequent US occupation of Cuba. Theodore Roosevelt played midwife to Panama's separation from Colombia in 1903, and two years later issued a corollary to the Monroe Doctrine that allowed Washington to "exercise international policy power" to keep countries in the region solvent, which served as the justification to impose an American "economic adviser" in the Dominican Republic in 1905. The US Marine Corps maintained a garrison in Nicaragua almost permanently between 1912 and 1933, until FDR's Good Neighbor Policy tried to soften Washington's military profile in the region.[3]

World War II initiated Washington's first serious attempts to strengthen Latin American militaries and hence laid the foundation for the Cold War counterinsurgency outreach that was to follow. US military missions to Latin American expanded in earnest from 1938 in an attempt to undermine historic German influence in many regional forces. Military contact accelerated from 1940 as lend-lease agreements were eventually concluded with eighteen Latin American states that bartered $500 million in military equipment and economic assistance against commitments to uphold hemispheric defense.[4] Defense cooperation was accompanied by an upsurge of intelligence collection by the FBI, the Special Intelligence Service (SIS) created by Roosevelt to gather information on Axis agents and sympathizers, and police training programs. An Emergency Advisory Committee for Political Defense assembled representatives from Argentina, Brazil, Chile, Mexico, Uruguay, Venezuela, and the United States in Montevideo in an effort to extirpate Axis influence in the region through internment of German nationals. "The SIS program put in place a new science and technology of surveillance and social control," write Menjivar and Rodriguez, "a bureaucratic method of following 'suspects,' gathering information from 'informants' or 'interrogations,' keeping 'files,' constructing 'lists,' and centralizing 'data' at high administrative levels to develop counter-action strategies for lower-level agency personnel to carry out."[5]

The Rio Pact of 1947 was followed by the 1951 Mutual Security Act which earmarked over $38 million to upgrade Latin American militaries to defend the hemisphere from external attack, just as the Korean War and the advent of the Cold War found the CIA issuing warnings about potential communist designs on the region. The shift from external to internal defense of Latin America grew with the Cold War. The Bolivian revolution of 1952 was a source of deep worry in the Eisenhower administration which decided to recognize the new government because it had redeemed itself in Washington's eyes by purging itself of communists. The Jacobo Árbentz regime in Guatemala was not so fortunate, and instead succumbed to a CIA orchestrated coup in 1954.[6] However, the overthrow of the Batista regime in Cuba in 1959 appeared to confirm that the region balanced on the cusp of revolution.

Had the analysts looked closer, however, they might have concluded that it was the revolutionaries who were deceived by Castro's success.

"A conspiracy of heroes": Mao, Castro, Guevara, and the romanticism of peasant revolution

For Latin American revolutionaries of the 1950s and 1960s, Mao's peasant-centric strategy seemed perfectly adapted to an introverted, fragmented, parochial Latin America where extreme economic inequality, plantation economies, racial and class divisions, the absence of democratic forums and civic values, a predilection for messianic language, and the weakness of the rule of law stunted the evolution of liberal democratic traditions and facilitated *caudillismo* rule by charismatic strong men.[7] In this environment, Mao's revolutionary vision proved unbearably attractive to revolutionaries like the Argentine Ernesto Che Guevara, who while still a young medical student had become sensitized to Latin America's grinding poverty and income inequality during a tour of South America, a condition which he blamed on imperialism and capitalism. In 1955, Che met Raúl and Fidel Castro in Mexico City. All were eager to escape the diktat of classical Marxism's – and the Kremlin's – insistence that revolution await a bourgeois capitalist transitional phase that would lay the groundwork for a workers' revolution. In November 1956, they sailed to Cuba to foment the overthrow of the regime of General Fulgencio Batista. From their base in the Sierra Maestra Mountains, the revolutionaries recruited and trained insurgents, carried out hit-and-run operations, and, in the final weeks of 1958, commenced a march toward Havana. Batista fled the island on January 1, 1959, which threw open Havana to the advancing revolutionaries, greeted by the population as heroes for having rid Cuba of the unlamented Batista.

Cuba's fairly quick and painless revolution seemed to confirm both the vulnerability of Latin American governments and that classic communism's insistence on a preliminary "bourgeois phase" before proceeding to upheaval needlessly retarded revolution in Latin America. Castro's 1959 triumph in Cuba fell on Latin America like a bombshell, although as Daniel Moran notes, the success of his insurrection owed more to Mussolini than to Mao. The December 1958 revolutionary stroll toward Havana by Che and the Castro brothers was no people's war.

Rather, it more closely replicated the *coup d'état* of Mussolini's October 1922 March on Rome when a few thousand fascist *squadristi* forced King Victor Emanuel to name him prime minister. As in Il Duce's Italy, the ingredients of Castro's coup combined regime ineptitude, spinelessness, and unpopularity with the deliberate ambiguity of Castro's goals, which disarmed potential opposition until it was too late.[8]

But the legend of the Sierra Maestra recounted that Castro had assembled Cuban *campesinos* for a people's war against the Batista regime. As Castro's companion in revolution, Che Guevara extracted best practices from their experience, which he published in a 1959 treatise *Guerrilla Warfare*. Che's assertion was that popular forces – later dubbed the *foco* or "center" by his French disciple Régis Debray – can, by launching guerrilla attacks on regular armies in the Latin American outback, create revolutionary conditions on an accelerated schedule, rather than patiently awaiting the ripening capitalist-induced class warfare as traditional communist parties admonished.[9] Che's message was that "revolutionary conditions" were endemic in Latin America in the form of profound economic inequality enforced by unpopular authoritarian regimes that had consolidated across the region in the 1940s and 1950s. The precipitous collapse of the Batista regime was merely the harbinger.

But Batista was an exception. Latin America was not China between 1937 and 1949, where a combination of anti-Japanese nationalism, a power vacuum of authority caused by the KMT eclipse, the Soviet invasion of Manchuria, and the arms bonanza presented by the Japanese surrender combined with the strategic mistakes of Chiang to allow Mao to consolidate his power base and triumph over a weakened and delegitimized KMT. However, Che and co. were little interested in a historical analysis of how and why Mao had triumphed. The important point was that, with Soviet support in the form of arms and resources, Cuba could become the launch pad of Latin American revolution.

Unfortunately for Castro, the shock of his 1959 Havana coup left Washington in no mood to sit passively as revolutionaries picked off vulnerable client states. In March 1961, John F. Kennedy initiated the Alliance for Progress, a program to promote democracy, literacy, land redistribution and economic growth, and raise the per capita income in Latin America with the goal of defusing economic and political discontent in the region that theorists believed was the source of popular unrest. The Military Assistance Program (MAP) provided training and equipment to prepare regional militaries to counter internal subversion, supplemented by Agency for International Development (AID) money to improve police mobility and intelligence collection to assist COIN operations. In military terms, this approach propagated COIN theories that incorporated development programs under the rubric of *acción cívica*.

A different trend was at work in the Southern Cone of South America where in the 1950s an advance party of right-wing French clerics gathered in an organization called *La Cité Catholique*, heirs of the royalist and pro-Vichy *Action française*, put down roots in Argentina. They were pre-positioned to welcome a wave of *Algérie française* refugees forced out of France as Charles de Gaulle consolidated the Fifth Republic. In 1959, the French President signed a convention with Buenos Aires to send French veterans of the Algerian War as advisers to the Argentine military. In the early 1960s, they were followed by fugitives from the *Organisation de armée secrète*, disaffected French counterinsurgents intent on assassinating de Gaulle, that included two French officers, Georges Grasset and Jean Gardes, and Robert Pincemin, a former commander in the Vichy *milice*. These men were welcomed by the deeply politicized officers of an Argentine military ripe for conversion to the concept of *la guerre subversive*. The idea that Latin America, like Indochina and Algeria, was a target of an international communist conspiracy was introduced into the curriculum at the Navy Mechanics School, which was to become torture central during Argentina's dirty war launched in 1976, as well as in those of other Argentine military schools, through French officers dispatched as visiting professors as a result of the 1959 accord. The result was to confer moral validation and doctrinal rationalization for dirty war tactics. "Under the cover of a Christian pardon accorded to executors of State terror," writes Mario Ranalletti, "everything was permitted in order to vanquish and assure the triumph of defenders of established authority, who were protecting the 'natural order' desired by God."[10] From Buenos Aires, their influence eventually spread through right-wing Catholic circles and military exchanges to the armies of other Southern Cone countries following the 1964 coup in Brazil, and the 1973 coups in Chile and Uruguay, while their outlook was institutionalized in the dirty war that followed in the wake of Argentina's 1976 coup.[11]

Anti-subversive missions supported by counterinsurgency doctrine imported by military advisers found a propitious environment in Latin America in great part because counterinsurgency, or more accurately anti-subversion theories, tapped into an intellectual tradition of geopolitical thinking inspired by General Karl Haushofer's *Lebensraum* concepts imported in the early twentieth century on the coat-tails of German military missions to Latin America. Geopoliticians view states as living entities formed by geographical and historical factors locked in a social Darwinian competition for survival with other states and nations in the region for land or resources. Geopolitics spawned the National Security Doctrine, "an interrelated set of concepts about state, development, counterinsurgency warfare, and, above all, security" taught in Latin American military colleges by the 1960s that easily adapted the threat perception in the Cold War from interstate competition to communist-inspired subversion. According to this view, "insurgents" and "subversives" directed by foreign powers conspired against "Western civilization and ideals" by uniting political, social, economic, psychological, and military resources to mobilize a popular base to subvert the state. Because democracies are vulnerable to these "invading microbes" that manipulate concepts like individual rights, free speech, and the right to peaceful protest to penetrate and destabilize institutions, the state must organize to defend itself with campaigns of repression and state terror.[12] This mindset, already apparent in most colonial armies in the interwar years, translated easily in the atmosphere of Cold War big power rivalry into the concept of an authoritarian National Security State organized to combat internal communist subversion.[13] A COIN doctrine sold as a panoply of methods to bolster Western Christian values against communist ideological challenges enjoyed far more resonance in Latin America than it did in non-Western countries, where COIN often presented a clash of civilizations dichotomy.[14] The face of COIN in Latin America – like everywhere – was more often that of repression and coercion than hearts and minds and population-centric benevolence. The difference was that very few Latin American soldiers seemed troubled by the "moral ambiguity" of counterinsurgency, or its effects, which were stabilization through atomization and the deliberate polarization of society.

Critics have at least two complaints about Cold War era security assistance – first, that security assistance caused Washington to forfeit the moral high ground by bolstering anti-democratic regimes that repressed their own people. Security assistance put an overwhelmingly military face on US foreign aid in the region. In doing so, it provided the justification, resources, and training that allowed militaries in Latin America, but also in Korea, Pakistan, and Turkey to overthrow democratically elected governments. It was also irresponsible, even immoral, in that Latin American soldiers instructed in the intricacies of *la guerre révolutionnaire* by French veterans of Algeria or alumni of that alma mater of Human Rights malfeasance known as the US Army School of the Americans too often engaged in a "brutal, lawless struggle" to preserve Christian societies from Marxist-Leninist "progressivism" exported by Havana. The murder, torture, and disappearance of their own people was therefore undertaken in the name of national security.[15]

A second complaint advanced by institutional learning specialists that focuses specifically on US security assistance is that it was misguided, and predictably so especially in the aftermath of Vietnam, because it imported big-battalion conventional war military models ill adapted to counterinsurgency scenarios. These accusations retain plausibility across the political spectrum, for while the Latin American left attempted to make US interference in the region a motivation for insurgency, the right feared that Washington might abandon them as it had Cuba and Vietnam, which made them willing customers of US security assistance and avid converts to a "high-option" version of COIN.[16]

Placing Latin American conflicts in an international context

The debate over the responsibility of outsiders for the violence that Latin American governments inflict on their own people is an old one. Indeed, geopolitical thinking and the National Security Doctrine were viewed as an attempt to legitimize parochial disputes by fitting them into a larger intellectual framework.[17] An admittedly early critic of the morality argument, John M. Baines, argued in 1972 that the link between US security assistance and military misbehavior in Latin America was a tenuous one. Basically, the Latin American military had its own culture and behavior patterns, and sense of the required force levels based on intensity of internal political violence, that security assistance was largely powerless to alter. Coups, for instance, formed a perhaps regrettable but nevertheless robust feature of Latin American civil-military relations irrespectively of the amount of cash Washington dumped on a country. Baines wrote:[18]

> *Given the nature of most Latin American constitutions, the*
> *relative weakness of democratic processes, and the*
> *professional socialization of military officers, the military*
> *views itself not only as the embodiment of nationalism, but*
> *the moral and juridical guarantor of the constitution and civil*
> *order as well. It is doubtful that military assistance programs*
> *have fostered these anti-democratic sentiments on the part of*
> *the military. Nor has military assistance altered these*
> *views ... It is clearly reasonable to conclude that military*
> *coups would occur without U.S. military assistance.*

A second point is that security assistance and outside actors can act as a brake on local violence, by making aid contingent on good behavior. Despite some deplorable examples in which security assistance increased violence discussed below, individual agencies, ambassadors, NGOs, technicians, and others may work to improve human rights, or increase the professionalism of the military or intelligence agencies so that they will rely less on torture and brutality against the population and adopt a more informed and measured approach as well as a more professional attitude compatible with the profession of arms.[19] A third point made by Baines and David Pion-Berlin is that the response of the militaries in states like Venezuela, Peru, Bolivia, and Colombia in the 1960s through the 1980s to the challenge of insurgency was to focus on community development – to become advocates of economic and social transformation through *acción cívica*, a program of economic and social activism inspired by JFK's Alliance for Progress. This sometimes put them at odds with oligarchs in their respective governments.[20] Indeed, two chiefs of staff of the Colombian army were sacked by conservative presidents when they argued that the absence of social and economic reform was a major factor in sustaining Colombia's endemic insurgencies.[21]

In contrast, military leaders in Southern Cone countries like Augusto Pinochet regarded hearts and minds COIN as an "intrinsically perverse" approach that validated Marxist theory that revolution is a product of economic and social inequality. They preferred counter-terrorist crackdowns inspired by French *guerre révolutionnaire* practitioners like Charles Lacheroy and Roger Trinquier who thought it pointless to try to win the hearts and minds of terrorists, who were simply evil people with an anti-Western agenda. Best simply to torture and exterminate them. This is not to say that soldiers in Colombia, Peru, and Venezuela in the 1960s and beyond did not on occasion fall off the *acción civica* bandwagon and adopt a counter-terrorist approach. But in general, Southern Cone security services earned an unrivaled reputation for prosecuting campaigns of counter-terror defined by "gross violation of human rights, neoconservative economics, and intelligence paranoia,"[22] the most infamous of which was Operation CONDOR.

CONDOR was a program in effect between November 1975 and the fall of the Argentine junta in 1983 coordinated among the governments and intelligence services of Argentina, Chile, Uruguay, Paraguay, Bolivia, and Brazil to track, apprehend, torture, and disappear an estimated tens of thousands of leftists, or those thought to be such, across the region. Critics of security assistance note that while the bloodthirsty behavior of Latin American security services may be endemic, and that violence may be a product of the belief in "the necessary massacre" to terrorize the population, intimidate the tribe, and secure the land title, or whatever, such a sophisticated, systematic, well-financed transfrontier operation as CONDOR would have been impossible without the active participation of the United States intelligence services acting with the support of National Security Adviser and Secretary of State Henry Kissinger, as well as technical refinements supplied by French operatives. Assets supplied by US security assistance helped to internationalize parochial Latin American conflicts by redefining them as fronts in the East–West struggle and legitimating their dirty war methods as requirements for intelligence gathering and the defense of the state.[23]

From counter-terrorism to counterinsurgency

The end of the Vietnam War saw an influx of US advisers with counterinsurgency experience to Latin American countries. Institutional learning specialists searching for impediments to doctrinal change and military adaptation found that to be a central problem in post-Vietnam US security assistance to Latin America. According to this view, the last quarter of the twentieth century found the US military to have evolved into a self-satisfied, careerist, conformist, bureaucratic, complacent, and unimaginative organization that was self-righteously hostile to politicians and condescending to a civilian society that lacked the stomach to fight long wars. Hence, the US military's "never again" and "no more Vietnams" mindset predisposed it to repeat the Indochina missteps when

13 Castro visits North Vietnam in 1973. Soviet leader Leonid Brezhnev condemned the "adventurism" of Latin American radicals like Castro and Che Guevara who believed insurrection to be the product of "a conspiracy of heroes."

confronted with new asymmetric challenges. This was especially worrying because Latin America witnessed "below the threshold of conventional conflict" proxy confrontations between Washington and Moscow. These were not a replication of nineteenth-century imperialism, in that these wars were fought by clients who seldom reflected the strategic interests of their sponsors. This was particularly true of Castro, whose agenda in Latin America announced the cautious pursuit of ideological and political independence from his Moscow sponsors.

If the US Army in particular was as hopelessly conventional and adaptation challenged as the institutional learning specialists led by Richard Duncan Downie claim, then logically it would have responded poorly to Latin American insurgencies. The truth, however, is that despite the endemic structural weaknesses and contested legitimacy of Latin American states, the US security assistance effort in Latin America has proven a fairly successful enterprise not the least because Latin American revolutionary movements were and continue to be as fatally infatuated with Maoist peasant revolution as are counterinsurgents and Special Operators smitten with Lawrencian romanticism. Che Guevara offers a case in point.

In 1966, Guevara traveled to Bolivia to test his *foco* theories in the Santa Cruz region of Bolivia. The fact that he chose to launch his revolution in a place where "land hunger," which many Latin Americanists believe the main incentive for peasant–guerrilla cooperation, was absent serves as testimony to Che's artlessness, lack of local knowledge, and to the fact that he was captive to revolutionary romanticism. Following the Bolivian Revolution of 1952, the government had established universal suffrage, nationalized the mining industry, and instituted an extensive program of agrarian reform. For these reasons, and because many of the older peasants had served in the army during the Chaco War (1932–1935) between Bolivia and Paraguay, both the army and the Bolivian President, General René Barrientos, were popular in Santa Cruz. The Cubans and even the Bolivians in Che's band were outsiders. Therefore, because the "moral economy" of Santa Cruz was purportedly in balance, they proved unable to strike a rapport with the indigenous population, collect intelligence, or craft a program designed to exploit what turned out to be a dearth of local grievances. If that were not enough, Che isolated himself by snubbing other left-wing groups, especially the Bolivian Communist Party. Finally, while Che certainly proved courageous and dedicated, his military know-how, such as it was, had been acquired in the course of a few months in the Sierra Maestra and during an unsuccessful sojourn in the Congo in 1965. As a guerrilla leader, Che proved to be detached, arrogant, humorless, and frequently abusive, even murderous, whose command style owed much to Robespierre and Stalin.[24] Therefore, neither the strategic environment of Santa Cruz nor Che's revolutionary vision and leadership augured well for the success of his venture.

Given these circumstances, a dollop of security assistance sufficed to isolate and capture Che and his band. Washington dispatched a team of fifty-three advisers that included men from the CIA's Special Activities Division and a sixteen-man Military Training Team of US Special Forces to train the Bolivian Rangers, some helicopters, light weapons, and C rations to the Bolivian army.[25] For all of these reasons, Che's *foco* disintegrated as the peasants ratted him out. Pursuit by the US-trained Bolivian Rangers kept him hungry and on the run, and those fighters who survived became progressively demoralized. Che was eventually run to ground and captured in a skirmish with Bolivian soldiers who executed him in October 1967.

Rather than discredit his vision, however, Che's early death secured his celebrity, much as Lawrence's premature demise helped to shroud his reputation in the afterglow of the Arab Revolt. In fact, both men shared traits of stardom that helped to promote their claim that, with proper vision and leadership, remote and backward peoples might be mobilized in support of a larger, international project. Both were nonchalant, reflective media personalities, each sartorial in an eccentric way, each addicted to speed and motorbikes in a mode that proclaimed an infatuation with risk and death. Idealistic men of conviction, they muddled myth with history to become iconic symbols. They maneuvered in disguise through a world of murk and moral ambiguity that was destined to betray them. Each died the romantic icon of his cause[26] – Lawrence, a latter-day Chinese Gordon soldier of fortune, while Che made the Maoist myth of peasant revolution and people's war trendy, if not entirely convincing.

Leonid Brezhnev, then General Secretary of the Soviet Communist Party, spoke for communist orthodoxy when he condemned the "adventurism" of people's war-besotted Latin American radicals who nurtured a romanticized view of an imaginary peasantry, and who believed insurrection to be "a conspiracy of heroes" rather than an enterprise organized by a Marxist vanguard once "the necessary objective conditions" for revolution were present.[27] However, rather than interpret Che's October 1967 demise as a thumping demonstration of the "hubris and naiveté" of his ideas,[28] Latin American revolutionary groups continued to argue that prolonged popular war, punctuated by heroic gestures, dramatic coups, and bold actions, could by itself create the necessary objective conditions for insurrection,[29] thereby dispensing with the requirement to solicit the Kremlin's preliminary blessing.

The problem for Latin American insurgents was that the ideological fervor associated with the people's war ideal offered neither a strategy nor a tactical doctrine for victory. Revolutionaries combined ideological gullibility with sub-par military skills. In Colombia, to take but one example, both the *Ejército de Liberación Nacional* (ELN) and M-19 sent guerrillas to Havana in the 1970s for training; these fighters were then redeployed back in Colombia to ignite revolution, with (for the guerrillas) disastrous results. For instance, in the summer of 1973, around seventy Cuban-trained ELN guerrillas installed themselves in the Anorí region north of Medellín, Colombia. The Colombian army deployed a classic, British-style COIN campaign against them that included arbitrary arrest and internment of suspects; food, animal, and population control; the occupation of chokepoints; trackers; mobile patrols; and coordinated intelligence collection. The ELN was defeated, but not by COIN tactics. Rather, like Che in Santa Cruz, the ELN's real problem was that Anorí had been a conservative bastion during *la Violencia*, the bloody civil war between liberals and conservatives that had raged for a decade in Colombia from 1948 to 1958. The population was deeply religious and pro-military. The ELN defeat was sealed after the army summoned the local bishop, who reminded his flock that the guerrillas were simply the heirs of the liberals. Denounced by the peasants, the guerrillas were quickly swept up by the army in Anorí in the space of barely three months in early 1974, without US assistance. Subsequent Cuban attempts to train and reinsert guerrillas into Colombia met similar fates.[30]

There were several ironies lurking here: first, the main protagonists of people's war in Latin America, and subsequently Africa – Castro and Che – owed neither their success, nor their survival, to people's war. Castro was allowed to linger unmolested on his island because he was backed by Soviet conventional and nuclear arms. Their attempts to export people's war to Latin America and Africa flopped completely, and not just because of US security assistance. Second, the Sino-Soviet split after 1960 deepened the Kremlin's allergic reaction to people's war, which helps to explain Moscow's impatience with Havana's heroic conspiracies. But despite his lack of success in exporting people's war, Castro continued to believe that Cuba had the ability to "inflict a heavy defeat to the entire policy of the imperialists (and) . . . free Africa from the influence of the Americans and Chinese."[31] Until the collapse of the USSR forced him to repatriate his troops and technicians, superpower assistance in the form of hardware was bound to be more effective in promoting or hindering insurgency than enthusiastic people's warriors armed only with slogans from the red book of the day.

Revolutionary success increasingly became a long shot as Latin American regimes, middle classes, armies, and the United States, on the *qui-vive* against Castroite subversion, coalesced. In fact, Latin America in the age of Castro offered a promising counterinsurgency laboratory for several reasons. First, although the counterinsurgent methods were fairly rudimentary, *consolidación*, roughly translated as population control, was the historic mission of Latin American armies since the advent of the Spanish Empire. Therefore, there was no need to seduce them away from ingrained conventional doctrines designed for trans-national war. In its updated 1960s hearts and minds idiom, *consolidación* translated into *acción civica*, a battery of programs to raise peasant standards of living and hence through activist government and increasing prosperity supposedly inoculate them against revolutionary infection.

So, one may question how important security assistance was to the defeat of revolution in Latin America where peasants for the most part turned a deaf ear to calls for insurrection, especially when they came from middle-class, frequently international revolutionary romantics. Nor did Latin American insurgents prove to be particularly proficient guerrilla fighters. Rank-and-file guerrillas were only superficially indoctrinated, and quick to defect if given the opportunity. Like many insurgent organizations, they targeted the population and survived by hiding in remote locations, or because the government army was small, unaggressive, or inept. The decision of insurgencies like Peru's Shining Path or Colombia's *Fuerzas Armadas Revolucionarias de Colombia – Ejército del Pueblo* (FARC-EP) to go into the drug trade has given them resources, while at the same time diluting their ideological cohesion and reducing their popular base to coca growers, and their allies to drug cartels who process and market their product. The combination of insurgent political isolation and low guerilla military skills meant that a small dose of US security assistance in the form of weapons and training in *kleiner krieg* tactical, technical, and organizational skills offered to regular Latin American militaries could usually tip the balance against the insurgents. Agent infiltration, GPS, cell phones, air-power, and smart bombs have made the concentration of significant guerrilla forces a suicidal decision, as the FARC-EP discovered from the late 1990s.

Second, unlike in Vietnam, and subsequently in Iraq and Afghanistan, the fact that US forces acted as advisers, remained small in number, and avoided engaging in combat became a plus, because it put a local face on the counterinsurgency, distanced US advisers from the human rights abuses that inevitably accompany COIN, and avoided the racialized antagonism that, despite cultural and language training, habitually erupts between better-trained, equipped, and disciplined US troops and their understandably resentful in-country allies.[32] Finally, while institutional learning is certainly important on the tactical level, where timely adaptation increases combat efficiency and saves lives, there is no evidence that conventional soldier advisers have proven ineffective in Latin America's small wars arena. Besides, the ability to create COIN-centric armies is overrated as an explanation for the strategic outcome in counterinsurgency operations. This has been the case in Latin America as it was in Vietnam, where the evolution of the strategic environment, not merely the acquisition of weapons and tactical finesse, offers a more plausible explanation for intervention outcomes. A dose of US security assistance delivered by small teams of advisers was usually sufficient to increase the combat efficiency of government forces to the point that they could overcome what in most cases amounted to weak, ill-prepared, unrealistically optimistic insurgent challenges.[33]

This proved to be the case in both El Salvador and Peru. Plan Colombia, a package of security assistance developed in 1999, provided the critical margin and the incentive that allowed Bogotá to rein in the human rights abuses of its intelligence services and military, coordinate and modernize their command structures and procedures, upgrade the training, weaponry, and mobility of Colombian forces, and go on the offensive against a collection of insurgencies, right-wing paramilitary groups, and criminal cartels that threatened at the turn of the twenty-first century to bring the Colombian state to its knees. This has not transformed Colombia into a salsa version of Switzerland. But it has bought time for the government to consolidate its authority. In contrast, large infusions of US troops in places like Vietnam, Iraq, and Afghanistan arguably were counterproductive and politically destabilizing in great part because the tactics used in the stabilization process helped to convince the locals that American soldiers were "violent, reckless, intrusive, arrogant, self-serving, profane, infidel bullies hiding behind high technology."[34]

The problem with security assistance induced civic action was that it roiled civil-military relations. And as the French discovered in Syria in the 1920s, in places like Guatemala civic action projects anchored in modernization theory broke down traditional social relationships in the countryside, sometimes mechanized the peasants out of a job, and alienated powerful elites.[35] So, rather than improve the life of the peasantry, enlist the upper classes in a national project to spread democracy, stabilize society, and solidify civil-military relations, civic action could and did actually prove counterproductive in some places.

El Salvador as a failure to learn

The case that most closely justified Che's faith in a *foco* strategy was Nicaragua, where a near universal loathing for the Somoza dynasty, generalized across class, race, party, and countries in the region, combined with the inability of the Carter administration to convince Anastasio Somoza to liberalize, boosted the Sandinista National Liberation Front (FSLN) to power in 1979. The Sandinistas then funneled Soviet arms to neighboring El Salvador, threatened in 1981 by an offensive orchestrated by the *Farabundo Martí National Liberation Front* (FMLN). In response, at the request of San Salvador, President Ronald Reagan ordered fifty-three US advisers, the most permitted by a US Congress anxious to avoid another open-ended Vietnam troop commitment, to rescue San Salvador from the FMLN threat.

On the face of it, US security assistance to El Salvador can be termed a success in that it stabilized a government that in 1981 appeared on the road to downfall. US advisers forced the Salvadorian army out of their barracks and onto the offensive, and eventually brought the war to an end with a negotiated settlement that drew the FMLN into the political process. Not so fast, says "learning" theorist Richard Duncan Downie, for whom the notion that a conventional US Army could successfully choreograph El Salvador's response to an asymmetric threat environment constitutes COIN-dinista heresy. Downie concedes that the US effort increased the Salvadorian military (ESAF) from 12,000 to 56,000 men, revamped its organization and intelligence structure, improved air reconnaissance and small-unit tactics, established a National Campaign Plan, and so on. However, he complains that US advisers did not apply a population-centric, "whole of government"

COIN doctrine that coordinated social and economic development with military clear-and-hold operations. Instead, US security assistance converted the Salvadorian armed forces from a timorous, undermanned, poorly trained constabulary into a conventional force armed with heavy weapons inappropriate for COIN missions. Such a response, according to Downie, was to be expected from a US army whose officers proved unable to achieve "organizational consensus" that would have allowed the application of a coherent COIN approach. Because the US Army had deleted Vietnam from its operational memory, its advisers had no small wars repertoire of solutions to draw on in El Salvador. The war stumbled to an exhausted termination, according to Downie, not because the US-directed COIN campaign had been effective, but rather war termination flowed from the electoral defeat of the FMLN's Sandinista supporters in Nicaragua, the collapse of the USSR which curtailed support from Cuba, and by pressure from Washington embarrassed by the persistent human rights violations of the Salvadorian military.[36] Writing in 1998, Downie complained that the United States had invested $4 billion over a decade-long conflict in El Salvador, largely in a misguided military assistance effort that, because of its conventional warfare approach, was able only to produce a stalemate.[37]

Downie's assertion that soldiers trained in conventional conflict lack the mindset to adapt to irregular warfare because they fail to apply institutional learning and develop an organizational consensus simply reformulates Bugeaud's 1840 critique of Vallée in Algeria, or the post-Vietnam accusation that Westmoreland's conventional, search and destroy operational approach had forfeited victory in Vietnam, in a more academically sophisticated, social scientific jargon. The fundamental learning organization assumption that a civil-military fused, hearts and minds approach offers the single formula for success against insurgencies is simply lifted from Lyautey's romanticized, when not intentionally misleading, vision of conquest as a process of peaceful penetration, rather than a kinetic reflex of metropolitan soldiers.

There are several questionable assumptions behind the assertion that COIN approaches offer a more successful way to counter people's war. A guiding premise of this book is that historically conventional soldiers are more likely to adapt to counterinsurgent challenges than COIN-dinistas to conventional conflict. So, even if US advisers brought a conventional mindset to the fight in El Salvador in the 1980s or Colombia in the first decade of the twenty-first century, this did not necessarily make their approach wrong-headed and inefficient. They were simply fighting a war on a different level, employing persuasion, cash, diplomatic pressure, and organizational skills to elicit the cooperation of Salvadorian and Colombian militaries that knew the country, and had their own agendas, set of priorities and practices, to reform their strategy, operational methods, and tactics. In other words, transforming a host-country military seeks to sharpen its fundamental military skills and improve its operational efficiency through education, training, and organizational adaptations. These modifications are not specific to conventional or COIN-focused armies, but are merely foundational. The calculation is that better equipment, training, discipline, and leadership will lead to tactical success, which should help to curtail human rights abuses and the requirement to ally with paramilitary thugs.

The objection is that, by focusing on improving the fundamental skills of the military, security assistance loses sight of the ideal COIN vision of a fused, coordinated, civil-military interagency, "whole of government" approach. This is not necessarily true. But the problem becomes that the extra-military dimensions of pacification, difficult for poor, institutionally weak Latin American governments to resource and coordinate in the best of times, become especially challenging in intense combat environments. In El Salvador, as Downie admits, the level of violence made it difficult to carry out pacification programs with civilian agencies, while a lack of resources and troops made a clear-hold-build approach tough to sustain. Violence and resource disputes created disagreements that made it difficult to achieve and maintain a bureaucratic and political consensus around a policy and a strategy backed by appropriate tactics. Nor, even had a "whole of government" strategy been followed, would it likely have achieved its ultimate goal, which was "legitimacy" for the government. In fact, among the contradictions that lurk at the heart of COIN as applied in Latin America, Hal Brands notes that the short-term goal of bolstering government stability and longer-term democratic and social reform may be at odds. Modernization that seeks to improve the life of the peasants and hence the legitimacy of the government can backfire if it breaks down social patterns, worsens economic and social conditions, and alienates elites.[38]

A third problem is that COIN approaches that require a devolution of responsibility to the lowest command level may not be as culturally suited to every military organization as Downie imagines, especially those in Latin America. The problem of transforming Latin

American armies into efficient counterinsurgency forces begins with the fact that, because the local citizenry may be divided in their political loyalties, force expansion requires caution. Historically, many Latin American armies represent a faction or a political viewpoint, so that officers are drawn from a certain social group, even from a limited number of military families. Because connections and political loyalty are considered paramount virtues, these military organizations seldom embrace a Napoleonic "career open to talent" that can increase organizational efficiency by promoting the best men to the top. Instead, Latin American militaries tend to be socially and racially layered, under-officered organizations, with no tradition of a strong NCO corps, and a largely leaderless soldiery. Conscripts may lack the motivation or incentive to fight. Units expected to train their own soldiers may lack resources to teach basic soldiers skills like marksmanship, water survival, and small-unit tactics, or they may neglect them out of fear that soldiers will defect to the insurgents upon discharge. This limits organizational efficiency because decentralized command and control may lead to a lack of initiative and underperformance, which provides neither lessons nor mechanisms to encourage institutional learning.

Fourth, aggressive, small-unit tactics may be discouraged by a lack of mobility, firepower, an intelligence apparatus to identify targets and risks, and above all by an absence of medical support, all of which are more likely to be generated in larger, centrally organized force structures. For these reasons, venturing outside the wire, especially in small groups that lack efficient lower-level tactical leadership and fire-power, carries great risks and may be career ending for hard-hitting officers who encounter adverse circumstances like ambushes or IEDs that proliferate in small wars environments. As a result, the most sensible tactic for these armies is to operate in large, conventionally organized units, saturate an area, clean it up, and move on. Or, given their levels of inefficiency and the perils of security assistance/NGO oversight, they may cooperate with paramilitary criminals whose "war among the people" best practices lean more toward terrorism than quiet persuasion.

For these reasons, COIN campaigns are more likely to be prosecuted using dirty war rather than by hearts and minds methods. Human rights violations, at the very least massive population displacement, become an endemic feature of counterinsurgency operations due to a relative absence of civilian control and the racial/cultural/tribal/ideological/religious/class animosities mobilized in a civil war setting. This was certainly the case in El Salvador, which helped to undermine Congressional support for the war in Washington. The potential for abuse is increased when pressure on the military to get results translates into body counts, not to mention massacres, disappearances, and "false positives" – murdered civilians passed off as guerrilla kills. Nor is it easy to prevent, because by committing to uphold a client government, the intervening power places itself at the mercy of local actors who may have different goals as well as elastic legal and human rights standards.

Downie's assumption that insurgencies are best contained when they are confronted by COIN tactics applied by militaries adept at institutional learning is faulty. Rather, insurgencies are more likely to cease combat when the strategic environment changes, so that they conclude that their goals can best be achieved through political, rather than violent, means. In a perverse way, US security assistance did help to bring about the end of the Salvadorian conflict. But whether security assistance was COIN or conventionally focused made no difference in the end. Rather, the Salvadorian military became so large, well-armed, and politically empowered by US assistance that even conservatives saw accommodation with the rebels as the only way to bring an increasingly predatory and politically assertive soldiery into line.[39] Finally, writing in 2012 while costly COIN commitments in Iraq and Afghanistan are only just winding down, what US citizen would not call a political settlement achieved with a *soupçon* of security assistance and $4 billion a bargain? All of these problems, Hal Brands opines, "indicate that some healthy skepticism might have a salutary influence on contemporary debates over counter-insurgency strategy."[40]

8 BUILDING THE "MOST SUCCESSFUL COUNTERINSURGENCY SCHOOL": COIN AS THE BRITISH WAY OF WAR

The COIN-dinista gospel asserts that there is a right way and a wrong way to fight insurgencies. In Algeria the French were too brutal, in the process solidifying Muslim support for the FLN, constricting government policy options, undermining support for the war at home and abroad, and politicizing French counterinsurgents to the point of mutiny. The US military failed in Vietnam for different, but equally systemic reasons – the "American way of war," the counterinsurgents' argument goes, dictates a conventional, firepower-focused force structure that is ill-matched to a COIN environment. Only the British, this argument continues, managed the intellectual and operational transition from imperial small wars to contemporary COIN. Thus, while the COIN-dinistas' shared memory starts with Vietnam, their folklore begins with Sir Robert Thompson's 1966 book, *Defeating Communist Insurgency*. Thompson boasted impeccable COIN credentials – an RAF officer who had fought as a Chindit under Orde Wingate in Burma during World War II, he graduated through the small wars hierarchy during the Malaya Emergency (1948–1960) serving successively as staff officer to Sir Harold Briggs, Director of Operations in Malaya in 1950–1951, as coordinating officer for security under Briggs' successor, Sir Gerald Templer, and Deputy Secretary for Defence after Malayan independence in 1957, moving to Permanent Secretary for Defence in 1959. He subsequently advised both Presidents Kennedy and Nixon during the Vietnam War. Thompson argued that in Malaya, which in the COIN-dinista view set the gold standard of post-World War II counterinsurgency, the British achieved the correct balance of persuasion and force by establishing some basic principles. These principles continue to bulk large in British and US COIN doctrine: The government must have clear aims; it must be both "reasonably efficient" and "uncorrupt"; it must conduct counterinsurgency operations within the limits of the law; it must apply a "whole of government" strategy that coordinates the civil, police, and the military effort; it must prioritize defeating political subversion by focusing on insurgent support structures, rather than concentrating on killing guerrillas; finally, in the guerrilla phase of the insurgency, the government must concentrate on securing its base areas first, in part through the pursuit of economic, political, educational, and infrastructure reforms to point up the benefits of supporting the incumbent power.[1]

British historian David French concedes that *Defeating Communist Insurgency* was a breakthrough book, in which Thompson advertised an "ideal type" COIN approach institutionalized in principle in the British Army by 1957, one compatible with modern Western notions of war among the people, conducted efficiently, humanely, and with minimum force. However, while French notes that Thompson's precepts have helped to guide works like *FM 3–24*, he cautions that Thompson must be read as a didactic, aspirational treatise rather than as a statement of fact.[2] This admonition has not prevented historians from confusing Thompson's "low-option" counterinsurgency guidelines with the British Army's actual conduct of post-1945 small wars.

The most articulate, comprehensive, and sympathetic academic restatement of the application of Thompson's principles to British counterinsurgency was supplied by Tom Mockaitis' 1990 *British Counterinsurgency*, which basically argues that London institutionalized the idea of minimum force, civil-military cooperation/aid to the civil, and tactical flexibility based on decentralized decision-making in their counterinsurgency operations. These were the guidelines for British conduct in Malaya, which was "by any standards . . . an impressive victory" that could not be attributed to contingent factors unique to the theater such as Malaya's ethnic divisions, its geographical isolation, or the fact that the insurgency went off half-cocked. Rather, success in Malaya was the product of the application of Thompson's minimalist principles of selective force reiterated in official writings and staff college instruction. Mockaitis concedes that British hearts and minds approaches were firmly anchored in a paternalistic, "white man's burden" sense of racial superiority, and that poorly trained, locally recruited police reservists or Home Guards in Kenya especially might occasionally have resorted to vigilantism in response to insurgent provocation. Overall, however, the "most successful counterinsurgency school was built" that brought successes in Malaya and Kenya especially, mythologized by COIN-dinistas as the Austerlitz and Jena-Auerstadt of hearts and minds.[3]

Richard Duncan Downie's 1998 *Learning from Conflict* reinforced Mockaitis' argument that COIN is a canon that has to be transmitted from generation to generation via institutional learning. He puts down the US Army's alleged failure to do that to the fact that the institution is simply too large and bureaucratic to develop a "learning cycle" that allowed it to build a consensus to adapt its doctrine to the exigencies of counterinsurgency warfare. US commanders are reluctant to accept suggestions from subordinates, while the US military lacks socializing institutions like the British regimental mess that allow officers to interact in less formal settings.[4] The British MOD swanked in 2001: "The experience of numerous small wars has provided the British Army with a unique insight into this (COIN) demanding form of conflict,"[5] a boast that a generation of Northern Irish Catholics and subsequently Basra Shi'as might dispute.

John Nagl's 2002 *Learning to Eat Soup with a Knife* reinforced the Mockaitis and Downie argument about the superiority of British counterinsurgency, in the process resurrecting the 1970s debate about the nature of the Vietnam War. Nagl argues that Briggs and Templer blazed a counterinsurgency trail in Malaya "after conventional strategy failed" with a formula that, had it been applied in Vietnam, could have led to victory for the Americans there. The British were more adaptable in counterinsurgency than was the larger US Army because it was "a small quasi-tribal collection of regiments," for whom Callwell's *Small Wars* and its successors – Charles Gwynn's *Imperial Policing* (1934) and H. J Simson's *British Rule and Rebellion* (1937) – became staff college staples into the post-World War II years.[6]

There are several problems with the COIN-dinista arguments, but let's begin by challenging the Mockaitis–Nagl assertion that the British military broke the code on counterinsurgency in the interwar years and managed to become an exemplary learning organization that transmitted its minimum force/aid to the civil wisdom through the generations. As has been seen, the British Army did not have a particularly exemplary record at COIN or at any warfare, for that matter, at the time of Malaya. It had been run out of Ireland in 1921 – not as Mockaitis states, because they failed to coordinate an effective counterinsurgent plan until the spring of 1921, by which time it was too late.[7] In fact, British action in Ireland combined tactical success with strategic disaster. Michael Collins admitted that the IRA was "dead beat" by June 1921. But the program of collective reprisals, house burnings, internment, summary executions, and other COIN refinements crystallized support for separation among Irish Catholics many of whom disapproved of the IRA's methods, while it undermined backing for Lloyd George's "mean and unnecessary war" among a British public shamed by the excesses of the RIC and the Auxiliaries.[8] Nor had Palestine been a resounding success. To be fair, no evenhanded policy was likely to work given the incompatible interests of Arab and Jew. But as in Ireland, ham-fisted British counterinsurgency tactics in Palestine applied in a political vacuum only served to unite moderates in the Jewish Agency and the Haganah with the extremist groups in a common cause to drive the British from Palestine. Given this fairly dismal track record of imperial policing failure, how then did the British recover suddenly to cop the prize as the world's foremost counterinsurgents?

The British Army as a learning organization

John Nagl argues that the British Army was successful at counterinsurgency because it was an "efficient learning organization" that cultivated an attitude that they must "correct quickly the things that are wrong" because it was small and had a culture honed in colonial wars.[9] In fact, the charge against the British Army was that it was very slow to adapt because it lacked solid leadership and a tradition of operational and tactical problem-solving. "Indifferent," "amateur," "the mockery of the world" are some of the kinder descriptions that Max Hastings applied to World War II British generals.[10] Of course, he was referring to the British Army's wooden approach to conventional operations, which are more difficult to coordinate than counterinsurgency ones. But it is not clear that regimental-centric decentralization made the British any more adaptable in imperial police actions. In fact, the post-1945 British Army faced many of the same Cold War distractions that allegedly impeded "organizational learning" for counterinsurgency in the French and American armies, the constant recycling of two-year National Servicemen and the requirement to train for conventional warfare in Europe and even the Middle East among them. Adaptation was further impeded by the loss of the Indian army in 1947 that historically had executed imperial "sovereignty missions." While like most armies, the British had a system of recording campaign "lessons learned" and translating them into doctrinal manuals, one of the drawbacks of a decentralized, regimentalized command structure is that the transmission of techniques from conflict to conflict really rather depended on the receptiveness of the battalion commander. This explains the persistence of large-scale sweeps and "cordon-and-search" operations despite their drawbacks. Even Mockaitis concedes that counterinsurgency lessons were more likely to be transmitted outside of official channels by word of mouth or through the books of Thompson and General Frank Kitson.[11]

Even if the army managed to pass on "traditional wisdom" organized around the three principles of minimum force, civil-military cooperation, and tactical flexibility,[12] the Colonial Office on whom a "whole of government" approach depended was in the opinion of David French a "forgetting organization." In any case, the Colonial Office and the police often lacked the personnel or cash to implement "best practices" even if they recognized what should be done.[13] Because each colony was expected to bear the costs of the counterinsurgency campaign and because it might reflect poorly on their leadership, colonial governors were often slow to admit that they faced a problem, take preventative measures, and call for help. Which is why they relied upon, even encouraged, cost-effective but politically risky ethnic or sectarian police forces and paramilitary organizations of settlers in Malaya and Kenya and other ad hoc creations. One reason that Briggs and Templer were able to create such an elaborate counterinsurgency apparatus was that Malaya was a wealthy colony able to finance it. The financial burden combined with the highly publicized violence in the British-run detention camps during the Kenyan Emergency helped to convince Prime Minister Harold Macmillan that the lawless brutality of British counterinsurgency had forfeited London's moral right to rule African colonies.[14] Decentralization, far from facilitating "organizational learning," too often translated into a lack of supervision, lapses of discipline, racist attitudes, and abuse of the population – as General Bobby Erskine discovered upon his arrival in Kenya.[15]

Britain's small wars

Not surprisingly, historians taking a closer look at post-World War II British counterinsurgency campaigns have drawn less laudatory conclusions. As for national styles of counterinsurgency, Chris Bayly and Tim Harper writing of decolonization in Southeast Asia and David Anderson's masterful book on the Mau Mau have revealed them as wars every bit as repressive – even "dirty" – as those fought by the French.[16] Rather than win by applying Mockaitis' three COIN principles, the formula for victory in Malaya's "model conflict" relied on far more repressive methods. Of Malaya's 5.3 million people in 1945, roughly half were Malays who lived in *kampongs* under the governance of British-appointed headmen. About 38 percent were Chinese immigrants imported by the British to work in the Peninsula's tin mines and rubber plantations. Eleven percent were Indians, mainly Tamils, paid starvation wages by white planters who governed their vast rubber estates like feudal kingdoms. Twelve thousand Europeans, mostly British, supplied the executive and managerial class. The only thing that united these disparate communities was their poverty, deepened by wartime destruction and dislocation, and the conviction that Britain's failure to defend Malaya and Singapore from the 1941 Japanese invasion had delegitimized the imperial mandate. Otherwise, communal tensions ran high, with Malay nationalists scapegoating Indian moneylenders and Chinese shopkeepers, whom they blamed for their community's poverty.[17]

Postwar violence that swept South and Southeast Asia was fed in Malaya by consternation over London's glacial postwar conversion of Malaya to Commonwealth status. At first glance, the Chinese were best placed to take advantage of it – the overwhelmingly Chinese-dominated Malayan Communist Party (MCP) had organized powerful unions from the 1930s and seized on the invasion to form the SOE-supported Malayan People's Anti-Japanese Army (MPAJA), a force of several thousand men that emerged at war's end to inflict a reign of terror on "collaborators" and police that stoked communal violence in which hundreds died. The prospect of opposition from Muslim Malays, not fear of the British who were thin on the ground and who in any case had their hands full in India and Burma, dissuaded the MCP from declaring a provisional government in 1945. Instead, the MCP disbanded the MPAJA and cooperated with the British Military Administration in the

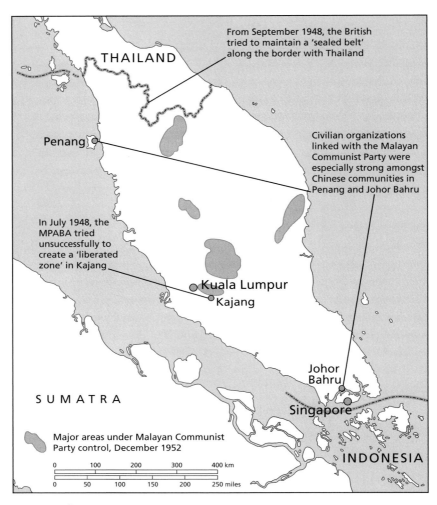

THAILAND

From September 1948, the British tried to maintain a 'sealed belt' along the border with Thailand

Penang

Civilian organizations linked with the Malayan Communist Party were especially strong amongst Chinese communities in Penang and Johor Bahru

In July 1948, the MPABA tried unsuccessfully to create a 'liberated zone' in Kajang

Kuala Lumpur
Kajang

Johor Bahru

SUMATRA

Singapore

Major areas under Malayan Communist Party control, December 1952

| 0 | 100 | 200 | 300 | 400 km |

| 0 | 50 | 100 | 150 | 200 | 250 miles |

INDONESIA

Map 5 Malaya

hope that they could leverage their strong political base in the unions to carve out a powerful position in the proposed multiethnic Malayan Union.[18] It proved a missed opportunity, for in 1946 the British abandoned a multiracial concept of Union citizenship in favor of a Malay-dominated Federation of Malaya, promised independence at some distant future date. With the citizenship, and hence political future, of Malaya's Chinese community in doubt, the unions under siege by employers and police, and legal avenues slammed shut, the MCP stepped up protests and labor unrest, and began to prepare camps in the jungle, which the British correctly interpreted as a prelude to insurrection.[19]

But the MCP was experiencing serious problems of leadership, finances, and internal divisions even before June 16, 1948, when the killing of three European plantation managers announced the beginning of hostilities. The "White Terror" against the Chinese community unleashed by the State of Emergency outlawed the Chinese-dominated trade unions, arrested many left-wing leaders, and imposed what one author has called "a veritable police state on Malaya." Extra-judicial detention and deportation were the preferred methods because the government wanted to show firmness, because authorities seldom collected evidence that would hold up in court, and because trials would have attracted both in-country and international protests. In Malaya, 226 people were officially executed, while 31,245 "communists" were eventually deported to China, where many may have been executed.[20]

Indeed, fear of detention and deportation proved the prime recruiter for the 5,000-strong Malayan People's Anti-British Army (MPABA), renamed the Malayan People's Liberation Army (MPLA)[21] on February 1, 1949 in an unsuccessful attempt to broaden its support base. But rebranding failed to transform the MPLA into an effective guerrilla army or expand its appeal to the South Asian community.[22] MPLA units seldom coordinated operations. They failed to establish a presence in the towns where 27 percent of the population lived. Instead, insurgents survived by creating logistical networks from 1949, called Min Yuen, in camps where Chinese squatters lived as miners, loggers, and peasant farmers on the jungle's fringe. But lack of food kept units small, while an arsenal of antiquated Japanese weapons limited their actions to assassinations, small-scale ambushes, destroying identity cards, and slashing rubber trees. British pressure progressively fragmented the insurgents and drove them deeper into the jungle.[23]

Despite MCP disorganization and the fact that imperial authorities had been obsessed by the prospect of a communist insurrection for some time,[24] the British proved remarkably ill-prepared to confront an insurgency that their divide and rule policies had ignited. Malaya was garrisoned by ten understrength, poorly trained infantry battalions in 1948, together with 12,000, mainly Malay police. Counterinsurgency tactics were Boer War redux – when sweeps by large units guided by maps that had not been updated since 1928 failed to yield results, the British turned to detentions, settlement burning, and summary executions of Chinese laborers passed off as "insurgents" because they were found in possession of rice, cups, batteries, or simply because they had failed the "callus test."[25] Indeed, brutal and indiscriminate army reprisals against the population convinced High Commissioner Sir Henry Gurney to expand the police from 1948 and give them the operational lead.[26] But while the "police" were reinforced by five hundred constables imported from Palestine and ad hoc formations of settler volunteers, most of whom were army veterans, and Malay *kampong* auxiliaries, "aid to the civil" was notable by its absence – while the police and the army were meant to coordinate operations, an absence of administrative structures, different service cultures, or personality clashes meant that each often preferred to operate on their own. Nor did they share intelligence, in part because the diminutive Special Branch contained few Mandarin speakers. Thus "support to the civil" actually left soldiers legally less constrained than had they operated under the laws of war.[27]

The counterinsurgency narrative recounts that the turnaround in British fortunes was engineered by Sir Harold Briggs, appointed Director of Operations in April 1950 by Gurney precisely to control the army and better coordinate its operations with those of the police,[28] and consolidated by General Sir Gerald Templer, who combined the Director of Operations with the post of High Commissioner after Gurney's death in an insurgent ambush from December 1951. The actions of these men to centralize the planning and coordination of the civil and military element of the counterinsurgency campaign in Malaya have become legendary in the literature of counterinsurgency.[29] Nagl argues that these two men rescued the bungled "conventional strategy" of their predecessors with an organization and tactics more appropriate to war among the people, thus solidifying the British Army's colonial policing and administration vocation.[30] Thompson, who as Permanent Secretary for Defense in Malaya acted as the Boswell to these two COIN-dinista Johnsons, chronicled the reorganization of the British effort in Malaya which he sold as a template for successful COIN anywhere, but most particularly in Vietnam. "Winning the population can tritely be summed up as good government in all its aspects," which prioritized schools, democratic transparency, self-help projects, and security provided by close cooperation of the police and the army.[31]

The army was doubled to twenty-one battalions, more men than the British had seen fit to deploy to defend Malaya and Singapore against the Japanese in 1941. The definition of terrorism was expanded.

"Malaysian Scouts," specially formed Special Forces units, perfected deep penetration raids guided by information gleaned by an improved intelligence organization. Propaganda units worked the internment camps. Infiltrators revealed the coordinates of MPLA jungle camps that could be bombed by the RAF. But this was a slow process that left London impatient for tangible evidence of progress, especially as collective punishments, aerial fumigation of food crops, and poor conditions in the camps raised questions in Parliament and the press.[32] The key to success in Malaya, in Thompson's view, was population resettlement, a program launched by Briggs in June 1950 after Mao's victory in the Chinese Civil War made deportation more problematic. Nor had deportations, while viewed as a "ruthless" response, lessened insurgent violence.[33] The goal was to move half a million Chinese into "new villages," which turned out to be crime-infested "rural ghettos" guarded by barbed wire enclosures and searchlights that combined all the comforts of Kitchener's concentration camps minus the "Ladies Committee." A further 650,000 plantation and mine workers were also forced to live behind barbed wire, subjects of owners who seized the opportunity to extinguish the last vestiges of union representation. Communities were divided, families scattered, sequestered, and starved.[34]

One recent historian of the Malaya campaign concluded that the MCP "lost because of the scale of the difficulties they faced and because the British exploited those difficulties." The resettlement of the Chinese population, although slow and expensive, separated the insurgency from its base. The army's increasingly efficient jungle warfare skills, and the Special Branch's better intelligence collection and exploitation combined with the support of the Malay population which supplied home guards, police, and soldiers in a campaign of relentless attrition isolated the MCP/MPLA.[35]

Another view, however, holds that the insurgency was basically isolated, dislocated, and whipped by "conventional tactics" before the Briggs Plan was put into action and Templer imposed coherence and method onto a hitherto flailing and improvised British counterinsurgency campaign. The insurgency simmered in the jungle without hope of victory because the MPLA was able neither to broaden its social base, nor increase the level of violence, nor break out of its geographical isolation.[36] It was not "model counterinsurgency" tactics that ultimately extinguished the war in Malaya. Rather, it was the realization by Churchill's Conservative government, elected in

November 1951, that insurrection was rooted in local loyalties and concrete grievances – the lack of opportunity and upward mobility, and political and economic insecurity in an ethnically and socially stratified Malay society. The fundamental causes of the insurgency had not been addressed by the Emergency because the British saw the MPLA as a collection of "misfits maladjusted to normal society, the selfish, the too ambitious, and the discontented or the ill-advised minorities" rooted in some mystical Chinese "secret society complex,"[37] and because any political concessions to the Chinese community risked alienating the Malays.

This situation began to change with the June 1950 outbreak of the Korean War that sent prices for tin and especially rubber skyward, which raised living standards across all communities. In February 1952, Templer was ordered to offer the Chinese citizenship in an independent Malaya, in part because London feared that France's deteriorating situation in Indochina might over time end MCP/MPLA isolation. This allowed what Bayly and Harper call a "new generation" of Malay, South Asian, and Chinese leaders willing to circumvent British divide and rule tactics and forge the multiethnic Alliance Party in 1953 to take advantage of "a world of rapidly expanding horizons." The Alliance Party stormed to power in the July 1955 elections on a platform of self-government that undercut the appeal of the MCP and its insurrection.[38] In the final analysis, British policies had provoked the insurgency, while communal favoritism coupled with counterinsurgency tactics had succeeded only in proliferating misery and "personal tragedy" rather than seeking to win hearts and minds. COIN tactics had served only to make the Emergency nastier and more costly in lives and resources than it need have been, not to resolve its fundamental causes.

Kenya

As in Malaya, in Kenya the British counterinsurgency strategy also made little attempt to win the hearts and minds of the 1.4 million Kikuyus who made up roughly 28 percent of the Kenyan population, concentrated in the highlands close to Nairobi. Instead, in the words of British historian of that conflict David Anderson, "between 1952 and 1956, when fighting was at its worst, the Kikuyu districts of Kenya became a police state in the very fullest sense of that term."[39] The roots of the Kenyan Emergency

Map 6 Kenya

can be traced to the arrival of white settlers and missionaries at the turn of the twentieth century. Settlers progressively displaced the Kikuyu, especially in the so-called "White Highlands" where coffee was introduced in 1912, and cattle post-World War I. As more settlers arrived, Kikuyu were forced into crowded reserves under the authority of British appointed "chiefs" required to keep order, collect taxes, administer justice, produce corvée labor for roads and railway projects, and stifle political opposition.[40] Others "squatted" on *shambas*, small plots carved out of white estates, which were far from models of Karen Blixen, "Out of Africa" paternalistic harmony.

Mission schools became the stepping-stone for many ambitious Kikuyu boys unable to find work or wives in the reserves to jobs as telephone operators, clerks, and tradesmen in Nairobi, which had become a racially segregated boomtown by the 1920s in which black Africans were denied the right of permanent residence. Therefore, swarms of rootless young males huddled in makeshift shantytowns that were periodically demolished by municipal authorities who correctly recognized them as intersections of politics and criminality, and a form of resistance to imperial racial boundaries. From the 1920s, conservative chiefs began to clash with nationalistic "mission boys" from less well-to-do families like Jomo Kenyatta, the unions, and the Kikuyu Central Association (KCA), who denounced them as imperial collaborators.[41]

Windfall profits reaped by white settlers during World War II who raised cattle, or grew coffee, tea, or maize, were shared by few Africans on the reserves who were reduced to famine by inflated prices for basic foodstuffs, which failed to drop in the immediate postwar years. Mechanization of agriculture and the arrival of more white settlers forced the relocation of 100,000 squatters from the White Highlands to the reserves between 1945 and 1952, which became rural slums filled with young men unable to marry because they could not pay the bride price. Others crowded into makeshift urban neighborhoods in Nairobi where the color barrier and vexatious pass laws were strictly enforced.[42]

"Oathing" – a traditional Kikuyu practice meant to bind men together in the face of hardship – began spontaneously in the 1940s and spread rapidly, especially among the 75,000 Kenyan veterans of World War II. White settlers called this oath "Mau Mau," an invented, meaningless term that nevertheless conveyed the official view that Kikuyu discontent represented a resurgence of African primitivism rather than a perfectly comprehensible protest against an increasingly intolerable white settler/chief condominium. Perhaps more important was the politicization of young men in the towns by the East African Trades Union Congress (EATUC) which had called for independence on May 1, 1950, a declaration quickly followed by a general strike. The police crushed both the strike and the EATUC, which drove its more radical leaders into the ranks of the hitherto moderate KCA and the Kenya Africa Union (KAU), constitutionally recognized as representing black Kenyans. Under this more insurrectionary leadership, the oathing movement spread into Nairobi, while the original talk of civil disobedience gave

14 Kikuyu cattle rounded up by the British in Kenya in March 1953 to deprive the population of a livelihood and hence starve the so-called Mau Mau insurgency.

way to violence against opponents. The governor, hoping to slip quietly into retirement with an unblemished record, failed to alert the Colonial Office of the deteriorating situation. However, in June 1952, the government imposed collective fines and punishments in areas affected by oathing, and pressured loyalist chiefs and moderate heads of the KAU to denounce Mau Mau.

On October 20, 1952, Operation Jock Scott inaugurated a State of Emergency. Jomo Kenyatta and other prominent leaders numbered among 8,000 arrested in the first month of an Emergency that essentially declared the Kikuyu a "criminal tribe." In keeping with East Africa's long history of judicial violence against the indigenous population, Kenyatta was convicted of complicity with the rebellion and given a seven-year sentence although no evidence could be produced of his guilt.[43] But the decapitation strategy only succeeded in triggering a January 1953 declaration of war from a group called the Council of Freedom that organized underground committees to supply the Land and Freedom Armies whose soldiers, inflated by Jock Scott refugees, had begun to muster in the jungles of the Aberdare mountains and Mount Kenya in Central Province.[44]

As in Malaya, neither side was prepared to fight a protracted guerrilla war. The Mau Mau were, if anything, less unified and organized than had been the hapless MCP in 1948, without money, weapons, a command structure, military bases, or a strategy. While the Mau Mau enjoyed significant sympathy among most Kikuyu in Nairobi and on the reserves in the Rift Valley, support beyond the Central Province was lacking. Vague political demands summed up in the motto "land and freedom," which were variously interpreted to mean expropriation of white settler land, an end to discrimination in hiring, freedom for trade unions, and national independence, hardly qualified Mau Mau as one of Thompson's "communist insurgencies." Nevertheless, the British declaration of an Emergency without the troops and police to enforce it left Mau Mau bands free to range through the reserves often hacking "loyalist" villagers to death because machete-like *pangas* were the only weapons they had, but seldom attacking white settlers.[45] By the end of the conflict, only 100 Europeans and 1,800 loyalists had been killed, against an official total of 11,000 Kikuyu deaths. Caroline Elkins puts the real number of African deaths in the hundreds of thousands and so qualifies the British COIN in Kenya as "a murderous campaign to eliminate the Kikuyu people" in the name of Britain's civilizing mission.[46] In fact, the Mau Mau emergency was a Kikuyu civil war that featured communal violence, not a race war. This did not prevent white settlers, police, and loyalist Home Guards from competing to inflict staggering levels of violence on the Kikuyu population, claiming that they faced an anti-modern, atavistic, racially inferior foe, a stance that allowed them to dismiss the legitimate grievances that sparked the insurrection. Beating prisoners to extract information and "confessions," the execution of wounded, mutilation of corpses, taking bodies of alleged Mau Mau from village to village to demonstrate the consequences of rebellion, or even putting heads on stakes in front of police stations were common. The Kenyan Police Reserves and the Special Branch were even accused of organizing murder squads to "disappear" suspects.[47]

Only in June 1953 did General Bobby Erskine, a veteran of Palestine, arrive to impose some order on a hitherto improvised imperial counter-revolution. His immediate task was to rein in army and police violence which had begun to attract attention in Britain, but which put him at odds with the white settler community, one well represented in the

King's African Rifles officer corps and in the Kenya Police Reserve.[48] For the next six months, 20,000 troops swept the reserves, and the "Prohibited Areas" of the Aberdares and Mount Kenya, shooting Africans on sight. But a Westminster commission concluded in January 1954 that Nairobi was effectively controlled by insurgents, while the rebellion had begun to contaminate other tribes, especially the Kamba who furnished railway workers, police, and soldiers, and even some Masai in the south of the country. Faced with these challenges, Erskine deployed the usual panoply of counterinsurgency measures – photo identification cards, shanty clearings, roadblocks, closing down businesses suspected of supplying food or funds to the insurgency, and emergency courts with expansive powers to dispatch to the gallows anyone who met the yawning definition of an "insurgent."[49] In April 1953, Special Branch gutted what remained of the Trades Union leadership in Nairobi. The opposition found no effective counter, and were reduced to boycotting buses and South Asian-owned shops, and refusing to buy British cigarettes and beer.

However, as in Malaya, the British put their money on internment as the strategy for breaking the back of the insurgency. Operation Anvil in April 1954 massed 25,000 troops and police to cordon off Nairobi, a city of roughly 95,000 people. Screening teams of the colonial officials and the Kenya Police Reserve aided by hooded informants detained 27,000 mainly Kikuyu men and women, some as young as twelve, and deported a further 20,000 back to the reserves. Internment violated the European Convention on Human Rights to which London had put its signature. However, lawyers claimed that the Convention did not apply to Africans, and that article 15 of the Convention allowed detention without trial during a "public emergency threatening the life of the nation."[50] Swept up in this bureaucratic dragnet was the Mau Mau Central Committee and what was left of the militant trade union leadership, together with business work forces, entire church congregations, and parents of children who were left to fend for themselves on the streets. Authorities, however, declared their ethnic cleansing of the capital a counterinsurgency triumph – Nairobi was declared Mau Mau-*frei* as members of other tribes streamed in to occupy formerly Kikuyu-owned businesses and houses.[51]

Forced "villagization" shifted to the reserves. Inspired by Templer's incarceration of Chinese in Malaya, Kenyan officials swept through the countryside torching Kikuyu huts and transferring over a million terrified Kenyans into what is described as "little concentration camps" – 800 settlements surrounded by trenches, barbed wire, and watchtowers, and patrolled by armed guards where the population could be "rehabilitated" by a regime of starvation and forced labor while sleeping rough and unsheltered, punctuated by regular beatings by club- and whip-wielding Home Guards designed to break the spirit of Kikuyu men.[52] Starvation rations made pellagra endemic while unsanitary conditions caused periodic outbreaks of typhoid and other diseases. Erskine "resettled" a greater percentage of the population than did any other counterinsurgency campaign, including the French in Algeria or the Portuguese in Mozambique.

With the Mau Mau locked out and their Kikuyu subjects locked in, corrupt chiefs and compliant Home Guards, who numbered 25,600 by November 1954, were joined by mission-organized vigilantes who extorted bribes from Kikuyu eager to avoid incarceration, or looted the homes of detainees. Resettlement became a form of counter-terror and intimidation. Kikuyu were persuaded to enlist in the Home Guards with exemptions from taxes, communal labor, pass laws, fines, and with opportunities to plunder, settle personal or family grudges, or simply upgrade their family's meager food rations. Refusal to enlist was taken as a sign of Mau Mau sympathies, and an occasion to pile on all of the above. Confiscating the land of Mau Mau supporters and transferring titles to loyalists provided an important inducement to support the British, who also lifted the bitterly resented prohibition on Africans growing coffee, which both raised the value of land in coffee-growing areas and increased rural revenue.[53] Home Guard transgressions were seldom prosecuted for fear that they would desert to the Mau Mau.[54] However, Home Guards were more valuable as a counter-mobilization strategy than as a military organization with bite, except when released to retaliate against the local population. In March 1954, the Police Commissioner recommended that Home Guard abuses combined with the fact that the chiefs employed them to pursue their own local political agendas should lead to their abolition.[55]

Meanwhile, suspect Kikuyu males were introduced to the Pipeline, a system of classification introduced in 1953 that allowed them to progress through a series of camps to release based on compliant behavior, a willingness to confess to the crime of belonging to the insurgency, and to implicate others in the conspiracy against British rule. Confessions were both a psyops and an intelligence-gathering tactic anchored in the theories of Louis Leakey and Dr. J. C. Carothers, a psychiatrist who claimed special insight into the "African mind," who argued that inducing confessions would break the hold of the oath on the Mau Mau as a step toward reintegration into the Kikuyu social system on which their mental health depended.[56] Screening teams interrogated suspects and organized "confessional baranzas" where Mau Mau sympathizers were forced publicly to recant their sins and identify co-conspirators. Many confessed just to gain release. But by 1956, the brutality of these camps which featured solitary confinement and starvation for even minor offenses had succeeded in turning even lukewarm Mau Mau into hard-core resistors. Embarrassed that 30,000 Mau Mau persisted in their refusal to recant, in 1957 the British launched Operation Progress, a program of systematic beatings and horrific tortures in the camps permitted under regulations that allowed guards to used "compelling force" to gain inmate compliance, which included hanging suspects upside down, filling their mouths with mud, group assaults, and something called "bucket fatigue" whereby inmates were forced to carry buckets of water or sand on their heads while their knees were bent, until they collapsed. In 1958, the government called off Progress after press reports of brutality in the camps elicited embarrassing questions from Labour MPs. However, when an inquiry in March 1959 revealed that ten inmates had died in the Hola detention camp from beatings, even the Conservative anti-immigration MP Enoch Powell criticized Westminster's "pitiful yearning to cling to the relics of a bygone system."[57]

As the oil spot of government control of Nairobi and the fortification of villages on the reserves expanded, the loose confederacy of Mau Mau bands assembled under the grand title of the Land and Freedom Army were forced further into the bush and away from the reserves. Resettlement, internment, and the Home Guards dried up recruitment. Erskine mustered detainees to cut tracks into the bush and establish base camps for army patrols. Subsisting on a diet of maize porridge and jungle meat, and with few weapons, the remnants of the Land and Freedom Army were stalked with sweeps and pseudo-gangs of captured and turned Mau Mau, a tactic imported from Palestine and Malaya by Captain Frank Kitson which proved remarkably effective. By the end of 1956, with the leader of the Land and Freedom Army captured and hanged, the Mau Mau rebellion was effectively over. A victory which COIN-dinistas rank in the annals of British arms with Waterloo and El Alamein had been won in a war in which official executions, extra-judicial killings, the torture of prisoners especially by the settler-dominated Kenya Police Reserve but also by the army, and incarcerations, Anderson estimates, exceeded anything carried out by the Dutch in Indonesia or the French in Algeria.[58]

It is possible to argue, as does Elkins, that Britain's apparent operational success in Kenya in fact led to strategic defeat, because the brutality of its COIN tactics carried out with a deliberate disregard, even flaunting, of legal constraints, mocked the legitimacy of Britain's claim to rule Kenya.[59] So, in a perverse way, the Mau Mau forced the pace of transition to majority rule in an independent Kenya. There was also a fear that if Britain did not take steps to transition power in Kenya, they might face Mau Mau round two. This is because the application of hearts and minds techniques fundamental to COIN theory assumes an ability to establish a commonality of interests between the counterinsurgent and the target population. The British instead allied in true imperial small wars fashion with minority settlers and their loyalist collaborators against the interests of a legitimately aggrieved Kikuyu majority. In the absence of a program that removed economic and social grievances, allowed for the creation of forums for political expression and reform to convince the population to supply the British with intelligence, recruits, and political support to isolate the insurgents, counterinsurgency as practiced by the British boiled down to unalloyed repression and torture inflicted in the name of inculcating a culture of "Britishness" in the African population. All of these considerations speeded the decision to disengage. The British government allowed direct election of the African members of the Legislative Assembly in 1957, increased African representation in the Legislative Assembly in January 1960, and granted complete independence in December 1963, far ahead of schedule.[60] Those in the white settler community who cared to leave were compensated generously by the government.

COIN tactics as applied in Palestine, Malaya, and Kenya had demonstrated the high costs of empire, both financially and morally, to a country struggling to recover from the effects of World War II. Post-war schemes to make Africa profitable had failed. The Kenya Emergency had cost the Exchequer £55 million, at a time when 32,000 British troops aided by 8,000 mainly Turkish Cypriot auxiliaries deploying deportations, decapitation, torture, pseudo gangs, police violence, and sweeps, and encouraging inter-communal friction between Greeks and Turks appeared unable to corral a handful of Greek Cypriot insurgents on an island the size of Wales. These COIN tactics failed in a strategic environment in which the sympathies of roughly 400,000 Greeks, who made up 82 percent of the island's population, lay with the *Ethniki Organosis Kyprion Agoniston* (National Organization of Cypriot Fighters, or EOKA) fighting for union with Greece. Police reinforcements sent from the UK were both ignorant of local languages and behaved with a callousness experienced by other colonial subjects, that further staunched the intelligence flow. "If [Field Marshal Sir John] Harding [the Governor of Cyprus] carefully had planned to alienate the entire Greek population of the island and push the moderate Greeks into full support of EOKA, he could not have done better than by his policy of unleashing a horde of untrained, poorly-led Turkish police on the population," concludes Lieutenant Colonel James S. Corum.[61] Unfortunately, Cyprus was hardly the exception, but merely confirmed the pattern of British COIN, which sought to intimidate the population through tactics of violence.

The brutality of Britain's post-World War II counterinsurgency campaigns combined with the 1956 Suez fiasco seriously to damage the high regard in the international community which Britain's heroic wartime conduct had earned it. In February 1960, Macmillan delivered his "winds of change" speech to the South African Parliament in Cape Town, which outlined the British government's intention to shed its African possessions. Cyprus was granted independence in August, after the government concluded that, with the loss of India, Palestine, and Suez, it no longer needed a base in the Eastern Mediterranean. Some Conservatives objected. But the Devlin report in October 1960, which accused the British of using "police state" tactics in Nyasaland, left even many Conservatives with the feeling that empire, and the repressive COIN campaigns required to sustain it, had become an electoral liability.[62]

Conclusion

Thompson and Mockaitis argue that the British laid the foundations in the interwar years for a new counterinsurgency approach that focused on minimum force, aid to the civil power, and tactical flexibility in which examples of brutality were atypical events perpetrated by settler police auxiliaries and semi-trained conscripts. In *The Politics of the British Army*, Hew Strachan argues that victories in British colonial campaigns were bought with timely political concessions, not earned through the efficiency of British COIN tactics.[63] Claims of British COIN success based on minimum force and acting with the bounds of legality rest on wobbly historical foundations: David French's *The British Way in Counter-Insurgency* culminates at least a decade of scholarship that challenges the claims of Mockaitis, Richard Duncan Downie, and John Nagl that the British broke the counterinsurgency code in the interwar years and transmitted their successful tactical formula into the post-World War II era. The British can justifiably claim to have succeeded in Malaya, Kenya, and Nyasaland, although by employing methods that strain the dictionary definitions of "aid to the civil power" and "minimum force," not to mention the tender connotations of hearts and minds. These were also insurgencies that claimed such a narrow support base, limited resources, and sclerotic strategic vision that their chances of success would have been problematical even with less competent or ruthless opposition. Cyprus was a quasi-success in that London prevented *Enosis* – union with Greece – and retained bases on the island, although the Greek Cypriot rebellion forced it to concede sovereignty over an island that, after departure from Palestine in 1948, Westminster viewed as a vital strategic enclave in the Eastern Mediterranean. Likewise, Oman became a do-over project because COIN-induced stability failed to stick. Palestine, the Suez Canal Zone, and Aden slip into the lost column.[64] And Mockaitis to the contrary, British success where it occurred depended on contingent factors like ethnic divisions, geographic isolation, the political mistakes of insurgent leaders, or the granting of political concessions by the British that deflated the rebellion. In short, were Britain's post-1945 won–lost record that of a football team, the coach would most assuredly be searching for alternative employment.

Strachan notes that aid to the civil was not imperial practice. Rather, a fusion of civil and military authority was the rule in post-Mutiny India because the army was recognized as the central pillar of British power in places where British presence was not welcomed. A "whole of government" approach that combined administrators, soldiers, and policemen of the sort that eluded the French was instituted in Malaya by General Sir Harold Briggs in 1950 and perfected during Templer's time as High Commissioner there (1952–1955). But by that time, the system of civil-military councils simply put the ribbon on a counterinsurgency campaign against an ill-prepared, ethnically and geographically isolated, financially strapped, and incompetently led MCP whose defeat had already been sealed by robust military action.[65] The British never evolved a systematic structure of committee governance that migrated from crisis to crisis, in large part because the Colonial Office as the lead agency in the colonies never instituted a system of lessons learned. On the contrary, the Colonial Office response to crises was invariably ad hoc, improvised, and tardy, for several reasons: colonial governors were loath to admit that the security situation was out of hand lest it reflect badly on their governance; they lacked loyal local allies on whom to base a stabilization strategy; or because colonial civil servants were unwilling to concede powers to the military.[66] Therefore, rather than offering an exceptional example of an organization that evolved a system to police and control colonial populations within legal constraints, British counterinsurgency operations suffered the same problems of brutality, adaptation, and patterns of checkered success as did those of the French and Americans.

9 BRITAIN'S THIRTY YEARS' WAR IN NORTHERN IRELAND

It is difficult to square John Nagl's praise of the British Army's capacity for organizational learning with its poor early performance in Northern Ireland after 1969. As Irish historian John Bew notes, while the British Army views their intervention in Northern Ireland as "a rare success," in fact, the application of the army's historically coercive COIN tactics there in the months from 1970 proved to be the least successful phase of the thirty-year campaign. When combined with Westminster's early policy of neglect and delayed intervention, the army's actions most certainly gave unrest momentum[1] by helping to transform a political confrontation into an inter-communal conflict that endured for more than three decades. The British experience in Northern Ireland also reinforces Clausewitz's dictum that war is politics, and that small war tactics applied in the absence of a political strategy designed to isolate extremists by presenting viable alternatives to the majority of the population offer a recipe for repression or prolonged stalemate, which is exactly what Northern Ireland became after 1970.

The crisis that evolved in Northern Ireland in the late 1960s was the product of a collision between the post-Great War "Troubles" with the 1960s civil rights movement. The Catholic minority in Ulster, which made up slightly more than one-third of the population, viewed the partition of the island in 1921 as a denial of full national self-determination. However, although they were subject to electoral, housing, health care, educational, and employment discrimination by Protestant-dominated local councils, neither IRA attempts to harness German assistance to provoke rebellion during World War II, nor the so-called "Border Campaign" of the 1950s

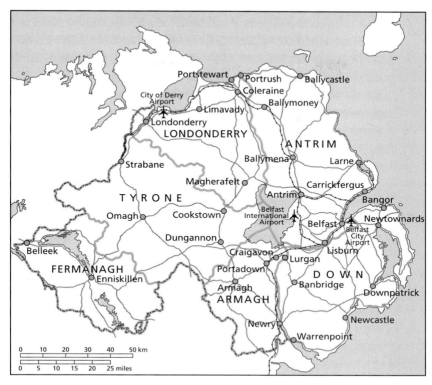

Map 7 Northern Ireland

had encountered more than a whisper of popular support among Catholics in the North, many of whom viewed the IRA as "guys who would take the eye out of your head and say you'd look better without it."[2] When from 1963, the leader of the Northern Ireland Assembly at Stormont, Terence O'Neill, realizing that Ulster had to jettison its historic legacy of religious tribalism as a condition for modernization, had tried to mitigate discrimination, he met intractable opposition from hardline Unionists (so-called because they supported the Act of Union with the UK) and members of the sectarian Orange Order. Meanwhile, inspired by the civil rights campaign in the United States and 1960s student radicalism, a growing middle class of grammar-school-educated Catholic activists working through organizations like the Campaign for Social Justice, the Northern Ireland Civil Rights Association, and the Derry Housing Action Committee pressed for an end to discrimination. They found support in Britain's Labour Party, elected to office in 1964 under Harold Wilson.

A vicious October 5, 1968 assault by the Royal Ulster Constabulary (RUC) on a small but peaceful civil rights march in Londonderry announced that a Catholic push for an end to discrimination would not go unchallenged by Protestant hardliners, who suspected the IRA of steering the civil rights movement. To diffuse the situation, O'Neill introduced a five-point plan designed to assuage Catholic discontent and sacked his Home Secretary, who had been critical of the civil rights movement. However, when a radical, mainly Marxist fringe sought to replicate the Selma to Birmingham march in Alabama with a Londonderry to Belfast march, O'Neill allowed it to proceed, even though the mainline civil rights movement opposed it as provocative. When on January 1, 1969 the civil rights marchers were attacked by Protestants on the Burntollet Bridge, many of them members of the Special Constabulary, called 'B' Specials, the Protestant-dominated RUC predictably looked on with folded arms, so that Catholics began to wonder how far peaceful protest would take them. The answer came four days later when the RUC carried out what can only be described as a police riot in Bogside, a working-class Catholic neighborhood in Londonderry.

The assertion by Unionist hardliners that the civil rights movement was simply an IRA front became a self-fulfilling prophesy. In March and April, Protestant paramilitaries carried out a number of bomb attacks on public utility sites which they blamed on the IRA in a successful attempt to force O'Neill's resignation. In fact, the Catholic civil rights movement and the Protestant backlash it incurred caught the IRA completely by surprise and severely compromised their strategy, adopted in the 1960s in the wake of the "Border Campaign" failure, of attempting to unite Protestant and Catholic workers around common economic grievances. The no-show "I Ran Away" IRA was derided by Catholic youths. Although the civil rights movement scaled back its demonstrations to calm the situation, O'Neill's hardline replacement, James Chichester-Clark, allowed the traditional July–August Protestant "marching season," deliberately calculated to remind Catholics of their defeat and subjugation since the seventeenth century, to proceed. The consequences were predictable – Catholic youths attacked the Protestant marchers, which touched off two months of riots in Belfast and Londonderry. Catholics barricaded their neighborhoods to protect them against Protestant rampages abetted by the RUC. In December 1969, a splinter group of IRA activists vowed to enter the struggle to protect the Catholic population under the name of the Provisional IRA.[3]

When the collapse of police control in Northern Ireland prompted the British government to dispatch British soldiers to Belfast and Londonderry in mid August 1969 to separate the two communities, problems were bound to arise. In the first place, Westminster had no policy for Northern Ireland beyond viewing itself as an honest broker between the two communities, a self-perception that anyone with the most superficial knowledge of Irish history must have considered delusional, and a vague faith that job creation would alleviate unrest. Neither Prime Minister Harold Wilson nor his Tory successor from 1970, Edward Heath, were keen to be drawn into an "Irish bog," so that British policy for Northern Ireland was confused, reactive, and informed by "an alarming ignorance" of the situation on the ground.[4] In truth, Westminster did have views on the causes of the conflict, but they remained a fusion of contradictory clichés: On the one hand, London politicians considered Ireland a backward island inhabited by mulish tribes whose intractable, centuries-old blood feuds remained bafflingly Balkanesque. On the other, it assumed that the agitation was the work of a few hundred extremists on each side who could be isolated by mobilizing the moderate majority in each community. "The British government believed itself to be an outsider in what was an Irish conflict, and the best it could do was to assist the Irish in bringing about a solution themselves," writes Peter Neumann. And as the people of Northern Ireland, agitated by Nationalist and Protestant extremists, appeared incapable of compromise in 1969, the government strategy was to showcase its neutrality and eliminate Northern Ireland as a factor in British politics. However, devolving security decisions to the General Officer Commanding (GOC) who assumed control of all security services in the province over the heads of Stormont and the RUC was not the best way either to demonstrate London's neutrality, or to remove Northern Ireland as a focus of British political concerns. This "stood on its head all the doctrine and precedent about military aid to the civilian power." As a consequence, the army, basically left to create order in a policy vacuum, "operated blindly."[5]

While Prime Minister Harold Wilson apparently understood that the arrival of the British Army might be seen as a provocation by the Catholic community,[6] the dispatch of nearly 15,000 British troops to Belfast without firm policy guidelines and clear mechanisms of civilian control is incomprehensible, especially given the British Army's historic connection to Protestant Ireland. Furthermore, many members of the

Labour government had protested British Army misconduct in Kenya, while in 1967, only two years before the deployment to Belfast and Londonderry, they had witnessed the well-publicized imposition of "Argyll Law" by Lieutenant Colonel Colin "Mad Mitch" Mitchell, commander of the Argyll and Sutherland Highlanders, who had entered the Aden Crater against orders and subsequently pacified it with methods that included accusations of wanton killing of Arabs in sadistic ways accompanied by widespread looting by undisciplined troops.[7] The expectation in Westminster in 1969 that the army could restore order mirrored similar delusions evident in the French Assembly in 1956, which had legislated the Special Powers Act of that year as a mechanism to restore order in Algeria and thus pave the way for communal reconciliation. Instead, they discovered that policy was sabotaged on the tactical level by French army violence against the Muslim population.[8] Likewise, it is difficult to credit that anyone in London, least of all Labour politicians, harbored illusions that doctrines of minimum force and legality would long be respected in Ireland, because they had been respected nowhere else, least of all during the earlier bout of the Troubles. Even a nodding acquaintance with the techniques of colonial counterinsurgency should have alerted political leaders in London that the central force-multiplier technique of small war success was to team up with local allies, the more ruthless the better. Nevertheless, London transformed delusion into disaster when it allowed Protestant Unionist leaders in Stormont to continue in power in the naïve expectation that its membership would evolve more tolerant "British" attitudes. Instead, Unionist-dominated Stormont clamored for suspension of legal and even human rights in the face of what they saw as Catholic provocation. As Neumann writes:[9]

> *Whilst telling the Army to act impartially, the British government tied its political authority to the Unionist government which had been made responsible for most of the grievances the civil rights movement of 1967 and 1968 had been protesting against. As a consequence, Westminster compromised its role as an 'honest broker' in what had started as an inter-communal conflict.*

To some army veterans standing between two apparently irreconcilable communities, Northern Ireland must have looked eerily similar to Palestine. While the army's immediate task was to protect Catholic neighborhoods, the Labour government's strategy in 1969 was to force reforms to make Stormont more representative and establish "neutral" policing in Northern Ireland. Even had Edward Heath and the Tories who deferred entirely to the Unionists on Irish matters not come to power in June 1970, Papist emancipation would have proven a hard sell to Ulster Presbyterians. For their part, Catholics remained justifiably skeptical that a Unionist-dominated Stormont that historically deployed Special Powers, the RUC which in the 1970s was actually commanded by a former member of the Palestine Police, and part-time police auxiliaries known as 'B' Specials to maintain a sectarian police state could ever achieve evenhandedness and "neutral policing."

Military occupation was initially welcomed by the Catholic community as preferable to the RUC. However, sensing a political vacuum, the Provisional IRA launched a campaign to end the "British occupational system" with rioting from May 1970. At this point, the army abandoned any pretense of neutrality and turned on the Catholic population who the Unionists claimed, with some justification, was harboring IRA activists in their midst. Clashes between the army and Catholic youths became more frequent in the summer of 1970. When the Orange Order marching season resumed in July–August 1970, the IRA retaliated with bombings. Stormont passed laws promising draconian penalties for those participating in riots, while the security forces invoked the 1922 Special Powers Act which gave them extensive powers to detain suspected terrorists, cordon and search neighborhoods, and impose curfews. Were this not reason enough, internment without trial introduced in August 1970 only validated the Provisional IRA claim that they, not Westminster, Stormont, or the army, were the true protectors of the Catholic community.[10]

Opinion differs as to whether the government faced a full-blown insurgency by mid 1970. One view is that, despite IRA claims that they spearheaded a republican insurgency, army presence prevented the evolution of protests into an insurrection. A contrary interpretation, however, argues that Catholic neighborhoods in Belfast and Londonderry had become un-policed IRA enclaves where Catholic youth enlisted in IRA ranks in droves. IRA propaganda in this period claimed that the organization sought to create a "people's army" of battalions and brigades for "one last push" to end British colonialism, which they assumed naïvely would fold as it had in Aden once the magic number of thirty-six British soldiers were killed.[11] In response to this deteriorating situation, in September 1970, the army invited Brigadier Frank Kitson, their counterinsurgency expert and veteran of Kenya, Malaya, Muscat and Oman, and Cyprus, to cast his Calvinist gaze on Northern Ireland. Kitson's arrival was perfectly in keeping with the pattern of British learning, according to Andrew Munford, which consisted of the deployment of personnel with "often outdated or inappropriate" best practices from other theaters. This British learning reflex was made necessary by the army's lack of "an authoritative doctrinal underpinning" for counterinsurgency operations.[12] It also proved baleful given the British Army's historic reliance on excessive force in COIN operations.

In common with other British officers, Kitson made no attempt to understand the causes of the conflict and concoct a political/military strategy to mitigate them.[13] Indeed, the British Army's official report on its actions in Northern Ireland concedes that "it could be argued that the Army did make the situation worse by, in practice, alienating the catholic [*sic*] community in 1970 and 1971," although it attributes the problem to "emotions, perceptions or deep-seated grievances and beliefs" rather than to the fact that the army made common cause with loyalists and hence forfeited neutrality in the eyes of the Catholic population.[14] Rather, Kitson arrived with the comfortable colonialist assumption that insurgencies were the work of a few troublemakers who used violence and intimidation to undermine "the natural loyalty of the people," which to be fair to him was also a prevailing view in Whitehall. Kitson's solution was to create a framework for operations that consisted of a coordinated campaign "at every level," a psyops program "for ensuring that the insurgents do not win the war for the minds of the people," an intelligence organization, and "a legal system adequate to the needs of the moment." The problem with Kitson's operational concept was that the requirements of intelligence collection and legal elasticity, not to mention the use of force which in counterinsurgency "should be used very largely in support of ideas," threatened to undermine "the war for the minds of the people."[15] In short, tactics pipped strategy.

No surprise, then, that Kitson lost the battle for the hearts and minds of the nationalist population. Because the RUC appeared unable to either control or collect intelligence in Catholic areas, Kitson pushed for the army to develop its own intelligence apparatus to identify and arrest members of the IRA and locate their arms dumps. Over time, British intelligence improved. In the short term, however, in keeping with Kitson's view that "the operational requirement is for a mass of

15 British troops search civilians in Belfast August 1971. Colonialized British Army counterinsurgency tactics applied in a vacuum of government policy against British subjects helped to transform a Catholic civil-rights movement into a full-blown IRA-led insurgency.

lower level information,"[16] soldiers established contact with the population through aggressive and confrontational tactics – roadblocks, house and vehicle searches, foot patrols, interrogations using stress techniques, mini-fortresses erected in Wild West Catholic neighborhoods, and undercover operations modeled on pseudo-gangs and proxy militias used in Malaya, Kenya, Cyprus, and elsewhere. Deferring to the "political control" of Stormont was correctly interpreted as allying with the Protestants, especially after the largely Catholic Social Democratic and Labour Party (SDLP) representatives withdrew from Stormont in July 1971, by supplying Protestant militias with intelligence, and giving them a free pass to murder or intimidate Catholics. Subsequent political attempts to negotiate compromises foundered on the opposition of hardline Unionists and the Protestant militias who were tacitly, when not actively, supported by the security services.[17] Catholic activist and Stormont MP Paddy Devlin designated Kitson as the man most responsible for consummating the divorce between the two communities,[18] and transitioning the character of the conflict, at least in the minds of many Catholics, from a struggle for civil rights to insurrection.

Even British Colonel Richard Iron, who argues plausibly that by the 1980s the security services had evolved effective tactics to contain the IRA that helped to create conditions for an eventual political resolution to the conflict, concedes that the army's Kitson-inspired coercive approach "created a radicalization of the Catholic communities that was to sustain the republican insurgency for much of the following thirty years." In this way, Iron echoes the conclusion of the army's official after action report *Operation Banner*.[19] The army also discovered that even when they could identify and eliminate IRA cadres in a neighborhood, the Protestant-dominated civil administration failed to fill the vacuum of governance, while the perception of army harassment, loyalist intransigence, and out-of-control Protestant militias like the Ulster Defense Association or the Ulster Workers' Council neutralized potential moderate Catholic interlocutors.[20] While it is certainly true that the IRA was the main driver of violence in Northern Ireland, it is equally true that army, RUC, and militia mayhem alienated friends, radicalized neutrals, and allowed people like IRA militant and eventual Sinn Féin MP Gerry Adams to claim to speak for the Catholic community:

> *No one could look on and passively accept having their doors kicked in, their houses wrecked, their family members beaten up. As military intervention in the neighbourhood increased in frequency and intensity so the local people, out of their own feelings of self-respect, outrage and resistance, organized more and more their own response to the military presence. The attitude and presence of British troops was also a reminder that we were Irish, and there was an instant resurgence of national consciousness and an almost immediate politicization of the local populace.*[21]

British COIN had been most successful when it could decapitate the insurgency, isolate the militants from their support base, and instill a culture of fear and intimidation in the subject population. Such tactics had quelled unrest in Malaya and Kenya, not to mention South Africa in 1900, when the British deported, interned, or resettled virtually the entire minority population, destroyed whole villages, issued identity cards, imposed calorie control, and so on. Because such methods designed for colonial folk of color were considered unacceptable for use against British subjects, limited internment without trial was instituted in

August 1971. In a rerun of the failed tactics used by the British against Zionists extremists in Palestine, despite warnings that it would only alienate Catholics and probably not impact the IRA, slightly under 2,000 Irish Catholics were interned by 1975. As a decapitation strategy internment failed, in part because Special Branch intelligence was so faulty that many of those interned were not IRA militants, at least not at the time of their arrest. Only eighteen of those interned were ever charged with offenses.[22] Innocence was no guarantee of protection, however, as many of them were beaten or otherwise abused and insulted by troops and police to extract intelligence, a process that "left bitter legacies," concludes Munford. "The intelligence dividend was negligible, and the social and political backlash against the treatment of detainees proved to be a catalyst to greater violence."[23] Sandhurst instructor Aaron Edwards argues that minimum force and unity of civil-military control, much less fighting the counterinsurgency within the framework of the law, were treated as alien concepts in Northern Ireland between 1969 and 1976, which contributed to the notorious "Bloody Sunday" massacre of January 30, 1972 when British paratroops opened fire on unarmed marchers in Derry protesting internment, killing fourteen and wounding twenty-eight.[24] Following this Amritsar on the Foyle, the entire Catholic community felt under attack, which the March 1972 assumption of direct rule by Westminster did nothing to change. The IRA became by default the defenders of Bogside, Londonderry's major Catholic enclave, and launched a retaliatory offensive with bombings and shootings. The number of deaths skyrocketed in 1971–1973.[25] Thanks to Frank Kitson, a trigger-happy British Army, and a strategically challenged set of policymakers in London furnished the IRA with the credibility – as had been the case with the Stern Gang, the MCP, the Mau Mau, and Colonel Grivas' Cypriots – to assemble enough popular support to pursue their murderous insurgency.

The British Army's self-assessment for this period was typically focused on the tactical and operational level, noting the failure to develop a unified campaign plan, create a single authority to coordinate political and military action, or to utilize an inter-agency, whole of government process, all fundamental tenets of COIN theory, but all quite futile if the counterinsurgency enjoys no legitimacy among the rebellious portion of the population. Even less comprehensible was the self-confessed lack of cultural awareness of the Northern Irish situation in the British Army.

"Such cultural issues ... are inherently difficult to comprehend," according to the *Banner* report. "In the absence of such deep understanding the British tended to underestimate the differences between the Irish and themselves. One commentator observed that Englishmen, especially, tend to view the Irishman as a variant of Briton rather than as a foreigner." The claim that the British counterinsurgency effort suffered from a gap of cultural understanding is disingenuous, given the fact that the English had been present in Ireland at least since Elizabeth I. Whitehall had no need to train linguists and assemble Human Terrain or Female Engagement Teams to communicate with the locals, or to create cells of regional experts to decipher the political, social, and sectarian dynamic of the island. What they required was a viable strategy, not a tutorial in language and culture.

Accordingly, the inability of the British to decide whether they were operating in the UK or in a foreign country made it difficult in the army's view to develop a viable strategic communications campaign. Operation Motorman witnessed the invasion of previously inviolate "no go" areas by the 31,000 troops and police following the July 21, 1972 Bloody Friday IRA bombing campaign in central Belfast.[26] Catholic neighborhoods like Londonderry's Bogside witnessed an Irish version of the Battle of Algiers as house searches virtually doubled to 36,617 in 1972. In the process, British soldiers raised in a culture of Glasgow's Celtic–Rangers and Liverpool's "No Pope in Everton" football rivalry devised their own "sort the Micks out" strategic communications campaign, in the process elevating football hooliganism to the level of COIN doctrine. This was especially true of "the Black Watch, a Scottish regiment which seemed to give most of its attention to breaking religious objects and symbols of the Glasgow Celtic football club," according to Stormont MP Paddy Devlin. Any lingering misconception that the British Army represented a neutral arbiter of Northern Ireland's communal conflict evaporated.[27]

In fact, the only COIN lessons that theorists led by Kitson managed to introduce, at least in the eyes of the Catholics, was "collusion, counter gangs, dirty tricks ... manipulation of the media, the criminal justice system and the apparatus of the state."[28] The British Army insisted that allegations of soldierly misconduct were fabricated by IRA sympathizers to discredit the security services. Nevertheless, the army made 410 cash payments to people alleging abuse at the hands of the military from 1972–1975, rather than contest these claims in court.

British historian Huw Bennett estimates that this was simply the tip of the iceberg – "evidence shows the army very probably committed hundreds of offenses against civilians in the 1972–5 period," he concludes. Bennett attributes this aggressive attitude toward civilians to the army's colonial experience, the soldiers' sense of impunity, judicial bias, perjured testimony, command cover-ups, and fear expressed by political and military leaders at least since the earlier bout of the Troubles and repeated in post-World War II Palestine that fighting within the law would undermine morale. Despite the fact that Westminster recognized that an absence of impartiality was undermining its policy, it appeared unable or unwilling to rein in its forces, as the Heath government was once again succeeded by Wilson in 1974. British military indiscipline and violence toward civilians, which by the early 1970s in Northern Ireland had become an endemic feature of the British Way of War, combined with a rise in officially tolerated, when not abetted, Protestant paramilitary violence helped to collapse the Sunningdale Agreement signed in December 1973 by moderate Unionists and the Catholic SDLP.[29]

From "one last push" to the long war strategy, 1975–1990

By 1975, the conflict had reached an impasse. The IRA's "one last push" strategy had failed while the "conveyor belt" justice system, guided by improved British intelligence, squeezed the leadership. Tensions grew between IRA organizations north and south of the border over the wisdom of a ceasefire adopted in 1974, while feuding between the Provisional and Official IRA created serious divisions in the resistance to British rule. Too many captured IRA operatives were "breaking" under interrogation, which in the minds of the leadership was evidence of insufficient preparation and weak indoctrination. Popular support for the IRA in Catholic communities receded in the wake of bombings that killed innocents, while Sinn Féin made little headway among the electorate. So, the IRA leadership began to transition from a "people's war" approach to a "long war" strategy supported by an atomized, and hence difficult to detect, structure based on cells of six or seven operatives whose names were known only by the cell leader that would fuse the political and military struggle against the British state. Although their initial optimism that 1972 would be the critical year that would break British resolve had evaporated, the IRA not unreasonably took heart from their perception that London's commitment to remain in Northern Ireland was fragile.[30] Unfortunately for them, this assumption came as Westminster reluctantly concluded the opposite – that Britain had no choice but to remain in Northern Ireland, even though polls in 1975 showed that 64 percent of the British public favored withdrawal. While the IRA showed no desire to compromise, London concluded that bloody communal violence would erupt in the wake of withdrawal. This view was quietly supported by Dublin, whose inability to cope with the political, financial, and military consequences of a British departure, and trepidation at seeing the IRA become a factor in southern Irish politics should their campaign gain success, made it a discreet advocate of a continued British presence.[31]

Westminster's new resolution to remain required new strategies. Realizing that internment and Kitson-inspired COIN had roiled Northern Ireland, further divided the Unionist and nationalist communities, and brought the conflict no closer to resolution, from 1974 the government began the shift to an anti-terrorist strategy modeled on Italian and German approaches to the Red Brigades and the Baader-Meinhof gang respectively. The idea was to attack the IRA self-image as nationalist warriors. The army's role was scaled back to deal with the insurgency in the rural border areas of North and South Armagh, while the Special Air Service (SAS), Force Research Unit (FRU), and 14 Intelligence Company would conduct a clandestine intelligence and special operations war against the IRA. The more visible campaign would be spearheaded by a revamped RUC backed by the locally recruited Ulster Defense Regiment created in 1970. The RUC acquired enhanced authority in the 1974 Prevention of Terrorism Act that allowed the arrest of IRA suspects who could be held for seven days without charge in interrogation centers in Belfast and Londonderry. Although this strategic shift signaled the failure of COIN to win Catholic hearts and minds or seriously dent the IRA, Kitson praised the new approach – variously called normalization, criminalization, or Ulsterization – as signaling that political violence would henceforth be treated as normal crime and prosecuted in special courts presided over by a single judge with special powers. According to British jurist Baron Diplock, the special counter-terrorist "Diplock courts" created in 1973 would avoid jury intimidation and "the danger of perverse acquittals,"[32] while delegitimizing the IRA as common criminals rather than freedom fighters. The logic was that no political settlement could be made to stick until security was established.

The strategy was to put pressure on IRA safe havens and their logistical networks by mobilizing the legal system as a counterinsurgency weapon, re-establish the legitimacy of the security forces by putting the police, rather than the army, in the forefront of the counterinsurgency campaign, minimize troop casualties, convince Unionists that Westminster was actually protecting them, while persuading the IRA to abandon violence and join the political process.[33]

But who exactly was "delegitimized" by these methods is open to question. The adoption of criminalization showed how confused, out of touch, ignorant of the failure of past policies, and strategically challenged Westminster remained even as it tried to readjust its approach to Northern Ireland. The British problem lay in the fact that concentrated but nonetheless significant pockets of the Catholic population before 1990 viewed Republicanism, Sinn Féin, and the IRA as legitimate political and military actors, not isolated groups of terrorists like the Red Brigades or Baader-Meinhof gang who assembled no constituency to share their anger. Criminalization allowed the IRA to define the political narrative of the conflict. It had created its own justice system in Catholic areas, so that even the British government had to concede that the IRA had come to represent the population in important nationalist areas of Belfast, Londonderry, and Armagh.[34] Nor was there anything "normal" about the tactics used to accomplish normalization. While the army argued plausibly that the legal system seriously attrited the IRA,[35] the Provisionals countered that the so-called Diplock courts mocked British claims to maintain their counterinsurgency campaign within a legal framework.

A second problem for London's strategy shift, at least in the short term, was that the police were both too few to take control of the streets from the army, largely because many policemen were part-time auxiliaries, while the overwhelmingly Protestant RUC was rejected as an impartial actor by the Catholic community. To bolster an understrength police force unprepared to apply normalization, in 1976, teams of SAS operatives were introduced as a force multiplier. At a stroke, Westminster resurrected Major Roy Farran and the Special Squads which had created nightmare PR problems in Palestine, not to mention the Kenyan Police Reserve and other out-of-control law enforcement amateurs that had shamed, delegitimized, and brutalized earlier British counterinsurgency endeavors. The deployment of SAS was a knee-jerk reaction pushed by Labour Secretary of State Roy Mason over the objections of the army command who claimed that SAS operations were too eye-catching and undermined the criminalization strategy. While arguably the SAS became more proficient at killing IRA operatives by the 1980s, largely because army and RUC intelligence became more precise, in the short term Westminster had to deal with the usual special operations embarrassments and strategic blowback, beginning in May 1976 when eight SAS men were arrested in the Irish Republic kitted out with sawn-off shotguns and other paraphernalia of murder. This provoked the greatest crisis in cross-border relations since the introduction of internment without trial, and dissuaded Westminster in the circumstances from asking for the right of cross-border hot pursuit.[36] The prominent SAS role in the new strategy further contradicted the British claims to police primacy and minimum force, while their actions often undermined legal guarantees of due process for British subjects.[37] The frontier justice served up in Diplock courts, sectarian police recruitment, stressful interrogations, and special operators masquerading as law enforcement replicated colonial COIN methods and provided further evidence that London viewed Northern Irish Catholics as just another criminal tribe on the fringes of empire. "The failure of Labour ministers, most notably the then Secretary of State for Northern Ireland, Roy Mason, to put a stop to this was to play an important part in the downfall of the Labour government in march 1979," writes Newsinger, and paved the way for the victory of the Conservatives under Margaret Thatcher.[38]

The Thatcher era, which began in May 1979, witnessed an unsuccessful full-on push by the British Army to end the normalization/criminalization strategy, reintroduce internment, and allow hot pursuit into the Republic, following a series of spectacular terrorist assassinations that included the murder of World War II hero, Conservative MP and the designated Secretary for Northern Ireland Airey Neave, Lord Mountbatten, and the Warrenpoint ambush in which eighteen British paratroopers died in what was viewed in the Catholic community as payback for Bloody Sunday.

The IRA repost to criminalization was the hunger strikes, organized among inmates in the Maze Prison from October 1980 in an attempt to gain recognition as political prisoners. Nationalist Ireland mobilized behind the strikers, whose sacrifice resonated in a tradition of Catholic martyrdom. One of the strikers, Bobby Sands, defeated the official Unionist candidate in Fermanagh-South Tyrone. Thatcher stood firm, insisting that "a crime is a crime. It's not political." But when Sands died,

100,000 people attended his funeral. Following the deaths of six IRA detainees, the families intervened to end the strike. On the surface, Thatcher's intransigence appeared to have defeated the strikers. But the price had been high – support for Sinn Féin, which had won its first parliamentary seat in modern times, soared in Catholic communities at the expense of the moderate SDLP, which in the view of some prolonged the conflict by a decade. The Unionist and nationalist communities were more polarized than ever. Relations between the Irish Republic and Westminster had been damaged as Dublin had been forced to adopt a more nationalist stance in the face of a groundswell of support for the hunger strikers. Criminalization had clearly failed as a strategy. In the view of the army, however, extreme polarization in the nationalist community of the sort seen in 1922 offered a sign that the Republicans were transitioning away from terrorism and into the political arena.[39]

The Thatcher era saw several innovations, beginning with the so-called "supergrass" initiative. Copied from the Italian success against the Red Brigades, this relied on convictions based on the testimony of turned IRA informants. This collapsed, however, when the appellate courts refused to go along with it because the evidence was uncorroborated, and after it was revealed that "supergrass" testimony was purchased with get out of jail free cards followed by resettlement on the Costa Brava or other exotic locations.[40] A second, more promising, initiative was the Anglo-Irish Agreement (AIA) signed in November 1985. Opinions are split on the value of the AIA, which brought the government of Eire into the peace process in an attempt to craft an Irish solution to the Troubles and win over the Catholic community. Whatever its long-term contribution, the AIA's short-term impact proved marginal – for instance, it failed to gain Dublin's immediate cooperation in securing the border as London had hoped, while Westminster pushed back on several of Dublin's demands, like a root-and-branch reform of the RUC and enlisting Dublin's input in the formulation of Northern Irish policy, because it impinged upon British sovereignty.[41] The AIA also produced a huge backlash in the Loyalist community that included strikes and riots in 1986, which were faced down by the RUC. Singer sees the AIA as the beginning of the end of the conflict that paved the way for the 1998 Good Friday Agreement which brought Sinn Féin into the Northern Ireland government. Other scholars of the conflict argue that the AIA accomplished few of its goals.[42] The Catholic community was given credible interlocutors in the government of Eire and a strengthened SDLP as substitutes for Sinn Féin and the IRA, denounced by some nationalists as having institutionalized the partition of Ireland in 1921. The RUC had weathered the Protestant revolt of 1986, thereby proving its discipline, loyalty, and value to the government as a law enforcement tool.

The security services were increasingly tightening the screws on the IRA, evidence that the IRA's shift to a secret army strategy from 1974 had not fared well. As John Bew explained to the author:

> *The IRA isn't the Taliban. These guys drink, they hang out in bars, speak English, do drugs, and go on holiday in Spain. There are about fifteen prominent IRA families. They all know each other, so the cell structure doesn't really guarantee anonymity. When one of their number is picked up, they all turn up for the court hearing.*[43]

The IRA's lack of security consciousness allowed British intelligence to penetrate them at the highest levels to the point that an estimated one in three top IRA officials were giving some information to authorities, which allowed the RUC to claim that by 1994 it was able to thwart eight out of ten IRA operations in Belfast.[44] The organization found its ability to kill soldiers diminishing, while a new generation of Protestant militants led by Johnny "Mad Dog" Adair and the Ulster Freedom Fighters launched a campaign of violence against nationalist militants from the late 1980s.

British success against the IRA was the product of a low-profile counterinsurgency approach by the intelligence services. Military intelligence was beefed up to include soldiers in plain clothes organized as the Military Reconnaissance Force, groups of IRA defectors known as Freds, the creation of a Military Intelligence Staff in GHQ Northern Ireland as well as intelligence and counter-intelligence sections in every battalion. Military intelligence personnel were attached to the police Special Branch. A Special Reconnaissance Unit organized covert operations from 1972. MI5 and MI6, Britain's domestic and foreign intelligence services respectively, also appeared in Belfast. These organizations emphasized intelligence gathering, covert operations, infiltration of IRA cells, and stricter border controls to prevent the importation of IRA weapons via Eire. Military training was improved to include instruction on how to search houses using sniffer dogs.[45] This replaced saturation crucifix smashing invasions of Catholic neighborhoods of the early 1970s and lowered the tension of confrontation, even if it failed to build trust in the Catholic community, in part because "shoot-to-kill" tactics of SAS and RUC Special Squads that felled unarmed IRA operatives, while relatively rare, continued to be denounced as demonstrations of excessive force in the Catholic communities.[46] Colonel Iron argues that the largely clandestine intelligence and special operations war against the IRA led to assassinations, arrests, and interceptions of perhaps a third of weapons importations from Libya and elsewhere. This counteroffensive balked the IRA's plan to replicate a Têt Offensive in the border areas that aimed to break British public will to continue operations.[47] Over time, the leadership of the Provisional IRA became disturbed by widespread penetration of their organization by army intelligence and convinced that Britain could not be induced to depart Ireland through military means. Loyalist death squads, guided by British Army intelligence or by collusion with Protestant volunteers in the Ulster Defence Regiment,[48] formed another element of intimidation. Increasingly denied hard police and army targets, in the late 1980s and early 1990s, the IRA resorted to bombings. When these invariably produced civilian casualties, including children, electoral support for Sinn Féin plummeted in the Catholic community. By the early 1990s, the nationalist strategy of "the Armalite (rifle) and the ballot box" had failed to realize its promise. Assassinating British soldiers and RUC constables had become prohibitively costly in IRA operatives, while the number of British soldiers killed annually after 1991 could be counted on the fingers of one hand. Meanwhile, bombings created collateral damage that cost Sinn Féin votes. On August 31, 1994, the Provisional IRA declared a ceasefire. This paved the way for the Good Friday Agreement of 1998, the result of war weariness, the marginalization of bitter enders on both sides, containment of the IRA by the security forces, and the decline of Sinn Féin fortunes at the ballot box.[49]

Both the British Army and the Provisional IRA proved to be "mythologizing organizations" rather than "learning" ones. The army mythologized a theory of victory based on successfully "securing the population and gaining and maintaining popular support."[50] In fact, classic counterinsurgency in the Kitson mode, re-enforced by a sectarian RUC, and the introduction of Special Operations Forces (SOF) actually inflamed the situation in the 1970s and, in the view of one human rights critic of the army, "betrays a profoundly colonial mindset towards the conflict here and those involved in it."[51] Even Peter Neumann, who in general offers a sympathetic appraisal of London's dilemmas in

Northern Ireland, agrees that the military response in the early days proved counterproductive because it was carried out in a political vacuum.[52] Faced with the failure of classic British COIN, Westminster switched to a "security strategy" from 1974, over the protestations of the army, in an attempt to gain a political compromise.[53] When Iron concedes that the army's adaptation to the conflict was ad hoc, tardy, and reactive, he simply repeats the conclusions of the army's official after action report that the army only engaged the IRA on the tactical level, and so did not "'win' in any recognizable way" with a COIN, whole of government approach, but instead with the RUC helped to create a military stalemate that paved the way for a political settlement.[54] While it is true that military action beginning with Motorman in 1972 did reduce violence, for Neumann it remains unclear whether this was the result of the successful application of petty war tactics, or because from 1974 the IRA adopted a long war strategy that sought to consolidate its hold over the Catholic population.[55]

> Arguably, the drop in IRA activity was largely due to structural and strategic changes within the Republican movement whose new leadership now asserted that there was "no quick solution to our British problem", and that the military instrument had to be reorganized to fight a protracted campaign, the so-called Long War. Whether the Long War doctrine was an immediate reaction to [Secretary of State for Northern Ireland Roy] Mason's security policies, or whether it had followed from the continued frustration of the IRA's military efforts ever since Operation Motorman, is difficult to say.

In essence, in the opening years of the Northern Ireland crisis, the army had filled a vacuum of strategic leadership with combinations of minor tactics that papered over policy drift, strategic confusion, and civil-military mistrust in London. Deprived of viable political context and applied with a view to intimidate rather than build a basis for trust and compromise, COIN tactics were shown to be counterproductive.

London had been forced to withdraw from southern Ireland in 1922, not because they had failed to repress the rebellion, but because their coercive methods alienated British public opinion while convincing the majority of Catholics that they had no future as part of the United

Kingdom. Irish fatigue also set in during the second bout of the Troubles – a 1988 *Economist* poll revealed that only 27 percent of Britons favored retaining Northern Ireland within the UK.[56] The Provisionals proved no more cognizant about the shortcomings of past strategies. The replication of a Têt offensive in the Catholic-dominated border areas, if that indeed is what was in the offing, would have decimated them as it had the Viet Cong. The difference, however, was that their revolution could not be salvaged as it had been in Vietnam by an invasion of a regular army. A strategy of random bombing attacks in Northern Ireland and England was in many respects the flip side of internment – as Michael Collins had realized in the Troubles, indiscriminate bombings that killed civilians angered Northern Irish Protestants and stiffened English resolve rather than undermined it, and steeled politicians to stay the course, while they also alienated their Catholic base and provoked retaliation from Protestant murder squads.[57] The insurrection, such as it was, was concentrated in a few Catholic majority areas in Belfast, Londonderry, and Armagh that could be contained by the army and the RUC. The failure of the Provisional long war strategy combined with the success of infiltration of IRA cells by the intelligence services, the difficulties of importing weapons, and improved army patrol tactics that made attacks on the security services simply too difficult convinced enough members of the IRA Army Council that they had no prospect of winning what had become a very dirty war.[58]

A forgetting army

The fumbled approach to this second eruption of the Troubles cast further doubt on Mockaitis' assertion that the British laid the foundation in the interwar years for a new counterinsurgency approach that focused on minimum force, aid to the civil power, and tactical flexibility. "Detention without trial, the forced relocation of elements of the local populace, and controversies surrounding excessive use of force have a long heritage" in British COIN, writes Munford.[59] The British Army's record in Northern Ireland, or in Iraq or Afghanistan after 2003 for that matter, fail to support the assertion that the British were able through institutional learning to develop a traveling circus technique to deal with insurgent challenges to imperial authority. While Westminster must bear a significant burden of responsibility for a fumbled political strategy in

Northern Ireland, the army must take at least some blame for making this harder than it might have been with its aggressive tactics and alliances with Protestant paramilitaries.

The British political opening beginning with the 1985 Anglo-Irish Agreement that created a framework for negotiation involving both the Republic and Westminster provided the keys to success, not merely the denial of victory to the IRA and the creation of stalemate. Among the impediments to organizational learning in the British Army, Huw Bennett lists the following: a regimental system that discourages systematic analysis; a requirement to prepare for conventional war; frequent deployments and turnover of personnel; poor intelligence that leads to flawed assessments that allow the insurgency to capture momentum early on; lack of resources and personnel; and the fact that transferring "lessons" from one insurgency to the next is largely pointless as each insurgency produces its own dynamic that depends on its ideology, organization, strategy, and tactics. In fact, "learning" may not only prove pointless, but might also become positively detrimental to success.[60] Neumann concluded that in Northern Ireland, "even supposed hardliners like Thatcher or Mason accepted the impossibility of defeating the IRA by military means alone, and in rejecting most of the measures that could have delivered a 'military defeat', they acted accordingly."[61] But the remarkable thing about Northern Ireland is how little the government grasped the political realities of the situation caused by the deep sectarian divide. Instead, it sought to compensate for a lack of a strategy with tactical solutions beginning with Kitsonized COIN. When this succeeded only in making matters worse, Westminster shifted to a normalization strategy under the sectarian RUC backed by SOF and special tribunals while claiming that there were no political prisoners in Britain, their operations conformed to legal norms, and that special operators unleashed among the population were innocent of deploying excessive force. Once Westminster abandoned the moral high ground through these tactics, it retained very little credibility among the various actors.[62] London only began to gain the upper hand from 1985 with a combination of political initiatives to isolate Sinn Féin and the IRA, and more low-key military and police tactics. But the fact that the strategy and tactics only began to evolve fifteen years into the conflict in a province that had been an integral part of the UK for centuries hardly serves as a thumping confirmation that the British government and its security services were exemplary learning organizations.

10 VIETNAM WITH A HAPPY ENDING: IRAQ AND "THE SURGE"

Reconstructing "the American way of war"

The end of the Vietnam War in 1975 found the US Army bitter, confused, "nearly broken," as was much of the country in a painful decade, for which warfare as an instrument of policy appeared to have lost legitimacy.[1] While George Decker's confident contention that "any good soldier can handle guerrillas" appeared hubristic in hindsight, no appetite existed to remodel the US military into a counterinsurgency force in the face of an arming Warsaw Pact in the second half of the 1970s and the putative lessons of the October 1973 Yom Kippur War on the acceleration of conventional war as interpreted below. On one level, Andrew Krepinevich captured the popular perception of a group of civilian military reformers of the 1970s that the US Army was inept, unimaginative, careerist, and hidebound, adjectives to which some on the left at the time might have added incompetent, racist, bloodthirsty, and imperialist.

But the book that found the widest readership three decades ago was Colonel Harry Summers' 1981 *On Strategy*. That Summers' counternarrative, levied against the counterinsurgency school, found more resonance in the newly all-volunteer US Army is hardly surprising. Many of the most respected senior soldiers, seized again as in the early 1950s after the Korean War of the "never again" school, saw counterinsurgency and nation-building as a fool's errand, a sort of semi- or quasi-war endeavor, and, like the post-1871 French army or the Reichswehr from 1919, devoted themselves to "the reconstruction of conventional war."[2] The situation of the late 1970s whereby events seemed to indicate a Soviet offensive in arms in Central Europe and Soviet-led proxy wars in Africa provided fertile ground for Summers' ideas of re-professionalization through a willful interpretation of the immediate past and the Anglo-Saxon reading of Clausewitz. Summers' Vietnam was a war in which American soldiers "never lost a battle," but instead were stabbed in the back by vague objectives, political micromanagement, "incrementalism," Congressional pusillanimity, and a drought of generational fortitude in contrast to the era of total war earlier in the twentieth century. The 1984 Weinberger Doctrine, later stiffened by General Colin Powell during his tenure as Chairman of the Joint Chiefs of Staff (1989–1993), which set up a series of six preconditions to be met by the nation and its government before military intervention could take place, was concocted in the wake of President Ronald Reagan's disastrous 1982–1983 intervention in Lebanon and fear that the army would be dispatched to El Salvador.[3] While Ronald Reagan's Manichean good versus evil view of the world and his insistence that Vietnam had been a noble cause betrayed by unpatriotic liberals conformed to the services' outlook, the assessment of public aversion to protracted, backwoods hostilities only affirmed a War College assessment of a decade earlier that revenue guzzling, Third World interventions beyond the bounds of US "vital interests" should be dropped from the nation's grand strategy and operational planning. Weinberger–Powell also evinced a sense of "martyrdom and entitlement" among soldiers that persisted well into the 1980s, in an era when warriors betrayed by their governments became a popular theme in literature and film and recalled the metanarrative of European colonialism and the disaffection with civil society.[4]

The refocus on conventional and/or operational warfare in the Cold War came none too soon, because a dispirited US military emerged from the Vietnam decade to confront an ominously up-gunned Warsaw Pact in Europe. The Soviet challenge combined with the 1973 Middle East War that featured highly lethal, fast-moving combinations of armored forces, mechanized infantry, artillery, and airpower allowed the US military, like that of France after 1962, to view COIN as an imperial anachronism. Conventional warfare on the operational level as visible in the 1970s was "real soldiering," with clear-cut frontiers between war and peace, where soldiers deployed force against opposing armies to achieve political objectives with a minimum of civilian micromanagement. A return to operational warfare allowed the American military to reestablish its professional identity and rebalance US civil-military relations with a reinvention of "the American way of war."

Perhaps the most significant post-Indochina reform was implemented within the US Army itself. The creation of Training and Doctrine Command (TRADOC) in 1973 aimed to rally the US Army around a common language and a doctrine that could serve as an operational center of gravity in the face of the fractures of the army's structure exposed by Vietnam. The revised version of *FM 100–5*, which appeared in 1976, admonished officers to "win the land battle" with a technique called "active defense." (The 1982 edition introduced the term AirLand Battle more or less wholly borrowed from the Wehrmacht via NATO.) The Army of Excellence was reimagined around Heavy Divisions that combined the "Big Five" weapons systems – the M1 Abrams tank, Blackhawk and Apache helicopters, Patriot air defense missiles, and the Bradley fighting vehicle in answer to Warsaw Pact modernization and the 1973 operational and tactical lessons of the Yom Kippur War.[5] While the late 1970s and the 1980s also had a profound nuclear dimension, the emphasis in the US Army and US Air Force on AirLand Battle revived professional core and focus for the land forces that, in turn, was financed with generous Reagan defense budgets.

The foundation for the narrative of the COIN-dinista rescue of a failed Iraq strategy was laid, somewhat ironically, with the apparent operational success of conventional arms in Operation Desert Storm in 1991. Although the Armageddon in the Fulda Gap as a prelude to nuclear war thankfully never materialized prior to 1989, the 1991 Gulf War convinced soldiers that they had been correct to organize around a joint, centrally planned, big battalions/"shock and awe" airpower combo, even if the junior varsity Iraqi enemy, ill equipped with inferior Soviet equipment and defective doctrine, didn't pack much of a punch and the end game had been mangled.[6] The neo Kursk tank battle of 73 Eastings on February 26, 1991 appeared to undo the stain of Vietnam and give AirLand Battle as applied to the Middle East its baptism of fire.

But as Andrew Bacevich has brilliantly demonstrated, for a group of soon-to-be-influential defense intellectuals in the years prior to September 11, 2001, Desert Storm in 1990–1991 offered a thumping demonstration of the limitations of the post-Vietnam defense reforms for both operational and political reasons: first, the operational focus on extended preliminary air bombardment followed by an invasion force of 540,000 soldiers organized around armored formations offered a remake of the Battle of the Bulge in the sands. Orthodox, plodding generals had ignored potentially transformative technical upgrades like long-range precision weapons and information systems that could collapse the enemy's command and control and unfold a true Blitzkrieg made possible by brilliant munitions, magical ballistics, and superior command and control. The task of adapting the US military to the information age by initiating what came in the early 1990s to be called in a misleading manner Revolution in Military Affairs (RMA) was spearheaded in the Pentagon by Andrew Marshall and the Office of Net Assessment, one of the original RAND Corporation figures and an enduring feature of the senior-most echelons of US defense thought. Convinced in the 1980s and 1990s that the Soviets and their successors might trump the United States with a future Pearl Harbor (despite the collapse of the USSR and the Warsaw Pact), Marshall funded scholars to examine interwar scenarios that demonstrated how Blitzkrieging Germans were able to seize the technological moment and evolve efficient operational systems to achieve "full spectrum dominance" over hapless Poles and French in 1939–1940. Anyone who bothered to read to the very end of the story in the year 1944–1945, however, might have concluded that putting faith in technology as a substitute for strategy leads to overstretch and defeat. But why spoil the RMA revelry? The RMA also offered a technological mirror of Mao and COIN, one that willfully factored out strategy in favor of a theory of victory in which he who grasps the prize via a unitary, supreme means ("the people"/"technology") will emerge victorious.

The idea of substituting technology for manpower to make divisions both slimmer and more lethal was hardly new – indeed, the 1970s Army of Excellence architects had discovered that technological upgrades created their own logistical, organizational, and budgetary demands that might run at cross-purposes with such desirable attributes as lightness, agility, affordability, and flexibility. Nor did TRADOC's obsession with the AirLand Battle appear particularly relevant to post-Cold War missions – irregular warfare, operations other than war, low-intensity conflict had been shoved to the back burner, to the point that some wondered if the army even considered irregular warfare "a legitimate form of conflict."[7] While micro interventions in the Falklands (1982), Lebanon (1982–1983), Grenada (1983), and Panama (1989) had showcased the need for a mid-range expeditionary capability, the so-called Light Divisions of the 1980s built around the high-mobility multipurpose wheeled vehicle (HMMWV) and tube-launched, optically tracked, wire command data link, guided missile (TOW) and airborne combinations proved too heavy for rapid deployment, and so in doctrinal terms usually ended up assigned secondary missions around the fringes of continental combat.[8]

More significant for the shape of doctrine and force structure at the end of the twentieth century and with portents for the resurgence of counterinsurgency, each service maintained its separate SOF establishment that for the army included Special Forces, Rangers, psychological operations, civil affairs, and aviation. The much ballyhooed disaster of Operation Eagle Claw, the failed April 1980 attempt to rescue American diplomats taken hostage in Tehran, combined with the Reagan administration's desire to combat communist subversion in Latin America and elsewhere to refocus interest on what at the time came to be known in the US Defense Department as "Low Intensity Conflict" or LIC. Nothing that occurred in Indochina, Algeria, or Vietnam altered the conclusions of World War II veterans that SOF was useful as an adjunct to conventional operations, not as a stand-alone force.[9] Indeed, the failure of Eagle Claw should have underscored the perils of forcing operational solutions onto strategic problems. However, SOF spokesmen lobbied successfully over the objections of the Chiefs of Staff to convince a group of reformers in the US Congress that conventional soldiers "misused" SOF. Under pressure, the army consolidated its SOF in October 1982, organized a Ranger regiment in 1984, and in 1987 ended SOF's Babylonian captivity by separating it from the infantry, and established US Special Operations Command (USSOCOM) at MacDill Air Force Base, Florida, with its own (secret) budget and control over all SOF forces.[10]

The triumph of the RMA in the strategic confusion of the 1990s required a strategic and intellectual context. Brian Lynn notes that the collapse of the Soviet Union left the United States with what some called a "display army" with neither a foe nor a mission, the Iraq campaign of 1991 notwithstanding. Big Battalions, excessive firepower, cumbersome logistics, and deep war doctrine failed to fit the new security environment of LIC, peacekeeping, humanitarian and security assistance. The post-1989 army shed 270,000 soldiers which made Heavy Divisions a challenge to man and maintain even as the campaign in Kuwait was launched in 1990. More significant for the subject of this study, however, critics complained that the 1993–1994 Somalia intervention offered a mini-replay of Vietnam featuring a muscle-bound army led by an "unthinking" officer corps unable to adjust its Cold War customs to quell a minor eruption of Mogadishu mayhem. War and command and staff colleges offered curricula featuring Civil War and World War II case studies to soon-to-be-RIFed (Reduction in Force) officers. Army brass could devise no coherent vision of what modern warfare would look like, and so constantly reorganized and re-acronyzed.[11]

That the US armed forces appeared unable to define a vision for future warfare might not have proven fatal had it not been for "unipolar moment" and "end of history" triumphalism in the early 1990s after the victory in Kuwait, itself the culmination of the conservative backlash against Vietnam, that combined fundamentalist theology, xenophobia, and romantic anti-modernism to assert that US wealth allied with an invincible military machine would allow Washington to remake the world in its image.[12] Bacevich notes that the link between fascism and the machine age in the interwar years had its contemporary corollary in the 1990s with the marriage of neo-conservatism and "information superiority" in economy and armaments as a vehicle for world transformation.[13] Such neo-imperialists as Max Boot, Robert Kaplan, Niall Ferguson, and the liberal internationalist Joseph Nye, few of whom had any real military experience of a serious kind, argued that the requirement for international order compels the West led by the United States once again to take up the "white man's burden," predicting that the universal appeal of Western values and the transferability of democratic institutions will cause right-thinking non-Western peoples to welcome invasion and occupation as a liberation. Ferguson, a talented and articulate historian with aspirations to celebrity and political influence, reaches into the past to correct the narrative of empire as the exploitation of indigenous peoples. Instead, he argues that the British Empire had been a modernizing enterprise that imported the rule of law, free markets, financial stability, and relatively incorrupt government to areas of the world that before had known none of it. He attributes the pervasiveness and quasi-universal acceptance of Western models of civilization not only to their superiority, but also to the fact that empire was a globalizing endeavor that exported Western knowledge and culture, European languages, institutions, and capital and whose ultimate impact was to benefit minorities and women, and to create an indigenous constituency for occupation through access to educational and commercial opportunities, without which empire would have become unsustainable.[14] Ferguson's was an interpretation tailored for the times to provide a beneficent mythology of empire to frame contemporary COIN, highly at odds with generations of scholarship that focused on the cultural destruction, economic exploitation, racism, and military repression at the heart of imperialism and its small wars.[15]

"From the doubts of the 1950s to the certitudes of the 1990s"

The second problem with Desert Storm in the eyes of the neo-conservatives in the years after 1991 and prior to 2001 was that operational dominance on the battlefield had failed to translate into strategic success – the legendary Republican Guard escaped destruction in a second decisive battle of myth and saga of February 1991, the Iraqi army retained their helicopters to suppress the Shi'a uprising, and Saddam clung to power largely because Powell and theater commander Norman Schwarzkopf took their feet off the gas pedal at the critical moment in war termination that put the lie to their brilliance in the weeks before. The mishandling of the Gulf War end game joined later with the debacle in Mogadishu and the agonies of limited force in Bosnia and Kosovo to convince what Bacevich labels the neo-conservative "war club" that the Weinberger–Powell Doctrine of overwhelming conventional force followed by a rapid "exit strategy" had become obsolete in the post-Soviet era. Soldiers who had painstakingly regained public stature by focusing on rehabilitating conventional warfare and excluding civilians from important wartime decisions were in reality a collective of timid, orthodox thinkers untutored in the transformative potential of military force in the post-Cold War era.[16] The collapse of the USSR had left the United States a free hand to remake the world in its image in this unipolar moment, which seemed to reappear in the wake of September 11, 2001 terror attacks if not at the time that Paul Wolfowitz first proposed such a security strategy in the early 1990s.

RMA proponents rhapsodized that speedy, synchronized attacks guided by precision cyber technology would lift the fog of war, expose the enemy to overwhelming force at the decisive point, and so realize revolutionary goals of a Global War on Terror etched into the 2002 *National Security Strategy*. Unfortunately, Lynn concludes that the 2001 *FM 1: The Army* and *Vision* of that year that supposedly encapsulated the RMA's fundamental principles, offered little more than a cascade of clichés.[17] Neo-cons, however, believed that the US military had lost the capacity to adapt to an evolving strategic environment, although they appeared unable to evaluate the degree to which the military had already folded technology into existing forces and combat capabilities.[18] September 11, 2001 and the declaration of the Global War on Terrorism, the war without end, offered the opening for defense civilians led by Donald Rumsfeld and Paul Wolfowitz to shatter the aura of strategic determinism and reticence based on post-Vietnam guilt that had surrounded Colin Powell as a political figure and the voice of military professionalism in American democracy. Their goal was to force hide-bound soldiers to build a lithe, lean, agile, technologically sophisticated military for total victory. The speed and ease with which a handful of SOF backed by airpower and in league with local warlord allies toppled the Taliban in Afghanistan in late 2001 appeared to confirm all of the neo-con/RMA assumptions.[19]

Defense specialist and White House confidant Eliot Cohen's immensely influential 2002 book *Supreme Command* argued that the success of great civilian wartime leaders – Lincoln, Clemenceau, Churchill, and Ben Gurion – resided in the fact that they imposed their will on often timorous or unimaginative military leaders.[20] It is difficult to know just how much influence Cohen's "war is too important to be left to generals" views carried in the Pentagon circa 2002, but they certainly provided the historical heft to the campaign by George W. Bush's security team to override the concerns of the regular soldiers in the highest echelons of command about the under-resourcing of the Iraqi Freedom campaign in 2003. Rumsfeld and Wolfowitz became the senior professional military's worst nightmare, like serial killers who insist to the court that they are competent to conduct their own defense. It was as if the ghost of Robert McNamara had returned to forfeit yet another war by meddling in the military's professional sphere of strategic and operational competence. But Cohen led a chorus of defense intellectuals, not all of them neo-cons by any means, who feared that the army's attachment to conventional war within limited war was symptomatic of the military's ossification and bureaucratization. It might also herald the onset of an authoritarian culture reinforced by the termination of conscription, lingering resentment over the "betrayal" of Vietnam, a distrust of politicians, and a disdain for a civilian society that soldiers considered unworthy of the professionally and ethically superior armed forces that protected them. Combined, these attitudes might make the armed services resentful, reluctant to take direction, and lacking the imagination to adapt to a fluid operational environment as had been the case since the close of the Indochina War and which was especially visible with Clinton as commander-in-chief in the 1990s.[21]

Indeed, the distilled fears of defense *cognoscenti* were that the decline in the number of Congressional members with military service, and the post-Vietnam die-off of Democratic Party defense expertise with the passing of senators Jackson, Stennis, and Nunn as a field of parliamentary excellence, combined with the Republicanization of the officer corps and the outsourcing of many hitherto military tasks to civilian contractors might have both weakened democratic civilian constitutional oversight and eroded military professionalism with politicization and a caste ethos among officers. In this view, the American military had set themselves up for the neo-con/RMA coup because their increasingly political stances on national issues, such as forcing President William Jefferson Clinton in March 1993 to retreat from his "gays in the military" initiative, endorsing (mainly Republican) political candidates, and, finally, openly rebelling in the election campaign of 2006 over the stalemate in Iraq, had crumbled the strictly professional, above the political fray barrier erected in the 1980s.

Nor for many keen observers of the brains of the army was the military's post-Vietnam withdrawal from politics compensated with an upgrade in professional competence as had been visible in an earlier epoch of the twentieth century. Instead, officers focused on "ticket punching" had become risk-averse, careerist, "action-oriented," and self-righteously anti-intellectual. Especially in the 1990s and into the present, war and command and staff colleges substituted "buzzword bingo" in the place of strategic education, much of it cadged from business schools or from Hollywood studios. Scandals that followed from the outbreak of war in 2001 – Pat Tillman's friendly-fire incident, Jessica Lynch's "capture" and "liberation" *à la* Spielberg's "Saving Private Ryan," the forced retirement of Major General Anthonio Taguba following his categorization of events at the Abu Ghraib prison as war crimes, the Walter Reed military hospital's inadequate treatment of wounded veterans – triggered an institutional circle-the-wagons, cover-up reflex. The absence of command support from senior generals reluctant to stand up to Rumsfeld's bullying in the Pentagon, in turn, discouraged initiative on the part of subordinates in Iraq. How different this fact was from the World War II generation who, in the words of Richard Kohn, demonstrated "remarkable success prior to and during World War II in creating and executing strategy in the largest and most complex war in human history." The fact that the "remarkable success" of George Marshall and Dwight Eisenhower in the years 1941–1945 relied on Red Army attrition of the Wehrmacht and FDR's insistence, at Churchill's behest, that the Americans learn to fight in the Mediterranean because they were unready in 1942–1943 for prime time in Northern Europe notwithstanding, Kohn's point is that the energy of US officers in the recent past and present has become solely concentrated on simply managing an unwieldy and routinized institution. "The result was the withering of strategy as a central focus for the armed forces, and this has been manifest in a continual string of military problems."[22]

The attacks of 9/11 demonstrated America's vulnerability and silenced voices that had cautioned against "clash of civilization" and neo-conservative adventurism in global minefields of national, tribal, and religious conflicts. In the wake of September 11, 2001, Headquarters, USSOCOM, and its subordinate forces were expanded to around 50,000 men, its budget increased by over one-third, and it executed a hostile take-over of the CIA's paramilitary functions.[23] The tale of how Republican Party macho and apparent love of warfare,[24] neo-conservative cultural hubris, George W. Bush's unilateralist impulse and perhaps other feelings of personal and professional inadequacy, a faith in RMA-guided preventative war, and the heroic ethos and warrior values of the US military[25] combined to produce Operation Iraqi Freedom in the year 2003 is an oft told one. While realists might argue that Saddam was an unattractive but necessary feature of Middle Eastern regional stability and that charges that he harbored nuclear ambitions appeared fanciful to well-informed critics of US policy and strategy in 2002, the case for intervention was hard to resist on a moral level, especially as the wizards of RMA in think tanks and the E ring of the Pentagon promised a quick and painless process with a joyful conclusion on the model of the invasion of Panama in 1989. Rumsfeld and Wolfowitz dismissed lumbering force requirement estimates provided by Army Chief of Staff Eric K. Sinseki, whose defense of the Weinberger–Powell Doctrine was accompanied by Powell's political suicide, on the occasion of the latter's witless attempt to prove to the UN Security Council the existence of weapons of mass destruction.

Rumsfeld directed, in turn, an invasion of Iraq with an understrength, overly mechanized ground force unprepared for the constabulary role, once rioting and subsequent occupation, stabilization, and counterinsurgency tasks became urgent in the weeks after April 2003. In his best-selling book, *The Gamble*, a sequel to his equally illuminating *Fiasco*, the Pulitzer Prize winning *Washington Post* journalist Tom Ricks established the COIN-dinista narrative of how General David Petraeus and a cohort of defense intellectuals, both in and out of uniform, designed a "surge" to rescue a failed coalition strategy in Iraq. *The Gamble* opens in Haditha, Iraq on November 19, 2005, the day that a squad of US marines, reacting to the detonation of an IED that had killed one of their members, went on a killing spree that, in a matter of minutes, left twenty-four Iraqis dead. The fact that some of them were women and children cast doubt on the marines' alibi that blamed the civilian deaths on the IED and the ensuing firefight with insurgents in the houses that lined the road. Eight marines were eventually charged with various crimes ranging from homicide to dereliction of duty. The charges were later dropped.

The incident attracted much attention at the time with an American and coalition public grown weary of the costs – human, monetary, and moral – of the Iraq War. Coming on the heels of the scandal of the mistreatment of internees at Abu Ghraib, the journalistic reflex was to liken Haditha to My Lai, the March 1968 murder of hundreds of Vietnamese civilians by soldiers of the infamous Americal Division. While commentators disagreed over whether Haditha was indeed "Bush's My Lai," studies revealed that the upward spiral of violence in Iraq had coarsened attitudes among US troops toward Iraqi civilians whom many saw as complicit with the insurgency. This chasm of distrust and hostility that had opened between coalition forces and Iraqi civilians jeopardized the US mission in Iraq. "In 2005 the United States came close to losing the war in Iraq," Ricks concluded.[26] The situation deteriorated seriously from July 2006 when Shi'a militias began to attack Sunni neighborhoods, and Sunnis, reinforced by al-Qaeda operatives, retaliated with car bombs.

Taking a page from the script of counterinsurgency boosters of the past and present, Ricks assembled a familiar small wars rap-sheet for "defeat," beginning with the persistence of a conventional war mindset in a coalition for whom counterinsurgency "was just a slogan." That the institutional pathologies that had "lost" Vietnam resurfaced in Iraq came as no surprise, given US forces' attachment to a "dominant American military tradition that tends to view war only as battles between conventional forces of different states." Daytime sweeps and mounted patrols run out of large Forward Operating Bases known as "super FOBs" equipped with all the comforts of home offered a strategy of "retreat in place." The US military, dominated by complacent, careerist generals who failed to ask hard questions, were obsessed with "force protection," and who lacked the imagination to create more innovative solutions, had ceased to be a "learning organization." "The American tradition also tends to neglect the lesson, learned repeatedly in dozens of twentieth-century wars, that the way to defeat an insurgency campaign is not to attack the enemy but instead to protect and win over the people," Ricks opined.[27] Iraq in 2005 looked just like Vietnam minus the napalm and Agent Orange.

Ricks' story line, which imitates that of journalists who have long made common cause with colonial soldiers in the battle for the public mind at home, with an identifiable cast of heroes and villains, and a happy ending, runs as follows: As the situation in Iraq deteriorated in the summer of 2006 with ethnic cleansing and skyrocketing attacks on US forces, President George W. Bush came under increasing pressure to change the strategy of entrusting Iraq's internal security to the Iraqi army and police force. This proved difficult as the "Iraqization" of the war had the support of Vice President Dick Cheney, the Secretary of Defense Donald Rumsfeld, and their handpicked military commanders.[28] But help was in the wings, in the form of a team of maverick officers and their dynamic leader, General David Petraeus in the US Army's TRADOC in Kansas, where the general had gone after his first Iraq tour. As Iraq smoldered in 2006, Petraeus supervised the writing of a new counterinsurgency manual, *FM 3–24*, which was published in December 2006. In February 2007, Petraeus returned with his command team and 20,000 reinforcements to "surge" out of the "super-FOBs" and saturate Baghdad neighborhoods in the spring of 2007 with small posts, blast barriers, and roadblocks.

The COIN-dinista narrative enshrined by Ricks is that, when the RMA failed in the period from 2004 until 2006, the "Petraeus guys" rode to the rescue with a self-reverential doctrine of a renewed American way of war for the twenty-first century, which in reality was anchored in the romanticism of nineteenth-century imperialism and a pornographic fixation on the strategic benefits of SOF, which had managed since the nadir of the essentially forgotten "Green Beret Affair" circa 1969 to rebrand themselves as the White Knights of American Exceptionalism.

What's wrong with this picture?

First, this book has argued that historically violence against the population has been central to a tactical approach to conflict that makes "malleable and calculating masses" the focus of war making and which seeks to liberate counterinsurgents from legal norms and civilian control that apply in conventional conflicts.[29] How, then, does one respond to Ricks' seductive, historical flip scenario of Petraeus riding to the rescue of a failed US strategy? One can begin by asking what, exactly, Ricks means by "losing the war in Iraq"? The original rationale for the war – weapons of mass destruction; the collaboration of Saddam Hussein with the perpetrators of the attack of September 11, 2001; and transforming Iraq into a beacon, if not the bow wave, of democracy in the Middle East – were already lost causes as early as late 2003 and surely by the year 2004. The surge came too late to rescue Republican hopes in the 2008 elections. Nor did it buy time for Iraqi politicians to form a government. So, what political and strategic goal exactly, did "the surge" accomplish?

Far from being a strategy for victory in Iraq, COIN in the context of 2005–2006 offered simply the latest promise of a strategic renaissance following on from the doctrinal disappointments of the AirLand Battle and especially the RMA. The apparent contradictions of the latter as a guide to policy and strategy never attracted sufficient criticism and analysis in the years of peace of the 1990s, only to fail with stupendous consequences in the Iraqi campaign of 2003, all claims by RMA diehards notwithstanding. The renaissance of COIN filled a strategic vacuum in Baghdad with at best a system of grand tactics and no grand strategy and papered over the civil-military crisis of leadership in Washington with empty promises to buy time so that Iraqis could reconcile their political and religious divisions. COIN appeared to be a breath of fresh air in a Washington made weary with Wolfowitzian hubris and Rummy's misquotation of Herman Kahn and the "known unknowns." And "unknown unknowns." Politically, the new doctrine was offered as a vaguely conservative Democratic comeuppance to the neo-con RMA.[30] The fact that Republicans embraced the very nation-building that they had denounced as "social engineering" at the outset of the Bush administration offers a measure of their desperation following the collapse of the RMA, a Global War on Terrorism (GWOT) gone awry, and the evaporation of any attainable US strategy and interests in Iraq beyond getting out. The reborn doctrine elevated to grand strategy offered COIN's vindication of what earlier had been a minority view among strategists that Vietnam could have been won if a "better war" counterinsurgency approach had been adopted. Counterinsurgency proponents argued that without Petraeus and the surge, the newsreels would soon close Iraqi Freedom's sad saga with pictures of the helicopter lifting off the embassy roof.[31] But what other outcome might one expect from a claque of timorous, bureaucratized, conventional soldiers – flashbacks of Lyautey blaming France's unimaginative, routinized, careerist, politicized metropolitan officer corps in the 1890s for the initiation and cover-up of the Dreyfus affair, at a time when the creative colonial soldiers led by Gallieni were pioneering the breakthrough oil spot technique in Tonkin – big and small warriors never seem to get along.[32]

A second problem with the Petraeus as savior narrative is that *FM 3–24: Counterinsurgency* of December 2006 failed to supply a blueprint for strategic reversal in Iraq beyond a compendium of predictable platitudes about requirements for "legitimacy" and "effective governance" lifted from British theory "with adjustments for contemporary context."[33] In the view of Andrew Bacevich, *FM 3–24* offers not so much a vision of a "new American way of war," as of no war at all – a Lawrence/Liddell Hart victory without battles formula. But fighting battles, winning wars is what soldiers do, not "armed social work." In Bacevich's view, COIN reflects the strategic confusion that has lately seized defense intellectuals in the United States in the protraction of the GWOT. *FM 3–24*'s formula for victory boils down to "imperial policing combined with the distribution of alms." But its real purpose, one must say, has been to legitimize Petraeus' cult of personality by discrediting the effort of "conventional" predecessors – indeed rejecting the notion that conventional war will play any part in the United States' imperial mission or in national security *tout court*.[34]

For all its talk of "culture" and pages filled with historical examples, the historian Edward Luttwak, well versed in the ways of the US Department of Defense, finds *FM 3–24* to be both culturally naïve and historically selective to the point of deliberate deception. "Christians" promoting democratic consensus seldom get a sympathetic hearing in historically fractured Islamic societies. Advocating women's rights as part of a modernization package, even female engagement in the counterinsurgency cause as both Galula and Kilcullen advocate,[35] sparks backlash and resentment. Professions of altruistic intentions inevitably meet skepticism among peoples with prior encounters with Western colonialism, and who measure all actions in the shadow of the United States' unflinching support of Israel and Zionists. "Development" often offers a path to corruption and waste, while collaborators will be viewed as opportunists and outsiders, which many of them are. Intelligence collection to identify and eliminate insurgents, an aspect of counterinsurgency that *FM 3–24* addresses at some length, provides no antidote to political and strategic problems. Given that "convincing models of success in defeating insurgents by military means" historically have combined various forms of official "terror," to include population concentration, calorie control, judicial complicity in internment and torture, house demolitions, pitting one group, tribe, or faction against another, and so on, *FM 3–24* represents a backward evolution in counterinsurgency doctrine, "from the doubts of the 1950s to the certitudes of the 1890s." In Luttwak's view, *FM 3–24* offers no strategy for success, only a compendium of practices, procedures, and tactics that discount the fact that insurgencies are political phenomena. As such, "its prescriptions are in the end of little or no use and amount to a kind of malpractice."[36]

Indeed, the underlying assumption of "population-centric warfare" is identical to that of Mao – that popular collaboration is both a prerequisite and the determining factor for victory in people's war. Kilcullen defines counterinsurgency as "a competition with the insurgent for the right and the ability to win the hearts, minds and acquiescence of the population."[37] This generalization is historically inaccurate. Better strategies, leadership, coercion, and contingent circumstances in their variety, not popular support, determined victory in small wars/insurgencies. The revived counterinsurgency doctrine is also anti-Clausewitzian because in its determinism, it denies the interactive nature of conflict as manifest in the will, chance, and anger of conflicting parties as in the duel. Finally, *FM 3–24* was superfluous because the army in the final decades of the twentieth century was both deployable and flexible, while US soldiers possessed an intellectual framework that allowed them to adapt to the changing nature of the conflict at least eighteen months before *FM 3–24: Counterinsurgency* hit the bookstores.

"The pivot from conventional to unconventional operations"

The general evolution of combat in the Iraqi campaign of 2003 went as follows according to official US Army historian John Sloan Brown: From 2002, the build-up of forces in theater progressed far more rapidly than for Desert Storm a decade earlier because of prepositioned stocks, improved sea and airlift, lighter units, and deployment rehearsals, which meant that Heavy Divisions in some cases beat paratroops into the theater. Firepower improvements meant that the advance on Baghdad could be undertaken with fewer units than during Desert Storm. The

Stryker Brigades, introduced by General Shinseki, proved to be the most flexible and adaptable units given the mix of missions required in Iraq. Light and airborne units bulked up with armor and helicopters from prepositioned stocks. The major oversights of the invasion proved to be the inadequate provision of trucks (like the Wehrmacht in the Russian campaign), so that the advance quickly outran its supply base in Kuwait, and unreliable civilian support contractors. But once the invasion was complete, the application of modular organization, distribution-based logistics, and computer tracking proved to be one of the success stories of the Army of Excellence, despite the fact that supply convoys were a particularly favorite insurgent target. (The Afghanistan deployment, in turn, offered a different mix of air-transported SOF and conventional forces.) But the army official history declared the deployment and invasion phases to be "impressive displays of expeditionary force projection." All this was surely true on the tactical and operational level, with a view backward to the experience of 1991. But in the event, it was more or less meaningless at the strategic level. On the downside, although Baghdad fell quickly in April 2003 in a conventional campaign of maneuver and fire, "shock and awe" had failed to live up to its press notices. Nevertheless, while the RMA proved to be a work in progress, cyber technology greatly improved command and control, GPS navigation, communications, joint operations, and logistics as well as allowing US forces to adapt quickly to changes in enemy tactics and dispositions. Precision weapons struck through sandstorms and honed in on the thermal signatures of Iraqi vehicles hiding in urban areas or vegetation. In sum, Iraqi Freedom in 2003 overran a larger areas than had Desert Storm in 1991 with half the troops at a price of about a third of the casualties.[38]

The "Mission Accomplished" triumphalism of the fall of Baghdad in April 2003 had soured by the spring of 2004, as attacks on supply lines ballooned into full-scale Shi'a uprisings in Sadr City, Najaf, and Basra, while Sunni militants became active in Samarra, Ramadi, and Fallujah. The collapse of law and order cleared the way for a proliferation of criminal gangs, ethnic cleansing, a generalized settling of scores, kidnappings, and property seizures. As we have seen, COIN proponents complained that the insurgency caught the army and marines flat-footed and at a loss as how to respond. This statement is an exaggeration. While the army official history concedes that only SOF specialized in LIC, and line units had concentrated on the top end of the conflict spectrum, LIC remained part of the army's tactical repertoire because stability operations often exceeded SOF capabilities, as had been the case in the post-conflict and security-building operations in Kurdistan and Somalia in the 1990s. Virtually every combat brigade had deployed somewhere in the decade before Iraqi Freedom, so that such units contained veterans of Kurdistan and Somalia, as well as of operations in Haiti and the Balkans. Afterwards, Action Reviews from these operations were written for the Center for Army Lessons Learned, from which "low-end" combat scenarios were adapted and incorporated into training. The basic principles of COIN were grasped in such units, the army had updated LIC doctrine periodically in the 1990s, and kicked off Iraqi Freedom by issuing *FM 2–07: Stability Operations and Support Operations* in February 2003.[39] The fact that David Petraeus, John Nagl, and H. R. McMaster had focused their PhD research on counterinsurgency topics in the post-Vietnam era testifies to a continuity of interest in COIN in the years of conventional warfare dominance in which a school of strategic thought and practice on this aspect of war continued to operate along with many others.

Iraq surely did not indicate that the US Army and US Marine Corps failed as "learning organizations." Eric Shinseki, who had served in both Vietnam and Bosnia, understood the extensive manpower requirements of an occupation force, in part because the Center of Military History had been tasked to study force ratios for twenty twentieth-century US occupations, as well as the "collateral requirements" of occupation, to include humanitarian relief, peacekeeping, law and order, and nation-building. Not only was Shinseki's estimate that "something in the order of several hundred thousand soldiers" would be required for the occupation of Iraq rejected by Rumsfeld and Wolfowitz. But also, the manpower shortfall became catastrophic when Ambassador Paul Bremer unilaterally disbanded the Iraqi army. This decision, which has become the alibi of a nation in the years since 2003, also meant that the problem of demobilization of Iraqi security forces was added to the already violent and lawless cohort of those resisting the US/coalition occupation in 2003–2004. A hundred and ninety-five thousand constantly rotating coalition troops with few interpreters and scant knowledge of the country were too thin on the ground to execute the multiple missions of securing Iraq's borders, maintaining order, creating the basic structures of government, and keeping services going inside a country of 30 plus million factious souls with a barely functioning infrastructure ravaged by decades of war. The situation began to slide toward chaos in 2003–2004 as those who initially cooperated with the Americans were killed or intimidated, insurgent attacks became more audacious, and locally recruited security forces evaporated or turned hostile. The official history admits that the invasion force's initial reaction to this deteriorating situation actually made things worse. The top-down intelligence structure designed for conventional combat operations proved unable to supply the grassroots knowledge and information required for stability. Therefore, US soldiers swept up and imprisoned young men Battle of Algiers style, which soon found detention centers at Camp Bucca and Abu Ghraib overflowing and severely damaged relations with the locals. A bloated command and control center stretching back to CENTCOM in Tampa and a bumbling, clueless Coalition Provisional Authority proved slow to respond to a deteriorating local situation. With poorly defined rules of engagement, thrust into an alien and increasingly hostile environment, US troops often fired first and asked questions later.[40]

Insurgent tactics evolved slowly in the face of the coalition forces. Ambushes of American patrols invited detection by thermal sights, night-vision goggles, sensors, and overhead surveillance by drones. And if this arsenal was unleashed in full, the result was usually annihilation, not only by the firepower of the troops attacked, but also by pile-on swarms of GPS-directed reinforcements firing laser-guided munitions. Most Coalition offensive operations occurred at night, both to avoid media coverage and to take full advantage of US night-vision capabilities. Uprisings in Najaf, Samarra, and Fallujah in 2004 convinced insurgents that trying to defend ground against US forces was suicidal. So they turned increasingly to IEDs, most fabricated from explosives lifted from Saddam's weapons dumps that had remained unsecured during the invasion and long after due to the lack of troops,[41] a dearth compounded by the Bush administration's diversion of soldiers to search for nonexistent caches of WMDs in the weeks following the invasion. But, contrary to the claims of some that the forces were incapable of "learning," GIs quickly adopted IED defense measures that included electronic jammers, drone surveillance, networks of Iraqi lookouts supplied with cell phones, and "spider web" entrapment techniques to isolate and surround snipers and bombers, better training to recognize and deal with IEDs, and armoring of HMMWVs. Forensic examination of detainees for traces of explosives and the creation of extensive databases of suspects allowed many cells to be broken up, which was particularly important as the increasing frustration with the impotence of IEDs pushed insurgents toward vehicle and individual suicide bombing. These measures meant that while IED attacks tripled between 2004 and 2006, casualties remained steady. Individual brigades and divisions began to organize locally recruited paramilitary organizations, which in April 2004 were grouped under the rubric of Iraqi National Guard. And while the military capabilities of these forces was limited, they served as a sort of counter-mobilization that helped to dry up potential insurgent recruits and solve, in part, the problem of demobilization and the creation of military desperados.[42] George Decker was vindicated when conventional warriors, whom the critics described as incapable of innovation and improvisation in the sense of Clausewitz's genius, proved that they knew how to handle guerrillas!

So, bottom line, the US Army argues that: "The pivot from conventional to unconventional operations proved problematic, largely because of a dearth of manpower to cope with recognizably manpower-intense requirements," not because its soldiers lacked the tactical skills to handle guerrillas. "Transformation enabled the United States to dispatch conventional foes handily and to sustain prolonged major counterinsurgencies with relatively few casualties and a small volunteer Army," concludes US Army historian John Sloan Brown.[43] In his study of the adaptation of five "conventional" US Army and US Marine Corps battalions to the asymmetric challenges of post-invasion Iraq, Naval Postgraduate School Professor James Russell confirmed the official history's verdict that US units proved to be fast learners in part because doctrine, even though "conventional," provided an organizational and methodological framework and common understanding upon which the units drew to build COIN competencies. By the time the Petraeus COIN-centric staff officer circus arrived in the spring of 2007, US units had proven able to step down from conventional to unconventional operations by spontaneously evolving successful small war tactics, most dramatically in Anbar where innovations, begun in late 2005 with little direction from higher military and civilian authorities, had started to show results by the fall of 2006: "None of the units examined herein received what could be considered command-level guidance from headquarters level on how to structure their counterinsurgency operations," Russell writes.[44]

Because the policy in Washington on the Panama 1989 paradigm à la Rumsfeld and Wolfowitz was to transition security responsibility as quickly as possible to Iraqi Security Forces (ISF), the priority of

16 Members of the US-backed Neighborhood Patrol Awakening Council in August 28, 2008. Critics of General David Petraeus' 2007 surge in Iraq argued that arming the "Sons of Iraq" offered "an eerie echo of British imperial policies" of "divide and rule" that undermined nation-building and opened the US Sunni allies to reprisals by the Shi'a-dominated government.

in-country commanders-in-chief Generals John Abizaid and George W. Casey had been to withdraw forces to large bases as a prelude to repatriation. In the meantime, units had to generate a tactical response to the deteriorating situation on the ground. "The process began in what could be described as tactical, ad hoc adaptation in which individual leaders reacted to local circumstances cycling through different ways of employing their units and equipment on the battlefield," Russell found. For instance, in Ramadi, units had begun to split out of super FOBs into smaller combat outposts by the fall of 2006 with beefed-up battalion intelligence (B2), an increase in foot patrols, and the application of police techniques to keep order, all of which helped them to develop a better feel for the local political climate. They had already begun to work with local sheiks to raise a police force. This innovation was possible because these conventional units were composed of highly trained and educated soldiers led by imaginative commanders willing to delegate authority, who encouraged a free flow of information within and across their organizations whose structures they proved willing to change and adapt, and who utilized digital technology and analytical methods to increase efficiencies and aid decision-making. None of these ad hoc tactics amounted by themselves to a formula for victory – that depended on the evolution of a more favorable political situation and the formulation of strategy at the highest levels and theater command. But Russell's point is that the absence of a COIN doctrine or structure scarcely hindered adaptation of conventional units to counterinsurgency tasks, contrary to what has later been claimed by the COIN doctrine people. And this tactical and operational flexibility appeared, despite the fact that the US military had been set up for failure by the Bush administration's inability to formulate and coordinate coherent policy-strategy-operational objectives on the national and theater level, and to devise a plan backed by a civil-military structure to implement them.[45]

Ricks might argue that the surge, by showing the insurgents that they could not win, offered a step toward "sustainable security."[46] That may be. But Rachel Schneller, State Department representative in Basra in 2005–2006, argued that Petraeus and co. had become largely irrelevant to the events that unfolded in Iraq in 2007: "We frequently deluded ourselves into attributing positive developments in the country to our own efforts, when instead it was deal-brokering between Iraq's political parties and militias that was largely responsible for everything that happened outside the Green Zone, and certainly outside of Baghdad." In short, Ricks offered a history of the surge with the Iraqis factored out, an American habit of strategic myopia that had operated in Indochina as well whereby the Vietnamese frequently disappeared from strategic debate in the 1960s. By the time the surge kicked in, Shi'a death squads had cleansed Baghdad and created a Sunni diaspora whose dimensions are disputed but which at a minimum is over a million strong in Jordan, Syria, and Lebanon – refugee camps abroad obviated the requirement for population concentration in Iraq.[47] Sadrist militias concluded a ceasefire with the Iraqi government in August 2007. The so-called "Sunni Awakening," for which the COIN proponents took credit, was already underway before the surge began and violence was on a downward trend. The Awakening did not occur simply because al-Qaeda was making unacceptable demands on the Sunni tribes, but because they were under great pressure from ISF and Shi'a militias. Petraeus and his acolytes merely boarded a train that had already left the station at least six months earlier. Al-Qaeda presence in the Sunni tribal areas had been exaggerated by the US military, who were basically arming the "Sons of Iraq" to defend themselves against the US-created government and its

Shi'a-dominated security forces, not al-Qaeda – in short, arming civil war, not nation-building.[48] The fact that State Department Provincial Reconstruction Teams (PRTs), civilian specialists embedded with military units, had also begun to operate by 2007 goes unmentioned by Ricks in a more than telling manner. Schneller believes that PRTs "arguably had as much effect as the military surge itself" in that they distributed economic assistance more broadly than had the military, demonstrated the benefits of development over violence, and helped to mitigate the excesses of a hitherto largely operational-tactical driven policy. For Schneller, *The Gamble* offers a stunted, overly militarized, "Hollywoodesque" history of 2005–2008 that "sacrifices accuracy" to a morality tale story line and whose effect is to restore a damaged soldierly ethos in the face of uncontrolled political violence.[49]

A second critic, London School of African and Oriental Studies' Laleh Khalili, properly captures *The Gamble*'s gothic quality as "an eerie echo of British imperial policies," in which US officers convinced themselves that the surge's success flowed from the concept of tribes as Iraq's "tectonic plates." She notes the self-conscious, even self-reverential, Orientalism of Petraeus' counterinsurgency team, down to their admiration of the patrician anthropologist Gertrude Bell, a T. E. Lawrence contemporary and Arab *aficionada* who helped guide the imposition of Britain's post-Great War imperial straitjacket on the Middle East, the font of so many contemporary problems in the region. The Australian David Kilcullen's "Twenty-Eight Articles" of counterinsurgency reproduce a highly tactical, Lyautey-light checklist that treats the local population as an abstraction, similar to T. E. Lawrence's twenty-seven nostrums issued almost a century earlier.[50] While one advantage of this "cultural" approach is that it does not mistake indigenous folk for Westerners in training, the danger, as Patrick Porter argues, is that it treats them as culturally static, "archaic curiosities or medieval throwbacks fixed in another time," whose behavior is dictated by culturally derived factors like feuds, honor or kinship ties, and denies them the presumption of rational calculation of benefit and risks.[51] Counterinsurgency becomes adult intervention into a schoolyard of bullied children. Such soothing terms of the post-September 11 conflict as "stability," "development," "nation-building," and "democracy" merely front for a "white man's burden," "civilizing mission" ideology of conquest. In a replication of British divide and rule imperial tactics, US officers rewarded cooperating tribes with weapons and bags of cash, while denying such benefits to "terrorist" ones. *The Gamble* in Khalili's view simply offers the latest, updated installment of Lugard's *Dual Mandate*, "a new managerial handbook of imperial rule."[52] And like the British Empire, all the US effort is likely to leave behind is a factious and fragile state. Indeed, while acknowledging the requirement for security, Schneller worries that Baghdad has no interest in achieving it through democratic negotiation and consensus. Rather, as in Basra in 2008, the new Iraqi government will, like Saddam, employ the forces sired by US Security Assistance in a civil war to repress its own people.[53]

But no one seems to have picked up that the subtext of *Fiasco* and *The Gamble* is Vietnam with a happy ending – Prince Hal comes to his senses, banishes Fat Jack, and sallies forth to win Agincourt. One problem with COIN, as Petraeus realized in his Princeton thesis, is that a strategy of "victory without battles" lacks the drama of a decisive outcome which is the common grammar of war and its interpretation by military professionals and by civil society. If COIN video games have yet to flood the market, it is because COIN is perceived as a slow, ambiguous process lacking in Good versus Evil drama.[54] The surge saturated Iraqi cities with US forces as a PR exercise to create the perception of an about face of American fortunes.[55] The role of Ricks, an affiliate of the Center for New American Security, Washington's COIN-dinista K Street "stocked up on influential reporters,"[56] is that of Krepinevich in a *keffiyeh*. Following in the footsteps of other small wars-friendly journalists since the time of Bugeaud, Ricks must make COIN sexy by representing Petraeus' Baghdad arrival, in the manner of Lawrence's appearance in the Hijaz, as a game-changing epiphany of US strategy. To do this, he resurrects all the hoary, *déjà vu* indictments of unimaginative, bureaucratic "heavy army" warriors and their "whizz kid" Pentagon bosses who had to be rescued from defeat after the misapplied practices of formerly glorious AirLand Battle and the Revolution in Military Affairs declared bankruptcy in Iraq by nimble, dazzling, "soldier-scholars" with PhDs in history and anthropology and their "light infantry army" leader.[57] In fact, the complete "Petraeus guys" narrative does not begin with Haditha but with its mirror image – the 1969 "Green Beret Affair."[58]

Therefore, a closer examination of the US experience in Iraq exposes the three components of myth and legend that together, in the view especially of the advocates of COIN as a grand strategy and American way of war, attribute "victory" in Iraq to the surge – the appearance of *FM 3–24* in December 2006; Petraeus decisively reoriented American tactics to

COIN; a 20,000 troop surge miraculously imposed order in the spring of 2007 – to be, to put it kindly, incomplete.[59] Nor can the surge, especially as it reinforced the Anbar Awakening or Kurdish separatism, meet even a broad definition of nation-building. Rather, these events of 2006–2007 simply resurrected the divide and rule tactics of small wars and imperial rule. What the surge did was to underline the PR and propaganda dimensions of small wars, especially in the civil-military links between imperial soldiers in the field, their publicists, journalists, and an imperialist readership at home. Like Lyautey, the "Petraeus guys" proved to be propagandists able to brand small wars for the age of mass politics. They mythologized the campaigns even as they happened in a polarized era of domestic politics in which imperial glory also has had a domestic political role with the celebration of soldiers and combat by very demilitarized civilians. Petraeus and his clique of counterinsurgency colonels with PhDs mobilized the US Army's TRADOC as a booster organization to reinforce their own conventional narrative of the failure of a managerial elite of conventional soldiers, itself a story recast as a business school case study retold in desert camouflage of bad management which fails to modernize and embrace lean sigma six principles or just-in-time logistics. In other words, training and doctrine are substituted for strategy. *FM 3–24* offers a vision of strategic idealism appropriate for a neo-imperial age in which the real sources of organized political violence are made to disappear in a puff of Western values and beneficent population-centrism. The authors of the *FM 3–24* serve up an old story of soldiers on the fringe, those in exile from big army – small warriors, SOF, counterinsurgents, self-styled "mavericks" – attempting to inflate the importance of their role by belittling the garrison, establishment military organization that "wouldn't listen," was too bureaucratic, unimaginative, politicized, "conventional," while advancing exaggerated claims for the strategic impact of their skills.

In November 2012, the David Petraeus formula of marketing COIN triumphs by cultivating a Hollywood image of martial stardom collapsed in a tawdry, cyber-snooping scandal. Some journalists wondered how they could have been seduced into touting to a skeptical democracy a "brutal enterprise" that included arming thugs and abandoning former local allies to their fates, much as the French had done to the *harkis* in Algeria. A sales strategy based on "hiding the truth, on deception, on building a false image," through cultivating an incestuous relationship with a compliant media and booster organizations would have been familiar to Wolsey, Kitchener, Lyautey, Leonard Wood, and

T. E. Lawrence. Using similar methods, Petraeus deployed his political clout first to force President Barak Obama to approve the 2009 Afghan "bound to fail surge," then to communicate the impression of strategic progress by leaking "exclusive documents . . . that made the general seem driven by data and not ideology." "[Paula] Broadwell . . . was an attractive package to push Petraeus and his counterinsurgency ideas" and, when required, to defend the brutality of his methods by dismissing the "theatrics" of Afghans who objected to their houses being destroyed and their family members killed by Petraeus-sanctioned pacification methods. "Another irony that Petraeus' downfall reveals is that some of us [journalists] who egotistically thought our coverage of Petraeus and counterinsurgency was so sophisticated were perpetuating myths without fully realizing it," concluded Spencer Ackerman, perhaps disingenuously. *New York Times* columnist Maureen Dowd understood that, in COIN, reputations fabricated on trickery quickly transition to tragedy: "So many more American kids and Afghanistan civilians were killed and maimed in a war that went on too long. That's the real scandal."[60]

"All the troubles in the world": Britain's Basra homecoming

Meanwhile, the British Army's title-hold on COIN triumph was further challenged by its performance in Iraq, where by the late spring of 2007 its 5,000-man force had all but surrendered its primary base in the southern Iraqi city of Basra, and, according to Thomas Ricks, was "hiding in the airport."[61] What can only be called the Britain's COIN collapse in Iraq is particularly surprising as Britain's ability twice in 1920 and 1941 to vanquish uprisings in that country with relative ease gave them the "self-assurance and comfort with foreign culture derived from centuries of practicing the art of soldier diplomacy and liaison."[62] Unfortunately, the British characteristics on display in Basra combined brutality toward the population, to include torture of suspects à la Kenya, Aden, and Belfast, with tactical and operational lethargy. When the British finally launched Operation Sinbad between September 2006 and February 2007 to reclaim the city from the gangs, tribal and sectarian militias, smugglers, and vigilantes that dominated it, they failed utterly, much to the frustration of their American coalition partners who had endured for some time British swaggering about their COIN superiority.[63] "British officials confess not to know how to tackle the problem Operation Sinbad was supposed to resolve," the International Crisis Group concluded in 2007[64] – so much for the "most successful counterinsurgency school"! When the British withdrew in the wake of Sinbad, Major General Jalil Khalaf, the Basra police commander, complained that "they left me militia, they left me gangsters, and they left me all the troubles in the world."[65] "Basra is a mess, and the exit strategy attempted there has failed," the Brookings Institution's Michael O'Hanlon seconded. "It is, for the purposes of future Iraq policymaking, an example of what not to do. Basra has gone far towards revising the common American image of British soldiers as perhaps the world's best at counter-insurgency."[66] British military performance in Iraq so disappointed expectations that Iraqi Prime Minister Nouri-al-Maliki fired the British Army from the April 2008 Operation Charge of the Knights organized to reassert government control over Basra.[67] Nor was Britain's military reputation redeemed by its actions in Helmand Province, Afghanistan in the same period, where its soldiers negotiated local truces with Taliban forces and assumed a defensive crouch.[68] Fault has been laid at the feet of senior commanders who neglected to advise the Secretary of State for Defence that the army lacked adequate troops to carry out operations in both Iraq and Afghanistan, a lack of flexible planning, and poor intelligence.[69]

Colonel Alexander Alderson, the lead author of the British Army's 2010 counterinsurgency doctrine, believes that the shortcomings evidenced by the British in Basra and Helmand began with the army's failure to integrate counterinsurgency lessons learned into a Manoeuvrist Approach to operations and training after 1994, assuming that it could "step down" from maneuver warfare to counterinsurgency if required.[70] In 2003, Basra seemed peaceful, which removed any sense of urgency to create a plan to coordinate military operations with national and provincial officials, or to prepare for Phase IV stability operations. Expecting a speedy transition to Iraqi authority, the British recruited soldiers and policemen indiscriminately without proper vetting. They soon discovered that the very security services upon whom they relied were thoroughly infiltrated by sectarian militias.[71] However, Rachel Schneller, who served as the US State Department representative in Basra in 2005–2006, was told by her Foreign Office counterpart that Northern Ireland had taught them that "the presence of soldiers on the streets actually enflamed the local population." Because the British Army could devise no "population-centric" solution to keep order, Basra soon degenerated into a battleground.[72]

According to Alderson, the absence of a legal framework for operations led to breakdowns of discipline and mistreatment of the population, a behavior endemic to COIN operations.[73] Cases of abuse combined with too few troops, and a high level of turnover especially among senior commanders meant that the British were unable to build local relationships, secure the population, or mount an effective strategic communications plan. They therefore operated in an intelligence desert and so were incapable of identifying and targeting Shi'a insurgent and criminal groups that infested the city and infiltrated the Iraqi security forces. The British remained convinced that aggression was directed solely at them, when in fact an estimated 20,000 Iraqis died from generalized violence in Basra in 2007.[74] (Schneller notes that "hundreds of politicians, government workers, academics, humanitarian aid workers and anyone else brave enough to enter our compound" visited "The Palace" in Basra to plead with the British to act, only to be met with a "let Iraqis sort themselves out" attitude.) Alderson admits that the US military also faced similar problems of adaptation but nevertheless managed to overcome them, as symbolized by Petraeus' 2007 surge. The British, however, never recovered from their initial miscalculations for many of the reasons mentioned above, but mainly because the army was "intellectually unprepared" and lacked a "common philosophical foundation." Anderson concluded that:

> *Continuity, the watchword in Northern Ireland, became institutionalized discontinuity as the campaign veered from being cast as nation-building, to peace support, to stability operations, to – eventually – counterinsurgency, and then counter-corruption, crucially, with no underpinning intelligence database, or established connections with the Baswari population.*[75]

If this had been the first time an insurgency had caught the British flat-footed and flailing for a response before opting for a Kitsonized coercive operational approach, one might accept Alderson's contingent circumstances explanation. But this has been the pattern of British COIN in Palestine, Malaya, Kenya, Cyprus, Northern Ireland, and lately in Iraq and Afghanistan.[76] It is also true that the British suffered from the same muddled strategic environment as did American forces – the failure of the Bush administration to lay out clear political goals in Iraq, a dysfunctional Coalition Provisional Authority, and under-resourced operations among them. "Aid to the civil power" failed in Basra because the police were infiltrated and corrupt, and because the British lacked language skills or "cultural understanding."[77] But neither language skills nor cultural understanding were lacking in Northern Ireland, where the British Army adapted slowly after egregious initial mistakes. Faced with many of the same problems to include poor planning, inadequate troop numbers, best case assumptions about indigenous cooperation and governance capacity, and leadership failures, US forces appeared to recover at least tactically largely because of initiative shown by lower unit commanders.[78]

This book has argued that the fumbled response in Basra is part of a pattern that the British Army appears unable to "learn" its way out of – almost all of the shortcomings identified by Alderson were also recognized by the *Operation Banner* report on Northern Ireland. The British called their counterinsurgency effort in Ireland "framework operations." But by "framework," they meant "covert operations," code for "dirty war." The reality is that the British Army has no framework, no intellectual system to solve problems posed by the adaptive challenges of war. Sure, tactics are a plus, but *Banner* acknowledged that insurgencies must be engaged on the operational and strategic level as well. "The British Army simply did not have the vocabulary to articulate a campaign plan," Colonel Iron conceded about Northern Ireland, and only began to develop a conceptual approach as the campaign drew to a close.[79] Two observers of British operations in Iraq and Afghanistan concluded that the British Army's professionalism was compromised by the fact that it is "also extraordinarily psychologically self-contained, used to muddling through and expecting little else."[80] If six weeks is a long time in politics, thirty years is an eternity in war, during which people are killed, precious resources are exhausted, time is wasted, and opportunity squandered. In neither Belfast nor Basra did the British Army develop a concept. Indeed, "institutionalized discontinuity," not "organizational learning," may be the only identifiable common thread running through the history of British counterinsurgency.

So, in the final analysis, the British failed in plain sight in Iraq, while the Americans salvaged institutional pride with the fig leaf of the surge. But the mythology of the surge has failed to gain traction for counterinsurgency to claim the title of "the new American way of war" because few thinking people alive to the strategic problems of the present are convinced that "armed social work" builds nations at an acceptable cost. The issues that counterinsurgency tactics are meant to resolve are too complex and defy political solutions; net assessments are notoriously unreliable in byzantine environments in which altruistic motives may be misinterpreted; setting priorities, coordinating institutions, and mustering and sustaining resources for a comprehensive approach is too difficult; and COIN missions are carried out in places where Western powers have few interests, vital or otherwise, and where the evangelical propagation of Western mores remains a non-starter. They place too much strain on the social fabric of participating nations, especially in a democracy, but also even in totalitarian countries (i.e. Axis Europe and the Warsaw Pact). COIN operations force democracies to compromise the very freedoms and values that they are meant to export abroad. Promoted as a means for the armed forces and the nation to reinvigorate and renew itself through strategic idealism that is at once blind to the deeper forces of war in their dimension of political purpose, chance, and hatred and anger, COIN sullies the altruistic self-image of nations when, in fact, military institutions rely on torture and concentration camps to prevail, a process that causes the military professional to become rotten and coarsen into an executioner. "War among the people" makes civilians the central objective of war making. The argument that COIN is a separate category of warfare that requires special skills and a suspension of the laws of war – or of laws *tout court* – because terrorists cannot be treated as lawful combatants and civilian laws and courts are inadequate to deal with them is an attempt to liberate COIN from the legal restrains of due process and Western political culture. Nor are military organizations convinced that assertions that counterinsurgency is a discrete category of warfare serve anything more than the special interests of a subcategory of soldiers, who had heretofore existed on the fringes of military institutions in a resentful posture. On the contrary, war is an endeavor that is prosecuted on several levels, depending on the enemy, the geography, and the politics of the situation, to say nothing of the values and political culture of the combatant nation-state and the tradition of the army in conflict – war is war!

11 CONCLUSION

This book has made several arguments: First, the claim that COIN constitutes a separate category of warfare, one made at least since the 1840s by generations of small wars enthusiasts, is contentious at best. The assertion that COIN be considered in its own conflict category is rooted in a rejection of the Clausewitzian character of war in favor of a Jominian posture of determinism with tactics and operational methods (grand tactics), or a half-baked culturalist or meta-anthropological approach substituting for a cohesive, balanced policy and strategy rooted in sound constitutional practice and statecraft. Tactically and operationally, colonial warfare, of which COIN is the lineal descendant, required forces designed for mobility, an aptitude for independent small-unit actions, and the ability to master logistical challenges over great distances. Its adherents were and continue to be tacticians who eschew the imponderables of war made up of politics and mass psychology. Beyond these order of battle prescriptions, the hearts and minds methods of the nineteenth century based on the self-advertised cultural knowledge required for the peaceful penetration and governance of colonial territories boiled down to nothing more than the application of an Orientalized Western view of indigenous societies as immutable tribal affiliations that had either to be "improved" or preserved from contamination, depending on the political views of the respective officer-administrator. COIN writings of both the mid twentieth and the twenty-first centuries have followed these nineteenth-century trailblazers to a remarkable degree, in that they emphasize the political character of their population-centric, information warfare, Phase IV/Stability Operations, hearts and minds, aid to the civil power, and so on, tactics. But like their imperial predecessors, contemporary COIN-dinistas are basically romantics, whose strategic communications target politics and society at home while they profess to apply paternalistic theories onto biddable populations required to show gratitude for their improved conditions by outing pistoleros, bandits, terrorists, and insurgents in their midst.

Today as in the past, COIN proponents and their "new wars" offspring claim that the propensity of conventional soldiers to treat COIN as an inferior form of strategy and military organization in the post-Cold War era is self-defeating, because counterinsurgency has become the norm of conflict – specifically, going forward, future war will mean asymmetrical conflict which, in an echo of the mid-nineteenth-century practitioners of small wars, means that Clausewitzan analysis of the interaction of war, armies, and society, and its impact on strategy formulation are henceforth old think.[1] But none of the doctrinal pre-scriptions and info war accretions of past and present COIN contradicts Decker's assertion that, "any good soldier can handle guerrillas." Those uninformed by the history upon which this study has attempted to generalize too often assume that COIN missions are more complex than more "straightforward" conventional wars.[2] Indeed, nineteenth-century French colonial soldiers complained that metropolitan military tourists who cashed in on colonial stopovers to collect a campaign ribbon with "feats of war" failed to recognize that counterinsurgency fused the business of war with the business of government in the complex coordination of tribal analysis, political negotiation, economic develop-ment, and kinetic encouragement that underpinned imperial consolida-tion.[3] The truth, however, was that imperial soldiers willfully fabricated and assigned attributes to "tribes" as a way better to categorize and control an otherwise undifferentiated mass of humanity, appointed "chiefs" willing to collaborate with the occupier in large part because certain social and economic advantages accrued to them, and, in turn, criminalized dissenters who disputed their legitimacy. This method of control was then marketed through compliant journalists, nationalistic politicians, and imperial pressure groups to the homeland – and the rest of the military – as a specialized endeavor to fulfill professional goals within the ranks of the service as well as provide a tool to manage civil-military relations. But when this method of control came unstuck in the teeth of reality, which it invariably did because small war dominance institutionalized foreign occupation anchored in minority rule, political and cultural hubris, and economic exploitation, then hearts and minds quickly gave way to the cudgel and machine gun, which was the case following both world wars in a variety of bloody counterinsurgency campaigns that continue through those prosecuted most recently in Iraq and Afghanistan.[4]

Little evidence of such small wars and of their strategists supports the contention that soldiers on imperial service were better at learning than were their comrades in continental home garrisons and staff schools, or even that learning by military organizations ultimately made any difference to the outcome of conflicts. Of course, this fact raises the question of learning on what level – on the battlefield, in the intellect of armies, and of their strategic culture as a whole? Hoche, Bugeaud, Gallieni, and the French generally were very adept at mastering the tactics of counterinsurgency. The British Army drew on its long small war experience in Ireland in 1920–1921 and eventually evolved small-unit jungle warfare in Malaya and Kenya in the 1950s, and patrol and interception techniques in Northern Ireland by the late 1970s to make IRA ambushes prohibitively costly. In the first decade of the new century, Americans successfully developed small-unit and counter-IED tactics in Iraq to the point that insurgent options were reduced to large-scale suicide attacks against the population. All of this, however, falls into the category of what Hoche, Wellington, and Bugeaud (and no doubt Decker had the expression still enjoyed currency in the 1960s) would have categorized as petty war, small-unit tactics included in any conventional soldier's field service regulations and "how to fight" manuals.

But insurgencies are political events carried out with violence to achieve a goal. And it is on the political and strategic level, not the tactical, that counterinsurgencies are won or lost. Insurgents may be too isolated politically, ethnically, religiously, or geographically, their message too unpopular or methods too brutal, to swell and sustain support for a particular political, social, economic, or religious agenda. In which case, the counterinsurgent can simply pick a side in a civil war, or roll up an insurgency's infrastructure, incarcerate its support base, decapitate its leadership, and destroy its economy to prevail, as was the case in both Malaya and Kenya, the two signature successes of British COIN in the 1950s. However, this tactic failed in Palestine in 1946–1947 and backfired in Northern Ireland two decades later where the British Army teamed up with Protestant paramilitaries, at a stroke transforming a civil rights protest movement into a full-blown insurgency. Nor did things work out as planned in the Salvadorian civil war in the 1980s. William Deane Stanley argues that the build-up of a large and powerful Salvadorian military through US security assistance in the 1980s to defeat the FMLN actually frightened conservatives into cutting a deal with their ideological opponents.[5]

The surge – the belated 2007 decision to throw support to Sunni tribes in Anbar province – is trumpeted as the event that rescued the US project in Iraq from failure, vindicated the counterinsurgency school of warfare so long denigrated by big war soldiers, and confirmed the strategic brilliance of General David Petraeus. The truth, however, is that the surge impacted hardly at all the strategic dynamic of a conflict that witnessed the unprecedented consolidation of Shi'a power in Iraq through ethnic cleansing and political exclusion, which a tactical adaptation through organizational learning of a few battalions of US soldiers in a bypassed Sunni province did nothing to deter. Whether the Anbar Awakening has mobilized sectarian tensions to put the erstwhile Sunni collaborators at risk in the long term and whether US security assistance has contributed to sustainable state-building is open to doubt.[6] Nor did the surge transfer to Afghanistan where General David Petraeus' reliance on decapitation and scorched-earth tactics supported by warlords and their networks of militia mafias to stabilize a manifestly corrupt and illegitimate regime in Afghanistan laid bare the vacuity of sunny COIN hearts and minds formulae for seducing biddable populations with benevolent acts and good governance.[7] When there were impediments to the application of divide and rule strategies of occupation, as against Zionists in Palestine in the 1940s or Greek Cypriots in the 1950s, or the minorities on which one relies – Turkish Cypriots, or *montagnards*, Catholics, and Cao Dai in Indochina also in the 1940s through 1960s – are simply too diminutive or insufficiently aggrieved to swing the balance of the conflict, then the counterinsurgent may be deprived of important tools for victory, and collaborators expose themselves to reprisals.

In which case, the counterinsurgent can just play for time and hope that the insurgency will implode because it miscalculates levels of popular support, mistimed its insurrection, is too isolated geographically, lacks resources or ideological appeal, is politically inept, too brutal, or a strategy of protraction simply fails to work in its favor. Insurgencies in the Philippines, Malaya, and Latin America have failed due to a combination of these factors. It is equally true that naïve, poorly prepared, or miscalculating insurgencies may be salvaged, or at the very least sustained, by racial/ethnic stereotyping and by draconian counterinsurgent tactics, or by a refusal to make political concessions that might alleviate fundamental grievances that underpin rebellion. Criminalization or normalization strategies that seek to stigmatize insurgents as mere congeries of outlaws may in fact allow them free rein to define the political parameters of the conflict and portray themselves as martyrs to the cause when they are condemned by a customized, fast-track justice system and executed. This fact may consolidate a constituency for the insurgents that the intrinsic appeal of their message or methods would not otherwise merit – Zionist radicals, the Algerian FLN, and the Troubles in Southern and Northern Ireland come immediately to mind. Even poorly prepared insurgencies can be sustained through bad times, even rescued by outside support – rebellions in Algeria and Aden survived in part by associating themselves with the broader cause of Arab nationalism which gave them safe havens and financial support, while the victory of the Viet Minh/Cong might have been unlikely without the direct intervention of China, the USSR, and North Vietnam.

If strategy, not tactics, provides the key to victory, why then have such practitioners and scholars as Thompson, Kitson, Galula, Trinquier, Mockaitis, Nagl, and Downey among others put so much emphasis on institutional learning by COIN-centric forces as a key to victory in counterinsurgency, and why have some of them claimed, furthermore, that historically the British have adapted most quickly to counterinsurgency challenges? Of course, tactical adaptation is preferable to ineptitude, because it saves lives and may set up conditions in the right strategic and operational environment for negotiation and political settlement. But little evidence exists to support the view that small warriors or British colonial soldier-governors were better at tactical adaptation in counterinsurgencies, or that the transfer of lessons learned and best practices by whatever institutional mechanism from one counterinsurgency to another actually helped, rather than impeded, a successful outcome. Imperial military organizations were often unwilling or unable to adapt to the strategic, cultural, or tactical environment in which they operated. Elite white regiments "too famous to learn" looked upon local insurgents with condescension. They regarded the political officer, meant to be their cultural and political interlocutor, as a military failure, captivated by his tribal clients, and useful only for targeting. Impatient with the "political" approach, the reflex of senior officers was to militarize the policy and blood the troops.[8]

David French classifies the post-1945 British Army, Colonial Office, and colonial police as "forgetting organizations," in the style of Colonel Blimp, that invariably failed to transfer lessons from conflict to conflict despite doctrinal manuals and staff college studies. Instead, reorganization following two world wars, conflicts between the War and Colonial Offices, budgetary constraints in the atomic age, economic decline, reliance on local settlers or minorities, short-service conscript armies, and personnel rotations joined a host of issues that meant that counterinsurgents tended to view each eruption of colonial violence as a unique phenomenon so that their initial reactions proved to be tardy, ad hoc, and harsh, especially if they incorporated settler pogroms against the natives as in Malaya, Kenya, and Algeria. Slow to recognize growing native discontent, they neither would nor could implement the political reforms that might have headed off a crisis. Instead, the British too often reacted to colonial unpleasantness like the post-1815 Bourbons, said by Talleyrand to have learned nothing and forgotten nothing – their reflex was to militarize, even SOFize, the police and rely on coercion to restore order. A combination of psychological denial, political paralysis, and overly zealous tactical reactions also characterized French responses to imperial uprisings in modern history. And when British and French COIN proponents did transfer lessons learned from other theaters, the severity of population-centric best practices often served to inflame the situation. In this manner, contemporary COIN-dinistas, locked in the embrace of their specious formulae, cocooned by sycophantic staffs and bilious media handlers who traffic journalistic access in exchange for favorable press, have produced a new generation of château generals, who refuse to listen when their soldiers catalogue for them in pragmatic fashion COIN's misleading assumptions.[9]

If the French mastered the fundamentals of counterinsurgency in its full population-centric magnitude under Bugeaud in the mid nineteenth century, Lyautey taught them how to repackage conquest for an era of mass democratic politics in the late nineteenth century as peaceful penetration through oil spot expansion of the civilizing mission. In this way, French COIN-dinistas manipulated both the tactical and the political dimensions of small wars, and lost nonetheless in mid-twentieth-century Indochina and Algeria. French counterinsurgents managed to spin off their *excès de zèle* techniques to the Southern Cone of Latin

America with baleful consequences, and even to the United States where the Phoenix Program of targeted killings in Vietnam boasted a French pedigree. That COIN proponents in the present fall for the discredited Galula "I won on my front" argument is testimony to a deep ignorance of the War for Algerian Independence, as well as the fact that French information operations were geared primarily at convincing their home audience in the Fourth and Fifth Republics that their methods were both professional and humane. It also reveals their conviction that, if the tactics are correct, then victory will inevitably follow, so long as the nation and its politicians do not sell them out. The French applied all of Galula's prescriptions, including reaching out to women. What Galula thought the French had to offer Muslim women, locked into resettlement camps with starving children, their husbands interned or otherwise deprived of a livelihood, under curfew, food rationing, their religion humiliated and land turned into a free-fire zone, seems to be limited to sewing classes and peripatetic medical clinics run by male doctors. This has not discouraged the US Marine Corps from assembling so-called Female Engagement Teams composed of truck drivers, mechanics, mess hall supervisors, and the like whose only qualification is that their gender allowed them access to Muslim women in Iraq and Afghanistan. The hope is that solace and aspirin will encourage these women to view the infidel invaders in a more positive light and so offer intelligence on the activities of their menfolk, at least until the next *ratonade* or door-shattering exercise in indigenous insult and humiliation – the SOF midnight raid.[10] The peculiar idea that women somehow hold the key to victory in counterinsurgency is more evidence that COIN-dinistas grasp at straws, often found in domestic politics, to concoct victory scenarios in the absence of an open admission that counterinsurgency success often depends on the systematic application of intimidation and divide and rule tactics on a grand scale, of which Human Terrain and Female Engagement Teams are simply another example.

Krepinevich argues that the US Army in Vietnam failed to make the transition from conventional warfare on the European model to COIN, and so lost. Of course, Krepinevich's assertion raises the question of whether it was in the strategic and doctrinal interest of an army whose primary mission throughout the Vietnam War years was to deter the Warsaw Pact in Central Europe to reorganize as a COIN-centric force? But the truth is that the US Army did not need to – the historical verdict is that the US military did attempt to apply tactics that ran the spectrum of conflict short of nuclear war in the 1960s. However, tactics in their diversity, counterinsurgent or search and destroy via the Ia Drang valley, made no difference to the outcome in Vietnam, where the real problem was the political and strategic context in which the war was fought. Neither a tactical nor operational adjustment, nor lashings of strategic hamlets, Combined Action Platoons, and Phoenix assassinations were going to buck up a corrupt and illegitimate South Vietnamese government and its morale-challenged military in the face of an enemy who enjoyed an inviolate sanctuary, nationalist legitimacy, solid political and military leadership, a motivated and adaptable military force, a command economy, and two powerful communist allies who supplied diplomatic cover and virtually unlimited *matériel*.

Ultimately, tactical adaptation in counterinsurgency depended on battalion-level commanders "who were given wide latitude to pick and choose what lessons they taught their men," in the opinion of David French.[11] And there is no evidence that colonial soldiers had a lock on adaptation, either through experience or because of the decentralized nature of their organization. On the contrary, conventional soldiers often proved better at solving the conundrums of small wars because they were more professional, better trained, more proficient tacticians, had an intellectual and doctrinal framework that facilitated problem-solving, and were unencumbered by Orientalist cant about alleged native behavior patterns. In the recent past, conventional US forces adapted rather quickly to the tactical requirements of small wars in Iraq and Afghanistan, even as strategic success remained elusive.[12] The flip of this problem of small versus big war has been that small warriors proved to be in over their heads in conventional conflicts. In turn, COIN-centric armies have, historically, adapted badly to conventional operations, not vice versa. This fate befell the French army in 1870, and the British in two world wars, because a fragmented, regiment-focused order of battle designed for sovereignty operations lacked a command, staff, and education structure, as well as familiarity with all arms combinations of divisions, corps, and armies in frequent *Kriegsspiel* and grand maneuvers to become top-down learning organizations, or to channel and assimilate bottom-up lessons learned in doctrine and training.

Small wars also lagged behind the historical mainstream, in part because laws creating protected categories of combatants and non-combatants and regulating types of weapons used in European battle zones only slowly filtered out to the colonies. While the British in particular have boasted that their counterinsurgency operations are conducted within the confines of legality, that framework has favored repression, not the protection of human rights. Indeed, as Chase Madar writes: "On the whole, the history of IHL is a long record of codifying the privileges of the powerful against lesser threats like civilians and colonial subjects resisting invasion . . . one more weapon of the strong against the weak."[13] British claims to confine repression within legal constraints were regarded as hypocrisy by those on the receiving end, as the family of Alexander Rubowitz discovered in 1947, along with tens, perhaps hundreds of thousands of Malay Chinese, Kikuyu, and Greek Cypriots in the same era. Westminster exploited a legal loophole in the European Convention on Human Rights, written to prevent a repeat of the atrocities inflicted during World War II, to justify detention without trial in Kenya in camps where thousands were tortured and murdered.[14] Even in Northern Ireland between 1972 and 1975, the government settled 410 cases brought against the Ministry of Defence out of court rather than proceed with investigations that would have undermined the army's fallacious claims to operate within the rule of law.[15] All of which demonstrates that British law, as interpreted in the context of imperial policing, aimed to facilitate and justify official violence, not constrain it. British colonial constabularies were militarized organizations that regarded even peaceful political activity as a form of insurrection and whose salient task was to collect intelligence on the populations they oversaw as a hedge against rebellion. In any case, foreign soldiers fighting a "war among peoples" whom they little understood, in turn, felt under siege, on edge, traumatized, and demoralized. As discipline eroded, they became desensitized and inured to mistreating, torturing, and killing civilians, or disrespecting insurgent dead, even as this enraged the local population whose hearts and minds were in play.[16] Emergencies, therefore, required that law and human rights be ignored or shaped in favor of the counterinsurgent, not simply to quell insurrection, but also to preserve discipline and morale among the counterinsurgents. Far from providing a legal framework for COIN, therefore, martial law has expanded the definition of lawful behavior as a mechanism to prevent or contain escalations of soldierly vigilantism.

It is hardly surprising, then, that when population-centric techniques were transferred between theaters by COIN specialists like Kitchener, Thompson, Kitson, Argoud, or Trinquier, their fundamental assumption was that the counterinsurgents enjoyed impunity which exempted them from the laws and standards of conduct that apply in conventional conflict. This was reinforced by the sentiment, especially prevalent among French devotees of *la guerre subversive* and their Latin American acolytes, that theirs was a holy crusade to protect Christian civilization against demonic indigenous forces. They considered the rule of law, the central pillar of Western civilization and the legitimizing element of imperial rule, an inadequate tool that hindered effective pacification which justified, even required, campaigns of generalized terror and torture to compel popular compliance. The fatal contradiction of terror was that an absence of legal constraints combined with the view that defeat was "synonymous with the decline of Christian civilization," which excused manifestly un-Christian behavior, helped to solidify popular support behind the Viet Minh and FLN insurgents. Not only did the exemplary brutality of COIN bolster insurgent fortunes, be they Zionists, FLN, IRA, or now, it seems, Taliban.[17] But also, harsh tactics undermined support for COIN among populations at home shocked that counterinsurgent crusades promoted in the name of freedom, fair play, or *liberté* justified open-ended states of exception, torture, targeted killings, night raids, drone and air strikes, indefinite internment, a suspension of legality, and alliances with unsavory, corrupt, and illegitimate local actors, even disappearances and massacres in the name of national security. Nations that acquiesce to counterinsurgency "wars on terror" because the threat seems credible and the enemy weak and easily overcome must realize that small wars are long, dirty affairs fought most often in remote places among peoples little inclined to see the arrival of Western forces as liberation. Even when they are achieved, military victories in small wars seldom come at an acceptable political, diplomatic, legal, moral, and financial cost.

In the final analysis, Callwell's definition of COIN as "an art by itself" basically boils down to a mastery of small-unit tactics, the acquisition of tactical Intel (which is really what hearts and minds is about), and a capacity to drink endless glasses of tea with tribal sheiks as they exact their price for cooperation. Orde Wingate decried such political service "peddlers of war material and cash" who aim to produce "the rush of tribesmen, the peasants with billhooks."[18] The truth, however, is that not only do such population-centric, people's war methods constitute inefficient Wingatian "hugaboo." They are also heartless and inhumane because they place the crosshairs on the people in a process of escalation inherent in war and are seldom population-friendly. The people are not so much biddable as they become targets of force and coercion, and the competition devolves not into one of governance but into intimidation by both sides perhaps enshrined nowhere more vividly than in Gillo Pontecorvo's cinematic 1966 interpretation of the Battle of Algiers.[19] Protection and isolation of the population from the insurgents usually boiled down to campaigns of counter-terror that included internment without trial, torture, deportation, creating refugee tsunamis, or curfew and concentration camp lockdowns supplemented by calorie control. French author Alexis Jenni qualifies French counterinsurgency success in Algiers in 1957 in novelistic but accurate fashion as a tactical victory bought at exorbitant human and strategic costs:[20]

> *We remained masters of a devastated city, emptied of men whom we could talk to, haunted by electrocuted phantoms, a town where hatred, atrocious pain, and generalized fear reigned. The solution that we discovered showed this very recognizable aspect of French genius ... Generals Massu and Salan applied their principles to the letter ... draw up lists, analyze the situation, to create disasters.*

Such tactics also led to the establishment of counterinsurgent forces that included paramilitary police, settler vigilantes, and warlord militias, sometimes romanticized and legitimized as resistance fighters like the Nicaraguan Contras or "awakened" inhabitants of Anbar Province, who amounted to little more than state-sponsored terrorists in uniform. That is why the application of COIN tactics often served to unite the population against the counterinsurgency and bestow a lesser of two evils legitimacy on fringe groups whose fanaticism or brutality might otherwise marginalize them, as in Palestine, Indochina/Vietnam, Cyprus, Algeria, Aden, Ireland (twice), and Afghanistan. Attempts to conceal coercive population-centric tactics behind an information operations facade of hearts and minds humanity aim to shift the focus of the mission from the benefits of stability and reconstruction campaigns for the homeland, which are far from obvious, to the rescue and rehabilitation of grateful natives.

This peripheral focus alters the question from "what's in it for us," to "what will be the consequences for them if we leave?" Since the 1830s when French politicians suggested terminating the occupation of Algiers originally organized as a short-lived putative expedition, calls for withdrawal invariably meet objections that retreat will sacrifice in-country collaborators, benefit the terrorists by according them safe havens,[21] short-circuit a project that is on the cusp of victory, betray our dead, and advertise the lack of backbone at home – in short, a stab in the back. One forgets that this dubious military idea of civilian betrayal arose from French colonial warfare in the nineteenth century, and not as is usually believed from Hindenburg's testimony to the Reichstag in 1919 on the causes of German defeat in World War I and from the pages of Hitler's *Mein Kampf*. In this way, stab in the back by an indifferent and ungrateful civilian population is an idea with a democratic civil-military pedigree firmly rooted in the small wars tradition. The default position of French soldiers in the final phase of the Algerian War was predictably that they were betrayed by President Charles de Gaulle and the French people in the years 1958–1962. But as de Gaulle reminded his Algerian praetorians, *l'armée pour l'armée* is not a national strategy, any more than a conspiracy of heroes forms a sound foundation for revolution. That proponents for staying the course in Iraq and Afghanistan have latterly presented COIN as a comprehensive political-military strategy for realizing national objectives speaks to their own enduring angst over defeat in Vietnam in the 1970s, and their search for a mission and a doctrine to unify the US military in the absence of a conventional threat as in the era of total war.

The anthropological update of COIN with Montgomery McFate, David Killcullen, and the spectacle of "anthropologists who have never done fieldwork in the Muslim world, let alone in Iraq, Afghanistan" parachuting into those countries to advise frontline troops on how to connect culturally with the natives amounts, in the eyes of some, to professional malpractice because it has more to do with targeting than underpinning cultural understanding as a prerequisite to the application of hearts and minds techniques. This latest parade of cultural experts into war zones is merely a scholastic update of an older and equally specious small wars deferral to "the man who knows the country" in the Arab Bureau, the Indian Political Service, William Sleeman whose self-proclaimed cultural fluency allowed him first to invent and subsequently crush a Thugee brotherhood, as well as other recreational cultural connoisseurs such as Chinese Gordon, T. E. Lawrence, and Gertrude Bell. It is also a strategic communications technique mobilized by a military whose soldiers tend to be at best suspicious, when not totally contemptuous of the cultures of populations they are tasked to control.

Indeed, the mutual dislike shared by US forces and their Afghan partners that has erupted into so-called Green-on-Blue fratricide in 2012 probably topped that between GIs and the ARVN forty-plus years earlier.[22]

Despite a fulsome rhetoric of hearts and minds and cultural sensitivity, the population constitutes for the counterinsurgent little more than "a terrain obstruction that one pushes aside, like sharp rocks, mangrove roots, or maybe mosquitoes," writes Jenni.[23] Indeed, the small wars habit of viewing the population as a topographical obstacle persists in the aptly named Human Terrain Teams deployed in Iraq and Afghanistan. These modern versions of the Arab Bureau and Indian Political Service collect "cultural and social data" with a view to meddle in local politics and "find, fix and finish the enemy" rather than understand indigenous culture and values, minimize collateral damage, and so win over popular support.[24]

COIN offers a doctrine of escapism for many relevant personalities and institutions – a flight from democratic civilian control, even from modernity, into an anachronistic, romanticized, Orientalist vision that projects quintessentially Western values, and Western prejudices, onto non-Western societies. Strategic goals like exporting freedom and democracy abroad are at best vague, when not totally destabilizing policy prescriptions around which to reorder society at home as well as in the insurgent country. The good news for the COIN-dinistas is that insurgents, too, often nurture their own illusions about the revolutionary potential of a class, religion, or ethnicity. Insurgency is seldom equated with poverty. Indeed, insurgents often fight for resource-rich areas – opium, coca, gold, diamonds, oil – which means that the frontier between insurgency and criminality becomes difficult to delineate. An insurgency's popular base may be composed of people who make a living producing or trafficking illegal goods and substances, which means that neither the insurgency nor its popular base are biddable, likely to be seduced by incentives that add up to good governance but which take away their major sources of income or threaten their lifestyle. Economic development may prove an antidote to insurgency – surging demand for rubber and tin with the Korean War created a wave of trickle-down prosperity in Malaya that helped to diminish the allure of insurgency there, while also funding counterinsurgency operations. However, the success of strategies of occupation anchored in developmental theory that seek to purchase loyalty, bolster legitimacy and good governance with economic or infrastructure improvements remain unproven.

Modernization may unbalance traditional economic and social relationships, while populations often remain blind to the advantages of infrastructure improvements, especially when they are accomplished by
forced labor with a goal of improving the operational mobility of occupation forces. A shortage of funds, the corruption or violence of the
environment which discourages investment, the inability or the unwillingness of the military to implement improvements, or the fact that no
support structure or capacities exist to maintain them – no teacher is
provided for the school, or the electric pump breaks down in a matter of
weeks for lack of spare parts or technicians to repair it – are among the
factors that may make development difficult to integrate into a unitary
COIN strategy. And, in the end, the citizens of states like France before
1962 may be persuaded that counterinsurgency wars are an anachronism, a rocky and expensive path to grandeur that in fact acts as an
impediment to progress. Small wars must end as a precondition for
prosperity and so that a nation may embrace its epoch.[25]

Modern COIN-incentivized development programs that seek
to evangelize liberal capitalism are often unsuited to insurgent-ravaged
areas. Even a card-carrying COIN-dinista like General H. R. McMaster
is forced to concede that the influx of international aid "into [an Afghan]
government that lacked mature institutions" converted a backwater
failed state into a casino of corruption that has further delegitimized
the Karzai regime.[26] The same is also true of Iraq, a relatively advanced
country that lacked the expertise and institutions to invest, track, and
manage large infusions of capital to apply liberal capitalist notions of
development, even had Iraqis understood them. Loose talk of implementing Marshall Plans in underdeveloped regions is founded on ignorance.[27] In the first decade of the twenty-first century, nation-building is
no longer carried out between states that share similar political traditions, values, economic structures, and national aspirations to play a
vital role in the international system, as in the aftermath of World War II
when West Germany, Italy, and Japan hankered to regain their status as
respected Western countries. But "stability and reconstruction" as practiced today no longer seeks to implement the Marshall Plan as in 1947 – a
nation-state to nation-state engagement applied by social democrats and
moderates who believed in the power of government to do good
works. In the present era of the hegemony of the market and globalization, Stability and Reconstruction is outsourced to NGOs and
international corporations like Halliburton, DynCorp, the Rendon

Group, Triple Canopy, and Blackwater/Xe, who, if anything, are not unlike the military entrepreneur/soldiers of fortune of early modern European history in a postmodern form. Rather than strengthen and modernize the state, this quasi-privatized nation-building, such as it is, which is supposed to be central to COIN success, actually bypasses, undermines, and diminishes good government, weakens transparency, and the checks and balances of military and intelligence operations in wartime,[28] when billions of dollars go missing, the arbitrary power of warlords and other criminals is enhanced, and politicians appeal to sectarian divisions, to say nothing of the ill effects on citizenship and military professionalism. "Contractors are one of the most visible and hated aspects of the American presence in Iraq," P. W. Singer concluded in 2007, whose attitude of impunity put them at the center of some of the most notorious scandals that "help undermine the very justification for the U.S. effort in Iraq." Similar complaints were heard about Private Military Companies in Afghanistan accused of fueling discontent, undermining the whole of government approach that allegedly underpins nation-building, and further delegitimizing the government.[29] Meanwhile the actions and attitudes of policemen and soldiers in stability operations and state-building often decrease the legitimacy of the state, which in turn is unable to provide basic services or improve security and economic conditions. In short, the complaint is that the unregulated market free for a world of outsourced state-building deprives COIN of a strategic framework for success, so that it becomes merely a catch-bag of tactics and operational concepts mustered to achieve an incomprehensible and even undesirable strategic objective for most of the population.[30] How, then, does COIN create legitimacy and integrity in such an anarchic environment as Afghanistan?[31]

Given counterinsurgency's checkered past and unproven record of success, how does one account for the persistence of COIN advocates in strategic thought, military operations, and civil-military relations? One reason is that COIN-dinistas have misused history to support their case in bureaucratic and professional infighting and conflicted democratic civil-military relations. In the classical formation of military thought and practice, Clausewitz for one believed that military history, if appropriately applied in the formation of judgment, intellect, and character of soldiers, could supply a valuable tool to sharpen soldierly skills of leadership and command through the applied study of comparative historical examples. He also conceded, however, that history was more likely to be misused by soldiers and others in a prescriptive, deterministic way than applied in a responsible way to inform the analysis and the making of strategy in theory and practice.[32] Eliot Cohen writes of the importance of developing "historical-mindedness" among officers, strategists, and policymakers, who should be "trained to detect differences as much as similarities" between past and present analogies by considering them in their context and political-military complexity. Such a framework, Cohen argues, is particularly valuable in an age of rapid technological and political change, because it avoids an overreliance on facile and simplistic lessons learned or single-point comparisons lifted out of context for the purposes of blinkered doctrine and military-bureaucratic struggles that constitute the norm.[33]

The impediments to such a judicious use of history are many, however, especially in US political culture where the past has become an arsenal for political fights that have nothing to do with the kind of disinterested professional reflection and basis for action as envisioned by Clausewitz two centuries ago. Further, in this connection, there operates what Bacevich calls the "Wilsonians under arms" mentality of the post-Cold War right that argues that the world awaits liberation.[34] In Francis Fukuyama's "end of history" *tabula rasa* world, history has lost the value to inform strategy, because ideology, technology, and doctrine now substitute for strategy.[35] History, and military history in particular, has always had nostalgic, even inspirational, as well as utilitarian value. Neo-conservative historians – Victor David Hanson, Niall Ferguson, Max Boot, and Robert D. Kaplan among them – prepared the way for the triumph of COIN by their hyping of the benefits of imperialism, a belief in military power as "the chief emblem of national greatness," the efficacy of preemptive strategies, and the romanticization of soldiers as superior to civilians.[36] This military romanticism or outright militarism among academics and partisans prepared the stage for advocates of the United States as the successor to the Raj, and its soldiers, marines, and special operators remade in the image of Fightin' Freddy Funston dispatched to right the world's wrongs after September 11, 2001.

Unfortunately, this appealing scenario ignores many of small wars' less attractive characteristics, beginning with Hew Strachan's warning that the counterinsurgent is a highly political soldier who fuses the divide between civil government and military operations with an emphasis on the latter. Politicians who engage in nation-building endeavors with a counterinsurgency dimension must be prepared to deal with a collection of men (and now women, in the years to come) who break the barriers separating the soldier and the politician, who are likely to be as estranged from their parent military institution and culture, and for whom the stab in the back forms the guiding principle of civil-military relations. These soldiers understand that they operate at a political disadvantage because counterinsurgency inevitably requires a strategy of attrition, often at high human and moral costs, which invites civilian intervention into the operational and tactical spheres. Therefore to succeed, they must create and, in turn, inflate a threat, assemble a supporting cast of academic, military, and media boosters to burnish their martial image and promote their strategic prescience, preach the benefits of counterinsurgency to the indigenous population, and mask the true costs of their operations by conducting them out of view and off budget. Above all, they must always hover on the cusp of success – COIN as a "process," "a rising tide of security," "seizing/breaking the momentum," or "this is the decisive year/month/week" currently top the charts of COIN-dinista cant, modern variants of the Vietnam War's "light at the end of the tunnel" sets of optimistic metrics marshaled to deflect or postpone popular impatience. They concoct a wartime story line of official optimism, claim progress and success with spinfests fueled by an annual $4.7 billion annual Pentagon PR budget that allows contracted media mercenaries attached to military staffs to maintain a confident narrative of counterinsurgency momentum, expand in-country goals, coax more men and resources out of skeptical governments, keep civilian policymakers off balance, and torpedo their military rivals with accusations that they "don't get COIN."[37] Such politicized soldiers of small wars will also concoct annihilationist scenarios, D-Day redux flood-the-zone swarms that are passed off in dispatches to home as soon to be superseded decisive turning points against the insurgency – *la prise de la smala d'Abd-el-Kader*, Operation Agatha, the Battle of Algiers, the Challe Offensive, Tet, Motorman, Tora Bora, Falluja, Tal Afar, the surge, Marja, Kandahar – even if the event proved over the long run to be far from decisive or its temporary tactical success, such as it was, had nothing to do with the tactics employed. COIN encourages a deceitful manipulation of civil-military relations, subterfuge, dishonesty, and betrayal, not only of one's citizens, but also of one's own soldiers.[38]

One of the apparent ironies is that the latest failed COIN experiments in Afghanistan and Iraq have actually augmented the status and influence of SOF. In the spirit of Mountbatten's 1944 observation about

Burma that "we're all Chindits now," and standing custom on its head, special operators are being promoted into senior commands to implement an organizational restructuring that will feature security assistance, raids and other SOF-spearheaded operations, with conventional units in support.[39] The elevation of petty war as the US Army's organization concept despite its limitations on the tactical and operational, not to mention strategic level, and the upgrade of USSOCOM's status and influence in the US military has several explanations, in this author's view, beginning with the fact that such a reaction is not unprecedented, especially in the wake of defeat or in moments of national frailty. Witness the fabrication of the T. E. Lawrence popular insurrection legend by Liddell Hart and others in the wake of Britain's Pyrrhic victory in the Great War and its post-Dunkirk resuscitation by Churchill in the SOE.

In such circumstances, SOF offer symbolic machismo, a national Rambo remake in the aftermath of two twenty-first-century wars that failed to go according to script, and the collapse of the 1990s "end of history" euphoria. For politicians, the attraction of SOF's "manly men, standing tall against terrorism," reinforced by drones and now cyberwarfare, opens the option of strategies of disruption, preventative war, and decapitation that aim to boost popular morale at home, allow politicians to posture as slayers of evil terrorists, and provide incremental victories in a long war scenario otherwise deficient in demonstrable evidence of progress or, in the case of the death of Osama Bin Laden, the political cover to begin a drawdown in Afghanistan.[40] However, while the overall usefulness of SOF to the military organizations in general is questionable, their strategic impact may be positively counterproductive. Decapitation strategies via SOF resurrects Marshal de Castellane's 1845 complaint that Bugeaud had personalized his vendetta with Abd-el-Kader. As a consequence, France was not fighting a war in Algeria, but was instead conducting a manhunt. Galula warned – correctly for once – that French decapitation operations against the FLN leadership in that country over a century later were counterproductive, because they narrowed political options, further radicalized the insurgency, and, like Southern Cone military dictators in the 1960s through the 1980s, reduced the complex social, economic, racial, religious, and political underpinnings of dialogue, protest, and resistance to a target list of bad guys whose elimination would restore societal harmony. One saw how well that worked when the US military replicated this contentious strategic approach to the stabilization of Iraq in 2003 with its much publicized deck of playing cards bearing the names of the top Baathist leaders to be killed or captured. One danger is that, like the Auxies, violence practiced as a team sport carries the risk that it will neutralize any individual sense of social and personal responsibility that can impact the success of the mission.[41] In Afghanistan, the counterinsurgency from the beginning has been dominated by drone and SOF-spearheaded "kill/capture missions" characterized, in the words of Thomas Johnson, by "culturally obtuse behavior, unnecessarily invasive and violent tactics, and a series of tragic incidents of 'collateral damage'" that have alienated populations on both sides of the Durand Line and provoked a quasi-war with Pakistan.[42] This is the primary reason why regional combatant commanders and ambassadors view the institutional and political empowerment of SOF cowboys encroaching onto their territory to carry out potentially politically catastrophic operations with trepidation.[43]

Rather than instruments of strategic success, drone and special operations coups offer an indicator of strategic slippage – a failure of diplomacy, a lack of leverage over an ally, a substitute for ineffective conventional or COIN operations, evidence of inviolate enemy safe havens, or of a particularly robust insurgent infrastructure and leadership cadre anchored in a significant popular support base. They often produce political blowback when inopportune strategic consequences from special operations far exceed their ephemeral tactical benefits. Moreover, special operators leverage the heroic image that allows nations to bask in the reflective glow of a flattering manliness which, combined with the secrecy surrounding their operations, discourages accountability and further undermines civilian oversight of a US military increasingly segregated from public life.

This state of affairs carries with it the potential of conceding the military too much influence over policy.[44] Robert Kaplan, yet another "reactionary populist" suffering delusions of Lawrencian romanticism, praises security assistance promoted by a new generation of SOF "imperial grunts" armed with "the martial evangelicalism of the South" who venture into "injun country" to teach COIN skills to indigenous militaries as a force multiplier. Kaplan fails to note that these men, trained by the United States, often have their own political, economic, or sectarian agendas, and may simply oppress their own people or their neighbors.[45] But the reality remains that, in counterinsurgency wars, win or lose, the counterinsurgent ends up feeling betrayed by civilians, as Michael Hastings notes:

The military culture was by nature authoritarian, and it was there they were most comfortable. Even if, as Special Forces operators, they pushed against its rigidness, they still felt more at home among their brothers on the inside than on the outside. In fact, with Special Forces, the element of separateness, the insulated feeling of superiority was even greater. They could do things other men couldn't do, and had done them. Good or bad – if it was the mission, then it was permissible. If it was for us against them, it was inherently right. If it took place in the arena, it was sublime. What wasn't permissible was breaking trust, or what they viewed as trust – straying outside the pack. The decade of war had hardened these feelings, creating an almost insurmountable boundary between them and the rest of society. The media just didn't play up this romantic image of warriors; the men held dearly to the romantic image themselves. They were willing to protect one another, to die for one another. That was the value that they cherished. And if you weren't part of the team, your motives were immediately suspect – impure, like the motives of politicians or diplomats. The base reasons that drove others – money and power – were not what drove them, or so they told themselves. They yearned for a pure relationship – it was a kind of love that could only be found in a world they saw reflected in themselves.[46]

Like Jean Lartéguy's *The Centurions*, small wars soldiers can become a rootless, disaffected, self-glorifying group estranged from a homeland that they regard as decadent and ungrateful, and from a military organization they see as bureaucratic and unresponsive.

All of the issues and questions analyzed in this study underline the requirement for historians as well as those makers of policy concerned with the essence of contemporary conflict to continue to establish the factual record so that mythologized, self-serving versions of the past are not offered as a grand strategic formula for the future. Assertions of COIN success based in shoddy research and flawed and selective analysis of cases are not only an historical error. Such an abuse of the record of the past as the basis for professional and institutional imperatives can lead to people getting killed because they fail to convey that each insurgency is a contingent event in which doctrine, operations, and tactics must support a viable policy and strategy, not the other way around.

My guess is that we are on the downside of the most recent episode of COIN enthusiasm for a variety of reasons, beginning with the fact that the liberal peace justification for intervention is becoming less attractive to Western populations, if for no other reason than that the campaigns in Iraq and Afghanistan have cost far too much in lives, money, and time amid a global financial crisis. Resistance in the second decade of the new century to Western modernity on the model of Fukuyama's discredited triumphalist thesis is becoming more fanaticized and globalized, less "accidental," and consequently more robust. Historically COIN succeeds, at least temporarily, by disrupting and fragmenting communities rather than by knitting them together, which rather defeats the proclaimed state-building purpose of modern intervention. Campaigns of counterinsurgency conducted by outsiders often fail because they create legitimacy gaps that are exploited by insurgents. Some argue that an increase in media and NGO scrutiny makes the coercive COIN practiced in the past more difficult to carry off today.[47] "There is no reason to believe that abuses in Iraq or Afghanistan have been worse or more frequent than they were in Malaya, for instance," opine two observers of British operations in Iraq and Afghanistan. "But the standards are perceived to be higher and, whereas in the days of vacuum tubes and steam ships, what happened in theater would have little immediate impact on the home audience, in the days of silicon chips and airliners, the links are direct and immediate."[48]

It may be true that civil society and democratic political culture manifest a greater counterweight today to the brutality of small wars than in the mid or early twentieth century.[49] But geographical and cultural remoteness, political indifference, and surely racism have muffled protests in the past. Following the example of the British in the Falklands campaign to curtail press reporting on war, successive US administrations have proven very successful in obscuring the true costs of the interventions in Afghanistan and Iraq by repatriating body bags in the dead of night and cloaking financial costs as off-line budget items, to say nothing of the burden of such fighting imposed on the all-volunteer armed forces which make up less than 1 percent of the US population. Besides, at least since Lyautey, savvy COIN-dinista generals have learned to master the media game to keep their political, diplomatic, and military rivals off balance for months by manipulating the truth and managing the counterinsurgency narrative. This has become a requirement for success because small wars were and continue to be prosecuted in the face of fragile public support. However, public opposition has stopped few counterinsurgency operations in the past even when their fanciful going-in assumptions and unacceptable tactical brutality were exposed, with the possible exception of Ireland in 1921. US pressure accentuated by the ham-fisted handling of the *Exodus* episode speeded Britain's exit from Palestine in 1947. However, while Bugeaud was vilified for his *enfumades* and *razzias* in the nineteenth century, public opposition succeeded in provoking only his defiance and that of his acolytes. Protests against the Anglo-Boer War, the German atrocities in German Southwest and East Africa at the turn of the twentieth century, the Indochina, Algerian, and Vietnamese wars, and British policies in Northern Ireland in the late twentieth century did little to alter the course of those conflicts, which were settled on the battlefield. The perpetrators went unpunished and might even be greeted as heroes, like Paul von Lettow-Vorbeck or Jacques Massu. Collateral killing of civilians, herding them into concentration camps, or driving them into exile is simply accepted as the unremarkable price of doing business in COIN. Excesses like Amritsar, My Lai, countless French and FLN massacres in Algeria, Bloody Sunday, Abu Ghraib, or Haditha are explained as the work of a few bad apples, a failure of leadership, or the product of split-second decisions made in the cauldron of a war in which insurgents are indistinguishable from civilians and the next car pulling up at the road block, even if it is filled with women and children, might be a suicide bomber.[50] But as Lalah Khalili notes, war among the people puts the people in the gun sights, because the counterinsurgent assumption is that subversion could not exist without the active support of the population, as French Lieutenant Colonel Patrice de Naurois noted in 1958:[51]

> *All the population without distinction of age or sex, is part of the "popular army," permanently ready for "the armed struggle." The population is not only an objective to conquer, but also a medium through which to continue and to expand the struggle. Everyone, men or women, old or young, participate actively in the struggle in accordance with their competence and their capacity; they will be combatants of death, soldiers of the Regular Army, guerrillas, sympathizers, agents of liaison or information, suppliers, etc. They will always be militants and propagandists.*

"Because the French/Argentine conception of the enemy was so broad, so all-inclusive, torture consequently became widespread," concludes Eric Stener Carlson.[52] Killing of civilians by counterinsurgents, sometimes for sport, torture, and other human rights and laws of war violations become part of the pattern, not the exception, and the soldiers are seldom punished for it. Legal constraints are not an absolute in COIN, but a subject for negotiation in a world where the insurgent is viewed as a coward and an assassin, an "enemy of all mankind," not a soldier who enjoys the protection of the laws of war. The counterinsurgent, on the other hand, is protecting society, and so is performing an honorable function even as he mobilizes dishonorable means. Those who criticize counterinsurgency methods are branded as hypocrites, ingrates, fellow travelers, enemies of Western civilization, and so on – in short, allies of subversion. War crimes become a normal cost of doing small war business with fateful implications for the ethos of the soldiers and the efficacy of military institutions in the long run.[53]

And the sacrifice of small wars is not only paid by populations abroad. War among the people is also prosecuted on the home front with equally fateful implications for state, citizenship, and society. Hannah Arendt noted, in her *Origins of Totalitarianism* as early as 1951 that the violence and racism of imperial conquest had a boomerang effect on the homeland. If Arendt's assertion has become a subject of debate, it is in part because she failed to develop her contention that the genealogy of the Holocaust lay in the sense of moral and racial superiority of German imperialists, the militarization of policy abroad, the politicization of colonial soldiers, and the belief that the rule of law in no way impeded imperial population transfers, massacres, and genocides. Critics argue that violence in Western societies had multiple roots, not simply colonial ones, a view with which Arendt herself surely agreed in her analysis of modern politics and society. Although Germany's Herero genocide in 1904–1907 proved to be the nadir of imperial malevolence and seemed to Arendt a warm-up for the Holocaust, no single nation monopolized colonial violence. The three quintessential imperial powers featured in this book – France, Britain, and the United States – avoided totalitarian tendencies, while Germany, Italy, and the Soviet Union, whose encounters with colonialism were less central to their national narrative, generated totalitarian regimes.[54]

However, none of this invalidates Arendt's contention that imperialism was hardly consequence free for imperial nations. Imperial armies became politicized when, as Hew Strachan has demonstrated even for the "apolitical" British Army, national needs became conflated with those of the imperial army. To begin with, the colonies witnessed political-military fusion as the barriers that separated political, bureaucratic, and military roles progressively tumbled. Imperial service was sought by the most ambitious British soldiers, so that the colonies became places where they perfected the art of political intrigue and media manipulation in defense of empire, skills repatriated to Britain and deployed in the political arena.[55] The same pattern can be detected in the French colonial army whose leaders orchestrated journalistic and political boosterism to expand and shield the French colonial enterprise. When that army concluded in 1958 that the Fourth Republic was prepared to sell out in Algeria, they overthrew it and continued to act out until closed down by Charles de Gaulle. The US defeat in Vietnam with its accompanying traumas of civilian protests witnessed a retreat into the All Volunteer, TRADOC-generated, Army of Excellence operational warfare doctrines, behind a Weinberger–Powell Doctrine Maginot Line in an attempt to deflect civilian interference, a factor that in their view had precipitated defeat in Vietnam. Initial miscalculations in Iraq and Afghanistan created the opening for "new school generals" like David Petraeus and Stanley McChrystal with a timely assist by John Nagl's 2005 *Learning to Eat Soup with a Knife* fantasy historical account of British COIN mastery to reassert a COIN narrative in hibernation since Vietnam. The goal was to discredit conventional warfare rivals, snag the top echelons of the US Army, and proceed to hijack the policy.[56]

Nor should one dismiss Arendt's suggestion that small wars with their concomitant curtailment of human rights abroad contribute to the erosion of civil liberties and human rights at home. The United Kingdom witnessed a severe curtailment of civil rights during both bouts of the Troubles. Excessive, public, and largely ineffective British measures against Zionist terrorism in Britain in the late 1940s only served to inflame anti-Semitism.[57] The post-1970 introduction of measures like internment and Diplock courts, saturating Catholic neighborhoods with troops who set up roadblocks and carried out unannounced, usually violent, house searches, and beating confessions out of IRA suspects in RUC police stations in Northern Ireland, not to mention the 1972 Blood Sunday massacre of unarmed civil rights protesters, were lifted straight out of the emergencies in Malaya, Kenya, and the Aden Crater, from which many British troops had just returned.[58] And at the time of writing, the current British government appears poised, years after the 2001 terrorist attack on New York and the 2005 bombings in London, to pass laws that, in the hallowed traditions of the British Empire and in the name of counter-terrorism, lift legal restraints to allow domestic intelligence agencies greater latitude to carry out domestic surveillance on British citizens.[59]

In Algeria, considered an integral part of metropolitan France, civil powers were surrendered to the army in 1956 under a Special Powers Act. Because the Algerian insurrection was classified as a criminal conspiracy, POWs had no right to humane treatment. Many captured FLN were initially guillotined or simply disappeared, while the civilian population was subject to reprisals, relocation, collective punishment to include wholesale massacres of villages, and other refinements of martial law. Nor did it take long for colonial violence anchored in the freebooter mentality developed in the French colonial military to reach the French mainland. What was called the "Algerianization" of the French state began when Maurice Papon, later convicted for having deported Jews to Germany during World War II, was brought back from Constantine, Algeria, in 1958 to serve as Paris Prefect of Police. Under Papon, colonial police techniques like arbitrary arrest, curfews for Muslim workers in France, the creation of massive detention centers, systematic violence, assassinations, torture, and general brutality that weakened the rule of law steadily escalated into the so-called Paris "police riots" of October 17, 1961 in which scores of Algerian migrant workers were killed. Police violence was not only limited to Muslim workers in France, but was also aimed at the growing opposition to de Gaulle's government from unions, the media, and the anti-war movement – for instance, nine people protesting right-wing OAS violence died at the hands of Papon's police in February 1962. De Gaulle was clearly more concerned about reeling in out-of-control COIN-dinistas in Algeria than protecting the rights of French citizens. Papon was only forced to resign in 1965 following the disappearance in Paris of Moroccan opposition leader Mehdi Ben Barka, almost certainly the result of a collaboration between French and Moroccan police and secret services.[60] This revenge of the periphery is noted by Jenni: "The colonial rot infects us, gnaws at us, comes to the surface . . . like a sewer stench." He watches the French police in his native Lyons in 2011 tumble out of armored vehicles in paratroop uniforms, shock battalion armaments, helmets, shields, and loudspeakers and proceed to "verify the identity" of the population according to an obvious color code, as if participating in a *Battle of Algiers* reenactment. "They do damage and leave ... The art of war hasn't changed."[61]

Nor has the United States escaped the domestic consequences of the GWOT which recall the British and French cases above. In the tradition of Simson and Gwynn, democratic dissent is first colonialized and then criminalized. Intelligence techniques worked out by the US Army in the Philippines at the turn of the twentieth century were turned against the US labor movement in the 1920s, against Italian and Japanese Americans in the 1940s, and against Hollywood filmmakers in the 1950s.[62] Similar applications of military technology developed during the Cold War were applied to urban populations, especially in the "ghetto unrest" that erupted in the wake of the Vietnam War.[63] Even the author's own institution, the Naval Postgraduate School, claims that there is a "significant overlap with how you deal with insurgencies and how you deal with cities that are under siege from gangs," and launched an initiative to apply counterinsurgency techniques evolved for Iraq and Afghanistan to the mean streets of near-by Salinas, California.[64] Nor are coercive COIN techniques restricted to anti-gang operations. Indefinite detention at Guantanamo and the assertion by the Obama administration that it retains the right to target US citizens for assassination "without a shred of due process" in the name of the GWOT worries civil libertarians, as have long prison sentences handed out to Muslims as a deterrent to those who even flirt with the rhetoric of jihad.[65] The 2012 National Defense Authorization Act has enshrined provisions that have been evolving under the previous administration of George W. Bush that undermine civil liberties – most notably, it authorizes indefinite detention of terrorist suspects; it outsources prosecution of terrorist suspects to military tribunals, stripping federal courts of most terrorist cases; finally, it bans detainees at Guantanamo from being transferred to jails on the US mainland or to friendly or allied nations who might take them.[66]

GWOT violence abroad also threatens to return to the homeland with what the *New York Times* has called "the militarization of the American police," which has featured the adoption of military-style tactics and equipment, and a more confrontational mindset among police officers that has become manifest in the civil strife in the wake of the financial crisis of 2007.[67] Is the United States in the shadow of the GWOT, are the security forces and branches of government, generally, evolving into a sort of paramilitary Royal Irish/Ulster Constabulary or

Palestinian Police Force where the focus is on prevention and punishment? The requirement for even small town police to add military armaments to their arsenals that include riot gear, heavy-duty weapons, armored vehicles with portals for automatic guns, and even tanks suggests that habituating the population to respect the law in the fashion of the Raj or the RIC has become valued above the liberty of the citizen and the sanctity of property.[68] Drones of the sort used in war zones in Iraq and Afghanistan have already been authorized for domestic use in the United States, which civil libertarians take as an indication of an expansion of the surveillance state. Some law enforcement specialists are even advocating that domestic drones be armed not only with surveillance cameras, but also with "nonlethal weapons such as Tasers or a bean-bag gun," or even lethal weapons. As happened in the mid twentieth century in the United States, wartime induces an authoritarian mindset in some politicians who emphasize the domestic nature of the terrorist threat, which is bolstered by defense contractors eager to open new markets for their drone technology.[69]

Perhaps the most convincing refutation of the COIN-dinista claims, however, comes from within the military where some officers argue that COIN doctrines are anchored in mythologized history and selective memory, fail to work at an acceptable price, and erode the core skills of conventional warriors.[70] Even in Petraeus' Afghanistan, population-centric strategies gave way to what two authors termed urban-centric strategies. In essence, the argument is that even Petraeus realized that Afghanistan was a nut too hard for COIN to crack – too big, too backward, too fanaticized, with insurgent safe havens on the borders. Therefore, the coalition in Afghanistan has basically focused on controlling the main towns and ring road that circles the country. There are at least two problems with this urban-centric approach, beginning with the fact that the insurgency is concentrated in the countryside where almost 80 percent of the population live, not in the cities. When US forces or allied forces do venture into the countryside, they build their bases outside the villages, sometimes in disadvantageous positions, far from air support, so that the village may become a staging area for attacks that can become quite costly. A second problem is that this strategy was tried before by the Soviets in the 1980s and led only to defeat.[71]

One result is that neo-containment of terrorist groups and the political entities that host them, not COIN, has become the preferred approach to places where intervention is required. This reverses a trend set in World War II and Vietnam that marries popular consolidation with SOF. Now COIN appears to have been jettisoned as slow and ineffective, leaving SOF as a stand alone. It appears that we are back to Palestine in the late 1930s, when Lord Trenchard's bombers combined with Orde Wingate's Special Night Squads as a formula to subdue the Arab Revolt. A combination of coalition air campaigns like the one that destabilized Moammar Gaddafi's regime in Libya, predator drones whose effects are clean, proportionate, and morally defensible according to some, and SOF is less costly and casualty-heavy than are extended occupations and avoids traumatic draw downs.[72] The inevitable collateral damage produces tremendous levels of local resentment, but there is little indigenous peoples can do about bombs directed at them from unseen predators commanded from control stations in California. SOF and drones also offer more psychological appeal, because they restore heroism, legitimacy, righteousness, manliness, and a sense of technological finality to the battlefield, attributes that avoid the expensive quagmire of Bacevich's armed social work. Therefore, COIN as symbolized by *FM 3–24* and the ephemeral tactical triumphs of the Petraeus guys in Anbar join a succession of failed organizational concepts that include the Army of Excellence, the AirLand Battle, through the RMA, and now to SOF-led petty war with conventional units in support – we're all Chindits now! Not only does the special operations tail wag the conventional army dog in this model, it runs the risk of failing catastrophically in the face of a serious challenge, much as the French army collapsed in 1870. The idea that the latest reinvention of Giulio Douhet flying machines and Orde Wingate supermen, as seen in the commando operation that killed Osama bin Laden in the spring of 2011, can repair the imperfections of the international system, accomplish national goals with minimal effort, avoid the Vietnam syndrome, and restore decision to war is attractive to populations and policymakers, not the least because it offers the prospect of war on the cheap.[73] This combination is pursued despite the fact that the US military's May 2012 *Decade of War* after action report on operations in Iraq and Afghanistan complained that "general purpose forces as the battlespace owners were left managing the second-order effects of SOF targeting operations," which caused a "significant disruption of their battlespace in the aftermath of those operations."[74] Whatever their tactical benefits or moral justifications, SOF and drone attacks have served to spread anti-America sentiment and roiled the strategic relationship with Pakistan, and now it seems with Yemen as well.[75] This sort of vicarious, video game, decapitation derby manhunt promises to avoid COIN's indecisiveness. In the end, however, it is just a makeover of Liddell Hart's victory without battles that is no more likely to provide a formula for security than have deceptive measures of progress that accompany and sustain the illusory promise of COIN success.

NOTES

Preface

1 Thomas E. Ricks, *The Gamble: General David Petraeus and the American Military Adventure in Iraq, 2006–2008* (New York: Penguin, 2009).
2 Douglas Porch, "The Dangerous Myths and Dubious Promise of COIN," *Small Wars & Insurgencies*, 22:2 (May 2011), 239–57.

1 The small wars prologue

1 As will be argued, Germany after 1871 was something of an outlier because of its stunted colonial experience before 1914, the ad hoc character of its expeditionary forces, and the fact that Bismarck shielded the German army constitutionally, budgetarily, and socially from democratic influences.
2 David A. Petraeus and James F. Amos, *FM 3–24: U.S. Army/Marine Corps Counterinsurgency Field Manual* (Washington, DC: Headquarters Department of the Army, December 2006), 7–11.
3 John Grenier, *The First Way of War: American War Making on the Frontier* (Cambridge University Press, 2005), 221–25.
4 Edward Luttwak, "Dead End: Counterinsurgency Warfare as Military Malpractice," *Harpers* (February 2007), www.harpers.org/archive/2007/02/0081384.
5 "Karzai Sharply Criticizes U.S. over Shooting Inquiry," *New York Times*, March 16, 2012, www.nytimes.com/2012/03/17/world/asia/karzai-lashes-out-at-united-states-over-inquiry-on-massacre.html?hp; "Afghanistan. The Horror," *The Economist*, March 12, 2012, www.economist.com/blogs/newsbook/2012/03/afghanistan.

6　C. E. Callwell, *Small Wars: Their Principle and Practice* (Omaha: University of Nebraska Press, 1996), 21.

7　Michael Few, "Interview with Dr. John Arquilla: How Can French Encounters with Irregular Warfare in the 19th Century Inform COIN in our Time?" *Small Wars Journal* (November 30, 2010), http://smallwarsjournal.com/blog/journal/docs-temp/608-arquilla.pdf.

8　Callwell, *Small Wars*, 41, 147.

9　Callwell, *Small Wars*, 147.

10　The name was taken from the *nom de guerre* of one of the insurrection's leaders, Jean Cottereau. Jacques Godechot argues that the Vendée revolt and the *Chouans* were separate phenomena; the former a genuine popular movement organized in large military formations, and the latter a pro-royalist insurgency. He also argues that the *Chouans* both preceded the Vendée revolt and outlasted it. However, he admits that the *Chouans* participated in the Vendée revolt and also recruited survivors after its December 1793 defeat. Godechot, *The Counter-Revolution: Doctrine and Action 1789–1804* (London: Routledge & Kegan Paul, 1972), 224–27.

11　Quoted in Godechot, *The Counter-Revolution*, 225.

12　Reynald Secher, *A French Genocide: The Vendée* (South Bend, IN: University of Notre Dame Press, 2003). The original French text appeared in 1986.

13　Godechot, *The Counter-Revolution*, 229; on the landings of 1795, 256–60; on 1799, 353–55; on degeneration of *Chouans* into common bandits, 366–67.

14　Timothy H. Parsons, *The Rule of Empires: Those Who Built Them, Those Who Endured Them, and Why They Always Fall* (Oxford University Press, 2010), 251.

15　John Arquilla, in Few, "Interview with Dr. John Arquilla"; see also Arquilla, *Insurgents, Raiders, and Bandits: How Masters of Irregular Warfare Have Shaped Our World* (Chicago: Ivan R. Dee, 2011), 44.

16　Quite apart from psychological operations designed to alter value systems and behavior, and convince a target audience that their interests and those of the counterinsurgent/occupier coincide, contemporary IO also incorporates intelligence collection, disinformation and deception techniques, and counter-intelligence that aim to distort the enemy's decision-making process (www.au.af.mil/info-ops/what.htm).

17　John Lawrence Tone, *The Fatal Knot: The Guerrilla War in Navarre and the Defeat of Napoleon in Spain* (Chapel Hill: University of North Carolina Press, 1994), 170.

18　Louis-Gabriel Suchet, *Suchet: War in Spain, The War Times Journal On-line*, www.wtj.com/archives/suchet/suchet10b.htm; Don W. Alexander, *Rod of Iron:*

French Counterinsurgency Policy in Aragon during the Peninsular War (Wilmington, DE: Scholarly Resources, 1985), 102.

19 Alexander, *Rod of Iron*, 49–61, 229–41.

20 Parsons, *The Rule of Empires*, 260.

21 Christopher Hibbert, *Wellington: A Personal History* (Reading, MA: Addison-Wesley, 1997), 44.

22 Hibbert, *Wellington*, 44, 46.

23 Hibbert, *Wellington*, 96–97, 139–40.

24 Richard Holmes, *Wellington: The Iron Duke* (London: HarperCollins, 2003), 81.

25 Callwell, *Small Wars*, 78.

26 Callwell, *Small Wars*, 57.

27 Alexis Jenni, *l'Art française de la guerre* (Paris: Gallimard, 2011), 12.

28 Ironically, John Arquilla celebrates Bugeaud's defeated adversary, Abd-el-Kader, and not Bugeaud, as one of the "masters of irregular warfare" who "shaped our world." *Insurgents, Raiders, and Bandits*, Chapter 6.

29 Charles-André Julien, *Histoire de l'Algérie contemporaine*, Vol. I: *La conquête et les débuts de la colonisation (1827–1871)* (Paris: PUF, 1964), 166.

30 Hannah Arendt, *The Origins of Totalitarianism* (New York: Harcourt, Brace, Jovanovich, 1973), 155.

31 "French Conquerors and Colonists," *Blackwood's Edinburgh Magazine*, Vol. 65, January 1849, 21, http://books.google.com/books?id=6fpFAAAAcAAJ&pg=PA21&lpg=PA21&dq=bugeaud+in+Algeria+man+hunt&source=bl&ots=pVoRqPfDaB&sig=ocwBRGzp13yjWekPdqiFJ4rZX20&hl=en#v=onepage&q=bugeaud%20in%20Algeria%20man%20hunt&f=false.

32 Julien, *Histoire*, 231–58.

33 Grenier, *The First Way of War*, 5, 12.

34 Arquilla, in Few, "Interview with Dr. John Arquilla." Arquilla defines "swarming" as "a deliberately structured, coordinated, strategic way to strike from all directions, by means of a sustainable pulsing of force and/or fire ... designed mainly around the deployment of myriad, small, dispersed, networked maneuver units (what we call 'pods' organized in 'clusters')." John Arquilla and David Ronfeldt, *Swarming and the Future of Conflict* (Santa Monica, CA: Rand Corporation, 2000), vii; "Swarming" has spawned a minor think tank industry – see, for instance, Sean J. A. Edwards, *Swarming and the Future of Warfare* (Santa Monica, CA: Rand Corporation, 2005).

35 Thomas Rid, "Razzia: A Turning Point in Modern Strategy," *Terrorism and Political Violence*, 21:4 (September 2009), 618.

36 Louis Charles Pierre de Castellane, *Souvenirs de la vie militaire en Afrique* (Paris: Victor Lecou, 1852), 229.

37 Rid, "Razzia," 618.

38 Julien, *Histoire*, 320.

39 Paul Thureau-Dangin, *Histoire de la monarchie de juillet,* Vol. VI (Paris: Plon, 1892), 347. The French army counted around 375,000 men in 1833. Figures in Douglas Porch, *Army and Revolution: France 1815–1848* (London: Routlege & Kegan Paul, 1974), 85.

40 Paul Thureau-Dangin, *Histoire de la monarchie de juillet,* Vol. V (Paris: Plon, 1890), 274–75; Vol. VI, 342. "French Conquerors and Colonists," 21.

41 Henry D'Ideville, *Le Maréchal Bugeaud d'après sa correspondance intime* (Paris: Firmin-Didotet, 1882), Vol. III, 155.

42 Thureau-Dangin, *Histoire de la monarchie de juillet* ,Vol. V, 346–55.

43 Callwell, *Small Wars*, 83.

44 "French Conquerors and Colonists," 21.

45 Thureau-Dangin, *Histoire de la monarchie de juillet,*Vol. VI, 345.

46 Julien, *Histoire*, 194–209.

47 Hannah Arendt, "Reflections on Violence," *New York Review of Books,* February 27, 1969, 12.

48 Isabel V. Hull, *Absolute Destruction: Military Culture and the Practices of War in Imperial Germany* (Ithaca and London: Cornell University Press, 2005), 134–35, 155–56, 324–25.

49 *FM 3–24* describes insurgents as "elusive, unethical and indiscriminate foes" operating in an "environment . . . characterized by violence, immorality, distrust and deceit," 7–10, 7–11.

50 Thom Shanker and Graham Bowley, "Images of G.I.s and Remains Fuel Fears of Ebbing Discipline," *New York Times,* April 18, 2012, www.nytimes.com/2012/04/19/world/asia/us-condemns-photo-of-soldiers-posing-with-body-parts.html?_r=1&hp.

51 Geoffrey Wheatcroft, "Send Forth the Best Ye Breed," *New Statesman,* July 5, 1999, www.newstatesman.com/199907050017.htm.

52 Rid, "Razzia," 629–30.

53 Julien, *Histoire*, 315.

54 Anthony Thrall Sullivan, *Thomas-Robert Bugeaud, France and Algeria 1784–1849: Politics, Power, and the Good Society* (Hamden, CT: 1983), 127–31.

55 Hull, *Absolute Destruction*, 332.

56 Thureau-Dangin, *Histoire de la monarchie de juillet,* Vol. VI, 343–44; Julien, *Histoire*, 106–107, 315–21.

57 Jules Harmand, *Domination et colonisation* (Paris: Flammarion, 1910), 317.

58 Julien, *Histoire*, 99–100.

59 Hew Strachan, *The Politics of the British Army* (Oxford: Clarendon Press, 1997), 80, 101.

60 Sullivan, *Bugeaud*, 130.

61 Quoted in Strachan, *The Politics of the British Army*, 97–98.

62 Melvin Richter, "Tocqueville on Algeria," *Review of Politics*, July 25, 1963, 377; Thureau-Dangin, *Histoire de la monarchie de juillet*, Vol. VI, 413–14.

63 Julien, *Histoire*, 322–23.

64 Julien, *Histoire*, 223.

65 Patrick Porter, *Military Orientalism: Eastern War through Western Eyes* (New York: Columbia University Press, 2011), 6.

66 Jacques Frémeaux, *Les bureaux arabes dans l'Algérie de la conquête* (Paris: Editions Denoël, 1993), 29–31. The *bureaux arabes* were abolished in 1870 when Algeria ceased to be under War Ministry jurisdiction and reverted to civilian administration, although French officers continued to administer the tribal territories in the south. The *bureaux* resurfaced when Tunisia was invaded by France in 1881 and subsequently in Morocco after the turn of the twentieth century as the *Service des Renseignements* (Intelligence Service, SR) transformed into the *Affaires indigènes* (Native Affairs) in the interwar years, and the *Sections Administratives Spécialisées* (SAS) during the Algerian War of 1954–1962. Kenneth J. Perkins, *Qaids, Captains and Colons: French Military Administration in the Colonial Maghrib 1844–1934* (New York and London: Africana, 1981), 21–26, 56–65; Moshe Gershovich, *French Military Rule in Morocco: Colonialism and Its Consequences* (London: Frank Cass, 2000), 85–88.

67 "U.S. Military, Oblivious of Iraqi Culture, Enlists Anthropologists for Occupation," *Middle East Online*, January 19, 2008, www.alternet.org/waroniraq/74326/. See also Ben Connable, "All Our Eggs in a Broken Basket: How the Human Terrain System Is Undermining Sustainable Military Cultural Competence," *Military Review*, March–April, 2009; Elizabeth Bumiller, "For Female Marines, Tea Comes with Bullets," *New York Times*, October 2, 2010, www.nytimes.com/2010/10/03/world/asia/03marines.html?pagewanted=all.

68 Catarina Kinnvall, *Globalization and Religious Nationalism in India: The Search for Ontological Security* (Abingdon, UK: Routledge, 2006), 58.

69 Marc Howard Ross, *Cultural Contestation in Ethnic Conflict* (Cambridge University Press, 2007), 49. Patrick James Christian, *A Combat Advisor's Guide to Tribal Engagement: History, Law and War as Operational Elements* (Boca Raton, FL: Universal Publishers, 2011), 29, 81.

70 Julien, *Histoire*, 165–66.

71 Grenier, *The First Way of War*, 13.

72 Porter, *Military Orientalism*, 33.

73 Rid, "Razzia," 627–28.

74 Strachan, *The Politics of the British Army*, 80–81; Christian Tripodi, *Edge of Empire: The British Political Officer and Tribal Administration on the North-West Frontier 1877–1947* (Farnham, Surrey and Burlington, VT: Ashgate, 2011), 21–27.

75 Terence Creagh Coen, *The Indian Political Service: A Study in Indirect Rule* (London: Chatto & Windus, 1971), 5, 10, 35, 37.

76 C. A. Bayly, "Knowing the Country: Empire and Information in India," *Modern Asian Studies*, 27:1 (February 1993), 4.

77 Christian Tripodi, "Peacemaking through Bribes or Cultural Empathy? The Political Officer and Britain's Strategy toward the North-West Frontier, 1901–1945," *The Journal of Strategic Studies*, 31:1 (2008), 128.

78 Simon Anglim, *Orde Wingate and the British Army 1922–1944* (London: Pickering & Chatto, 2010), 20–21, 27.

79 Anna Simons, "Anthropology, Culture, and COIN in a Hybrid Warfare World," in Paul Brister, William Natter, and Robert Tomes (eds.), *Hybrid Warfare and Transnational Threats: Perspectives for an Era of Persistent Conflict* (New York: CENSA, 2011), 83–91.

80 Tripodi, "Peacemaking through Bribes or Cultural Empathy?" 139; Anglim, *Orde Wingate*, 215.

81 Julien, *Histoire*, 336–37.

82 Frémeaux, *Les bureaux arabes*, 57–61.

83 Coen, *The Indian Political Service*, 203.

84 T. E. Lawrence, *Seven Pillars of Wisdom: A Triumph* (New York: Doubleday, Doran & Company, 1935), 38. Quoted in Porter, *Military Orientalism*, 59; an ill-informed, cliché-ridden view of the natives betrayed an ignorance that meant that insurrections like the Indian Mutiny of 1857 often caught Europeans totally by surprise. Bayly, "Knowing the Country," 37.

85 Elizabeth Burgoyne, *Gertrude Bell from Her Personal Papers* (London: Ernest Benn, 1958), Vol. II, 172.

86 Strachan, *The Politics of the British Army*, 81.

87 Frémeaux, *Les bureaux arabes*, 98–99.

88 Julien, *Histoire*, 337–41; Richard Bernstein, *The East, the West, and Sex: A History of Erotic Encounters* (Westminster, MD: Knopf, 2009), 140–41; Frémeaux, *Les bureaux arabes*, 99, although he does point out that many of these accusations were motivated by civilian resentment of military control of Algeria until 1870, 65.

89 Strachan, *The Politics of the British Army*, 79–80.

90 Parsons, *The Rule of Empires*, 221–22.

91 Tripodi, *Edge of Empire*, 225–28.

92 Coen, *The Indian Political Service*, 17, 56.

93 Bernstein, *The East, the West, and Sex*, 128, 133.

94 Julien, *Histoire*, 336–37.

95 Christian, *A Combat Advisor's Guide to Tribal Engagement*, 52.

96 Christian, *A Combat Advisor's Guide to Tribal Engagement*, 115.

97 Frémeaux, *Les bureaux arabes*, 270.

98 Bayly, "Knowing the Country," 35–39.

99 Denis Judd, *Empire: The British Imperial Experience from 1765 to the Present* (New York: Basic Books, 1996), 229.

100 Porter, *Military Orientalism*, 39.

101 Callwell, *Small Wars*, 50.

102 Porter, *Military Orientalism*, 6. Porter does not actually mention Sleeman, but discusses other manifestations of what he calls "the anthropological approach to war."

103 Kim A. Wagner, "The Deconstructed Stranglers: A Reassessment of Thuggee," *Modern Asian Studies*, 38:4 (2004), 933; also, Tom Lloyd, "Thuggee, Marginality and the State Effect in Colonial India, circa 1770–1840," *The Indian Economic and Social History Review*, 42:2 (2008), 201–37.

104 Porter, *Military Orientalism*, 39.

105 Mike Dash, *Thug: The True Story of India's Murderous Cult* (London: Granta, 2005), argues that Sleeman pioneered modern intelligence methods by ferreting out a cult of ritual stranglers. Others cite Sleeman's campaign as evidence of imperial suspicion of native secrecy and treachery, fear of "not knowing," and total misinterpretation of data, among them Martine van Woerkens, *The Strangled Traveler: Colonial Imaginings and the Thugs of India* (University of Chicago Press, 2002) and Patrick A. Kelley, *Imperial Secrets: Remapping the Mind of Empire* (Washington, DC: National Defense Intelligence College, 2008), 27–38.

106 Porter, *Military Orientalism*, 41–42.

107 "The chosen traumas embedded in the host tribe's historical narrative contain the seeds for much of the conflict to be reduced or mitigated by the engagement mission," writes US Army Colonel Patrick Christian. "[O]ne tribe's glory is another tribe's humiliation …. Insurgency and rebellion are normal outcomes of breakages in generational memory" caused by rapid social-structural changes. Christian, *A Combat Advisor's Guide to Tribal Engagement*, 7, 17, 29–30.

108 Porter, *Military Orientalism*, 15.

109 David H. Price, *Weaponizing Anthropology* (Oakland, CA: AK Press, 2011), 182–83.

110 Simons, "Anthropology, Culture, and COIN in a Hybrid Warfare World."

111 T. O. Ranger, "African Reactions in East and Central Africa," in L. H. Gann and Peter Duignan (eds.), *Colonialism in Africa 1870–1960*, Vol. I: *The History and Politics of Colonialism 1870–1914* (Cambridge University Press, 1969), 304–305.

112 Porter, *Military Orientalism*, 15–16.

113 Parsons, *The Rule of Empires*, 239–40.

114 Bayly, "Knowing the Country," 38–39.

115 Parsons, *The Rule of Empires*, 199–204, 219–24.

116 Geoffrey Wheatcroft, "The NS Essay – Send Forth the Best Ye Breed," *New Statesman*, July 5, 1999, www.newstatesman.com/199907050017.htm.

Wheatcroft argues that even though the European left increasingly saw imperialism as a capitalist racket and objected to the mistreatment of peoples of color, no one believed that any society outside of Europe had created a civilization that could rival that of Europe.

117 Julien, *Histoire*, 322–23.

2 The road from Sedan

1 Hannah Arendt, *Imperialism* (New York: Harcourt, Brace & World, 1968), 4–5.
2 www.nytimes.com/1863/03/14/news/the-mexican-war-and-the-jecker-bonds. html; the same was the case for Tunisia in 1881. A. S. Kanya-Forstner, *The Conquest of the Western Sudan: A Study in French Military Imperialism* (Cambridge University Press, 1968), 107.
3 Between 1815 and 1875, France had relied on an annual conscription lottery to fill army ranks. Those who drew a "bad number" and who could not afford to pay a replacement to serve in their stead were condemned to serve for five to seven years, depending on the combat arm. This requirement essentially meant that France had a professional army in this period, as at the end of their legal period of service many soldiers re-enlisted to qualify for pension benefits or sold themselves as replacements. Therefore, while France did create specialized units for colonial warfare, the conquest of Algeria and the Mexican campaign were fought in the main by regiments of long-service French conscripts. Therefore, because the pre-1870 French army had been a regimentally organized, professionalized force predominately experienced in fighting small wars, the pre-Sedan differences between colonial and continental war had been narrowed.
4 Douglas Porch, *The March to the Marne: The French Army 1871–1914* (Cambridge University Press, 1981), 16, Chapter 2.
5 Isabel Hull, *Absolute Destruction: Military Culture and the Practices of War in Imperial Germany* (Ithaca, NY and London: Cornell University Press, 2005), 132.
6 Hew Strachan, *The Politics of the British Army* (Oxford: Clarendon Press, 1997), 97.
7 Kanya-Forstner, *The Conquest of the Western Sudan*, 205.
8 Kanya-Forstner, *The Conquest of the Western Sudan*, 263.
9 Paul Thureau-Dangin, *Histoire de la monarchie de juillet* (Paris: Plon, 1890), Vol. v, 361.
10 Richard Holmes, *The Road to Sedan: The French Army 1866–1870* (London: Royal Historical Society, 1984), 31–32, 53–54, 208–33.
11 Hubert Lyautey, "Le rôle social de l'armée," *Revue des deux mondes* (March 15, 1891).
12 Porch, *The March to the Marne*, 152–53.

13 Strachan, *The Politics of the British Army*, 79.

14 Hull, *Absolute Destruction*, 133.

15 Arendt, *Imperialism*, 69–71.

16 Gwyn Harries-Jenkins, *The Army and Victorian Society* (London: Routledge & Kegan Paul, 1977), 143, 147.

17 W. S. Hamer, *The British Army: Civil-Military Relations 1885–1905* (Oxford University Press, 1970), 82, 90; Edward M. Spiers, *The Army and Society, 1815–1914* (London: Longman, 1980), 209–10.

18 Edward Paice, *Tip and Run: The Untold Tragedy of the Great War in Africa* (London: Phoenix, 2008), 51.

19 Arendt, *Imperialism*, 16.

20 Strachan, *The Politics of the British Army*, 80–81.

21 Carl von Decker, *Algerien und die dortige Kriegsführung* (Berlin: Friedrich August Herbig, 1844), 162. Quoted in Thomas Rid, "The Nineteenth Century Origins of Counterinsurgency Doctrine," *Journal of Strategic Studies*, 33:5 (October 2010), 727–58.

22 C. E. Callwell, *Small Wars: Their Principle and Practice* (Omaha: University of Nebraska Press, 1996), 23, 256–85.

23 Callwell, *Small Wars*, xiv.

24 The commonly accepted reason for Lyautey's sudden assignment to Tonkin was that it was punishment for his article, "Le role social de l'officier," which castigated the metropolitan officer corps for indifference to conscripts, rather than fulfilling the army's mission as the "school of the nation." But as the "punishment" fell fully four years after the offense, a more likely explanation was that Lyautey's homosexuality had become an embarrassment.

25 For the Tonkin campaign, see Douglas Porch, *The French Foreign Legion: A Complete History of the Legendary Fighting Force* (New York: HarperCollins, 1991), 235–44; also Le Commandant Emmanuel P. G. Chabrol, *Opérations militaires au Tonkin* (Paris: Charles-Lavauzelle, 1896), 251.

26 Chabrol, *Opérations militaires au Tonkin*, 250.

27 Marc Michel, *Gallieni* (Paris: Fayard, 1989), 143–72.

28 Kanya-Forstner, *The Conquest of the Western Sudan*, 207.

29 Henri Brunschwig, *Mythes et réalités de l'impérialisme colonial français, 1871–1914* (Paris: Colin, 1960), 73–81.

30 For Lyautey, see Douglas Porch, *The Conquest of Morocco* (New York: Farrar, Straus, Giroux, 2005); William A. Hoisington, Jr., *Lyautey and the French Conquest of Morocco* (New York: Palgrave, 1995).

31 John Arquilla, in Michael Few, "Interview with Dr. John Arquilla: How Can French Encounters with Irregular Warfare in the 19th Century Inform COIN in our Time?" *Small Wars Journal* (November 30, 2010), http://smallwarsjournal.com/blog/journal/docs-temp/608-arquilla.pdf.

32 David G. Marr, *Vietnamese Anti-Colonialism, 1885–1925* (Berkeley, Los Angeles, and London: University of California, 1971), 72–75. Gallieni's networks in upper Tonkin were easily furled by an October 1950 Viet Minh offensive that cost the French 6,000 troops, a prelude to the loss of the ultimate "node" at Dien Bien Phu four years later. This defeat was a direct, if delayed, consequence of Gallieni's decision to arm minority groups of *montagnards* while facilitating their entry into the opium trade as a stabilization tactic. The result was a network of French-sponsored, opium-financed warlords in upper Tonkin who increasingly set their own agenda and who preyed on the population as much as the pirates of the 1890s ever had. For the *politique des races* dimension of Dien Bien Phu, see Douglas Porch, *The French Secret Services* (New York: Farrar, Straus, Giroux, 1995), Chapters 13 and 14.

33 Porch, *The Conquest of Morocco*, 128–30, 183–88.

34 Porch, *The Conquest of Morocco*, 157, 159–60.

35 Patrick James Christian, *A Combat Advisor's Guide to Tribal Engagement. History, Law and War as Operational Elements* (Boca Raton, FL: Universal Publishers, 2011), 50.

36 For instance, General Jacques Massu's 1957 roll-up of FLN networks in Algiers failed to win the Algerian War for the French, or even assure French control of the Kasbah, which erupted in pro-independence demonstrations three years later.

37 P. Heidsieck, *Le Rayonnement de Lyautey* (Paris: Gallimard, 1947), 186–87.

38 Kanya-Forstner, *The Conquest of the Western Sudan*, 200–201.

39 Jean Sévilla, *Historiquement correct: pour en finir avec le passé unique* (Paris: Perrin, 2003), 258; Yves Benot, *La modernité de l'esclavage: essai sur la servitude au cœur du capitalisme* (Paris: La Découverte, 2003), 241; Denise Bouche, *Les villages de liberté en Afrique noire française, 1887–1910* (Paris: EHESS, 1968).

40 Christian Tripodi, "'Good for One but Not the Other': The 'Sandeman System' of Pacification as Applied to Baluchistan and the North-West Frontier, 1877–1947," *The Journal of Military History*, 73:3 (July 2009), 767. Tripodi argues that "indirect rule" might have pacified the North-West Frontier had it not been undermined by policy changes in New Delhi that followed the removal of the Russian threat to India after 1919, personal disputes and jealousies within the Indian administration, inter-service rivalry between the army and the RAF after World War I, financial constraints, and arguments over the applicability of "indirect rule" in all areas.

41 Marc W. D. Tyrrell, "What to Know before You Go: 10 Questions to Ask before, and during, a Mission," pre-conference discussion draft, *Small Wars Journal*, 2008, http://smallwarsjournal.com/blog/what-to-know-before-you-go.

42 Parsons, *The Rule of Empires*, 224.

43 Parsons, *The Rule of Empires*, 170.

44 Tripodi, "The 'Sandeman System'," note 13.

45 William A. Hoisington, Jr., *The Casablanca Connection: French Colonial Policy 1936–1943* (Chapel Hill: University of North Carolina Press, 1984), 105.

46 Tripodi, "The 'Sandeman System'," 787, 790–97.

47 Porch, *The Conquest of Morocco*, 258–62.

48 Gavin Maxwell, *Lords of the Atlas: The Rise and Fall of the House of Glaoua, 1893–1956* (London: Eland, 2004).

49 Tripodi, "The 'Sandeman System'," 794.

50 Brian McAllister Linn, *The Echo of Battle: The Army's Way of War* (Cambridge, MA: Harvard University Press, 2007), 69–75, 85.

51 Brian McAllister Linn, *The Philippine War 1899–1902* (Lawrence: University of Kansas Press, 2000), 323.

52 http://en.wikiquote.org/wiki/Philippine-American_War.

53 A. J. Birtle, "The U.S. Army's Pacification of Marinduque, Philippines Islands, April 1900–April 1901," *The Journal of Military History*, 61 (April 1997), www.ulongbeach.com/US_Arny_Pacification.html, 4, 9–10, 12–13, 19; Linn, *The Philippine War 1899–1902*, 213; Alfred W. McCoy, *Policing America's Empire: The United States, the Philippines, and the Rise of the Surveillance State* (Madison: University of Wisconsin Press, 2009), 89, 104.

54 Linn, *The Philippine War 1899–1902*, 214–15, 220–24, 323–28.

55 Birtle, "The U.S. Army's Pacification of Marinduque," 19.

56 McCoy, *Policing America's Empire*, 94–95, 271.

57 McCoy, *Policing America's Empire*, 89, 96, 138–42, 522–23.

58 McCoy, *Policing America's Empire*, 318–46.

59 Thomas Pakenham, *The Boer War* (New York: Random House, 1993), 9.

60 Many of the foreign volunteers were guest workers in the Rand when hostilities commenced. See Pakenham, *The Boer War*, 106, 389.

61 www.sahistory.org.za/dated-event/emily-hobhouse-addresses-public-meetings-britain-concentration-camps; for the full report, see http://library.stanford.edu/depts/ssrg/africa/pplc13.html.

62 Pakenham, *The Boer War*, 504–505, 514–18.

63 David F. Trask, *The War with Spain in 1898* (London and Lincoln: University of Nebraska Press, 1981), 8–10, 53–54. In fact, far more people were estimated to have died in Weyler's camps than in those of the British in South Africa. www.spanamwar.com/proctorspeech.htm.

64 Pakenham, *The Boer War*, 461–572, 581.

65 Pakenham, *The Boer War*, 511–15, 566–69.

66 Pakenham, *The Boer War*, 551, 575–76.

67 Pakenham, *The Boer War*, 561–62, 571–72.

68 Jeremy Sarkin, *Colonial Genocide and Reparations Claims in the 21st Century: The Socio-Legal Context of Claims under International Law by the Herero against Germany for Genocide in Namibia, 1904–1908* (New York: Praeger 2008), 142.

69 Hull, *Absolute Destruction*, 91–108, 153–58, 188–94.

70 Thomas Weber, *Hitler's First War: Adolf Hitler, the Men of the List Regiment, and the First World War* (Oxford and New York: Oxford University Press, 2010), 38–40.

71 One reason it fizzled was because Kitchener refused to provide statistics on mortality rates in the camps, thus hiding the true scope of the problem from doubters. Pakenham, *The Boer War*, 509–11.

72 French and international complaints about the brutality of French repression in Syria in 1924–1925, especially of indiscriminate air bombardment of Damascus, caused the recall of General Maurice Sarrail and induced the French to offer amnesty to the rebels. Michael Provence, *The Great Syrian Revolt and the Rise of Arab Nationalism* (Austin: University of Texas Press, 2005), 125–27; David Slavin notes that the racism and ignorance of French Communist Party rank and file, many of whom appear to have believed that Muslims were cannibals, made it difficult for the party to mobilize against the Riff Rebellion. "The French Left and the Riff War: Racism and the Limits of Internationalism," *Journal of Contemporary History*, No. 1 (January 1991), 5–32. The fact that much of French repression in Algeria took place out of public view and that in France there was general hostility to North Africans, combined with the fact that the French left had other priorities and was simply too divided to unite against the Algerian War, muted the popular response to that conflict. Most French bought into the government view that projected French soldiers and police as victims of the FLN. Jim House and Neil MacMaster, *Paris 1961: Algerians, State Terror and Memory* (Oxford University Press, 2006), 194–222.

73 Weber, *Hitler's First War*, 38–39.

74 Hull, *Absolute Destruction*, 191; for a discussion of colonial pressure groups in France, see Christopher M. Andrew and A. S. Kanya-Forstner, *France Overseas: The Great War and the Climax of French Imperial Expansion* (London: Thames and Hudson, 1981), 23–24.

75 Prosser Gifford and William Roger Louis (eds.), *Britain and Germany in Africa: Imperial Rivalry and Colonial Rule* (New Haven, CT and London: Yale University Press, 1967), 560–71.

76 Porch, *The Conquest of Morocco*, 132–36.

77 Jacques Frémeaux, *Les bureaux arabes dans l'Algérie de la conquête* (Paris: Editions Denoël, 1993), 59; Charles-André Julien, *Histoire de l'Algérie contemporaine*, Vol. I: *La conquête et les débuts de la colonisation (1827–1871)* (Paris: PUF, 1964), 1848 illustration facing p. 336: "Cavaignac quitte l'Algérie pour appliquer en France la discipline Africaine"; Porch, *The French Foreign Legion*, 168–69.

78 Hull, *Absolute Destruction*, 117–19, 124, 131.

79 John D. Fage, "British and German Colonial Rule: A Synthesis and Summary," in Gifford and Louis (eds.), *Britain and Germany in Africa*, 700.

80 Julien, *Histoire*, 491.

3 Counterinsurgency in the shadow of the Great War

1 Patrick Porter, *Military Orientalism: Eastern War through Western Eyes* (New York: Columbia University Press, 2009), 71.

2 David W. Hogan, Jr., "Head and Heart: The Dilemmas of American Attitudes toward War," *Journal of Military History*, 75:4 (October 2011), 1037.

3 David French, *The British Way in Counterinsurgency 1945–1967* (Oxford University Press, 2011), 61.

4 Hogan, "Head and Heart," 1041–42.

5 John Arquilla, *Insurgents, Raiders, and Bandits: How Masters of Irregular Warfare Have Shaped Our World* (Chicago: Ivan R. Dee, 2011).

6 Arquilla, *Insurgents, Raiders, and Bandits*, 147, 155.

7 Hew Strachan, "German East Africa Campaign (1914–1918)," in Richard Holmes (ed.), *The Oxford Companion to Military History* (Oxford and New York: Oxford University Press, 2001), 359–61.

8 Charles Townshend, "Guerrilla Warfare," in Holmes (ed.), *The Oxford Companion to Military History*, 383.

9 "The total was certainly not less than 350,000 men, women and children, and it is inconceivable that the death rate among them was no lower than one in seven," concludes British historian Edward Paice. "Furthermore, in stark contrast to common practice in the British colonies, these carriers were seldom paid anything for their service; and when famine, caused by the wholesale 'theft of food, cattle and men' by the military authorities, descended on many parts of the country the people were simply left to starve." *Tip and Run: The Untold Tragedy of the Great War in Africa* (London: Phoenix, 2007), 398, 5–6, 18–22.

10 Niall Ferguson, *Empire: The Rise and Demise of the British World Order and the Lessons for Global Power* (New York: Basic Books, 2004), 253.

11 On the issue of modernization through Ottomanization, see Ussama Makdisi, "Ottoman Orientalism," *The American Historical Review*, 107:3 (June 2002), 768–96; Selim Deringil, "'They Live in a State of Nomadism and Savagery,' the Late Ottoman Empire and the Post-Colonial Debate," *Comparative Studies in Society and History*, 45:2 (April 2003), 311–42.

12 Ottomanization included Istanbul's plan to connect Mecca to Medina by rail, end the Hijaz's exemption from conscription into the Ottoman army, and curtail the administrative autonomy of the Hijaz. William Ochsenwald, "Arab Nationalism in the Hijaz," in Rashid Khalidi, Lisa Anderson, Muhammad Muslih, and Reeva S. Simon (eds.), *The Origins of Arab Nationalism* (New York: Columbia University Press, 1991), 194–96, 199–201; Mary C. Wilson, "The Hashemites, the Arab Revolt, and Arab Nationalism," in Khalidi *et al.* (eds.), *The Origins of Arab Nationalism*, 219; Istanbul's "borrowed" colonial thinking argued that railways, conscription, public works

projects, administrative reform, education, etc. would help to "civilize [the Arab] and make him useful." Deringil, "'They Live in a State of Nomadism and Savagery,'" 318–19; 327. Ottomanization also meant racialization of the empire, by which Arabs in general were viewed by Turkish modernizers as a fanatical and ignorant minority who needed Turkish help to prevent a decline into utter chaos. The Wahabbis of Mecca and Medina were considered "as purveyors of error and deceit, corruption and sedition – as faithless heretics," the latter opinion shared by many urban Arab nationalists. Makdisi, "Ottoman Orientalism," 785, 788, 790–91, 793.

13 Quoted in Jeremy Wilson, *Lawrence of Arabia: The Authorized Biography of T. E. Lawrence* (New York: Atheneum, 1990), 313.

14 James Barr, *A Line in the Sand: Britain, France and the Struggle for Mastery of the Middle East* (New York: Simon & Schuster, 2011), 37–41.

15 Wilson, *Lawrence of Arabia*, 313–17.

16 Barr, *A Line in the Sand*, 41–44.

17 David Fromkin, "The Importance of T. E. Lawrence," *The New Criterion Online*, September 10, 1991, www.newcriterion.com/articles.cfm/ The-importance-of-T-E-Lawrence-4416, 7.

18 Barr argues (*A Line in the Sand*, 44) that Lawrence did not sever the rail link because the British would end their support for the Arab Revolt. But this is implausible as Lloyd George saw the revolt as central to his plans to leverage the French out of the Middle East.

19 Barr, *A Line in the Sand*, 59–61.

20 Wilson. *Lawrence of Arabia*, 504.

21 Wilson. *Lawrence of Arabia*, 458, 549–50, 555–56.

22 Polly A. Mohs, *Military Intelligence and the Arab Revolt: The First Modern Intelligence War* (London and New York: Routledge, 2008), 43–55, 107–108, 134. One argument is that Lawrence gave up on capturing Medina because he feared that the British would lose interest in the Arab Revolt once that objective had been taken. So he took Aqaba as a base for the advance north to associate Faisal with the advance into Syria.

23 Simon Anglim, *Orde Wingate and the British Army 1922–1944* (London: Pickering & Chatto, 2010), 50–51.

24 But in the Hijaz, the Hashemites justified their rebellion as a defense of Islam, not nationalism. Wilson, "The Hashemites, the Arab Revolt, and Arab Nationalism," 204–206, 212–15.

25 Anglim, *Orde Wingate*, 49.

26 Mohs, *Military Intelligence and the Arab Revolt*, 162–63.

27 Fromkin, "The Importance of T. E. Lawrence," 11–12, 17, 18.

28 Mechanized warfare, another alternative, offered an equally illusory recipe for making conventional warfare more efficient, less casualty heavy, less attritional, and more "decisive." The Germans in the wake of Versailles flirted with the idea

of *Volkskrieg*, based on the fictionalized ancestral memories of Prussian resistance to Napoleon, as well as with tanks as a form of strategic deterrence. But when they tried to wargame it as a defense scenario, it proved disastrous. Michael Geyer, "German Strategy, 1914–1945," in Peter Paret (ed.), *The Makers of Modern Strategy from Machiavelli to the Nuclear Age* (Princeton University Press, 1986), 557, 560–62.

29 Arquilla, *Insurgents, Raiders and Bandits*, 159.

30 Fromkin, "The Importance of T. E. Lawrence," 10. Even Lawrence worried that "[Liddell Hart] uses me as the stalking horse to air the merits of his ideas and this makes even the well-founded parts of his book feel improbable." Wilson, *Lawrence of Arabia*, 909, 907.

31 T. E. Lawrence, "The Science of Guerrilla Warfare," in *Encyclopedia Britannica*, 14th edn. (London, 1929), 953.

32 Forward by Sir Basil Liddell Hart in Mao Tse-tung and Che Guevara, *Guerilla Warfare* (London: Cassell, 1961), x.

33 Peter Paret, *French Revolutionary Warfare from Indochina to Algeria: The Analysis of a Political and Military Doctrine* (New York: Praeger, 1964), 6.

34 Geyer, "German Strategy, 1914–1945," 548.

35 Geyer, "German Strategy, 1914–1945," 557.

36 Geyer, "German Strategy, 1914–1945," 555–61.

37 Geyer, "German Strategy, 1914–1945," 543; see also Brian Bond and Martin Alexander, "Liddell Hart and De Gaulle: The Doctrines of Limited Liability and Mobile Defense," in Paret (ed.), *The Makers of Modern Strategy*, 598–623.

38 Christopher M. Andrew and A. S. Kanya-Forstner, *France Overseas: The Great War and the Climax of French Imperial Expansion* (London: Thames and Hudson, 1981), 247.

39 Daniel Moran, *Wars of National Liberation* (London: Cassell, 2001), 39–40.

40 Eugen Weber, *The Hollow Years: France in the 1930s* (New York: W.W. Norton, 1996), 11.

41 Martin Thomas, *Empires of Intelligence: Security Services and Colonial Disorder after 1914* (Los Angeles, Berkeley, and London: University of California Press, 2008), 294.

42 Thomas, *Empires of Intelligence*, 145–57.

43 To be fair to Lyautey, Churchill had contemplated using mustard gas bombs on Iraqi insurgents in 1920. Barr, *A Line in the Sand*, 113.

44 William A. Hoisington, Jr., *The Casablanca Connection: French Colonial Policy, 1936–1943* (Chapel Hill: University of North Carolina Press, 1984), 105–107, 111; William A. Hoisington, Jr., *Lyautey and the French Conquest of Morocco* (New York: St. Martin's Press, 1995), 186, 195–96, 205–206; Martin Thomas, *The French Empire between the Wars: Imperialism, Politics and Society* (Manchester and New York: Manchester University Press, 2005), 212–18.

45 On the disorder in 1919–1920, see James L. Gelvin, *Divided Loyalties: Nationalism and Mass Politics in Syria at the Close of Empire* (Berkeley, Los Angeles, and London: University of California Press, 1998), 35–47. In 1892, the Ottomans set up a Tribal School in Istanbul where sons of leaders on the frontiers of the empire would receive a totally free education. This aimed to instill loyalty in the future leaders of the empire. Michael Provence, *The Great Syrian Revolt and the Rise of Arab Nationalism* (Austin: University of Texas Press, 2005), 38–42, 46–47.

46 Stephen Longrigg, *Syria and Lebanon under French Mandate* (Oxford University Press, 1958), 11.

47 Thomas, *Empires of Intelligence*, 159, 161.

48 Provence, *The Great Syrian Revolt*, 67.

49 S. H. Roberts, *A History of French Colonial Policy* (London: P. S. King 1929), 602, quoted in Birgit Schaebler, "Coming to Terms with Failed Revolutions: Historiography in Syria, Germany and France," *Middle Eastern Studies*, 35:1 (January 1999), 34.

50 On the conditions leading to the Great Revolt, see Philip S. Khoury, *Syria and the French Mandate: The Politics of Arab Nationalism* (Princeton University Press, 1987), 151–59; also Joyce Laverty Miller, "The Syrian Revolt of 1925," *International Journal of Middle East Studies*, 8:4 (October 1977), 545–63.

51 Lenka Bokova, *La confrontation franco-Syrienne à l'époque du mandate 1925–1927* (Paris: Editions L'Harmattan, 1990), 72–75; Provence, *The Great Syrian Revolt*, 150.

52 The French would define the frontiers, could intervene in juridical and administrative affairs, approve all elections and governors, laws, budgets, and have exclusive oversight of technical, financial, economic, and military matters. They would handle foreign affairs and could fire the governor. In return, they would defend the Druze, exempt them from military service, allow them to carry arms, and not intervene in religious affairs. Bokova, *La confrontation*, 97–98.

53 Provence, *The Great Syrian Revolt*, 15, 26, 29, 33, 50–51; Thomas, *Empires of Intelligence*, 162–72.

54 Khoury, *Syria and the French Mandate*, 620; Provence, *The Great Syrian Revolt*, 141–42; Schaebler, "Coming to Terms with Failed Revolutions," 31–39.

55 Denis Judd, *Empire: The British Imperial Experience from 1765 to the Present* (London: Basic Books, 1996), 263.

56 Charles Tripp, *A History of Iraq* (Cambridge University Press, 2000), 30–45; Barr, *A Line in the Sand*, 104–127.

57 Florence O'Donaghue, *No Other Law (The Story of Liam Lynch and the Irish Republican Army 1916–1923)* (Dublin: Irish Press Ltd., 1954), 148–51; Joost Augusteijn, *From Public Defiance to Guerilla Warfare: The Radicalisation of the Irish Republican Army – A Comparative Analysis, 1916–1920* (Amsterdam: Centrale Drukkerij Universitet van Amsterdam, 1994), 244.

58 Richard Bennett, *The Black and Tans* (Boston: Houghton Mifflin, 1960), 27.

59 David Neligan, *The Spy in the Castle* (London: Prendeville Publishing, 1999), 184. I thank William Fuller for this reference and observations.

60 Francis Costello, *The Irish Revolution and Its Aftermath 1916–1923: Years of Revolt* (Dublin: Irish Academic Press, 2003), 129; Jim Maher, *Flying Column, West Kilkinney 1916–1921* (Dublin: Geography Publications, 1987), 92, 111.

61 C. S. Andrews, *Dublin Made Me* (Dublin: Lilliput Press, 2002), 129.

62 Peter Hart (ed.), *British Intelligence in Ireland, 1920–21: The Final Reports* (Cork University Press, 2002), 30–31, 36, 42, 43–44.

63 C. J. C. Street, *Ireland in 1921* (London: Philip Allan & Co., 1922), 102.

64 William Fuller argues in his forthcoming book that De Valera's strategy was to provoke the British into a level of retaliation that would demonstrate that England was "the accursed oppressor of nations." David W. Miller, *Church, State and Nation in Ireland 1898–1921* (University of Pittsburgh Press, 1973), 396. This would result in Ireland being put on the Versailles agenda that would result in international pressure to force Westminster to grant Irish independence. But Wilson's priority was the passage of a League of Nations for which he needed London's support. De Valera's arrogance divided Irish-American opinion, while Wilson, whom Irish-American voters tended to boycott in any case, was annoyed by his meddling in US domestic politics. The success of De Valera's US swing was also undercut by the accusation that Irish nationalists had been pro-German in the war.

65 D. G. Boyce, *Englishmen and Irish Troubles: British Public Opinion and the Making of Irish Policy 1918–22* (Cambridge, MA: MIT Press, 1972), 99; D. M. Leeson explores similar arguments, *The Black and Tans: British Police and Auxiliaries in the Irish War of Independence* (Oxford University Press, 2011), 194.

66 Thomas Pakenham, *The Boer War* (London: Weidenfeld & Nicolson, 1979), 511. For the failure of Montgomery's firm hand in Palestine, see John Newsinger, *British Counterinsurgency from Palestine to Northern Ireland* (New York: Palgrave, 2002), 225.

67 See Andrews, *Dublin Made Me*, 188; Andrew Boyle, *The Riddle of Erskine Childers* (London: Hutchinson, 1977), 271. I thank William Fuller for these observations.

68 Boyce, *Englishmen and Irish Troubles*, 52–53.

69 Leeson, *The Black and Tans*, 159, 194–96.

70 Georgina Sinclair, *At the End of the Line: Colonial Policing and the Imperial Endgame 1945–1980* (Manchester and New York: Manchester University Press, 2006), 14.

71 Hew Strachan, *The Politics of the British Army* (Oxford: Clarendon Press, 1997), 111

72 Thomas, *Empires of Intelligence*, 231.

73 Strachan, *The Politics of the British Army*, 116–17.

74 Leeson, *The Black and Tans*, 33.

75 Strachan, *The Politics of the British Army*, 165–66.

76 Michael Hopkinson, *The Irish War of Independence* (Montreal: McGill-Queen's University Press, 2002), 94.

77 Leeson, *The Black and Tans*, 195–97, 223.

78 Boyce, *Englishmen and Irish Troubles*, 55.

79 William Sheehan, *A Hard Local War: The British Army and the Guerrilla War in Cork 1919–1921* (Stroud: The History Press, 2011), 107.

80 Leeson, *The Black and Tans*, 192–93, 197, 199, 203, 212–14, 217–23.

81 Sheehan, *A Hard Local War*, 78–79.

82 Sheehan, *A Hard Local War*, 107, 113.

83 Sheehan, *A Hard Local War*, 108.

84 Sheehan, *A Hard Local War*, 168.

85 Boyce, *Englishmen and Irish Troubles*, 99, 102, 141, 180: Benjamin John Grob-Fitzgibbon, *Turning Points of the Irish Revolution: The British Government, Intelligence, and the Cost of Indifference, 1912–1921* (Gordonsville, VA: Palgrave Macmillan, 2007), 118.

86 Hart (ed.), *British Intelligence*, 28.

87 Boyce, *Englishmen and Irish Troubles*, 80–81, 131, 180–81.

88 Hopkinson, *The Irish War of Independence*, 201–203. More classic treatments of Irish independence include Charles Townshend, *The British Campaign in Ireland, 1919–1921* (Oxford University Press, 1975); David Fitzpatrick, *Politics and Irish Life 1913–1921: Provincial Experience of War and Revolution* (Dublin: Gill & Macmillan 1977); Charles Townshend, "In Aid of the Civil Power: Britain, Ireland and Palestine 1916–48," in Daniel Marston and Carter Malkasian (eds.), *Counterinsurgency in Modern Warfare* (Oxford: Osprey, 2008), 21–27.

89 Winston Churchill, *The Aftermath* (London: Thornton, 1929), 297.

90 Isabel V. Hull, *Absolute Destruction: Military Culture and the Practices of War in Imperial Germany* (Ithaca, NY and London: Cornell University Press, 2005), 33, 184–87.

91 John Keegan "Introduction," in Sir Robert Thompson (ed.), *War in Peace: Conventional and Guerrilla Warfare since 1945* (New York: Harmony Books, 1981), vi.

92 Douglas Porch, *The French Foreign Legion* (New York: Knopf, 1991), 508–10.

93 Terence Creagh Coen, *The Indian Political Service* (London: Chatto & Windus, 1971), 189.

94 Thomas, *Empires of Intelligence*, 238–40.

95 Anglim, *Orde Wingate*, 23.

96 Townshend, "In Aid of the Civil Power," 27.

97 Hart (ed.), *British Intelligence*, 65, 75, 86, 96.

98 Leeson, *The Black and Tans*, 228.

4 British counterinsurgency in the World War II era

1 Thomas R. Mockaitis, *British Counterinsurgency, 1919–60* (New York: St. Martin's Press, 1990), 17–21, 87.

2 Mockaitis, *British Counterinsurgency*, 9–11, 13–14, 17–18, 55–57.

3 Sir Robert Thompson, *Defeating Communist Insurgency. The Lessons of Malaya and Vietnam* (New York: Praeger, 1966); John A. Nagl, *Learning to Eat Soup with a Knife: Counterinsurgency Lessons from Malaya and Vietnam* (London and Chicago: University of Chicago Press, 2005); Richard Duncan Downie, *Learning from Conflict: The U.S. Military in Vietnam, El Salvador, and the Drug War* (Westport, CT: Praeger, 1998).

4 Hew Strachan, *The Politics of the British Army* (Oxford University Press, 1997), 181; John Newsinger, *British Counterinsurgency from Palestine to Northern Ireland* (New York: Palgrave, 2002), 1–2; Christopher Bayly and Tim Harper, *Forgotten Wars: The End of Britain's Asian Empire* (London: Penguin, 2007); David Anderson, *Histories of the Hanged: Britain's Dirty War in Kenya and the End of Empire* (London: Weidenfeld & Nicolson, 2005); David French, *The British Way in Counter-Insurgency, 1945–1967* (Oxford University Press, 2011).

5 Simon Anglim, *Orde Wingate and the British Army 1922–1944* (London: Pickering & Chatto, 2010); David Cesarani, *Major Farran's Hat* (Cambridge, MA: Da Capo Press, 2009).

6 Brian McAllister Linn, *The Echo of Battle: The Army's Way of War* (Cambridge, MA: Harvard University Press, 2007), 85.

7 Jean-Yves le Naour, *La honte noire: L'Allemagne et les troupes coloniales françaises 1914–1945* (Paris: Hachette, 2004); Raffael Scheck, *Hitler's African Victims: The German Army Massacres of Black French Soldiers in 1940* (Cambridge University Press, 2006).

8 Scheck, *Hitler's African Victims*.

9 Benjamin Madley, "From Africa to Auschwitz: How German South West Africa Incubated Ideas and Methods Adopted and Developed by the Nazis in Eastern Europe," *European History Quarterly*, 35:3 (2005), 429–64; Ben Kiernan, *Blood and Soil: A World History of Genocide and Extermination from Sparta to Darfur* (New Haven, CT: Yale University Press, 2007), 36. There were also many direct links between the Herero and the Holocaust. For instance, the father of the first commandant of Auschwitz, Rudolf Höss, had served with von Trota in German Southwest Africa, while Höss had been with the Ottomans at the time of the Armenian massacres.

10 John Horne and Alan Kramer, *German Atrocities 1914: A History of Denial* (New Haven, CT: Yale University Press, 2001), 93–113; Isabel V. Hull, *Absolute Destruction: Military Culture and the Practices of War in Imperial Germany* (Ithaca, NY and London: Cornell University Press, 2005), 117–28. On the other

hand, Thomas Weber, who has tried to turn much of this discourse on its head in a novel way, argues that colonial atrocities were a European imperial phenomenon, not a uniquely Teutonic peccadillo. While all colonizing countries carried out colonial massacres, only Germany and its Axis allies engaged in European genocide. Few leading proponents of the Holocaust had served in the Great War, much less in Africa. Rather, Weber blames the radicalization of violence on: "the lethal cocktail of ethnic conflict, extreme economic volatility, and empires in decline; as well as the transformation of a European state system of multi-ethnic empires to modern ethnically defined nation states and an obsessive fear of Bolshevism in general, and Hitler's paranoid anti-Semitism in particular." *Hitler's First War* (Oxford University Press, 2010), 336–37.

11 Strachan, *The Politics of the British Army*, 166, 169.

12 This argument, originally made by Hannah Arendt in *On Violence* (New York: Harcourt, Brace and World, 1970), 80, is developed more fully in Hull, *Absolute Destruction*, 325.

13 This is codified in British Army doctrine as Military Aid to the Civil Power (MACP). The Military is allowed to come to the aid of civilian authorities who lack resources or capacity to deal with certain situations and emergencies. The assumption is that the military is called in as a last resort and that operations will be conducted within the confines of civil and military law. Christopher Bellamy, "Aid to Civil Power," in Richard Holmes (ed.), *The Oxford Companion to Military History* (Oxford University Press, 2001), 206–207.

14 Georgina Sinclair, *At the End of the Line: Colonial Policing and the Imperial Endgame, 1945–1980* (Manchester and New York: Manchester University Press and Palgrave, 2006), vi, 9 note 21.

15 Christian Tripodi, *Edge of Empire: The British Political Officer and Tribal Administration on the North-West Frontier 1877–1947* (Farnham, Surrey and Burlington, VT: Ashgate, 2011), 231.

16 Sinclair, *At the End of the Line*, 11–20.

17 Mockaitis, *British Counterinsurgency*, 47–48.

18 Sinclair, *At the End of the Line*, 223, 156–60, 167–72; French, *The British Way in Counter-Insurgency*, 16–19.

19 Sinclair, *At the End of the Line*, 19.

20 French, *The British Way in Counter-Insurgency*, 29–31.

21 French, *The British Way in Counter-Insurgency*, 109.

22 Sinclair, *At the End of the Line*, 189–204; French, *The British Way in Counter-Insurgency*, 19–27.

23 Strachan, *The Politics of the British Army*, 169–70, 185–86; Major General Sir Charles W. Gwynn, *Imperial Policing* (London: Macmillan, 1934), 6–9, 11, 17, 23, 31. H. J. Simson, *British Rule, and Rebellion* (Salisbury, NC: Documentary Publications, 1977), 36–37, 64–65, 77, 101.

24 David Galula, *Pacification in Algeria 1956–1958* (Santa Monica, CA: Rand Corporation, 2006), v.

25 French, *The British Way in Counter-Insurgency*, 129–32, 137, 152.

26 Charles Townshend, *Britain's Civil Wars: Counterinsurgency in the Twentieth Century* (London: Faber & Faber, 1986), 61. Quoted in Strachan, *The Politics of the British Army*, 164.

27 Martin Thomas, *Empires of Intelligence: Security Services and Colonial Disorder after 1914* (Berkeley, Los Angeles, and London: University of California Press, 2008), 239.

28 Simon Anglim, *Orde Wingate and the British Army 1922–1944* (London: Pickering & Chatto, 2010), 32.

29 Sinclair, *At the End of the Line*, 189.

30 French, *The British Way in Counter-Insurgency*, 60–62.

31 Gwynn, *Imperial Policing*, 6–9, 11, 17, 23, 31. For a brief critique of Gwynn, see Strachan, *The Politics of the British Army*, 169–70.

32 Simson, *British Rule, and Rebellion*, 36–37, 64–65, 77, 101.

33 Simson, *British Rule*, 80.

34 Anglim, *Orde Wingate*, 85, 89–91; M. Hughes, "The Banality of Brutality: British Armed Forces and the Repression of the Arab Revolt in Palestine, 1936–39," *English Historical Review*, 124:507 (2009), 314–54.

35 Newsinger, *British Counterinsurgency*, 4.

36 Strachan, *The Politics of the British Army*, 170–71, 180.

37 Mockaitis, *British Counterinsurgency*, 22.

38 French, *The British Way in Counter-Insurgency*, 76–82; Benjamin John Grob-Fitzgibbon, *Imperial Endgame: Britain's Dirty Wars and the End of Empire* (New York: Palgrave Macmillan, 2011), 137–38.

39 Townshend, "In Aid of the Civil Power," 27–33; Hughes, "The Banality of Brutality," 331–54; M. Hughes, "The Practice and Theory of British Counterinsurgency: The Histories of Atrocities at the Palestine Villages of al-Basa and Halhul, 1938–1939," *Small Wars & Insurgencies*, 20 (2009), 313–54; J. Norris, "Repression and Rebellion: Britain's Response to the Arab Revolt in Palestine of 1936–39," *Journal of Imperial and Commonwealth History*, 36 (2008), 25–45.

40 Anglim, *Orde Wingate*, 28–29.

41 Anglim, *Orde Wingate*, 50.

42 Polly A. Mohs, *Military Intelligence and the Arab Revolt: The First Modern Intelligence War* (London and New York: Routledge, 2008), 43, 162–63; Anglim, *Orde Wingate*, 18.

43 Anglim, *Orde Wingate*, 37–40, 171.

44 Mao Tse-tung and Che Guevara, *Guerilla Warfare* (London: Cassell, 1961), x; Anglim, *Orde Wingate*, 53.

45 M. R. D. Foot, *SOE in France* (London: Her Majesty's Stationery Office, 1966), 438, 440. See Porch's discussion of the French Resistance in *The French Secret Services: A History of French Intelligence from the Dreyfus Affair to the Gulf War* (New York: Farrar, Straus, Giroux, 1995), Chapter 10.

46 Alan Milward, "The Economic and Strategic Effectiveness of Resistance," in Stephen Hawes and Ralph White (eds.), *Resistance in Europe* (London: Penguin, 1976), 193, 197.

47 Douglas Porch, *Path to Victory: The Mediterranean Theater in World War II* (New York: Farrar, Straus, Giroux, 2004), 638–39. One estimate calculates that of 100,000 active partisans, approximately 35,000 died, 21,000 were wounded and 9,000 were deported to Germany, or a 65 percent casualty rate. Paul Ginsborg, *A History of Contemporary Italy: Society and Politics 1943–1988* (London: Penguin, 1990), 16, 55–58, 70; David Ellwood, *Italy 1943–1945* (New York: Holmes and Meier, 1985), 163.

48 The situation in Yugoslavia was complicated by the extreme ethnic mix which meant that if one group chose to collaborate, its ethnic neighbors might choose to resist. Tito's Partisans played down their communist ideology and welcomed recruits of all ethnicities, including Jews. Partisan ranks swelled from 1944 as the Red Army entered Yugoslavia and Tito offered an amnesty to rival Chetniks who changed sides.

49 Norman Lewis, *Naples '44* (London: Collins, 1978), 143, 147–48.

50 Anglim, *Orde Wingate*, 142.

51 Ginsborg, *A History of Contemporary Italy*, 42.

52 Henry Rousso, *The Vichy Syndrome: History and Memory in France since 1944* (Cambridge, MA: Harvard University Press, 1991), 10.

53 Harold Macmillan, *War Diaries: The Mediterranean, 1943–1945* (New York: St. Martin's Press, 1984), 743.

54 John Arquilla, *Insurgents, Raiders, and Bandits: How Masters of Irregular Warfare Have Shaped Our World* (Chicago: Ivan R. Dee, 2011), 184–85.

55 William Slim, *Defeat into Victory* (London: Cassell, 1956), 546–49; see also Peter Meade and Shelford Bidwell, "Orde Wingate – Two Views," *Journal of Contemporary History*, 15:3 (July 1980), 401–404.

56 Anglim, *Orde Wingate*, 191–93, 207–12.

57 Cesarani, *Major Farran's Hat*, 36.

58 Newsinger, *British Counterinsurgency*, 16; Cesarani, *Major Farran's Hat*, 44, 210–11.

59 Newsinger, *British Counterinsurgency*, 23.

60 J. Bower Bell, *Terror out of Zion: The Fight for Israeli Independence* (New Brunswick, NJ: Rutgers University Press, 2009), 156.

61 Cesarani, *Major Farran's Hat*, 43, 53–55.

62 Cesarani, *Major Farran's Hat*, 46–53.

63 Cesarani, *Major Farran's Hat*, 63, 72.

64 Cesarani, *Major Farran's Hat*, 178.

65 D. M. Leeson, *The Black and Tans: British Police and Auxiliaries in the Irish War of Independence* (Oxford University Press, 2011), 217–22.

66 Cesarani, *Major Farran's Hat*, 176.

67 Cesarani, *Major Farran's Hat*, 60, 72, 129, 213–14.

68 Grob-Fitzgibbon, *Imperial Endgame*, 73, 80–85, 87–88; Newsinger, *British Counterinsurgency*, 28–30; Cesarani, *Major Farran's Hat*, 43, 53–54.

69 Newsinger, *British Counterinsurgency*, 22; Cesarani, *Major Farran's Hat*, 211–15.

5 From small wars to *la guerre subversive*

1 Henry Rousso, *The Vichy Syndrome: History and Memory in France since 1944* (Cambridge, MA: Harvard University Press, 1991), 75–76.

2 Mao Tse-tung, *On Protracted War* (Beijing: Foreign Language Press, 1967), Vol. II, 136–42; Daniel Moran, *Wars of National Liberation* (London: Cassell, 2001), 39.

3 Moran, *Wars of National Liberation*, 39.

4 Moran, *Wars of National Liberation*, 38–39.

5 Edward L. Dreyer, *China at War, 1901–1949* (New York: Longman, 1995), 185–89, 191–205

6 I thank William Fuller for providing me several chapters from a manuscript on a forthcoming work on terrorism.

7 Moran (*Wars of National* Liberation, 39–40) notes that both Frederick Engels and in particular Lenin established Clausewitz as the basis for Bolshevik military theory in the interwar years. Mao's contribution was to demonstrate the political dimensions of tactics as the "revolutionary fish swimming in the sea of the people."

8 Dreyer, *China at War*, 350–61.

9 William Wei, "'Political Power Grows out of the Barrel of a Gun,' Mao and the Red Army," in Robin Higham and David A. Graff (eds.), *A Military History of China* (Boulder, CO: Westview Press, 2002), 230–31.

10 Elizabeth Borgwardt, *A New Deal for the World: America's Vision for Human Rights* (Cambridge, MA: Harvard, 2005), 4–6.

11 Moran, *Wars of National Liberation*, 24–25.

12 David French, *The British Way in Counter-Insurgency 1945–1967* (Oxford University Press, 2011), 57.

13 David A. Petraeus and James F. Amos, *FM 3–24: U.S. Army/Marine Corps Counterinsurgency Field Manuel* (Washington, DC: Headquarters, Department of the Army, December 2006), 1–75.

14 Moran, *Wars of National Liberation*, 91.

15 Mark Atwood Lawrence, *Assuming the Burden: Europe and the American Commitment to the War in Vietnam* (Berkeley: University of California Press, 2005), 286.

16 While colonial amalgamations had worked well enough for pre-World War II sovereignty operations, they lacked the flexibility, cohesion, and numbers successfully to combat the Viet Minh, especially when the latter's force structure expanded in size and sophistication following Mao's 1949 victory in China.

17 Vincent Joly, *Guerres d'Afrique: 130 ans de guerres coloniales – L'expérience française* (Rennes: Presses Universitaires de Rennes, 2009), 254–62.

18 Joly, *Guerres d'Afrique*, 275. The Khmer Issarak was only formed in 1950 as a subsidiary of the Viet Minh and so may have lacked bona fide nationalist credentials in the eyes of some. Cambodia was given full independence by France in 1953, an important political concession which meant that the war in Cambodia was no longer an anti-imperialist struggle. The Khmer Issarak's Viet Minh patrons failed to negotiate a political role for it at the 1954 Geneva Conference that ended the Indochina War, which split the movement and led to its temporary eclipse. Nevertheless, some studies suggest that the Khmer Issarak, with Viet Minh help, controlled half of Cambodian territory in 1954. Donald M. Seekins, "The Historical Setting," in Frederica M. Bunge (ed.), *Burma: A Country Study* (Washington, DC: The American University Press, 1983), 1–71.

19 Moran, *Wars of National Liberation*, 183; Joli, *Guerres d'Afrique*, 276–77.

20 Moran, *Wars of National Liberation*, 183; Joli, *Guerres d'Afrique*, 276–77.

21 Peter Paret, *French Revolutionary Warfare from Indochina to Algeria: The Analysis of a Political and Military Doctrine* (New York: Praeger, 1964), 7.

22 Jules Roy, *The Battle of Dien Bien Phu* (New York: Carroll & Graf Publishers, 2002), xxv.

23 Raoul Salan, *Mémoires: fin d'un empire*, Vol. II: *Le Viêt-Minh mon adversaire* (Paris: Presses de la Cité, 1971), 225.

24 Simon Anglim, *Orde Wingate and the British Army, 1922–1944* (London: Pickering & Chatto, 2010), 187, 191–93, 207–12.

25 French Army Archives, Vincennes, 10H 338, 2e trimester 1953. Cited in Douglas Porch, *The French Secret Services* (New York: Farrar, Straus, Giroux, 1995), 331–32.

26 For the intelligence and special operations dimensions of Dien Bien Phu, see Porch, *The French Secret Services*, Chapters 12–14.

27 Jacques Juillard, "Le mépris de la modernité," in Jean-Pierre Rioux (ed.), *La guerre d'Algérie et les français* (Paris: Fayard, 1990), 158.

28 Perhaps the most egregious example was the army's decision on October 22, 1956 without government permission to hijack the Sultan of Morocco's plane to capture five FLN representatives on their way to the Tunis conference.

Martin Evans, *Algeria: France's Undeclared War* (Oxford University Press, 2012), 186–87.

29 Sylvie Thénault, *Histoire de la guerre d'indépendance Algérienne* (Paris: Flammarion, 2005), 164.

30 Lawrence, *Assuming the Burden*, 192.

31 Lacheroy document available at: http://bp2.blogger.com/_KRnfUFHNcdw/ R9QfDDuISQI/AAAAAAAABB4/Cgg4oqbl5IY/s1600-h/Lacheroy3.jpg.

32 Joly, *Guerres d'Afrique*, 256–57; on Lacheroy's social Catholicism, see Thénault, *Histoire*, 95.

33 Evans, *Algeria*, 134

34 Moran, *Wars of National Liberation*, 91.

35 Claude d'Abzac-Epezy, "La société militaire, de l'ingérence à l'ignorance," in Rioux (ed.), *La guerre d'Algérie et les français*, 247–48.

36 Ann Marlowe, "Forgotten Founder: The French Colonel Who Wrote the Book(s) on Counterinsurgency," *The Weekly Standard*, 15:5 (October 19, 2009), http:// m.weeklystandard.com/Content/Public/Articles/000/000/017/054kkhvp.asp; also Marlowe, *David Galula: His Life and Intellectual Context* (Carlisle Baracks, PA: Strategic Studies Institute Monograph, August 2010), 3–5, www. StrategicStudiesInstitute.army.mil/; A. A. Cohen, *Galula: The Life and Writings of the French Officer Who Defined the Art of Counterinsurgency* (Santa Barbara, CA: Praeger, 2012).

37 Grégor Mathias, *Galula in Algeria: Counterinsurgency Practice versus Theory* (Santa Barbara, CA: Praeger, 2011), 96.

38 Evans, *Algeria*, 138.

39 Interview of Aussaresses by Marie-Monique Robin in *Escadrons de la mort – l'école française*, www.mefeedia.com/entry/2926696; General Paul Aussaresses, *The Battle of the Casbah: Terrorism and Counter-Terrorism in Algeria, 1955–1957* (New York: Enigma Books, 2010).

40 In reality, however, even before the Algerian War ended, the Special Warfare Center at Fort Bragg hosted dirty warriors like Roger Trinquier and Paul Aussaresses whose insights are thought to have influenced the more kinetic aspects of the Phoenix Program in Vietnam. David Galula, *Pacification in Algeria 1956–1958* (Santa Monica, CA: Rand Corporation, 2006), 50. Marlowe notes that Galula worked closely with General Raoul Salan and Colonel Charles Lacheroy in psychological operations in 1958, and that his claims to have slept through the Salan-led May 13 coup in Algiers "seems disingenuous." *David Galula*, 44–45; on Trinquier and Aussaresses at Bragg, 41–42. On Algerian influence on US COIN, see Elie Tenenbaum, *L'influence française sur la stratégie américaine de contre-insurrection 1945–1972* (Paris: Ecole d'études politiques de Paris, Master de recherche de Sciences Po, June 2009). On disassociating himself from the brutality of French counterinsurgency in Algeria, Geoff Demarest suggests that Galula simply covered his tracks better than did Trinquier: "Let's

Take the French Experience out of U.S. Counterinsurgency Doctrine," *Military Review* (July–August 2010), Maurice Vaïsse, French historian of the April 1960 military mutiny against de Gaulle, notes that the "epidemic" of absenteeism among French officers was a major reason for its failure. *Comment de Gaulle fit échouer le putsch d'Alger* (Brussels: André Versaille éditeur, 2011), 210. Galula was the only French officer to participate in the RAND seminar of April 1962 of COIN luminaries which helped to lay the framework for the US counterinsurgency approach to the Vietnam War. Mathias, *Galula in Algeria*, 99–100.

41 Galula, *Pacification in Algeria*, xxii.

42 Mathias, *Galula in Algeria*, 93.

43 Mathias, *Galula in Algeria*, 96.

44 Galula, *Pacification in Algeria*, v.

45 André-Paul Comor, "L'adaptation de la légion étrangère à la nouvelle forme de guerre," in Jean-Charles Jauffret and Maurice Vaïsse (eds.), *Militaires et guérilla dans la guerre d'Algérie* (Paris: Editions complexes, 2001), 59–67.

46 Galula, *Pacification in Algeria*, ix, 1

47 Marlowe (*David Galula*, 39–40) agrees that French COIN adaptations in Algeria "represented continuity with the French military's intellectual tradition."

48 *Des guerres d'Indochine et d'Algérie aux dictatures d'Amérique latine.* Interview with Marie-Monique Robin, author of *Escadrons de la mort, école française* (Paris: La Découverte Poche/Essais no 268, 2008), www.ldh-toulon.net/spip. php?article1778.

49 d'Abzac-Epezy, "La société militaire," 248.

50 *Des guerres d'Indochine et d'Algérie aux dictatures d'Amérique latine.* Interview with Marie-Monique Robin, author of *Escadrons de la mort, école française* (Paris: La Découverte Poche/Essais no 268, 2008), www.ldh-toulon.net/spip. php?article1778. Both *Employment of Helicopter-Borne Units in Maintaining Order in French North Africa [Manual T.T.A. 152]* and *Opérations de contre guerrilla dans le cadre du maintien de l'ordre en AFN [Manual T.T.A. 123]* were translated by the US Army in 1956. Cited in Charles R. Shrader, *The First Helicopter War: Logistics and Mobility in Algeria 1954–1962* (Westport, CT: Praeger, 1999), 260–61. Laurent Henninger lists a number of official publications on "insurrectional" and "psychological" operations published in 1956 and 1957, as well as war college studies. *Histoire militaire et du sciences humaines* (Brussels: Complexe, 1999), 82 note 36.

51 Mathias, *Galula in Algeria*, 96–98.

52 Document available at http://bp2.blogger.com/_KRnfUFHNcdw/ R9QfDDuISQI/AAAAAAAABB4/Cgg4oqbl5IY/s1600-h/Lacheroy3.jpg.

53 http://bp1.blogger.com/_KRnfUFHNcdw/R9QeAzuISOI/AAAAAAAABBs/ lzBRcHTXaOE/s1600-h/Lacheroy1.jpg.

54 Joly, *Guerres d'Afrique*, 283; Marie-Monique Robin, *Les Escadrons de la mort, l'école française* (Paris: La Découverte, 2008), 113.

55 Jean-Charles Jauffret, "Une armée à deux vitesses en Algérie 1954–1962: reserves générales et troupes de secteur," in Jauffret and Vaïsse (eds.), *Militaires et guérilla*, 21–35.

56 Evans, *Algeria*, 168–71.

57 Raphaëlle Branche, *La torture et l'armée pendant la guerre d'Algérie 1954–1962* (Paris: Gallimard, 2001), 425.

58 Evans, *Algeria*, 338; on the government's decision to guillotine FLN captives, 181; http://en.wikipedia.org/wiki/Fernand_Yveton.

59 Evans, *Algeria*, 225.

60 Galula, *Pacification in Algeria*, v.

61 O. Carlier, "Le 1er novembre 1954 à Oran," 18, 23, 25; Charles-Robert Ageron, "L'insurrection du 20 août 1955 dans le Nord-Constantinois. De la résistance armée á la guerre du people," 20, 31–37, 47; Mahfoud Kaddache, "Les tournants de la guerre de libération au niveau des masses populaires," 51–54; in Charles-Robert Ageron (ed.), *La guerre d'Algérie et les Algériens 1954–1962* (Paris: Armand Colin, 1997).

62 Benjamin Grob-Fitzgibbon, *Imperial Endgame: Britain's Dirty Wars and the End of Empire* (New York: Palgrave Macmillan, 2011), 351–53.

63 Marie-Monique Robin, *Des guerres d'Indochine et d'Algérie aux dictatures d'Amérique latine*. On Sétif and the failure to reform, see Evans, *Algeria*, 91–94.

64 According to some accounts, warnings in October 1954 by police intelligence in Algeria that terrorist attacks were being planned for November 1 were not taken seriously by Paris. http://encyclopedie-afn.org/index.php/FLN.

65 Evans, *Algeria*, 138–43, 155, 162

66 Galula, *Pacification in Algeria*, v.

67 Evans, *Algeria*, 134, 219–20.

68 Guy Pervillé, "Le terrorisme urbain dans la guerre d'Algérie (1954–1962)," in Jauffret and Vïasse (eds.), *Militaires et guérilla*, 457–61; Evans, *Algeria*, 181–83, 201–203.

69 Pervillé, "Le terrorisme urbain dans la guerre d'Algérie," 460.

70 Evans, *Algeria*, 134, 209–15.

71 Marie-Catherine Villatoux and Paul Villatoux, "Le 5e Bureau en Algérie," in Jauffret and Vaïsse (eds.), *Militaires et guérilla*, 403–404; Evans, *Algeria*, 216–25.

72 Thénault, *Histoire de la guerre d'indépendance Algérienne*, 132–50; Charles-Robert Ageron argues that the impact on popular opinion was more ambiguous. In the short term, the "victory" over the FLN caused a blip of support for the war. But the long-term trend apparent by 1957 was one of pessimism over the future of *Algérie française*. The Battle of Algiers was one of several factors that began to shift public opinion against the war in 1956, that included the spring 1956 call-up of the reserves, the extension of conscription, and higher taxes to pay for the war. Ageron, "L'opinion française á travers les sondages," in Rioux (ed.), *La guerre d'Algérie et les Français*, 28–32.

73 Mathias, *Galula in Algeria*, 16, 29, 29–30, 47–49, 95.

74 Alistair Horne, *A Savage War of Peace: Algeria 1954–1962* (London: Macmillan, 1977), 220–21, 254, 332, 338–39.

75 Joly, *Guerres d'Afrique*, 277–78.

76 Mathias, *Galula in Algeria*, 94.

77 Thénault, *Histoire de la guerre d'indépendance Algérienne*; Jauffret and Vaïsse (eds.), *Militaires et guerilla*, 96–97.

78 Galula, *Pacification in Algeria*, v, xxi.

79 Galula, *Pacification in Algeria*, vi.

80 Evans, *Algeria*, 249–50

81 Evans, *Algeria*, 126, 173–75, 234, 249–50.

82 Evans, *Algeria*, ix, 94–95, 112, 254–55.

83 How can women feel liberated when their culture is under assault and their men humiliated and arrested, their families deprived of income and male protection? And what exactly did Galula mean by "emancipation"? The three female bombers portrayed in Gilio Pontecorvo's 1966 film *The Battle of Algiers* – Djamila Bouhired, Zohra Drif Bitat, and Hassiba Ben Bouali – were all "emancipated" women educated in French *lycées* and/or at university. The fact that they could "pass for French" is precisely why they were useful to the insurgency.

84 www.quotationspage.com/quote/38140.html.

85 Joly, *Guerres d'Afrique*, 22; Ted Swedenburg, *Memories of Revolt: The 1936–1939 Rebellion and the Palestinian National Past* (Minneapolis and London: University of Minnesota Press, 1995), 78–79, 193–94, 200–201.

86 Andrew J. Bacevich, *Washington Rules: America's Path to Permanent War* (New York: Metropolitan Books, 2010), 201.

87 Mathias notes that public works projects and medical visits were the most successful part of Galula's counterinsurgency strategy. But they were able to proceed only after a huge deployment of troops, and with the acquiescence of the FLN. Periodic budget gaps forced their suspension, which threw people out of work and made French promises of a better life ring hollow. And they failed to solved the basic political problems. *Galula in Algeria*, 27–28.

88 Andrew J. Bacevich, *The New American Militarism: How Americans Are Seduced by War* (Oxford University Press, 2005), 218.

89 Raphaëlle Branche, "La lutte contre le terrorisme urbain," in Jauffret and Vaïsse (eds.), *Militaires et guérilla*, 476–81. The police in Algeria were recruited principally among the *pied noir* population with whom they were in cahoots, and resisted incorporating reinforcements from metropolitan France whom they believed insufficiently devoted to the cause of *Algérie française*. Jacques Delarue, "La Police en paravent et au rampart," in Rioux (ed.), *La guerre d'Algérie et les français*, 257–63.

90 Galula, *Pacification in Algeria*, vi.

91 Evans, *Algeria*, 126.

92 Galula, *Pacification in Algeria*, vi.

93 Villatoux and Villatoux, "Le 5e Bureau en Algérie," 399–405.

94 Mathias, *Galula in Algeria*, 37.

95 Evans, *Algeria*, 128–30.

96 Social Catholicism dates from the nineteenth century as an outlook that espoused social justice within a conservative, paternalistic social order, without recourse to radical wealth redistribution and social re-engineering. Lacheroy was a member of both the Cité Catholique and the right-wing Action Française. Thénault, *Histoire de la guerre d'indépendance Algérienne*, 95.

97 Paret, *French Revolutionary Warfare*, 7, 25–28.

98 David Betz's contribution in Manea, "Pros and Cons on Galula Model," *Small Wars & Insurgencies* (November 23, 2010), http://smallwarsjournal.com/blog/pros-and-cons-on-galula-model.

99 By May 1959, 71 percent of Frenchmen polled wanted a negotiated end to the war. By January 1960, only 7 percent believed that the integration of Algeria and France was desirable. Ageron, "L'opinion française à travers les sondages," 34–35.

100 Joly, *Guerres d'Afrique*, 285–86.

101 Thénault, *Histoire de la guerre d'indépendance Algérienne*, 214

102 Jacques Vernet, "Les barrages pendant la guerre d'Algérie," 256–68; Sadek Sellam, "La situation de la wilaya 4 du moment de l'affaire Si Salah (1958–1960)," 181–83; Daho Djerbal, "Les maquis du Nort-Constantinois face aux grandes opérations de ratissage du plan Challe (1959–1960)," in Jauffret and Vaïsse (eds.), *Militaires et guérilla*, 199–215.

103 Stephen T. Hosmer and Sibylle O. Crane, *Counterinsurgency: A Symposium, April 16–20 1962* (Washington, DC: Rand Corporation, 2006). Quoted in Mathias, *Galula in Algeria*, 100.

104 Daniel Lefebvre, "L'échec du plan de Constantine," in Rioux (ed.), *La guerre d'Algérie et les français*, 320–24.

105 Paret, *French Revolutionary Warfare*, 96.

106 Galula, *Pacification in Algeria*, xxiii.

107 Constantine Melnick, *The French Campaign against the FLN* (Santa Monica, CA: Rand Corporation, 1967), 21. Quoted in Marlowe, *David Galula*, 38.

108 Thénault, *Histoire de la guerre d'indépendance Algérienne*, 165–68. For other interprétations, see Jean Lacouture, *De Gaulle: The Ruler 1945–1970* (New York: Norton, 1991), 243, 247, 330; Richard Vivinen, *France, 1934–1970* (New York: St. Martin's Press, 1996), 162.

109 Paret, *French Revolutionary Warfare*, 37, 77–80.

110 Thénault, *Histoire de la guerre d'indépendance Algérienne*, 197–204.

111 d'Abzac-Epezy, "La société militaire," 250.

112 Vaïsse, *Comment de Gaulle fit échouer le putsch d'Alger*, 297–98.

113 Paret, *French Revolutionary Warfare*, 21.

6 Vietnam and counterinsurgency

1 Richard Duncan Downie, *Learning from Conflict: The U.S. Military in Vietnam, El Salvador, and the Drug War* (Westport, CT: Praeger, 1998).

2 Peter D. Feaver, "The Right to Be Right: Civil-Military Relations and the Iraq Surge Decision," *International Security*, 35:4 (Spring 2011), 87–125.

3 Vincent Joly, *Guerres d'Afrique: 130 ans de guerres coloniales – l'experience française* (Rennes: Presses Universitaires de Rennes, 2009), 262.

4 David Kaiser, *American Tragedy: Kennedy, Johnson, and the Origins of the Vietnam War* (Cambridge, MA: Harvard University Press, 2000), 58–62, 125.

5 David W. Hogan, Jr., "Head and Heart: The Dilemmas of American Attitudes toward War," *The Journal of Military History*, 75 (October 2011), 1042–43.

6 Rostow was one of the founders of "developmental economics." Ha-Joon Chang, *Kicking Away the Ladder: Development Strategy in Historical Perspective* (London: Anthem Press, 2006), 7.

7 Kaiser, *American Tragedy*, 69, 461–62.

8 Mark Atwood Lawrence, *Assuming the Burden: Europe and the American Commitment to the War in Vietnam* (Berkeley: University of California Press, 2005), 284.

9 Lt. Col. Paul Yingling, "A Failure in Generalship," *Armed Forces Journal* (May 2007), www.afji.com/2007/05/2635198.

10 Downie, *Learning from Conflict*, 5–6, 11, 47, 51, 55.

11 Carl von Clausewitz, *On War*, ed. and trans. Michael Howard and Peter Paret (New York: Everyman's Library, 1993), 101.

12 Lewis Sorley, *Westmoreland: The General Who Lost Vietnam* (Boston and New York: Houghton Mifflin Harcourt, 2011), 78–81, 107.

13 John A. Nagl, "Counterinsurgency in Vietnam: American Organizational Culture and Learning," in Daniel Marston and Carter Malkasian (eds.), *Counterinsurgency in Modern Warfare* (Oxford: Osprey Publishing, 2008), 141.

14 F. J. West, Jr., *The Village* (New York: Harper and Row, 1972).

15 Nagl, "Counterinsurgency in Vietnam," 143; for a more sympathetic assessment of Abrams, see Lewis Sorley, *A Better War: The Unexamined Victories and Final Tragedy of America's Last Years in Vietnam* (New York and London: Harcourt Brace & Company, 1999).

16 Hogan, "Head and Heart," 1042–43, 1046.

17 Sandy Sandler, *To Free from Oppression: A Concise History of U.S. Army Special Forces, Civil Affairs, Psychological Operations, and the John F. Kennedy Special Warfare Center and School* (Fort Bragg, NC: US Army Special Operations Command, 1994), 56–65.

18 Probably the most succinct statement of this view is to be found in Nagl, "Counterinsurgency in Vietnam," 131–48, which is a restatement of his

conclusions in *Counter-insurgency Lessons from Malaya and Vietnam: Learning to Eat Soup with a Knife* (Westport, CT: Praeger, 2002), 115–90; also, Andrew Krepinevich, "Recovery from Defeat: The U.S. Army in Vietnam," in George Andreopoulos and Harold Selesky (eds.), *Aftermath of Defeat: Societies, Armed Forces and the Challenge of Recovery* (New Haven, CT: Yale University Press, 1994), 124–42. This is a more succinct summary of his conclusion in *The Army and Vietnam* (Baltimore, MD and London: Johns Hopkins University Press, 1986). See also George Herring, "The 1st Cavalry and the Ia Drang Valley, 18 October–24 November 1965," in Andreopoulous and Selesky (eds.), *Aftermath of Defeat*, 300–26; Sorley, *A Better War*.

19 The most thorough study was provided by Eric M. Bergerud, *The Dynamics of Defeat: The Vietnam War in Hau Nghia Province* (Boulder, CO: Westview Press, 1990), which in many respects was a direct rebuttal, although focused on one province, of Krepinevich, *The Army and Vietnam*.

20 Gregory A. Daddis, "Eating Soup with a Spoon: The U.S. Army as a 'Learning Organization' in the Vietnam War," paper delivered at the Annual Conference of the Society for Military History, 2011, 6–8, www.smh2011.org/program.html; Andrew J. Birtle, *U.S. Army Counterinsurgency and Contingency Operations Doctrine 1942–1976* (Washington, DC: US Army Center of Military History, 2007), 257, 261, 265; for a comprehensive overview of the 1960s COIN literature, see Anne Marlowe, *David Galula: His Life and Intellectual Context* (Carlisle Barracks, PA: Strategic Studies Institute, 2010), 13–20.

21 Paul Dixon, "'Hearts and Minds'? British Counter-Insurgency from Malay to Iraq," *Journal of Strategic Studies*, 32:3 (June 2009), 356–61.

22 Downie, *Learning from Conflict*, 50–57.

23 Daddis, "Eating Soup with a Spoon./www.smh2011.org/program.html."

24 On Westmoreland's support for pacification, see Birtle, *U.S. Army Counterinsurgency*, 387, 397; on lack of options, Dale Andrade, "Westmoreland Was Right," *Small Wars & Insurgencies*, 19:2 (June 3, 2008), 145–81.

25 Galula's area was judged to be "not very dangerous." The French maintained six battalions in the Kabylia that contained Galula's sector, plus a mobile counter-guerrilla unit that could come to the aid of distressed posts. Galula distributed his men in groups of twenty to twenty-five soldiers, strong enough to defend themselves against ALN who probably could muster no more than a platoon. Besides, the ALN were very poorly armed, in contrast to the VC/NVA. Grégor Mathias, *Galula in Algeria: Counterinsurgency Practice versus Theory* (Santa Barbara, CA: Praeger, 2011), 17, 19, 23, 92.

26 Bergerud, *The Dynamics of Defeat*, 33–38, 50–53.

27 Daddis, "Eating Soup with a Spoon," 18–19.

28 Jeffrey A. Lefebvre, "Kennedy's Algerian Dilemma: Containment, Alliance Politics, and the 'Rebel Dialogue'," *Middle Eastern Studies*, 35:2 (1999), 61–82,

www.jstor.org/pss/4284004. Kennedy did not oppose COIN per se, but he believed that France's efforts to hold onto Algeria jepoardized the West's standing in the non-aligned world.

29 Mao Tse-tung and Che Guevara, *Guerilla Warfare* (London: Cassell, 1961), xi–xiii, xvi.

30 Peter Paret, *French Revolutionary Warfare from Indochina to Algeria: The Analysis of the Political and Military Doctrine* (New York: Praeger, 1964), 7–8.

31 Bergerud, *The Dynamics of Defeat*, 55–56. Bergerud argues (325–35) that although he studies a single province, "Hau Nghia ...was quite typical of the entire upper Mekong Delta, the heartland of the insurgency... it was exactly the type of province within which the Americans and the GVN had to prevail, within a reasonable amount of time, in order to be victorious."

32 Peter Paret and John W. Shy, *Guerrillas in the 1960s* (New York: Praeger, 1962), 4–5, 60–61, 65–66, 71.

33 James H. Lebovic notes that promoting "coup fears" is a well-recognized tactic for enhancing host government influence over the intervener. *The Limits of U.S. Military Capability: Lessons from Vietnam and Iraq* (Baltimore, MD: Johns Hopkins University Press, 2010), 211.

34 Kaiser, *American Tragedy*, 126,150–52, 157–59, 161, 178, 193, 195.

35 Kaiser, *American Tragedy*, 153–57.

36 Stanley Karnow, *Vietnam: A History* (New York: Penguin, 1997), 246, 273–74.

37 Nagl, "Counterinsurgency in Vietnam," 135–36

38 Krepinevich, *The Army and Vietnam*, 24.

39 Kaiser, *American Tragedy*, 168–78, 208.

40 Sorley, *Westmoreland*, 301–303.

41 Daddis, "Eating Soup with a Spoon," 10–11.

42 Kaiser, *American Tragedy*, 181–85.

43 Kaiser, *American Tragedy*, 162, 347–48, 356.

44 Herring, "The 1st Cavalry and the Ia Drang Valley," 325.

45 Bergerud, *The Dynamics of Defeat*, 332.

46 Bergerud, *The Dynamics of Defeat*, 164–65. *The Dynamics of Defeat* goes unmentioned in Ann Marlowe's otherwise comprehensive historiographic review of the literature that shaped the strategy and interpretation of the Vietnam War, although far more than Summers, Bergerud provided the emphatic scholarly refutation of Krepinevich.

47 Bergerud, *The Dynamics of Defeat*, 141–42, 156–62, 166–67, 262–68.

48 Bergerud, *The Dynamics of Defeat*, 334.

49 Bergerud, *The Dynamics of Defeat*, 152–57, 171–73.

50 Lebovic, *The Limits of U.S. Military Capability*, 36–37, 101–104; Douglas Blaufarb, *The Counterinsurgency Era: U.S. Doctrine and Performance, 1950 to the Present* (New York: Free Press, 1977), 271–72.

51 Major General Nguyen Duy Hinh and Brigadier General Tran Dinh Tho, *The South Vietnamese Society* (Washington, DC: US Army Center of Military History, 1980); Lewis Sorley (ed.), *The Vietnam War: An Assessment by South Vietnam's Generals* (Lubbock: Texas Tech University Press, 2010), 723; Martin G. Clemis, "Violent Pacification: Force, Coercion, and the 'Other War' in Vietnam, 1968–1972," paper delivered at the 78th Annual Meeting of the Society of Military History, June 10, 2010; Bergerud, *The Dynamics of Defeat*, 178–79.

52 Kaiser, *American Tragedy*, 192.

53 Bergerud, *The Dynamics of Defeat*, 225–27, 268–72; Daddis, "Eating Soup with a Spoon," 10–11, 14–15.

54 Lebovic, *The Limits of U.S. Military Capability*, 207.

55 Bergerud, *The Dynamics of Defeat*, 327.

56 Hogan, "Head and Heart," 1046.

57 Krepinevich, *The Army in Vietnam*, 259; see also, Krepinevich "Recovery from Defeat," 125–34. Others who shared this view in the years immediately following the end of the war include William Colby, *Honorable Men: My Life in the CIA* (New York: Simon & Schuster, 1978) and *Lost Victory: A Firsthand Account of America's Sixteen-Year Involvement in Vietnam* (Chicago: Contemporary Books, 1989); Robert Komer, *Bureaucracy at War: U.S. Performance in the Vietnam Conflict* (Boulder, CO: Westview Press, 1986); Guenter Lewy, *America in Vietnam* (New York: Oxford University Press, 1980).

58 Harry Summers, *On Strategy: An Analysis of the Vietnam War* (Novato, CA: Presidio Press, 1982). For Krepinevich's criticisms, see *The Army in Vietnam*, 262–64.

59 Nagl, *Learning to Eat Soup with a Knife*, 27.

60 Lebovic, *The Limits of U.S. Military Capability*, 38–39, 207.

61 Bergerud, *The Dynamics of Defeat*, 327–28.

62 Bergerud, *The Dynamics of Defeat*, 323–24.

63 Bergerud, *The Dynamics of Defeat*, 332.

64 Bergerud, *The Dynamics of Defeat*, 335.

65 Lebovic, *The Limits of U.S. Military Capability*, 2–3.

66 Kaiser, *American Tragedy*, 128, 206–207, 493.

7 Counterinsurgency in Latin America

1 Miguel La Serna, *Corner of the Living: Ayachchu on the Eve of the Shining Path Insurgency* (Chapel Hill: University of North Carolina Press, 2012), 16, 124, 149, 182.

2 Cecilia Menjivar and Nestor Rodriguez (eds.), *When States Kill: Latin America, the U.S. and Technologies of Terror* (Austin: University of Texas Press, 2005), 5,

11–13; Eric Stener Carlson, "The Influence of French 'Revolutionary War' Ideology on the Use of Torture in Argentina's 'Dirty War'," *Human Rights Review* (July–September 2000), 71–84; David Pion-Berlin, "The National Security Doctrine, Military Threat Perception, and the 'Dirty War' in Argentina," *Comparative Political Studies*, 21:3 (October 1988), 382–407; David Pion-Berlin, "Latin American National Security Doctrines: Hard and Softline Themes," *Armed Forces & Society* 15:3 (Spring 1989), 411–29; John M. Baines, "U.S. Military Assistance to Latin America: An Assessment," *Journal of Interamerican Studies and World Affairs*, 14:2 (November 1972), 469–87.

3 Bryce Wood, *The Making of the Good Neighbor Policy* (New York: W.W. Norton, 1967).

4 Baines, "U.S. Military Assistance to Latin America," 471.

5 Menjivar and Rodriguez (eds.), *When States Kill*, 10.

6 Bryce Wood, *The Dismantling of the Good Neighbor Policy* (Austin: University of Texas Press, 1985), 150–55.

7 Felipe Fernandez-Armesto, *The Americas: A Hemispheric History* (New York: The Modern Library, 2003), 133–36.

8 Daniel Moran, *Wars of National Liberation* (London: Cassell, 2001), 144–45.

9 Timothy P. Wickham-Crowley, *Guerrillas and Revolution in Latin America: A Comparative Study of Insurgents and Regimes since 1956* (Princeton University Press, 1992), 313–14.

10 Horacio Verbitsky, "Breaking the Silence: The Catholic Church in Argentina and the 'Dirty War'," *Open Democracy* (July 28, 2005), 3–4, www.opendemocracy. net/content/articles/PDF/2709.pdf. Mario Ranalletti, "Aux origins du terrorisme d'état en Argentine," *Vingtième siècle*, No. 105 (January–March 2010), 45–56.

11 Menjivar and Rodriguez (eds.), *When States Kill*, 14–15; Martin Evans, *Algeria: France's Undeclared War* (Oxford University Press, 2012), 350.

12 Pion-Berlin, "The National Security Doctrine," 385–87.

13 Michel Foucher, *Fronts et frontières: un tour du monde géopolitique* (Paris: Fayard, 1991), 27; Jack Child, *Geopolitics and Conflict in South America: Quarrels among Neighbors* (New York: Praeger, 1985), 5, 7–8.

14 Menjivar and Rodriguez (eds.), *When States Kill*, 15.

15 Menjivar and Rodriguez (eds.), *When States Kill*, 5. The School of the Americans (SOA) evolved from the Latin American Training Center-Ground Division created in Panama in 1946, renamed SOA in 1963. It relocated to Fort Benning, GA, in 1984. Courses included sniper and commando training, psychological warfare and interrogation techniques. SOA was renamed the Western Hemisphere Institute for Security Cooperation in January 2001 with a curriculum that aimed to strengthen democratic governance, the rule of law, and human rights. Nevertheless, "SOA graduates have been among Latin America's worst human rights abusers, including the most notorious dictators of the region," according to Menjivar and Rodrigues (19–20). On the influence of

French military counterinsurgency theory of *la guerre révolutionnaire* on the Argentine military, see Prudencio García, *El Drama de la autonomía militar* (Madrid: Alanzia Editorial, 1995), 85–106; also a 2003 television documentary by Marie-Monique Robin, *The Death Squads: The French School*, and the book *Les Escadrons de la mort, l'école française* (Paris: La Découverte, 2004).

16 Child, *Geopolitics and Conflict in South America*, 11.

17 Menjivar and Rodriguez (eds.), *When States Kill*, 29.

18 Baines, "U.S. Military Assistance to Latin America," 483–84.

19 Menjivar and Rodriguez (eds.), *When States Kill*, 21.

20 Baines, "U.S. Military Assistance to Latin America," 479.

21 Pion-Berlin, "Latin American National Security Doctrines," 414–16. Army General Alberto Ruiz Novoa in 1965 and General Álvaro Valencia Tovar in 1975; Jorge E. Delgado, "Military Civic Action: Development of Strategy in the Colombian Army, 1955–65" (Master's thesis, King's College London, 2011), 17, 20.

22 David R. Mares, "The National Security State," in Tom Holloway (ed.), *A Companion to Latin American History* (Oxford: Blackwell, 2007), 387–88.

23 J. Patrice McSherry, "Operation Condor," in Menjivar and Rodriguez (eds.), *When States Kill*, 29–56, 92.

24 Wickham-Crowley, *Guerrillas and Revolution in Latin America*, 116–17, 129, 137, 150–51, 182–83, 204–205; see also Jon Lee Anderson, *Che Guevara: A Revolutionary Life* (New York: Grove Press, 1997).

25 Donald A. Selvage, "Che Guevara in Bolivia" (Quantico, VA: USMC Command and Staff College, April 1, 1985), http://casarrubea.files.wordpress.com/2008/09/us-marines-on-che-1985.pdf. For documents on Che's capture, see www.gwu.edu/~nsarchiv/NSAEBB/NSAEBB5/index.html#declass.

26 On Lawrence, see David Fromkin, "The Importance of T. E. Lawrence," *The New Criterion Online* (September 10, 1991), www.newcriterion.com/archive/10/sept91/fromkin.htm.

27 CIA report quoted in Henry Butterfield Ryan, *The Fall of Che Guevara: A Story of Soldiers, Spies, and Diplomats* (New York and Oxford: Oxford University Press, 1998), 164.

28 Anderson, *Che Guevara*, 752–53.

29 Wickham-Crowley, *Guerrillas and Revolution in Latin America*, 313.

30 Luis Alberto Villamarín, *Cóndor en el aire* (Bogotá: Talleres de TM Editores, 1999), 143, 280–83; Vera Grabe, *Razonas de vida* (Bogotá: Planeta, 2000), 142–46.

31 Piero Gleijeses, *Conflicting Missions: Havana, Washington, and Africa, 1959–1976* (Chapel Hill: University of North Carolina Press, 2002), 391–93.

32 Matthew Rosenberg, "Afghan Soldiers Step up Killing of U.S. Forces," *New York Times*, January 20, 2010, www.nytimes.com/2012/01/20/world/asia/afghan-soldiers-step-up-killings-of-allied-forces.html?_r=1&scp=2&sq=

afghanist; Jeffrey Bordin, "A Crisis of Trust and Cultural Incompatibility: A Red Team Study of Mutual Perceptions of Afghan National Security Force Personnel and U.S. Soldiers in Understanding and Mitigating the Phenomena of ANSF-Committed Fratricide-Murders," May 12, 2011, www.michaelyon-online.com/images/pdf/trust-incompatibility.pdf; on animosity between US and ARVN soldiers, see Bergerud, *The Dynamics of Defeat*, 226–34.

33 See Douglas Porch, "The Hunt for Martín Caballero," *The Journal of Strategic Studies* (2012), 1–28.

34 Dion Nissenbaum, "Report Sees Danger in Local Allies," *Wall Street Journal*, June 17, 2011, http://online.wsj.com/article/SB10001424052702303499204576389763385348524.html.

35 Hal Brands, "Reform, Democratization, and Counter-Insurgency: Evaluating the US Experience in Cold War-era Latin America," *Small Wars and Insurgencies*, 22:2 (May 2011), 299.

36 Richard Duncan Downie, *Learning from Conflict: The U.S. Military in Vietnam, El Salvador, and the Drug War* (Westport, CT: Praeger, 1998), 130–83.

37 Downie, *Learning from Conflict*, 130.

38 Brands, "Reform, Democratization, and Counter-Insurgency," 299.

39 William Deane Stanley, "El Salvador: State-Building before and after Democratisation, 1980–1995," *Third World Quarterly*, 27:1 (August 2006), 101–14.

40 Brands, "Reform, Democratization, and Counter-Insurgency," 311–13.

8 COIN as the British way of war

1 Sir Robert Thompson, *Defeating Communist Insurgency: The Lessons of Malaya and Vietnam* (New York: Praeger, 1966), 50–57; David French, *The British Way in Counter-Insurgency, 1945–1967* (Oxford University Press, 2011), 64. I would like to thank Professor French for generously sharing the proofs of his book with me.

2 French, *The British Way in Counter-Insurgency*, 3–5, 206, 247–48.

3 Thomas R. Mockaitis, *British Counterinsurgency, 1919–60* (New York: St. Martin's Press, 1990), 9–10, 13–14, 23, 45–47, 50, 52, 55–57, 63–64.

4 Richard Duncan Downie, *Learning from Conflict: The U.S. Military in Vietnam, El Salvador, and the Drug War* (Westport, CT: Praeger, 1998), 11–12; Mockaitis, *British Counterinsurgency*, 174–75. Mockaitis does argue (184–89) that decentralization and disdain for doctrine inhibited transmission of experience in the British Army in the inter- and postwar years.

5 Ministry of Defense, *Army Field Manual Volume 1 Combined Arms Operations, Part 10 Counter Insurgency Operations: Strategic and Operational Guidelines,*

B-2-1 July 2001. Quoted in French, *The British Way in Counter-Insurgency*, 251–52.

6 John A. Nagl, *Learning to Eat Soup with a Knife: Counterinsurgency Lessons from Malaya and Vietnam* (London and Chicago: University of Chicago Press, 2005), xiii, 216.

7 Mockaitis, *British Counterinsurgency*, 74–76.

8 D. G. Boyce, *Englishmen and Irish Troubles: British Public Opinion and the Making of Irish Policy 1918–22* (Cambridge, MA: MIT Press, 1972), 140, 180–81.

9 Nagl, *Learning to Eat Soup with a Knife*, 218.

10 Max Hastings, *Winston's War: Churchill 1940–1945* (New York: Knopf, 2010), 217 and *passim*.

11 Mockaitis, *British Counterinsurgency*, 188.

12 Mockaitis, *British Counterinsurgency*, 180.

13 French, *The British Way in Counter-Insurgency*, 210–13, 215–18, 248.

14 Timothy H. Parsons, *The Rule of Empires: Those Who Built Them, Those Who Endured Them, and Why They Always Fall* (Oxford University Press, 2010), 345; Caroline Elkins, *Imperial Reckoning: The Untold Story of Britain's Gulag in Kenya* (New York: Henry Holt, 2005), 353.

15 David Anderson, *Histories of the Hanged: Britain's Dirty War in Kenya and the End of Empire* (London: Weidenfeld & Nicolson, 2005), 257–61.

16 Christopher Bayly and Tim Harper attribute the British "victory" in Malaya to a policy of repression and deportation, and the egregious failure of the Malayan Communist Party to build a cross-communal coalition and collect the funds necessary to finance insurrection. *Forgotten Wars: The End of Britain's Asian Empire* (London: Penguin, 2007). Anderson (*Histories of the Hanged*, 6) argues that the British pursued a brutal war stripped of human rights protection "while maintaining the appearance of accountability, transparency, and justice."

17 Bayly and Harper, *Forgotten Wars*, 358–70.

18 Bayly and Harper, *Forgotten Wars*, 239–40; John Newsinger speculates that had the MCP/MPAJA attempted to take power in 1945, the British would have used Japanese troops against them, as they had in Indonesia. *British Counterinsurgency from Palestine to Northern Ireland* (New York: Palgrave, 2002), 34–35.

19 Newsinger estimates the decision to rebel was taken between the disappearance of MCP leader Lai Tek and November 1947. *British Counterinsurgency*, 39; Bayly and Harper, *Forgotten Wars*, 418.

20 After Mao's 1949 victory, Chinese officials were bribed to take deportees. French, *The British Way in Counter-Insurgency*, 110; Bayly and Harper (*Forgotten Wars*, 427, 433–35, 482–84, 512–14) note that nationalists troops came on board "armed to the teeth," while most deported Malayan Chinese assumed that deportation was a death sentence before 1949.

21 The British translated it as the Malayan Races Liberation Army (MRLA).

22 Malays in *kampongs* often saw Chinese squatters as intruding on their sovereignty. Bayly and Harper, *Forgotten Wars*, 422.

23 Newsinger, *British Counterinsurgency*, 41–45; Bayly and Harper, *Forgotten Wars*, 433–35, 473.

24 Bayly and Harper, *Forgotten Wars*, 427.

25 Bayly and Harper, *Forgotten Wars*, 448 *passim*.

26 Benjamin John Grob-Fitzgibbon, *Imperial Endgame: Britain's Dirty Wars and the End of Empire* (New York: Palgrave Macmillan, 2011), 119–24.

27 Bayly and Harper, *Forgotten Wars*, 317; on "White Terror," 433–35, on military veterans in the police, 438–39, 484–88, 479. On the lack of police/army cooperation, see French, *The British Way in Counter-Insurgency*, 101–103.

28 Grob-Fitzgibbon, *Imperial Endgame*, 126–27.

29 Mockaitis, *British Counterinsurgency*, 9.

30 Nagl, *Learning to Eat Soup with a Knife*, 216.

31 Thompson, *Defeating Communist Insurgency*, 111–13.

32 Grob-Fitzgibbon, *Imperial Endgame*, 160, 177, 198–201.

33 Grob-Fitzgibbon, *Imperial Endgame*, 116.

34 Bayly and Harper, *Forgotten Wars*, 490–98; Triads were given free rein in many settlements because the police saw them as a brake on MCP influence (491).

35 Newsinger, *British Counterinsurgency*, 58–59.

36 Moran, *Wars of National Liberation* (London: Cassell, 2001), 91.

37 Bayly and Harper, *Forgotten Wars*, 476.

38 Bayly and Harper, *Forgotten Wars*, 501–11; French, *The British Way in Counter-Insurgency*, 193–94, 198.

39 Anderson, *Histories of the Hanged*, 5.

40 Parsons, *The Rule of Empires*, 307, 324–27.

41 Anderson, *Histories of the Hanged*, 13–37; Parsons, *The Rule of Empires*, 329, 339.

42 Parsons, *The Rule of Empires*, 331–37.

43 French, *The British Way in Counter-Insurgency*, 93.

44 Newsinger, *British Counterinsurgency*, 63–64; French, *The British Way in Counter-Insurgency*, 115

45 Only 32 white settlers were murdered and 26 wounded during the emergency, compared to 1,819 loyalists officially killed and 916 wounded. Anderson, *Histories of the Hanged*, 84.

46 Elkins, *Imperial Reckoning*, xv–xvi.

47 French, *The British Way in Counter-Insurgency*, 60–62, 72, 147, 152, 154, 158.

48 An army-led inquiry blamed bad apples in the KPR for incidents of excessive violence. In any case, there was little stomach for prosecuting soldiers who the public felt had been put in a difficult situation. French, *The British Way in Counter-Insurgency*, 168–69, 222–24.

49 French, *The British Way in Counter-Insurgency*, 80.

50 Elkins, *Imperial Reckoning*, 314.

51 Anderson, *Histories of the Hanged*, 200–25. Wages also rose in the capital, although whether this was the result of a shortage of labor caused by Anvil, or the product of reforms suggested by the 1954 Carpenter Committee on African Wages and encouraged by the government sponsorship of a more moderate trades union movement is unclear. Newsinger, *British Counterinsurgency*, 75–76.

52 Elkins, *Imperial Reckoning*, xiv, 59, 235–65.

53 Newsinger (*British Counterinsurgency*, 76) seems to see the land transfer as part of a deliberate "carrot" strategy to create a Kikuyu rural middle class. Anderson (*Histories of the Hanged*, 271–72, 293–94) holds out the possibility that land transfer was a far less transparent process of power consolidation by the chiefs and even white settlers. French (*The British Way in Counter-Insurgency*, 194–96) argues that the British concluded that without land reform, the insurgency would drag on and the insurgents would continue to hold out in the bush.

54 French, *The British Way in Counter-Insurgency*, 109, 122, 163, 172, 186.

55 Anderson, *Histories of the Hanged*, 252–57, 270–71.

56 Anderson, *Histories of the Hanged*, 282–83.

57 Elkins, *Imperial Reckoning*, 316–50.

58 Anderson, *Histories of the Hanged*, 284–86, 292, 296–320.

59 Elkins, *Imperial Reckoning*, 353.

60 Newsinger, *British Counterinsurgency*, 82–83; French, *The British Way in Counter-Insurgency*, 232–38.

61 James S. Corum, *Training Indigenous Forces in Counterinsurgency: A Tale of Two Insurgencies* (Carlisle Barracks, PA: Strategic Studies Institute, March 2006), 32.

62 Elkins, *Imperial Reckoning*, 351; Newsinger, *British Counterinsurgency*, 85–107.

63 Hew Strachan, *The Politics of the British Army* (Oxford University Press, 1997), 181.

64 French, *The British Way in Counter-Insurgency*, 250–51.

65 French, *The British Way in Counter-Insurgency*, 6; Bayly and Harper (*Forgotten Wars*) attribute the British "victory" in Malaya to a policy of repression and deportation, and the egregious failure of the MCP to build a cross-communal coalition and collect the funds necessary to finance insurrection. Newsinger (*British Counterinsurgency from Palestine to Northern Ireland*, Chapter 2) argues that the MCP never developed an urban campaign nor reached out to the Malay community, but instead simply retreated into the jungle where their logistical problems and lack of military experienced doomed them to defeat.

66 French, *The British Way in Counter-Insurgency*, 101–102, 250.

9 Britain's Thirty Years War in Northern Ireland

1 John Bew, "The Limits of COIN and the Northern Ireland Experience," presentation given at "Reassessing Counterinsurgency: Theory and Practice" workshop hosted by the Robert S. Strauss Center for International Security and Law, University of Texas, June 7–9, 2012; on coercive counterinsurgency as part of the modus operandi of the British Army, see David French, *The British Way in Counter-Insurgency, 1945–1967* (Oxford University Press, 2012), 247–48.

2 Quoted in Maureen Dowd, "The Wearing of the Green," *New York Times*, June 30, 2012, www.nytimes.com/2012/07/01/opinion/sunday/the-wearing-of-the-green.html.

3 John Newsinger, *British Counterinsurgency from Palestine to Northern Ireland* (New York: Palgrave, 2002), 157–58.

4 John Bew, Martyn Frampton, and Iñigo Gurruchaga, *Talking to Terrorists: Making Peace in Northern Ireland and the Basque Country* (London: Hurst & Company, 2009), 36–37; Peter Neumann, *Britain's Long War: British Strategy in the Northern Ireland Conflict 1969–98* (Gordonsville, VA: Palgrave Macmillan, 2004), 65–67.

5 Neumann, *Britain's Long War*, 21, 26, 29, 32–33, 45.

6 Neumann, *Britain's Long War*, 51.

7 Newsinger, *British Counterinsurgency*, 128–29.

8 Martin Evans, *Algeria: France's Undeclared War* (Oxford University Press, 2012), xv.

9 Neumann, *Britain's Long War*, 27–29, 46.

10 Neumann, *Britain's Long War*, 55–57.

11 Interviews with John Bew and Paul Schulte, former member of the Northern Ireland Office, June 8, 2012, Austin, Texas.

12 Andrew Munford, *Puncturing the Counterinsurgency Myth: Britain and Irregular Warfare in the Past, Present and Future* (Carlisle Barracks, PA: Strategic Studies Institute, September 2011), 5.

13 Newsinger, *British Counterinsurgency*, 160.

14 Ministry of Defence, *Operation Banner: An Analysis of Military Operations in Northern Ireland* (London: MOD, 2006) 8.11, 8.3, 8.20–21, 8.5–6, www.vilaweb.cat/media/attach/vwedts/docs/op_banner_analysis_released.pdf. "Army Paper Says IRA Not Defeated," BBC News, July 6, 2007, http://news.bbc.co.uk/2/hi/uk_news/northern_ireland/6276416.stm.

15 Frank Kitson, *Bunch of Five* (London: Faber & Faber, 1977), Chapter 23.

16 Kitson, *Bunch of Five*, 286.

17 Newsinger, *British Counterinsurgency*, 177–78.

18 Newsinger, *British Counterinsurgency*, 170. To which Kitson's response was that the alternative was to do nothing, which would have worsened the situation. Second, that reports of the soldiers' excesses were exaggerated by "enemy propaganda," 293, 302.

19 Colonel Richard Iron, "Britain's Longest War: Northern Ireland 1967–2007," in Daniel Marston and Carter Malkasian (eds.), *Counterinsurgency in Modern Warfare* (London and New York: Osprey, 2008), 169; MOD, *Operation Banner*, 8.1, 8.2; 8.11, 8.3.

20 Aaron Edwards, "Misapplying Lessons Learned? Analyzing the Utility of British Counterinsurgency Strategy in Northern Ireland, 1971–1976," *Small Wars & Insurgencies*, 21:2 (June 2010), 316.

21 Gerry Adams, *Before the Dawn* (London: Brandon Books, 1997), 126. Quoted in Newsinger, *British Counterinsurgency*, 169.

22 Neumann, *Britain's Long War*, 57.

23 Munford, *Puncturing the Counterinsurgency Myth*, 14.

24 Edwards, "Misapplying Lessons Learned?" 318.

25 Newsinger, *British Counterinsurgency*, 159–67.

26 MOD, *Operation Banner*, 8.11–12, 8.3; 8.13–17, 8.4; 8.20–21, 8.6; Huw Bennett, "The Reluctant Pupil? Britain's Army and Learning in Counter-insurgency," RUSI Military History Circle Commentary (October 2009), www.rusi.org/analysis/commentary/ref:C4AD22F8DF284C/; Neumann, *Britain's Long War*, 78–79.

27 Paddy Devlin, *Straight Left: An Autobiography* (Belfast: Blackstaff Press, 1994), 129–30. Quoted in Newsinger, *British Counterinsurgency*, 162; MOD, *Operation Banner*, 8.43, 8.11; Neumann, *Britain's Long War*, 61.

28 Edwards, "Misapplying Lessons Learned?" 318.

29 Huw Bennett, "'Smoke without Fire'? Allegations against the British Army in Northern Ireland, 1972–5," *Twentieth Century British History* (2012), 1–30; Neumann, *Britain's Long War*, 77; Bew *et al.*, *Talking to Terrorists*, 44–47.

30 Bew *et al.*, *Talking to Terrorists*, 73, 76.

31 Bew *et al.*, *Talking to Terrorists*, 54–62.

32 Lord Diplock, Report of the Commission to consider legal procedures to deal with terrorist activities in Northern Ireland, para 37.

33 Neumann, *Britain's Long War*, 85, 98; Bew *et al.*, *Talking to Terrorists*, 66–72.

34 Neumann, *Britain's Long War*, 85–87, 107.

35 MOD, *Operation Banner*, 2.44, 2.15.

36 Bew *et al.*, *Talking to Terrorists*, 71–72.

37 Bew *et al.*, *Talking to Terrorists*, 67; Neumann believes that the SAS was unfairly accused of some excesses. Nevertheless, the British government soon recognized

the disadvantages of SAS activities and began to scale back the use of SAS in 1978. Neumann, *Britain's Long War*, 106–107, 130–32.

38 The event that changed critical Catholic votes was the publication of the Bennett report on police brutality in Northern Ireland. Newsinger, *British Counterinsurgency*, 181–83. Others might argue that public sector strikes were a more important factor in the Thatcher victory. MOD, *Operation Banner*, 2.40, 2.41, 2.14.

39 Bew *et al.*, *Talking to Terrorists*, 88–95; MOD, *Operation Banner*, 2.40, 2.41, 2.14.

40 Neumann, *Britain's Long War*, 130–31.

41 Neumann, *Britain's Long War*, 133–36.

42 Communication with John Bew, June 14, 2010.

43 Interview with John Bew, Austin, Texas, June 12, 2012.

44 Bew *et al.*, *Talking to Terrorists*, 76, 110.

45 Bennett, "The Reluctant Pupil?"

46 Newsinger, *British Counterinsurgency*, 188–90.

47 Edward Moloney, *The Secret History of the IRA* (London: Penguin, 2007), 18–23; Iron, "Britain's Longest War," 183.

48 Neumann, *Britain's Long War*, 159.

49 Bew *et al.*, *Talking to Terrorists*, 109, 112–13, 149–66; Newsinger, *British Counterinsurgency*, 191–94.

50 Octavian Manea, "Counterinsurgency as a Whole of Government Approach: Notes on the British Army Field Manual Weltanschauung: An Interview with Colonel Alexander Alderson," *Small Wars Journal* (January 24, 2011), 8, http://smallwarsjournal.com/jrnl/art/counterinsurgency-as-a-whole-of-government-approach.

51 "Army Paper Says IRA Not Defeated," BBC News, July 6, 2007, http://news.bbc.co.uk/2/hi/uk_news/northern_ireland/6276416.stm.

52 Neumann, *Britain's Long War*, 180.

53 Newsinger, *British Counterinsurgency*, 182.

54 Iron, "Britain's Longest War," 183; MOD, *Operation Banner*, 8.16, 8.4; 8.55, 8.15.

55 Neumann, *Britain's Long War*, 108.

56 MOD, *Operation Banner*, 8.51, 8.14.

57 Neumann, *Britain's Long War,* 28. On the other hand, John Bew believes that Irish bombing attacks in Britain, especially the October 1984 bombing of the Grand Hotel in Brighton that was hosting Margaret Thatcher and much of the Conservative Party, paved the way for the Anglo-Irish Agreement of November 15, 1985. Interview with the author.

58 Newsinger, *British Counterinsurgency*, 190–92.

59 Munford, *Puncturing the Counterinsurgency Myth*, 4.

60 Bennett, "The Reluctant Pupil?"

61 Neumann, *Britain's Long War*, 155.

62 Neumann, *Britain's Long War*, 182–83.

10 Vietnam with a happy ending: Iraq and "the surge"

1 Brian McAllister Linn, *The Echo of Battle: The Army's Way of War* (Cambridge, MA: Harvard University Press, 2007), 193; David W. Hogan, Jr., "Head and Heart: The Dilemmas of American Attitudes toward War," *Journal of Military History* 75:4 (October 2011), 1046–47, outlines the economic, intellectual, and political evolution of the 1970s.

2 Andrew Bacevich, *Washington Rules: America's Path to Permanent War* (New York: Metropolitan Books, 2010), 116, 155.

3 Jeffrey Record, "Back to the Weinberger-Powell Doctrine?" *Strategic Studies Quarterly* (Fall 2007), 80, www.au.af.mil/au/ssq/2007/fall/record.pdf.

4 Linn, *The Echo of Battle*, 194–97; Hogan, "Head and Heart," 1048–49.

5 These developments are described in Linn, *The Echo of Battle*, Chapter 7; and John L. Romjue, *The Army of Excellence: The Development of the 1980s Army* (Fort Monroe, VA: Office of the Command Historian, US Army Training and Doctrine Command, 1993); Andrew J. Bacevich, *The New American Militarism: How Americans Are Seduced by War* (Oxford University Press, 2005), 34–47; Major Paul H. Herbert, *Deciding What Has to Be Done: General William E. De Puy and the 1976 Edition of FM 100-5, Operations* (Fort Leavenworth, KS: Combat Studies Institute, 1988).

6 Linn, *The Echo of Battle*, 221.

7 Linn, *The Echo of Battle*, 213; James A. Russell, *Innovation, Transformation, and War: Counterinsurgency Operations in Anbar and Ninewa Provinces, Iraq, 2005–2007* (Stanford University Press, 2011), 3.

8 Linn, *The Echo of Battle*, 215, 228; Romjue, *The Army of Excellence*, 45–82, 111–25.

9 Simon Anglim, *Orde Wingate and the British Army 1922–1944* (London: Pickering & Chatto, 2010), 210–11.

10 Romjue, *The Army of Excellence*, 82–83; USSOCOM History and Research Office, *United States Special Operations Command History, 1987–2007* (USSOCOM/SOCS-HO: MacDill AFB, FL, 2007), 5–7.

11 Linn, *The Echo of Battle*, 9.

12 Hogan, "Head and Heart," 1048.

13 Bacevich, *The New American Militarism*, 168.

14 Niall Ferguson, *Empire: The Rise and Demise of the British World Order and the Lessons for Global Power* (New York: Basic Books, 2003), xxv.

15 Timothy H. Parsons, *The Rule of Empires* (Oxford University Press, 2010), especially Chapters 4 and 6 on the British Empire.

16 Bacevich, *The New American Militarism*, 60–65.

17 Linn, *The Echo of Battle*, 224–32; Romjue, *The Army of Excellence*, 16, 74–77; Bacevich, *Washington Rules*, 160–64.

18 Bacevich, *Washington Rules*, 171.

19 Bacevich, *The New American Militarism*, 93, 162–92.

20 Eliot A. Cohen, *Supreme Command: Soldiers, Statesmen, and Leadership in Wartime* (New York: Free Press, 2002).

21 Eliot A. Cohen, *Making Do with Less, or Coping with Upton's Ghost* (Carlisle Barracks, PA: Strategic Studies Institute, May, 26, 1995), 5, 7–9.

22 Richard H. Kohn, "Tarnished Brass: Is the Military Profession in Decline?" *World Affairs* 171:4 (Spring 2009), 73–83; Thomas E. Ricks, "Is American Military Professionalism Declining?" *Proceedings Magazine*, US Naval Institute, 124/7/1 (July 1998); Linn, *The Echo of Battle*, Chapter 7.

23 Eric Schmitt and Thom Shanker, "The Reach of War: Military; Special Warriors have Growing Ranks and Growing Pains in Taking Key Anti-terror Role," *New York Times*, August 2, 2004.

24 "I'm going to point a finger at my Republican colleagues. They like war. They like waging war. They like the notion of staying in war. They think we should like to spend money in war. They like the notion that we would engage our troops in combat to assert America's position in the world." Interview with Illinois Senator Richard Durban, "The Daily Show," August 4, 2011, www.thedailyshow.com/full-episodes/thu-august-4-2011-dick-durbin.

25 Linn believes (*The Echo of Battle*, 239) this was particularly the case of General Tommy Franks, CENTCOM commander and architect of the invasion. See also Hogan, "Head and Heart," 1052.

26 Thomas E. Ricks, *The Gamble: General David Petraeus and the American Military Adventure in Iraq, 2006–2008* (New York: Penguin, 2009), 8–9; Robert Parry, "Bush's My Lai," consortiumnews.com, May 30, 2006, www.consortiumnews.com/2006/052906.html; Christopher Hitchens, "The Hell of a War: Why Haditha isn't Mai Lai," *Slate*, June 5, 2006, www.slate.com/articles/news_and_politics/fighting_words/2006/06/the_hell_of_war.html.

27 Ricks, *The Gamble*, 8–9, 12, 14–15, 23.

28 Ricks, *The Gamble*, 31–57.

29 Laleh Khalili, "The Location of Palestine in Global Counterinsurgencies," *International Journal of Middle East Studies*, 42:3 (2010), 427.

30 Laleh Khalili, "The New (and Old) Classics of Counterinsurgency," *Middle East Report* (255) (June 7, 2010), http://eprints.soas.ac.uk/8609/.

31 Bacevich, *Washington Rules*, 186–91.

32 Douglas Porch, *The March to the Marne: The French Army 1871–1914* (Cambridge University Press, 2003), 58, 62.

33 David Betz and Anthony Cormack, "Iraq, Afghanistan and British Strategy," *Orbis* (Spring 2009), 322.

34 Bacevich, *Washington Rules*, 196–202.

35 David Kilcullen, "Twenty-Eight Articles: The Fundamentals of Company Level Counter-insurgency," *Small Wars Journal* (March 1, 2006), http://smallwarsjournal.com/documents/28articles.pdf, article 19.

36 Edward Luttwak, "Dead End: Counterinsurgency Warfare as Military Malpractice," *Harper's Magazine*, February 2007, www.harpers.org/archive/2007/02/0081384.

37 Kilcullen, "Twenty-Eight Articles."

38 John Sloan Brown, *Kevlar Legions: The Transformation of the U.S. Army, 1989–2005* (Washington, DC: US Army Center of Military History, 2011), 393, 395, 397–407, 412; on logistics and Stryker 433–37.

39 www.dtic.mil/doctrine/jel/service_pubs/fm3_07.pdf.

40 Brown, *Kevlar Legions*, 413–21.

41 Ann Scott Tyson, "GAO Faults Military Over Munitions in Iraq," *The Washington Post*, March 23, 2007, www.washingtonpost.com/wp-dyn/content/article/2007/03/22/AR2007032202017.html.

42 Brown, *Kevlar Legions*, 423–33, 439–40.

43 Brown, *Kevlar Legions*, 441–42.

44 James A. Russell, *Innovation, Transformation, and War: Counterinsurgency Operations in Anbar and Ninewa Provinces, Iraq, 2005–2007* (Stanford University Press, 2011), 3.

45 Russell, *Innovation, Transformation, and War*, 1–21, 27, 192–95, 207–208.

46 Michiko Kakutani, "The War in Iraq, Second in a Series," *New York Times*, February 9, 2009, www.nytimes.com/2009/02/10/books/10kaku.html?pagewanted=all.

47 Their story is told by Deborah Amos, *Eclipse of the Sunnis: Power, Exile, and Upheaval in the Middle East* (New York: Public Affairs, 2010).

48 John Burns and Alissa J. Rubin, "U.S. Arming Sunnis in Iraq to Battle Old Qaeda Allies," *New York Times*, June 11, 2007, www.nytimes.com/2007/06/11/world/middleeast/11iraq.html?pagewanted=1; Pierre Tristam, "The Sons of Iraq, or Iraqi Awakening: Iraq's Sunni Variable Insurgency or Conciliation? How the Sunni Awakening Challenges Iraq's Shiites," http://middleeast.about.com/od/iraq/a/meo80822.htm.

49 Rachel Schneller, "Do Surges Work?" *SAIS Review*, 30:1 (Winter–Spring 2010).

50 Kilcullen, "Twenty-Eight Articles."

51 Patrick Porter, *Military Orientalism: Eastern War through Western Eyes* (New York: Columbia University Press, 2009), 61, 193.

52 Khalili, "The New (and Old) Classics of Counterinsurgency."

53 Schneller's comments ("Do Surges Work?") come in the context of Operation "Charge of the Knights," the March 2008, U.S. assisted operation to extend government control over Basra.

54 According to the *New York Times* arts critic Seth Schiesel, video designers deliberately avoid themes that involve Iraq and Afghanistan "because the overall narratives of those conflicts don't seem particularly heroic or vindicating. The public understand that United States soldiers commit acts of heroism and bravery every day, but there doesn't seem to be a happy ending yet to America's recent wars, or any ending at all." "Recruiting the Inner Military Hero in Men Who Don't Face the Draft," *New York Times*, November 16, 2010.

55 Bacevich, *Washington Rules*, 194.

56 www.cnas.org/people website, accessed November 16, 2011; Michael Hastings, *The Operators: The Wild and Terrifying Inside Story of America's War in Afghanistan* (New York: Blue Rider Press, 2012), 81.

57 Ricks, *The Gamble*, 21.

58 www.time.com/time/magazine/article/0,9171,898517,00.html.

59 Russell, *Innovation, Transformation, and War*, 3.

60 Michael Hastings, "The Sins of General David Petraeus," *Buzzfeed Politics*, November 11, 2012, www.buzzfeed.com/mhastings/the-sins-of-general-david-petraeus; Spencer Ackerman, "How I Was Drawn into the Cult of David Petraeus," *Wired,* November 11, 2012, www.wired.com/dangerroom/2012/11/petraeus-cult-2; Maureen Dowd, "Reputation, Reputation, Reputation," *New York Times*, November 14, 2012, www.nytimes.com/2012/11/14/opinion/dowd-reputation-reputation-reputation.html?hp&_r=0. See also Paula Broadwell and David Loeb, *All In: The Education of David Petraeus* (New York: Penguin, 2012).

61 Ricks, *The Gamble*, 277.

62 "Army Transformation, Implications for the Future." Statement of Major General Robert Scales, House Armed Services Committee, July 15, 2004. Quoted in Porter, *Military Orientalism*, 58.

63 Andrew Munford, *Puncturing the Counterinsurgency Myth: Britain and Irregular Warfare in the Past, Present and Future* (Carlisle Barracks, PA: Strategic Studies Institute, September 2011), 8–9, 14.

64 International Crisis Group, *Where Is Iraq Heading? Lessons from Basra*, Middle East Report No. 67 (June 25, 2007), 17, www.crisisgroup.org/~/media/Files/Middle%20East%20North%20Africa/Iraq%20Syria%20Lebanon/Iraq/67_iraq___lessons_from_basra.pdf.

65 "UK has Left Behind Murder and Chaos Says Basra Police Chief," *Guardian*, December 16, 2007, www.guardian.co.uk/world/2007/dec/17/iraq.military.

66 Tim Shipman, "British Forces Useless in Basra," *Daily Telegraph*, August 19, 2007, www.telegraph.co.uk/news/worldnews/1560713/British-forces-useless-in-Basra-say-officials.html; Ministry of Defence, *Operation Banner: An Analysis*

of Military Operations in Northern Ireland, July 2006, www.vilaweb.cat/media/attach/vwedts/docs/op_banner_analysis_released.pdf, 8–8, 8–10.

67 Munford, *Puncturing the Counterinsurgency Myth*, 7.

68 Michael Smith, "British Troops in Secret Truce with the Taliban," *The Times*, October 1, 2006; Jason Burke, "Taliban Town Seizure Throws Afghan Policy into Disarray," *Observer*, February 3, 2007.

69 Presentation by John Bew, "Reassessing Counterinsurgency: Theory and Practice," The Robert S. Strauss Center, University of Texas at Austin, June 7–9, 2012.

70 The Maneuvrist Approach as the basis for British doctrine stressed finding and killing the target, rather than attrition or containment. Alexander Alderson, "The Validity of British Army Counterinsurgency Doctrine after the War in Iraq" (PhD dissertation, Cranfield University, UK, November 2009), 261.

71 International Crisis Group, *Where Is Iraq Heading*, 12–13.

72 Schneller also notes ("Do Surges Work?") that by 2005 a particularly lethal Explosively Formed Penetrator IED (EFP IED) had appeared in Basra which made a journey onto the streets a suicidal adventure even for armored British vehicles.

73 MOD, *Operation Banner*, 843, 8–11.

74 Bew, "Reassessing Counterinsurgency."

75 Alderson, "The Validity of British Army Counterinsurgency Doctrine after the War in Iraq," 261–69.

76 Huw Bennett, "The Reluctant Pupil? Britain's Army and Learning in Counter-Insurgency," Royal United Service Institute, www.rusi.org/analysis/commentary/ref:C4AD22F8DF284C/.

77 David Betz and Anthony Cormack, "Iraq, Afghanistan and British Strategy," *Orbis* (Spring 2009), 322, 333.

78 Jeffrey Smith, "U.S. Military Admits Major Mistakes in Iraq and Afghanistan," *The Atlantic*, June 11, 2012, www.theatlantic.com/international/archive/2012/06/us-military-admits-major-mistakes-in-iraq-and-afghanistan/258339/.

79 Colonel Richard Iron, "Britain's Longest War: Northern Ireland 1967–2007," in Daniel Marston and Carter Malkasian (eds.), *Counterinsurgency in Modern Warfare* (London and New York: Osprey, 2008), 177, 183; MOD, *Operation Banner* (8.12, 8.3 *passim*) drew the same conclusions: "From a military perspective, for most of the campaign there was little coherence and synergy. There was little evidence of a strategic vision and no long-term plan."

80 Betz and Cormack, "Iraq, Afghanistan and British Strategy," 336

11 Conclusion

1 Gian P. Gentile, "Learning, Adapting and the Perils of the New Counter-insurgency," *Survival*, 51:6 (December 2009–January 2010), 200; this is the argument made by Robert Kaplan, *Imperial Grunts: On the Ground with the U.S.*

Military from Mongolia to the Philippines to Iraq and Beyond (New York: Vintage, 2006); Bart Schuurman, "Clausewitz and the 'New Wars' Scholars," *Parameters* (Spring 2010), 89–100.

2 Former NSC official Kori Schake insisting that Petraeus' mission was more complex than Eisenhower's in World War II. "Win Wars? Today's Generals Must Also Meet, Manage, Placate, Politic, and Do P.R.," *New York Times*, August 13, 2010.

3 Douglas Porch, *The March to the Marne: The French Army 1871–1914* (Cambridge University Press, 2003), 160.

4 Michael Hastings, *The Operators: The Wild and Terrifying Inside Story of America's War in Afghanistan* (New York: Blue Rider Press, 2012), 356–57.

5 William Deane Stanley, "El Salvador: State-Building before and after Democratisation, 1980–95," *Third World Quarterly*, 27:1 (August 2006), 101–14.

6 Andrew E. Kramer, "U.S. Leaving Iraqi Comrades-in-Arms in Limbo," *New York Times*, December 14, 2011, A6; Tim Arango, "U.S. May Jettison Efforts to Train Iraq Police Units," *New York Times*, May 13, 2012.

7 Hastings, *The Operators*, 366–67; Stephen Biddle argues that in Afghanistan, no insurgents changed sides as in Anbar. In these circumstances, unlike Anbar, Afghan militias allied with US troops had no intelligence about an insurgency undiminished by defections. Biddle presentation, "Reassessing Counterinsurgency: Theory and Practice," The Robert S. Strauss Center for International Security and Law, University of Texas at Austin, June 7–9, 2012.

8 Christian Tripodi, "Peacemaking through Bribes or Cultural Empathy? The Political Officer and Britain's Strategy towards the North-West Frontier, 1901–1945," *Journal of Strategic Studies*, 31:1 (February 2008), 144–48.

9 Hastings, *The Operators*, Chapter 36, 315.

10 Major Maria Vedder, "Engaging the Female Populace," Headquarters International Security Assistance Force, www.google.com/#hl=en&sa=X& ei=TwJUT8mwMManiQKv2_yoBg&ved=0CBgQvwUoAA&q=Major+ Maria+Vedder,+%E2%80%9CEngaging+the+Female+Populace,%E2%80% 9D+Headquarters+international+Security+Assistance+Force,&spell=1&bav= on.2,or.r_gc.r_pw.,cf.osb&fp=43fcdc5b603cde22&biw=1016&bih=542; Elisabeth Bullmiller, "Letting Women Reach Women in Afghanistan," *New York Times*, March 6, 2010, www.nytimes.com/2010/03/07/world/asia/ 07women.html; LisaRe Brooks, "Female Engagement Teams (FET)," *Human Terrain Systems*, October 28, 2010, http://openanthropology.files.wordpress. com/2010/01/fet.pdf.

11 David French, *The British Way in Counter-Insurgency, 1945–1967* (Oxford University Press, 2011), Chapter 7.

12 See, for instance, James A. Russell, *Innovation, Transformation, and War: Counterinsurgency Operations in Anbar and Ninewa Provinces, Iraq, 2005–2007* (Stanford University Press, 2011).

13 Chase Madar, "'War Crime' Delusions," *Salon.com*, April 16, 2012, www.salon.com/2012/04/16/war_crime_delusions/singleton/

14 Caroline Elkins, *Imperial Reckoning: The Untold Story of Britain's Gulag in Kenya* (New York: Henry Holt, 2005), 314–15.

15 Huw Bennett, "'Smoke Without Fire'? Allegations against the British Army in Northern Ireland, 1972–5," *Twentieth Century British History* (2012), 1–30.

16 Thom Shanker and Graham Bowley, "Images of G.I.s and Remains Fuel Fears of Ebbing Discipline," *New York Times*, April 18, 2012, www.nytimes.com/2012/04/19/world/asia/us-condemns-photo-of-soldiers-posing-with-body-parts.html?_r=1&hp.

17 Lt. Col. Daniel L. Davis, "Truth, Lies and Afghanistan: How Military Leaders Have Let Us Down," *Armed Forces Journal*, February 2012, http://armedforcesjournal.com/2012/02/8904030; Rita Maran, *Torture. The Role of Ideology in the French-Algerian War* (New York: Praeger, 1989), 16.

18 Simon Anglim, *Orde Wingate and the British Army 1922–1944* (London: Pickering & Chatto, 2010), 142.

19 www.imdb.com/title/tt0058946/.

20 Alexis Jenni, *L'Art français de la guerre* (Paris: Gallimard, 2011), 191; a view echoed by Martin Evans, *Algeria: France's Undeclared War* (Oxford University Press, 2012), 234.

21 Hastings, *The Operators*, 378.

22 Anna Simons, "Anthropology, Culture and COIN in a Hybrid Warfare World," in Paul Brister, William Natter, and Robert Tomes (eds.), *Hybrid Warfare and Transnational Threats: Perspectives for an Era of Persistent Conflict* (New York: CENSA, 2011), 85–88; Jeffrey Bordin, "A Crisis of Trust and Cultural Incompatibility: A Red Team Study of Mutual Perceptions of Afghan National Security Force Personnel and U.S. Soldiers in Understanding and Mitigating the Phenomena of ANSF-Committed Fratricide-Murders," May 12, 2011, 4, www.michaelyon-online.com/images/pdf/trust-incompatibility.pdf; Hastings, *The Operators*, 270–73. On tensions between GIs and ARVN in Vietnam, see Eric M. Bergerud, *The Dynamics of Defeat: The Vietnam War in Hau Nghia Province* (Boulder, CO: Westview Press, 1991), 226–34.

23 Jenni, *L'Art français de la guerre*, 25.

24 *Human Terrain Team Performance: An Explanation* (Washington, DC, Center for Strategic Research, Institute for National Strategic Studies, National Defense University, April 13, 2012), 146–47. I am grateful to the authors, Dr. James Douglas Orton, Michael Davies, and Ted Pikulsky, for an early version of this important forthcoming study.

25 Evans, *Algeria*, 349.

26 David Feith, "H. R. McMaster: The Warrior's-Eye View of Afthanistan," *Wall Street Journal*, May 11, 2012.

27 See for instance, Dominique Strauss-Kahn, "Why We Need a Marshall Plan for Haiti," *Huffington Post*, January 22, 2010, www.huffingtonpost.com/dominique-strausskahn/why-we-need-a-marshall-pl_b_432919.html; or S. M. Krishna, "Afghanistan Needs a Marshall Plan," NDTV, December 5, 2011, www.ndtv.com/article/india/afghanistan-needs-a-marshall-plan-sm-krishna-in-bonn-155523.

28 Deborah Avant and Lee Sigelman, "Private Security and Democracy: Lessons from the US in Iraq," *Security Studies*, 19:2 (May 2010), 262.

29 P. W. Singer, "Can't Win With 'Em, Can't Go to War Without 'Em: Private Military Contractors and Counterinsurgency," Brookings Institution, Policy Paper No. 4 (September 2007), 5, 8; "Karzai Slams Private Security Firms," Al Jazeera, October 25, 2010, www.aljazeera.com/news/asia/2010/10/2010102593352891476.html.

30 See, for instance, Alex Marshall, "Imperial Nostalgia, the Liberal Lie, and the Perils of Postmodern Counterinsurgency," *Small Wars & Insurgencies*, 21:2 (June 2010), 233–58; Bob Herbert, "Worse than a Nightmare," New York Times, June 25, 2010, www.nytimes.com/2010/06/26/opinion/26herbert.html?ref=opinion.

31 David Betz and Anthony Cormack, "Iraq, Afghanistan and British Strategy," *Orbis* (Spring 2009), 332.

32 Gordon Craig, "Delbrück: The Military Historian," in Peter Paret (ed.), *The Makers of Modern Strategy* (Princeton University Press, 1986), 326; Peter Paret, *Clausewitz and the State: The Man, His Theories, and His Times* (Princeton University Press, 1985), 348–49.

33 Eliot A. Cohen, "The Historical Mind and Military Strategy," *Orbis*, 49:4 (Fall 2005), 575, 580.

34 Andrew J. Bacevich, *The New American Militarism: How Americans Are Seduced by War* (Oxford University Press, 2005), 16, 21. "Wilsonians under Arms" is the title of the first chapter of his book.

35 Francis Fukuyama, *America at the Crossroads: Democracy, Power, and the Neoconservative Legacy* (New Haven, CT: Yale University Press, 2006).

36 Victor Davis Hanson, "War & Reconstruction: For Bush's Critics, Even Hindsight is Cloudy," *National Review* Online, November 18, 2005; Niall Ferguson, *Empire: The Rise and Demise of the British World Order and the Lessons for Global Power* (New York: Basic Books, 2003). See also Niall Ferguson's *Colossus: The Rise and Fall of the American Empire* (New York: Penguin, 2005); Max Boot, *The Savage Wars of Peace* (New York: Basic Books, 2002); Kaplan, *Imperial Grunts*.

37 "Dereliction of Duty II: Senior Military Leaders' Loss of Integrity Wounds Afghan War Effort," January 27, 2012, www1.rollingstone.com/extras/RS_REPORT.pdf; Hastings, *The Operators*, 28, 37; see, for instance, McMaster's optimistic metrics for Afghanistan in David Feith, "H. R. McMaster: The Warrior's-Eye

View of Afghanistan," *Wall Street Journal*, May 11, 2012, http://online.wsj.com/article/SB10001424052702304451104577392281146871796.html.

38 In 2012, the father of a US soldier captured in Afghanistan complained that: "The [COIN] doctrine is fallacious. It doesn't achieve what they say it's going to achieve. It's a biometric data-gathering device – send the rabbits out there to get I.E.D.-ed so you can figure out who to kill at night. How ethical." Elizabeth Bumiller, "Idahoan's Unlikely Journey to Life as a Taliban Prisoner," *New York Times*, May 13, 2012.

39 Thom Shanker and Eric Schmitt, "Special Operations Veterans Rise in Hierarchy," *New York Times*, August 8, 2011; Thom Shanker, "Army Will Reshape Training, with Lessons From Special Forces," *New York Times*, May 2, 2012.

40 Hastings, *The Operators*, 379.

41 D. M. Leeson, *The Black and Tans: British Police and Auxiliaries in the Irish War of Independence* (Oxford University Press, 2011), 226–28.

42 Larry Goodson and Thomas H. Johnson, "Parallels with the Past: How the Soviets Lost in Afghanistan, How the Americans Are Losing," *Orbis*, 55:4 (Fall 2011), 589; "Beyond bin Laden: Inside the Military's Extraordinary, Secret Campaign to Take Out Thousands of Taliban and Al Qaeda Fighters," Frontline, PBS May 10, 2011, www.pbs.org/wgbh/pages/frontline/kill-capture/.

43 Eric Schmitt, Mark Mazzzetti, and Thom Shanker, "Admiral Seeks Freer Hand in Deployment of Elite Forces," *New York Times*, February 12, 2012.

44 "Hold the Military Accountable, ex-Ambassador to Afghanistan Tells Stanford Audience," *Stanford Report*, May 11, 2012,, http://news.stanford.edu/news/2012/may/eikenberry-military-acountability-051112.html.

45 Andrew J. Bacevich, "Robert Kaplan: Empire without Apologies," *The Nation*, September 26, 2005, www.thenation.com/article/robert-kaplan-empire-without-apologies.

46 Hastings, *The Operators*, 280–81.

47 French, *The British Way in Counter-Insurgency*, 253–54.

48 Betz and Cormack, "Iraq, Afghanistan and British Strategy," 331.

49 See, for instance, Gil Merom, *How Democracies Lose Small Wars* (Cambridge University Press, 2003).

50 For an example of a "heat of battle" argument that excused the US Marines from prosecution for Haditha, see Mackubin Owen, "Justice? Haditha Again," *The National Review On-line*, June 19, 2008, www.nationalreview.com/articles/224815/justice/mackubin-thomas-owens.

51 Patricio de Naurois, "Guerra Subversiva y Guerra Revolucionaria, *Revista de la Escuela Superior de Guerra* 331 (October–December 1958), 690. Quoted in Eric Stener Carlson, "The Influence of French 'Revolutionary War' Ideology on the Use of Torture in Argentina's 'Dirty 'War'," *Human Rights Review*, 1:4 (2000), 76.

52 Carlson, "The Influence of French 'Revolutionary War'," 76.

53 Michael S. Schmidt, "Baghdad Junkyard Gives up Secret Accounts of Wartime Massacre," *New York Times*, December 15, 2011.

54 Hannah Arendt, *Imperialism* (New York: Harcourt, Brace & World, 1968), 101; Richard H. King and Dan Stone (eds.), *Hannah Arendt and the Uses of History. Imperialism, Nation, Race and Genocide* (New York and Oxford: Berghan Books, 2007), 7–14.

55 Hew Strachan, *The Politics of the British Army* (Oxford University Press, 1997), 101, 116–17.

56 Hastings, *The Operators*, 8, 37–39.

57 David Cesarani, *Major Farran's Hat: The Untold Story of the Struggle to Establish the Jewish State* (Cambridge, MA: Da Capo Press, 2009), 148–49, 179–80.

58 John Newsinger, *British Counterinsurgency from Palestine to Northern Ireland* (New York: Palgrave, 2002), 161.

59 "From the Birthplace of Big Brother," *New York Times*, April 15, 2012, www.nytimes.com/2012/04/16/opinion/from-the-birthplace-of-big-brother.html?_r=1&hpw=&pagewanted=print.

60 Jim House and Neil MacMaster, *Paris 1961: Algerians, State Terror, and Memory* (Oxford University Press, 2006), 15, 27–31 and *passim*; for Ben Barka, see Douglas Porch, *The French Secret Services: From the Dreyfus Affair to the Gulf War* (New York: Farrar, Straus and Giroux, 1995), 417–20.

61 Jenni, *L'Art français de la guerre*, 175–76, 191, 253–55.

62 Alfred McCoy, *Policing America's Empire: The United States, the Philippines, and the Rise of the Surveillance State* (Madison: The University of Wisconsin Press, 2009), Chapter 9.

63 Jennifer Light, *From Warfare to Welfare: Defense Intellectuals and Urban Problems in Cold War America* (Baltimore, MD: Johns Hopkins Press, 2003).

64 "Cops Getting Military Help in Anti-Gang Attack," *Washington Post*, www.lineofduty.com/the-blotter/105729-ca-cops-getting-military-help-in-anti-gang-attack.

65 Glenn Greenwald, "NPR's Domestic Drone Commercial," *Salon.com*, December 6, 2011; Scott Shane, "Beyond Guantánamo: A Web of Prisons," *New York Times*, December 11, 2011.

66 Charles C. Krulak and Joseph P. Hoar, "Guantánamo Forever?" *New York Times*, December 13, 2011, A29; Glenn Greenwald, "Obama to Sign Indefinite Detention Bill into Law," *Salon.com*, December 15, 2011; Wendy Kaimer, "What Occupy and Tea Partiers Should Fear Most," *The Atlantic*, December 15, 2011, www.theatlantic.com/national/archive/2011/12/what-occupiers-and-tea-partiers-should-fear-most/249997/

67 Al Baker, "When the Police Go Military," *New York Times*, December 3, 2012.

68 Georgina Sinclair, *At the End of the Line: Colonial Policing and the Imperial Endgame, 1945–1980* (Manchester and New York: Manchester University Press

and Palgrave, 2006), 12–13; Arthur Rizer and Joseph Hartman, "How the War on Terror Has Militarized the Police," *The Atlantic*, November 7, 2011, www. theatlantic.com/national/archive/2011/11/how-the-war-on-terror-has-militarized-the-police/248047/; Arthur Rizer, "Asking Our Soldiers to Do Police Work: Why It Can Lead to Disaster," *The Atlantic*, January 17, 2012, www. theatlantic.com/national/archive/2012/01/asking-our-soldiers-to-do-police-work-why-it-can-lead-to-disaster/251380/.

69 Glenn Greenwald, "NPR's Domestic Drone Commercial," *Salon.com*, December 6, 2011; "The Growing Menace of Domestic Drones," *Salon.com*, December 12, 2011; Andrew Becker, "Cops Ready for War," *The Daily Beast*, December 21, 2011, http://news.yahoo.com/cops-ready-war-094500010.html.

70 One of the most vocal and informed opponents of COIN is Colonel Gian Gentile, "Our COIN Doctrine Removes the Enemy from the Essence of War," *Armed Forces Journal*, January 2008, www.armedforcesjournal.com/2008/01/3207722.

71 Goodson and Johnson, "Parallels with the Past," 577–99; Mark Bowden, "Echoes from a Distant Battlefield," *Vanity Fair*, 616, December 2011, 214 *passim*.

72 Briefing from NATO spokesman Dr. Jaime Shea, NATO Headquarters, Brussels, August 2011; Amitai Etzioni, "The Lessons of Libya," *Military Review* (January–February 2012), 45–54; "The Philosopher Making the Moral Case for US Drones: 'There's no Downside'," *Guardian*, August 2, 2012, www.guardian. co.uk/world/2012/aug/02/philosopher-moral-case-drones.

73 David W. Hogan, Jr., "Head and Heart: The Dilemmas of American Attitudes toward War," *The Journal of Military* History, 75:4 (October 2011), 1043.

74 Joint and Coalition Operation Analysis, *Decade of War: Enduring Lessons for the Past Decade of Operations*, June 15, 2012, http://blogs.defensenews.com/saxotech-access/pdfs/decade-of-war-lessons-learned.pdf.

75 Ibrahim Mothana, "How Drones Help Al Qaeda," *New York Times*, June 13, 2012.

SELECT BIBLIOGRAPHY

Adams, Gerry, *Before the Dawn* (London: Brandon Books, 1997).

Ageron, Charles-Robert (ed.), *La guerre d'Algérie et les Algériens 1954–1962* (Paris: Armand Colin, 1997).

Alderson, Alexander, "The Validity of British Army Counterinsurgency Doctrine after the War in Iraq," PhD dissertation, Cranfield University, UK, November 2009.

Alexander, Don W., *Rod of Iron: French Counterinsurgency Policy in Aragon during the Peninsular War* (Wilmington, DE: Scholarly Resources, 1985).

Amos, Deborah, *Eclipse of the Sunnis: Power, Exile, and Upheaval in the Middle East* (New York: Public Affairs, 2010).

Anderson, David, *Histories of the Hanged: Britain's Dirty War in Kenya and the End of Empire* (London: Weidenfeld & Nicolson, 2005).

Anderson, Jon Lee, *Che Guevara: A Revolutionary Life* (New York: Grove Press, 1997).

Andrade, Dale, "Westmoreland Was Right," *Small Wars & Insurgencies*, 19:2 (June 3, 2008), 145–81.

Andreopoulos, George and Selesky, Harold, *Aftermath of Defeat: Societies, Armed Forces and the Challenge of Recovery* (New Haven, CT: Yale University Press, 1994).

Andrew, Christopher M. and Kanya-Forstner, A. S., *France Overseas: The Great War and the Climax of French Imperial Expansion* (London: Thames and Hudson, 1981).

Andrews, C. S., *Dublin Made Me* (Dublin: Lilliput Press, 2002).

Anglim, Simon, *Orde Wingate and the British Army 1922–1944* (London: Pickering & Chatto, 2010).

Arendt, Hannah, *Imperialism* (New York: Harcourt, Brace & World, 1968).

On Violence (New York: Harcourt, Brace and World, 1970).

The Origins of Totalitarianism (New York: Harcourt, Brace, Jovanovich, 1973).

Arquilla, John, *Insurgents, Raiders, and Bandits: How Masters of Irregular Warfare Have Shaped Our World* (Chicago: Ivan R. Dee, 2011).

Augusteijn, Joost, *From Public Defiance to Guerilla Warfare: The Radicalisation of the Irish Republican Army – A Comparative Analysis, 1916–1920* (Amesterdam: Centrale Drukkerij Universitet van Amsterdam, 1994).

Aussaresses, General Paul, *The Battle of the Casbah: Terrorism and Counter-Terrorism in Algeria, 1955–1957* (New York: Enigma Books, 2010).

Avant, Deborah and Sigelman, Lee, "Private Security and Democracy: Lessons from the US in Iraq," *Security Studies*, 19:2 (May 2010), 230–65.

Bacevich, Andrew J., *The New American Militarism: How Americans Are Seduced by War* (Oxford University Press, 2005).

Washington Rules: America's Path to Permanent War (New York: Metropolitan Books, 2010).

Baines, John M., "U.S. Military Assistance to Latin America: An Assessment," *Journal of Interamerican Studies and World Affairs*, 14:2 (November 1972), 469–87.

Barr, James, *A Line in the Sand: Britain, France and the Struggle for Mastery of the Middle East* (New York: Simon & Schuster, 2011).

Bayly, C. A., "Knowing the Country: Empire and Information in India," *Modern Asian Studies*, 27:1 (February 1993), 3–43.

Bayly, Christopher and Harper, Tim, *Forgotten Wars: The End of Britain's Asian Empire* (London: Penguin, 2007).

Bell, J. Bower, *Terror Out of Zion: The Fight for Israeli Independence* (New Brunswick, NJ: Rutgers University Press, 2009).

Bennett, Huw, "The Reluctant Pupil? Britain's Army and Learning in Counter-Insurgency," *RUSI Military History Circle Commentary* (October 2009), www.rusi.org/analysis/commentary/ref:C4AD22F8DF284C/.

"'Smoke without Fire'? Allegations against the British Army in Northern Ireland, 1972–5," *Twentieth Century British History* (2012), 1–30.

Bennett, Richard, *The Black and Tans* (Boston: Houghton Mifflin, 1960).

Benot, Yves, *La modernité de l'esclavage: essai sur la servitude au cœur du capitalisme* (Paris: La Découverte, 2003).

Bergerud, Eric M., *The Dynamics of Defeat: The Vietnam War in Hau Nghia Province* (Boulder, CO: Westview Press, 1990).

Bernstein, Richard, *The East, the West, and Sex: A History of Erotic Encounters* (Westminster, MD: Knopf, 2009).

Betz, David and Cormack, Anthony, "Iraq, Afghanistan, and British Strategy," *Orbis* (Spring 2009), 319–36.

Bew, John, Frampton, Martyn, and Gurruchaga, Iñigo, *Talking to Terrorists: Making Peace in Northern Ireland and the Basque Country* (London: Hurst & Company, 2009).

Birtle, A. J., "The U.S. Army's Pacification of Marinduque, Philippines Islands, April 1900-April 1901," *The Journal of Military History*, 61 (April 1997), 255–82.

 U.S. Army Counterinsurgency and Contingency Operations Doctrine 1942–1976 (Washington: US Army Center of Military History, 2007).

Blaufarb, Douglas, *The Counterinsurgency Era: U.S. Doctrine and Performance, 1950 to the Present* (New York: Free Press, 1977).

Bond, Brian and Alexander, Martin, "Liddell Hart and De Gaulle: The Doctrines of Limited Liability and Mobile Defense," in Peter Paret (ed.), *The Makers of Modern Strategy from Machiavelli to the Nuclear Age* (Princeton University Press, 1986), 598–623.

Boot, Max, *The Savage Wars of Peace* (New York: Basic Books, 2002).

Bokova, Lenka, *La confrontation franco-Syrienne à l'époque du mandate 1925–1927* (Paris: Editions L'Harmattan, 1990).

Borgwardt, Elizabeth, *A New Deal for the World: America's Vision for Human Rights* (Cambridge, MA: Harvard, 2005).

Bouche, Denise, *Les villages de liberté en Afrique noire française, 1887–1910* (Paris: EHESS, 1968).

Boyce, D. G., *Englishmen and Irish Troubles: British Public Opinion and the Making of Irish Policy 1918–22* (Cambridge, MA: MIT Press, 1972).

Boyle, Andrew, *The Riddle of Erskine Childers* (London: Hutchinson, 1977).

Branche, Raphaëlle, *La torture et l'armée pendant la guerre d'Algérie 1954–1962* (Paris: Gallimard, 2001).

Brands, Hal, "Reform, Democratization, and Counter-insurgency: Evaluating the US Experience in Cold War-Era Latin America," *Small Wars & Insurgencies*, 22:2 (May 2011), 290–312.

Brown, John Sloan, *Kevlar Legions: The Transformation of the U.S. Army, 1989–2005* (Washington, DC: US Army Center of Military History, 2011).

Brunschwig, Henri, *Mythes et réalités de l'impérialisme colonial français, 1871–1914* (Paris: Colin, 1960).

Burgoyne, Elizabeth, *Gertrude Bell from Her Personal Papers*, Vol. II (London: Ernest Benn, 1958).

Callwell, C. E., *Small Wars: Their Principle and Practice* (Omaha: University of Nebraska Press, 1996).

Carlson, Eric Stener, "The Influence of French 'Revolutionary War' Ideology on the Use of Torture in Argentina's 'Dirty War'," *Human Rights Review*, 1:4 (2000), 71–84.

Castellane, Louis Charles Pierre (Comte) de, *Souvenirs de la vie militaire en Afrique* (Paris: Victor Lecou, 1852).

Cesarani, David, *Major Farran's Hat* (Cambridge, MA: Da Capo Press, 2009).

Chabrol, Le Commandant Emmanuel P.G., *Opérations militaires au Tonkin* (Paris: Charles-Lavauzelle, 1896).

Chang, Ha-Joon, *Kicking Away the Ladder: Development Strategy in Historical Perspective* (London: Anthem Press, 2006).

Child, Jack, *Geopolitics and Conflict in South America: Quarrels among Neighbors* (New York: Praeger, 1985).

Christian, Patrick James, *A Combat Advisor's Guide to Tribal Engagement: History, Law and War as Operational Elements* (Boca Raton, FL: Universal Publishers, 2011).

Churchill, Winston, *The Aftermath* (London: Thornton, 1929).

Coen, Terence Creagh, *The Indian Political Service: A Study in Indirect Rule* (London: Chatto & Windus, 1971).

Clemis, Martin G., "Violent Pacification: Force, Coercion, and the 'Other War' in Vietnam, 1968–1972," paper delivered at the 78th Annual Meeting of the Society or Military History, June 10, 2010.

Cohen, A. A., *Galula: The Life and Writings of the French Officer who Defined the Art of Counterinsurgency* (Santa Barbara, CA: Praeger, 2012).

Cohen, Eliot A., *Making Do with Less, or Coping with Upton's Ghost* (Carlisle Barracks, PA: Strategic Studies Institute, May 26, 1995).

Supreme Command: Soldiers, Statesmen, and Leadership in Wartime (New York: Free Press, 2002).

"The Historical Mind and Military Strategy," *Orbis* 49:4 (Fall 2005), 575–88.

Colby, William, *Honorable Men: My Life in the CIA* (New York: Simon & Schuster, 1978).

Lost Victory: A Firsthand Account of America's Sixteen-Year Involvement in Vietnam (Chicago: Contemporary Books, 1989).

Corum, James S., *Training Indigenous Forces in Counterinsurgency: A Tale of Two Insurgencies* (Carlisle Barracks, PA: Strategic Studies Institute, March 2006).

Costello, Francis, *The Irish Revolution and Its Aftermath 1916–1923: Years of Revolt* (Dublin: Irish Academic Press, 2003).

Craig, Gordon, "Delbrück: The Military Historian," in Peter Paret (ed.), *The Makers of Modern Strategy* (Princeton University Press, 1986), 326–53.

D'Ideville, Henry, *Le Maréchal Bugeaud d'après sa correspondance intime, 3 vols.* (Paris: Firmin-Didotet, 1882).

Daddis, Gregory A., "Eating Soup with a Spoon: The U.S. Army as a 'Learning Organization' in the Vietnam War," paper delivered at the Annual Conference of the Society for Military History, 2011, 6–8, www.smh2011.org/program.html.

Dash, Mike, *Thug: The True Story of India's Murderous Cult* (London: Granta, 2005).

Decker, Carl von, *Algerien und die dortige Kriegsführung* (Berlin: Friedrich August Herbig, 1844).

Delgado, Jorge E., "Military Civic Action: Development of Strategy in the Colombian Army, 1955–65," Master's thesis, King's College London, 2011.

Deringil, Selim, "'They Live in a State of Nomadism and Savagery': The Late Ottoman Empire and the Post-Colonial Debate," *Comparative Studies in Society and History* 45:2 (April 2003), 311–42.

Dixon, Paul, "'Hearts and Minds'? British Counter-Insurgency from Malaya to Iraq," *The Journal of Strategic Studies*, 32:3 (June 2009), 356–61.

Downie, Richard Duncan, *Learning from Conflict: The U.S. Military in Vietnam, El Salvador, and the Drug War* (Westport, CT: Praeger, 1998).

Dreyer, Edward L., *China at War, 1901–1949* (New York: Longman, 1995).

Edwards, Aaron, "Misapplying Lessons Learned? Analyzing the Utility of British Counterinsurgency Strategy in Northern Ireland, 1971–1976," *Small Wars & Insurgencies*, 21:2 (June 21, 2010), 303–30.

Edwards, Sean J. A., *Swarming and the Future of Warfare* (Santa Monica, CA: Rand Corporation, 2005).

Elkins, Caroline, *Imperial Reckoning: The Untold Story of Britain's Gulag in Kenya* (New York: Henry Holt, 2005).

Ellwood, David, *Italy 1943–1945* (New York: Holmes and Meier, 1985).

Evans, Martin, *Algeria: France's Undeclared War* (Oxford University Press, 2012).

Farrell, Theo, "Improving in War: Military Adaptation and the British in Helmand Province, Afghanistan, 2006–2009," *The Journal of Strategic Studies*, 33:4 (August 2010), 567–94.

Feaver, Peter D., "The Right to Be Right: Civil-Military Relations and the Iraq Surge Decision," *International Security*, 35:4 (Spring 2011), 87–125.

Ferguson, Niall, *Empire: The Rise and Demise of the British World Order and the Lessons for Global Power* (New York: Basic Books, 2003).

    Colossus: The Rise and Fall of the American Empire (New York: Penguin, 2005).

Fernandez-Armesto, Felipe, *The Americas: A Hemispheric History* (New York: The Modern Library, 2003).

Fitzpatrick, David, *Politics and Irish Life 1913–1921: Provincial Experience of War and Revolution* (Dublin: Gill & Macmillan 1977).

Foot, M. R. D., *SOE in France* (London: Her Majesty's Stationery Office, 1966).

Foucher, Michel, *Fronts et frontières: un tour du monde géopolitique* (Paris: Fayard, 1991).

Frémeaux, Jacques, *Les bureaux arabes dans l'Algérie de la conquête* (Paris: Editions Denoël, 1993).

"French Conquerors and Colonists," *Blackwood's Edinburgh Magazine*, 65, January 1849.

French, David, *The British Way in Counterinsurgency 1945–1967* (Oxford University Press, 2011).

Fromkin, David, "The Importance of T. E. Lawrence," *The New Criterion Online* (September 10, 1991), www.newcriterion.com/articles.cfm/The-importance-of-T-E–Lawrence-4416.

Fukuyama, Francis, *America at the Crossroads: Democracy, Power, and the Neoconservative Legacy* (New Haven, CT: Yale University Press, 2006).

Galula, David, *Counterinsurgency Warfare: Theory and Practice* (Westport, CT: Praeger, 2006).

    Pacification in Algeria 1956–1958 (Santa Monica, CA: Rand Corporation, 2006).

García, Prudencio, *El Drama de la autonomía militar* (Madrid: Alanzia Editorial, 1995).

Gelvin, James L., *Divided Loyalties: Nationalism and Mass Politics in Syria at the Close of Empire* (Berkeley, Los Angeles, and London: University of California Press, 1998).

Gentile, Gian P., "Learning, Adapting and the Perils of the New Counter-insurgency," *Survival*, 51:6 (December 2009–January 2010), 189–201.

Gershovich, Moshe, *French Military Rule in Morocco: Colonialism and Its Consequences* (London: Frank Cass, 2000).

Geyer, Michael, "German Strategy, 1914–1945," in Peter Paret (ed.), *The Makers of Modern Strategy from Machiavelli to the Nuclear Age* (Princeton University Press, 1986), 527–97.

Gifford, Prosser and Louis, William Roger (eds.), *Britain and Germany in Africa: Imperial Rivalry and Colonial Rule* (New Haven, CT and London: Yale University Press, 1967).

Ginsborg, Paul, *A History of Contemporary Italy: Society and Politics 1943–1988* (London: Penguin, 1990).

Gleijeses, Piero, *Conflicting Missions: Havana, Washington, and Africa, 1959–1976* (Chapel Hill: University of North Carolina Press, 2002).

Godechot, Jacques, *The Counter-Revolution: Doctrine and Action 1789–1804* (London: Routledge & Kegan Paul, 1972).

Goodson, Larry and Johnson, Thomas H., "Parallels with the Past: How the Soviets Lost in Afghanistan, How the Americans Are Losing," *Orbis*, 55:4 (Fall 2011), 577–99.

Grabe, Vera, *Razonas de vida* (Bogotá: Planeta, 2000).

Grenier, John, *The First Way of War: American War Making on the Frontier* (Cambridge University Press, 2005).

Grob-Fitzgibbon, Benjamin John, *Turning Points of the Irish Revolution: The British Government, Intelligence, and the Cost of Indifference, 1912–1921* (Gordonsville, VA: Palgrave Macmillan, 2007).

Imperial Endgame: Britain's Dirty Wars and the End of Empire (New York: Palgrave Macmillan, 2011).

Gwynn, Major-General Sir Charles W., *Imperial Policing* (London: Macmillan, 1934).

Hastings, Max, *Winston's War: Churchill 1940–1945* (New York: Knopf, 2010).

Hastings, Michael, *The Operators: The Wild and Terrifying Inside Story of America's War in Afghanistan* (New York: Blue Rider Press, 2012).

Hamer, W. S., *The British Army: Civil-Military Relations 1885–1905* (Oxford University Press, 1970).

Harmand, Jules, *Domination et colonisation* (Paris: Flammarion, 1910).

Harries-Jenkins, Gwyn, *The Army and Victorian Society* (London: Routledge & Kegan Paul, 1977).

Hart, Peter (ed.), *British Intelligence in Ireland, 1920–21: The Final Reports* (Cork University Press, 2002).

Heidsieck, P., *Le Rayonnement de Lyautey* (Paris: Gallimard, 1947).

Herbert, Major Paul H., *Deciding What Has to Be Done: General William E. De Puy and the 1976 Edition of FM 100–5, Operations* (Fort Leavenworth, KS: Combat Studies Institute, 1988).

Hibbert, Christopher, *Wellington: A Personal History* (Reading, MA: Addison-Wesley, 1997).

Higham, Robin and Graff, David A., *A Military History of China* (Boulder, CO: Westview Press, 2002).

Hitchens, Christopher, "The Hell of a War: Why Haditha Isn't My Lai," *Slate* (June 5, 2006), www.slate.com/articles/news_and_politics/fighting_words/2006/06/the_hell_of_war.html.

Hogan, David W., Jr., "Head and Heart: The Dilemmas of American Attitudes toward War," *Journal of Military History*, 75:4 (October 2011), 1021–54.

Hoisington, William A., Jr., *The Casablanca Connection: French Colonial Policy 1936–1943* (Chapel Hill: University of North Carolina Press, 1984).

Lyautey and the French Conquest of Morocco (New York: St. Martin's Press, 1995).

Holloway, Tom (ed.), *A Companion to Latin American History* (Oxford: Blackwell, 2007).

Holmes, Richard, *The Road to Sedan: The French Army 1866–1870* (London: Royal Historical Society, 1984).

Wellington: The Iron Duke (London: HarperCollins, 2003).

(ed.), *The Oxford Companion to Military History* (Oxford and New York: Oxford University Press, 2001).

Hopkinson, Michael, *The Irish War of Independence* (Montreal: McGill-Queen's University Press, 2002).

Horne, Alistair, *A Savage War of Peace. Algeria 1954–1962* (London: Macmillan, 1977).

Horne, John and Kramer, Alan, *German Atrocities 1914: A History of Denial* (New Haven, CT: Yale University Press, 2001).

Hosmer, Stephen T. and Crane, Sibylle O., *Counterinsurgency: A Symposium, April 16–20 1962* (Washington, DC: Rand Corporation, 2006).

House, Jim and MacMaster, Niel, *Paris 1961: Algerians, State Terror and Memory* (Oxford University Press, 2006).

Hughes, M., "The Banality of Brutality: British Armed Forces and the Repression of the Arab Revolt in Palestine, 1936–39," *English Historical Review*, 124:507 (2009), 314–54.

"The Practice and Theory of British Counterinsurgency: The Histories of Atrocities at the Palestine Villages of al-Basa and Halhul, 1938–1939," *Small Wars & Insurgencies*, 20 (2009), 313–54

Hull, Isabel V., *Absolute Destruction: Military Culture and the Practices of War in Imperial Germany* (Ithaca, NY and London: Cornell University Press, 2005).

Iron, Colonel Richard, "Britain's Longest War: Northern Ireland 1967–2007," in Daniel Marston and Carter Malkasian (eds.), *Counterinsurgency in Modern Warfare* (London and New York: Osprey, 2008), 167–84.

Jauffret, Jean-Charles and Vaïsse, Maurice (eds.), *Militaires et guérilla dans la guerre d'Algérie* (Paris: Editions complexes, 2001).

Jenni, Alexis, *l'Art française de la guerre* (Paris: Gallimard, 2011).

Joly, Vincent, *Guerres d'Afrique: 130 ans de guerres coloniales – l'expérience française* (Presses Universitaires de Rennes, 2009).

Judd, Denis, *Empire: The British Imperial Experience from 1765 to the Present* (New York: Basic Books, 1996).

Julien, Charles-André, *Histoire de l'Algérie contemporaine*. Vol. I: *La conquête et les débuts de la colonisation (1827–1871)* (Paris: PUF, 1964).

Kaiser, David, *American Tragedy: Kennedy, Johnson, and the Origins of the Vietnam War* (Cambridge, MA: Harvard University Press, 2000).

Kanya-Forstner, A. S., *The Conquest of the Western Sudan: A Study in French Military Imperialism* (Cambridge University Press, 1968).

Kaplan, Robert D., *Imperial Grunts: The American Military on the Ground* (New York: Random House, 2005).

Karnow, Stanley, *Vietnam: A History* (New York: Penguin, 1997).

Keegan, John, "Introduction," in Sir Robert Thompson (ed.), *War in Peace: Conventional and Guerrilla Warfare since 1945* (New York: Harmony Books, 1981).

Kelley, Patrick A., *Imperial Secrets: Remapping the Mind of Empire* (Washington, DC: National Defense Intelligence College, 2008).

Khalidi, Rashid, Anderson, Lisa, Muslih, Muhammad and Simon, Reeva S., *The Origins of Arab Nationalism* (New York: Columbia University Press, 1991).

Khalili, Laleh, "The Location of Palestine in Global Counterinsurgencies," *International Journal of Middle East Studies*, 42:3 (2010), 413–33.

"The New (and Old) Classics of Counterinsurgency," *Middle East Report* (255) (June 7, 2010), www.merip.org/mer255/khalili.html.

Khoury, Philip S., *Syria and the French Mandate: The Politics of Arab Nationalism* (Princeton University Press, 1987).

Kiernan, Ben, *Blood and Soil: A World History of Genocide and Extermination from Sparta to Darfur* (New Haven, CT: Yale University Press, 2007).

Kilcullen, David "Twenty-Eight Articles: The Fundamentals of Company Level Counter-insurgency," *Small Wars Journal* (March 1, 2006), http://small-warsjournal.com/documents/28articles.pdf.

The Accidental Guerrilla: Fighting Small Wars in the Midst of a Big One (Oxford University Press, 2009).

King, Richard H. and Stone, Dan (eds.), *Hannah Arendt and the Uses of History: Imperialism, Nation, Race and Genocide* (New York and Oxford: Berghan Books, 2007).

Kinnvall, Catarina, *Globalization and Religious Nationalism in India: The Search for Ontological Security* (Abington, UK: Routledge, 2006).

Kitson, Frank, *Bunch of Five* (London: Faber & Faber, 1977).

Kohn, Richard H., "Tarnished Brass: Is the Military Profession in Decline?" *World Affairs* 171:4 (Spring 2009), 73–83.

Komer, Robert, *Bureaucracy at War: U.S. Performance in the Vietnam Conflict* (Boulder, CO: Westview Press, 1986).

Krepinevich, Andrew, *The Army and Vietnam* (Baltimore, MD and London: Johns Hopkins University Press, 1986).

La Serna, Miguel, *Corner of the Living: Ayachchu on the Eve of the Shining Path Insurgency* (Chapel Hill: University of North Carolina Press, 2012).

Lacouture, Jean, *De Gaulle: The Ruler 1945–1970* (New York: Norton, 1991).

Lawrence, Mark Atwood, *Assuming the Burden: Europe and the American Commitment to the War in Vietnam* (Berkeley: University of California Press, 2005).

Lawrence, T. E., "The Science of Guerrilla Warfare," in *Encyclopedia Britannica* (London: 1929), 950–53.

Seven Pillars of Wisdom: A Triumph (New York: Doubleday, Doran & Company, 1935).

Le Naour, Jean-Yves, *La honte noire: l'Allemagne et les troupes coloniales françaises 1914–1945* (Paris: Hachette, 2004).

Lebovic, James H., *The Limits of U.S. Military Capability: Lessons from Vietnam and Iraq* (Baltimore, MD: Johns Hopkins University Press, 2010).

Leeson, D. M., *The Black and Tans: British Police and Auxiliaries in the Irish War of Independence* (Oxford University Press, 2011).

Lefebvre, Jeffrey A., "Kennedy's Algerian Dilemma: Containment, Alliance Politics, and the 'Rebel Dialogue'," *Middle Eastern Studies*, 35:2 (1999), 61–82, www.jstor.org/pss/4284004.

Lewis, Norman, *Naples '44* (London: Collins, 1978).

Lewy, Guenter, *America in Vietnam* (New York: Oxford University Press, 1980).

Light, Jennifer, *From Warfare to Welfare: Defense Intellectuals and Urban Problems in Cold War America* (Baltimore, MD: Johns Hopkins Press, 2003).

Linn, Brian McAllister, *The Philippine War 1899–1902* (Lawrence: University of Kansas Press, 2000).

The Echo of Battle: The Army's Way of War (Cambridge, MA: Harvard University Press, 2007).

Lloyd, Tom, "Thuggee, Marginality and the State Effect in Colonial India, circa 1770–1840," *The Indian Economic and Social History Review*, 42:2 (2008), 201–37.

Longrigg, Stephen, *Syria and Lebanon under French Mandate* (Oxford University Press, 1958).

Luttwak, Edward, "Dead End: Counterinsurgency Warfare as Military Malpractice," *Harpers* (February 2007), www.harpers.org/archive/2007/02/0081384.

Lyautey, Hubert, "Le rôle social de l'officier," *Revue des deux mondes* (March 15, 1891).

"Du rôle colonial de l'armée," *Revue des deux mondes* (January 15, 1900).

Madley, Benjamin, "From Africa to Auschwitz: How German South West Africa Incubated Ideas and Methods Adopted and Developed by the Nazis in Eastern Europe," *European History Quarterly*, 35:3 (2005), 429–64.

Maher, Jim, *Flying Column, West Kilkinney 1916–1921* (Dublin: Geography Publications, 1987).

Makdisi, Ussama, "Ottoman Orientalism," *The American Historical Review*, 107:3 (June 2002), 768–96.

Manea, Octavian, "Counterinsurgency as a Whole of Government Approach: Notes on the British Army Field Manual Weltanschauung – An Interview with Colonel Alexander Alderson," *Small Wars Journal* (January 24, 2011), 8, http://smallwarsjournal.com/jrnl/art/counterinsurgency-as-a-whole-of-government-approach.

Mao Tse-tung, *On Protracted War* (Beijing: Foreign Language Press, 1967).

Mao Tse-tung and Che Guevara, *Guerrilla Warfare* (London: Cassell, 1961).

Maran, Rita, *Torture: The Role of Ideology in the French-Algerian War* (New York: Praeger, 1989).

Marlowe, Anne, *David Galula: His Life and Intellectual Context* (Carlisle Barracks, PA, Strategic Studies Institute Monograph, August 2010), www.StrategicStudiesInstitute.army.mil/.

Marr, David G., *Vietnamese Anti-Colonialism, 1885–1925* (Berkeley, Los Angeles, and London: University of California, 1971).

Marshall, Alex, "Imperial Nostalgia, the Liberal Lie, and the Perils of Postmodern Counterinsurgency," *Small Wars & Insurgencies*, 21:2 (June 2010), 233–58.

Mathias, Grégor, *Galula in Algeria: Counterinsurgency Practice versus Theory* (Santa Barbara, CA: Praeger, 2011).

Maxwell, Gavin, *Lords of the Atlas: The Rise and Fall of the House of Glaoua, 1893–1956* (London: Eland, 2004).

McCoy, Alfred, *Policing America's Empire: The United States, the Philippines, and the Rise of the Surveillance State* (Madison: University of Wisconsin Press, 2009).

Meade, Peter and Bidwell, Shelford, "Orde Wingate – Two Views," *Journal of Contemporary History*, 15:3 (July 1980), 401–404.

Menjivar, Cecilia and Rodriguez, Nestor (eds.), *When States Kill: Latin America, the U.S. and Technologies of Terror* (Austin: University of Texas Press, 2005).

Merom, Gil, *How Democracies Lose Small Wars* (Cambridge University Press, 2003).

Michel, Marc, *Gallieni* (Paris: Fayard, 1989).

Miller, David W., *Church, State and Nation in Ireland 1898–1921* (University of Pittsburg Press, 1973).

Miller, Joyce Laverty, "The Syrian Revolt of 1925," *International Journal of Middle East Studies*, 8:4 (October 1977), 545–63.

Milward, Alan, "The Economic and Strategic Effectiveness of Resistance," in Stephen Hawes and Ralph White (eds.), *Resistance in Europe* (London: Penguin, 1976), 186–203.

Ministry of Defense, *Operation Banner: An Analysis of Military Operations in Northern Ireland* (London: MOD, 2006), www.vilaweb.cat/media/attach/vwedts/docs/op_banner_analysis_released.pdf.

Mockaitis, Thomas R., *British Counterinsurgency, 1919–60* (New York: St. Martin's Press, 1990).

Mohs, Polly A., *Military Intelligence and the Arab Revolt: The First Modern Intelligence War* (London and New York: Routledge, 2008).

Moloney, Edward, *The Secret History of the IRA* (London: Penguin, 2007).

Moran, Daniel, *Wars of National Liberation* (London: Cassell, 2001).

Munford, Andrew, *Puncturing the Counterinsurgency Myth: Britain and Irregular Warfare in the Past, Present and Future* (Carlisle Barracks, PA: Strategic Studies Institute, September 2011).

Nagl, John A., *Learning to Eat Soup with a Knife: Counterinsurgency Lessons from Malaya and Vietnam* (London and Chicago: University of Chicago Press, 2005).

Neligan, David, *The Spy in the Castle* (London: Prendeville Publishing, 1999).

Neumann, Peter, *Britain's Long War: British Strategy in the Northern Ireland Conflict 1969–98* (Gordonsville, VA: Palgrave Macmillan, 2004).

Newsinger, John, *British Counterinsurgency from Palestine to Northern Ireland* (New York: Palgrave, 2002).

Norris, J. "Repression and Rebellion: Britain's Response to the Arab Revolt in Palestine of 1936–39," *Journal of Imperial and Commonwealth History*, 36 (2008), 25–45.

Nguyen, Major General Duy Hinh and Brigadier General Tran Dinh Tho, *The South Vietnamese Society* (Washington, DC: US Army Center of Military History, 1980).

O'Donaghue, Florence, *No Other Law (The Story of Liam Lynch and the Irish Republican Army 1916–1923)* (Dublin: Irish Press, Ltd., 1954).

Ochsenwald, William, "Ironic Origins: Arab Nationalism in the Hijaz, 1882–1914," in Rashid Khalidi, Lisa Anderson, Muhammad Muslih, and Reeva Simon (eds.), *The Origins of Arab Nationalism* (New York: Columbia University Press, 1991), 189–203.

Paice, Edward, *Tip and Run: The Untold Tragedy of the Great War in Africa* (London: Phoenix, 2008).

Pakenham, Thomas, *The Boer War* (London: Weidenfeld & Nicolson, 1979).

Paret, Peter, *French Revolutionary Warfare from Indochina to Algeria: The Analysis of a Political and Military Doctrine* (New York: Praeger, 1964).

Clausewitz and the State: The Man, His Theories, and His Times (Princeton University Press, 1985).

(ed.), *The Makers of Modern Strategy from Machiavelli to the Nuclear Age* (Princeton University Press, 1986).

Paret, Peter and Shy, John W., *Guerrillas in the 1960s* (New York: Praeger, 1962).

Parry, Robert, "Bush's My Lai," *consortiumnews.com* (May 30, 2006), www.consortiumnews.com/2006/052906.html.

Parsons, Timothy H., *The Rule of Empires: Those Who Built Them, Those Who Endured Them, and Why They Always Fall* (Oxford University Press, 2010).

Perkins, Kenneth J., *Qaids, Captains and Colons: French Military Administration in the Colonial Maghrib 1844–1934* (New York and London: Africana, 1981).

Petraeus, David H. and Amos, James F., *FM 3–24: U.S. Army/Marine Corps Counterinsurgency Field Manual* (Washington, DC: Headquarters Department of the Army, December 2006).

Pion-Berlin, David, "The National Security Doctrine, Military Threat Perception, and the 'Dirty War' in Argentina," *Comparative Political Studies*, 21:3 (October 1988), 382–407.

"Latin American National Security Doctrines: Hard and Softline Themes," *Armed Forces & Society*, 15:3 (Spring 1989), 411–29.

Porch, Douglas, *Army and Revolution: France 1815–1848* (London: Routlege & Kegan Paul, 1974).

The March to the Marne: The French Army 1871–1914 (Cambridge University Press, 1981).

The French Foreign Legion: A Complete History of the Legendary Fighting Force (New York: HarperCollins, 1991).

The French Secret Services (New York: Farrar, Straus, Giroux, 1995).

Path to Victory: The Mediterranean Theater in World War II (New York: Farrar, Straus, Giroux, 2004).

The Conquest of Morocco (New York: Farrar, Straus, Giroux, 2005).

The Conquest of the Sahara (New York: Farrar, Straus, Giroux, 2005).

Wars of Empire (New York: Smithsonian Books, 2006).

"The Dangerous Myths and Dubious Promise of COIN," *Small Wars & Insurgencies*, 22:2 (May 2011), 239–57.

"The Hunt for Martín Caballero," *The Journal of Strategic Studies*, 35:2 (2012), 243–70.

Porter, Patrick, *Military Orientalism: Eastern War through Western Eyes* (New York: Columbia University Press, 2009).

Price, David H., *Weaponizing Anthropology* (Oakland, CA: AK Press, 2011).

Provence, Michael, *The Great Syrian Revolt and the Rise of Arab Nationalism* (Austin: University of Texas Press, 2005).

Ranger, T. O., "African Reactions in East and Central Africa," in L. H. Gann and Peter Duignan (eds.), *Colonialism in Africa 1870–1960*. Vol. I: *The History and Politics of Colonialism 1870–1914* (Cambridge University Press, 1969), 293–324.

Ranalletti, Mario, "Aux origines du terrorisme d'état en Argentine," *Vingtième siècle*, No. 105 (January–March 2010), 45–56.

Record, Jeffrey, "Back to the Weinberger-Powell Doctrine?" *Strategic Studies Quarterly* (Fall 2007), 80, www.au.af.mil/au/ssq/2007/fall/record.pdf.

Ricks, Thomas E., "Is American Military Professionalism Declining?" *Proceedings Magazine*, US Naval Institute, 124/7/1 (July 1998).

Fiasco: The American Military Adventure in Iraq (New York: Penguin Press, 2006).

The Gamble: General David Petraeus and the American Military Adventure in Iraq, 2006–2008 (New York: Penguin, 2009).

Rid, Thomas, "Razzia: A Turning Point in Modern Strategy," *Terrorism and Political Violence*, 21:4 (October 2009), 617–35.

"The Nineteenth Century Origins of Counterinsurgency Doctrine," *The Journal of Strategic Studies*, 33:5 (October 2010), 727–58.

Rioux, Jean-Pierre (ed.), *La guerre d'Algérie et les français* (Paris: Fayard, 1990).

Robin, Marie-Monique, *Les Escadrons de la mort, l'école française* (Paris: La Découverte, 2004).

Romjue, John L., *The Army of Excellence: The Development of the 1980s Army* (Fort Monroe, VA: Office of the Command Historian, US Army Training and Doctrine Command, 1993).

Ross, Marc Howard, *Cultural Contestation in Ethnic Conflict* (Cambridge University Press, 2007).

Russell, James A., *Innovation, Transformation, and War: Counterinsurgency Operations in Anbar and Ninewa Provinces, Iraq, 2005–2007* (Stanford University Press, 2011).

Ryan, Henry Butterfield, *The Fall of Che Guevara: A Story of Soldiers, Spies, and Diplomats* (New York and Oxford: Oxford University Press, 1998).

Sandler, Sandy, *To Free from Oppression: A Concise History of U.S. Army Special Forces, Civil Affairs, Psychological Operations, and the John F. Kennedy Special Warfare Center and School* (Fort Bragg, NC: US Army Special Operations Command, 1994).

Salan, Raoul, *Mémoires: fin d'un empire.* Vol. II: *Le Viêt-Minh mon adversaire* (Paris: Presses de la Cité, 1971).

Sarkin, Jeremy, *Colonial Genocide and Reparations Claims in the 21st Century: The Socio-Legal Context of Claims under International Law by the Herero against Germany for Genocide in Namibia, 1904–1908* (New York: Praeger 2008).

Schaebler, Birgit, "Coming to Terms with Failed Revolutions: Historiography in Syria, Germany and France," *Middle Eastern Studies*, 35:1 (January 1999), 17–44.

Scheck, Raffael, *Hitler's African Victims: The German Army Massacres of Black French Soldiers in 1940* (Cambridge University Press, 2006).

Schneller, Rachel, "Do Surges Work?" SAIS Review, 30:1 (Winter–Spring 2010), 151–55.

Secher, Reynald, *A French Genocide: The Vendée* (South Bend, IN: University of Notre Dame Press, 2003).

Seekins, Donald M., "The Historical Setting," in Frederica M. Bunge (ed.), *Burma: A Country Study* (Washington, DC: The American University Press, 1983), 1–71.

Selvage, Donald A., "Che Guevara in Bolivia" (Quantico, VA: USMC Command and Staff College, April 1, 1985), http://casarrubea.files.wordpress.com/2008/09/us-marines-on-che-1985.pdf.

Sévilla, Jean, *Historiquement correct: pour en finir avec le passé unique* (Paris: Perrin, 2003).

Sheehan, William, *A Hard Local War: The British Army and the Guerrilla War in Cork 1919–1921* (Stroud: The History Press, 2011).

Shrader, Charles R., *The First Helicopter War: Logistics and Mobility in Algeria 1954–1962* (Westport, CT: Praeger, 1999).

Simons, Anna, "Anthropology, Culture, and COIN in a Hybrid Warfare World," in Paul Brister, William Natter, and Robert Tomes (eds.), *Hybrid Warfare and Transnational Threats: Perspectives for an Era of Persistent Conflict* (New York: CENSA, 2011), 83–91.

Simson, H. J., *British Rule and Rebellion* (Salisbury, NC: Documentary Publications, 1977).

Sinclair, Georgina, *At the End of the Line: Colonial Policing and the Imperial Endgame 1945–1980* (Manchester and New York: Manchester University Press, 2006).

Singer, P. W., "Can't Win with 'Em, Can't Go to War without 'Em: Private Military Contractors and Counterinsurgency," Brookings Institution, Policy Paper No. 4 (September 2007).

Slavin, David, "The French Left and the Riff War: Racism and the Limits of Internationalism," *Journal of Contemporary History*, No. 1 (January 1991), 5–32.

Sorley, Lewis, *A Better War: The Unexamined Victories and Final Tragedy of America's Last Years in Vietnam* (New York and London: Harcourt Brace & Company, 1999).

Westmoreland: The General Who Lost Vietnam (Boston and New York: Houghton Mifflin Harcourt, 2011).

(ed.), *The Vietnam War: An Assessment by South Vietnam's Generals* (Lubbock: Texas Tech University Press, 2010).

Spiers, Edward M., *The Army and Society, 1815–1914* (London: Longman, 1980).

Stanley, William Deane, "El Salvador: State-Building before and after Democratisation, 1980–1995," *Third World Quarterly*, 27:1 (August 2006).

Strachan, Hew, *The Politics of the British Army* (Oxford: Clarendon Press, 1997).

Street, C. J. C., *Ireland in 1921* (London: Philip Allan & Co., 1922).

Suchet, Louis-Gabriel, *Suchet: War in Spain*, The War Times Journal On-line, www.wtj.com/archives/suchet/suchet10b.htm.

Sullivan, Anthony Thrall, *Thomas-Robert Bugeaud, France and Algeria 1784–1849: Politics, Power, and the Good Society* (Hamden, CT: 1983).

Summers, Harry, *On Strategy: An Analysis of the Vietnam War* (Novato, CA: Presidio Press, 1982).

Swedenburg, Ted, *Memories of Revolt: The 1936–1939 Rebellion and the Palestinian National Past* (Minneapolis and London: University of Minnesota Press, 1995).

Tenenbaum, Elie, *L'influence française sur la stratégie américaine de contre-insurrection 1945–1972* (Paris: Ecole d'études politiques de Paris, Master de recherche de Sciences Po, June 2009).

Thénault, Sylvie, *Histoire de la guerre d'indépendance Algérienne* (Paris: Flammarion, 2005).

Thomas, Martin, *The French Empire between the Wars: Imperialism, Politics and Society* (Manchester and New York: Manchester University Press, 2005).

Empires of Intelligence: Security Services and Colonial Disorder after 1914 (Los Angeles, Berkeley, and London: University of California Press, 2008).

Thompson, Sir Robert, *Defeating Communist Insurgency: The Lessons of Malaya and Vietnam* (New York: Praeger, 1966).

(ed.), *War in Peace: Conventional and Guerrilla Warfare since 1945* (New York: Harmony Books, 1981).

Thureau-Dangin, Paul, *Histoire de la monarchie de juillet*, Vol. v (Paris: Plon, 1890).

Histoire de la monarchie de julliet, Vol. vi (Paris: Plon, 1892).

Tone, John Lawrence, *The Fatal Knot: The Guerrilla War in Navarre and the Defeat of Napoleon in Spain* (Chapel Hill: University of North Carolina Press, 1994).

Townshend, Charles, *The British Campaign in Ireland, 1919–1921* (Oxford University Press, 1975).

Britain's Civil Wars: Counterinsurgency in the Twentieth Century (London: Faber & Faber, 1986).

"In Aid of the Civil Power: Britain, Ireland and Palestine 1916–48," in Daniel Marston and Carter Malkasian (eds.), *Counterinsurgency in Modern Warfare* (Oxford: Osprey, 2008), 21–27.

Trask, David F., *The War with Spain in 1898* (London and Lincoln: University of Nebraska Press, 1981).

Tripodi, Christian, *Edge of Empire: The British Political Officer and Tribal Administration on the North-West Frontier 1877–1947* (Farnham, Surrey, and Burlington, VT: Ashgate, 2011).

"Peacemaking through Bribes or Cultural Empathy? The Political Officer and Britain's Strategy towards the North-West Frontier, 1901–1945," *The Journal of Strategic Studies*, 31:1 (February 2008), 123–51.

"'Good for One but Not the Other': The 'Sandeman System' of Pacification as Applied to Baluchistan and the North-West Frontier, 1877–1947," *The Journal of Military History*, 73:3 (July 2009), 767–802.

Tripp, Charles, *A History of Iraq* (Cambridge University Press, 2000).

USSOCOM History and Research Office, *United States Special Operations Command History, 1987–2007* (USSOCOM/SOCS-HO: MacDill AFB, FL, 2007).

Woerkens, Martine van, *The Strangled Traveler: Colonial Imaginings and the Thugs of India* (University of Chicago Press, 2002).

Vaïsse, Maurice, *Comment de Gaulle fit échouer le putsch d'Alger* (Brussels: André Versaille éditeur, 2011).

Verbitsky, Horacio, "Breaking the Silence: The Catholic Church in Argentina and the 'Dirty War'," *Open Democracy* (July 2005), 3–4, www.opendemocracy.net/democracy-protest/catholicchurch_2709.jsp.

Villamarín, Luis Alberto, *Cóndor en el aire* (Bogotá: Talleres de TM Editores, 1999).

Vivinen, Richard, *France, 1934–1970* (New York: St. Martin's Press, 1996).

Wagner, Kim A., "The Deconstructed Stranglers: A Reassessment of Thuggee," *Modern Asian Studies*, 38:4 (2004), 931–63.

Weber, Eugen, *The Hollow Years: France in the 1930s* (New York: W.W. Norton, 1996).

Weber, Thomas, *Hitler's First War* (Oxford University Press, 2010).

Wei, William, "'Political Power Grows out of the Barrel of a Gun,' Mao and the Red Army," in Robin Higham and David A. Graff (eds.), *A Military History of China* (Boulder, CO: Westview Press, 2002), 229–48.

West, F. J., Jr., *The Village* (New York: Harper and Row, 1972).

The Wrong War: Grit, Strategy and the Way out of Afghanistan (New York: Random House, 2012).

Wickham-Crowley, Timothy P., *Guerrillas and Revolution in Latin America: A Comparative Study of Insurgents and Regimes since 1956* (Princeton University Press, 1992).

Wilson, Jeremy, *Lawrence of Arabia: The Authorized Biography of T. E. Lawrence* (New York: Atheneum 1990).

Wilson, Mary C., "The Hashemites, the Arab Revolt, and Arab Nationalism," in Rashid Khalidi, Lisa Anderson, Muhammad Muslih, and Reeva S. Simon (eds.), *The Origins of Arab Nationalism* (New York: Columbia University Press. 1991), 204–21.

Wood, Bryce, *The Making of the Good Neighbor Policy* (New York: W.W. Norton, 1967).

The Dismantling of the Good Neighbor Policy (Austin: University of Texas Press, 1985).

Yingling, Lieutenant Colonel Paul, "A Failure in Generalship," *Armed Forces Journal* (May 2007), www.afji.com/2007/05/2635198.

INDEX